The publisher gratefully acknowledges the generous contributions to this book provided by The Jane K. Sather Professorship in Classical Literature Fund and by the David Magie '97 Publication Fund of the Department of Classics of Princeton University.

SATHER CLASSICAL LECTURES

Volume Sixty-Five

Caesar's Calendar

CAESAR'S CALENDAR

CAESAR'S CALENDAR

*Ancient Time and
the Beginnings of History*

DENIS FEENEY

University of California Press
OCM 70718287
Berkeley   Los Angeles   London

University of California Press, one of the most
distinguished university presses in the United States,
enriches lives around the world by advancing
scholarship in the humanities, social sciences,
and natural sciences. Its activities are supported
by the UC Press Foundation and by philanthropic
contributions from individuals and institutions.
For more information, visit www.ucpress.edu.

University of California Press
Berkeley and Los Angeles, California

University of California Press, Ltd.
London, England

Library of Congress Cataloging-in-Publication Data
Feeney, D. C.
    Caesar's calendar : ancient time and the beginnings
of history / Denis Feeney.
        p.   cm.   —   (Sather classical lectures; v. 65)
    Includes bibliographical references and index.
    ISBN-13, 978–0-520–25119–9 (cloth : alk. paper)
    ISBN-10 0–520–25119–9 (cloth : alk. paper)
    1. Calendar, Roman.   2. Time—Social aspects—
Rome.   3. Time—Political aspects—Rome.
4. Chronology, Roman.   5. Synchronization.
6. Historiography—Rome.   7. Rome—
Historiography.   8. Rome—Social life and customs.
9. City and town life—Rome.   10. Rome—
Civilization—Greek influences.   I. Title.
CE46.F44   2007
529'.30937—dc22   2006023846

Manufactured in the United States of America

16   15   14   13   12   11   10   09   08   07
10   9   8   7   6   5   4   3   2   1

For Anna and Michael—
time for them

CONTENTS

ILLUSTRATIONS

PREFACE

Time became an obsession for me in more ways than one after I had the honor of being invited to deliver the Sather Lectures. Four years went by between receiving the invitation and arriving in Berkeley in spring 2004, and time's pressure grew remorselessly all through that period. It accelerated as the years dwindled, and "next year" finally became "this year." I moved into my office for the semester and began spending most of my waking hours facing out the window, looking at the beautiful Berkeley hills; framed against them was Sather Tower, with its inexorably advancing hands, and its bells tolling out the hours that were being sliced away from my deadline. Soon it was next month, and then next week, and then today, tonight.

Now, my first lecture is twenty-eight months in the past, and I can with a certain degree of tranquillity recollect the very happy semester I enjoyed in Berkeley. Everything you read in the prefaces to books in the Sather series is true: the friendliness and hospitality of the department and the university community are indeed wonderful, the physical surroundings are superb, the conditions for concentrated work are ideal. I owe a great debt of gratitude, first of all, to Robert and Carolyn Knapp. Robert was the perfect chairman, making everything run smoothly, and he and Carolyn made me feel immediately at home with their generous hospitality. The faculty were outstanding collective hosts; I must particularly thank Erich and Joan Gruen, Tony and Monique Long, and Nelly Oliensis and John Shoptaw. Steve Miller coached me on ancient agriculture and astronomy and took me to a

Cal rugby game (they lost, but only just). Crawford Greenewalt, my neighbor across the corridor in Dwinelle Hall, allowed me to borrow from his personal library and was always happy to help me find my way through the labyrinth of that building. The graduate students in my "Aetiologies" seminar were a delight to work with, and my Sather assistants (Chris Churchill, Athena Kirk, and Antonia Young) were models of patience and efficiency. Mark Griffith's daughter, Zoe, kindly lent me FAJ so that I could commute. My old friend Magen Solomon generously invited me to stay in her house in Oakland during my visit; my warm thanks to her for her kindness and thoughtfulness, and her great company. Until the last minute, my wife and I had hoped that all of us could come to Berkeley for the semester; I must thank Jude and my children for putting up with my absence when that proved impossible.

This book is fundamentally still the six lectures I gave at Berkeley. Even though I have documented and expanded the arguments, I have held on to the great opportunity the Sather Lectures provide of writing a book that maintains the freedoms of the lecture format. Without, I hope, falling into irresponsibility or cutting too many corners, I have tried to exploit the opportunity of opening up subjects that interested me even though I could not be comprehensive or exhaustive. Even so, at times I have felt overwhelmed by the magnitude of the subject, and by my sense of inadequacy in the face of all the skills that one really needs to work properly on the topic of time. I kept thinking of the savage attack that A. E. Housman makes on one of his predecessors, C. M. Francken, in the preface to his edition of Lucan: "The width and variety of his ignorance are wonderful; it embraces mythology, palaeography, prosody, and astronomy, and he cannot keep it to himself" (Housman 1927, xxxiv–v). Astronomy I must certainly count as one of my many areas of ignorance for the task before me, and I must include others too—astrology, mathematics, epigraphy, philosophy. I am all too aware that the great figures in the field of historical chronology and astronomy have established unmatchable standards of scholarship. I have still not fully recovered, for example, from the shock of realizing that when Felix Jacoby published *Apollodors Chronik,* a study that appears to embody a lifetime's learning, and that shows no areas of ignorance, he was twenty-five years old. Likewise, for someone who thought he knew something of Roman studies, it was a sobering experience properly to encounter the work of Mommsen for the first time.

I have, then, picked many brains. It is a pleasure to acknowledge and thank Bill Anderson, John Bodel, Ted Champlin, Emmanuele Curti, Emma Dench, John Dillery, Harriet Flower, Michael Flower, Tony Grafton, Erich Gruen, Tom Hare,

Sarah Harrell, Bob Kaster, Joshua Katz, Robert Knapp, Donald Mastronarde, Lloyd Moote, Steve Miller, Astrid Möller, Kathryn Morgan, Tessa Rajak, and Eviatar Zerubavel. The readers for the Press gave me helpful suggestions for improvement. Donna Sanclemente gave priceless assistance in preparing the artwork, figures, and final manuscript: I am greatly in her debt. Alessandro Barchiesi and Peter Brown read versions of the lectures, and I am most grateful to them for their responses and suggestions. I first tried some versions of these ideas on the members of the Department of Greek and Roman Studies at the University of Victoria, who invited me to give their Lansdowne Lectures in fall 1999; I must thank in particular Keith Bradley for his kindness on that visit. Since my semester at Berkeley other audiences have heard versions and given valuable reactions, at Boston University, Bryn Mawr College, the University at Buffalo, UCLA, Oxford University, Pennsylvania State University, the University of Washington at Seattle, and Yale University. I learned a lot from my colleagues in Princeton's Old Dominion Fellowship, who commented on a version of chapter 1, and from the members of the time seminar organized here by Miles Gilburne and Tony Grafton: this was a highly valuable experience as I began thinking about time in a concentrated way, and I thank Miles Gilburne for making it all possible. Of all the memorable moments in the course of the time seminar, the most vivid for me is still the silence that followed Jason Morgan's remark that modern time-keeping instruments were so acute they could measure the infinitesimal slowing-down in the rotation of the earth caused by the rising of sap and growth of leaves in spring in the Northern Hemisphere. Robert Hannah and Daryn Lehoux very generously made it possible for me to read their books on calendars and parapegmata before publication and responded patiently to my questions about these difficult topics.

My initial interest in the whole topic of Roman time was sparked by an inspirational paper delivered at Edinburgh by Andrew Wallace-Hadrill, which became his 1987 article "Time for Augustus: Ovid, Augustus, and the *Fasti*." At an important transitional stage of my thinking, I benefited greatly from stimulating correspondence with James Ker, and I look forward very much to the appearance of his own work on Roman time. My editor at UC Press, Laura Cerruti, has been an ally from the start and saved me when I was despairing of a title. I am deeply grateful to my project editor, Cindy Fulton, and to my copy editor, Marian Rogers, for their superb professionalism. Once again I am in the happy position of being able to thank Stephen Hinds, who read the lectures, and Tony Woodman, who read drafts of the chapters; as always, I am deeply in their debt for their frank and penetrating comments. Chris Kraus has also generously read the book in draft, and I have profited immensely from her acute responses. I have been very fortunate to have such friends assist me in this way. Finally, a debt of gratitude is due to another friend, Nicholas Horsfall, who has also commented on drafts, and who showed an interest in this project from the start, when it was still inchoate; over the last five years he has responded instantly to my queries and trial balloons, selflessly providing help and lines to follow up from his deep store of learning. None of the people mentioned here can be responsible for the use I have made of their generosity, but I know how much they have improved the book.

Acknowledgment is due to Carcanet Press for kind permission to quote from Les Murray's poem "The C19–20," from "The Sydney Highrise Variations," in *Collected Poems* (Carcanet Press: Manchester, 1991).

Abbreviations of periodicals follow the system of *L'année philologique;* citations of works and collections follow the system of *The Oxford Classical Dictionary,* 3rd edition.

I have taken over from Burkert (1995) the valuable convention of enclosing in quotation marks modern dates when they are used to correspond to an ancient author's system, as opposed to when they are used to give a date within our frame of reference. Thus I speak of Cicero referring to the events of "59 B.C.E." (the consulship of Caesar and Bibulus), whereas Robert Kaster refers to the events of 59 B.C.E.

Introduction

Someone writing a book on "time" is well advised not to type the word into a library catalogue search early on in the process. According to the bibliographic guide of S. L. Macey, some 95,000 books were published "on time-related subjects" between 1900 and 1990; in the fifteen years since then, boosted by the millennium, there have no doubt been at least another 35,000 at the rate of increase he charts.[1] As "the most widely used noun in the English language,"[2] "time" can take you in any direction, and it continually involves other subjects as it goes. "Place" and "space," to take just one example, are words regularly twinned with "time," producing titles such as *What Time Is This Place?* or *Timing Space and Spacing Time*.[3] We shall, accordingly, see throughout this study that Roman conceptions of time and of space are inextricably linked. When the Romans first started trying to map themselves into the larger Mediterranean world, their sense of where they belonged and how they fitted in was a challenge simultaneously to their sense of time and their sense of space; the charts they needed were geographical and chronological at once. Providing such charts was harder than it may appear, not least because charts of time and space do not always overlap harmoniously. Different parts of the world can appear to occupy different dimensions of time, "allochronies," as Johannes Fabian (1983) calls them, niches where the quality of time appears to be not the same as "ours," where the inhabitants are stuck in the past or are perhaps already ahead, in the future.

Roman society is a rich test case for the student of time, straddling as it does some of the usually accepted divisions in sociology. Rome was as highly developed in terms of social and technological organization as a premodern society could possibly be, with an accompanying battery of elaborate calendars, astronomical knowledge, and records and monuments of the past. At the same time, in its lack of clock regulation for synchronizing mass labor and travel, or of particular divisions of daily time beyond the fluctuating hour, it was a society that remained profoundly premodern and preindustrial in terms of the impact of time structures on the individual's lived experience.[4] Further, one may observe without undue romanticizing that even urban Romans were aware of their society's agrarian basis and of the patterns of recurrent life in the country, in a way that few modern city-dwellers are. Roman time structures, then, like so many other features of Roman society, are premodern and modern at once, resisting "the simple dualisms that have been used to characterise societies, including industrial versus pre-industrial, agrarian versus urban, cyclical versus linear time."[5]

Faced with a society so distinctively responsive to any avenue of inquiry within this large and all-embracing subject, I have had to be highly selective, concentrating on some clusters of interest and shutting out many others. In particular, I have deliberately concentrated on the more public as opposed to private dimensions of Roman time. This is of course a rough-and-ready division, which I shall follow the Romans in infringing at will, but it means that the book does not have much if anything to say about the rhythms of daily or weekly life, astrology, metaphors of experienced time, or individual memory, transience, and mortality. I have thought of these areas as the Bettini-Ker-Putnam terrain, in deference to three scholars whose stimulating work I have used as a kind of fence from my own.[6] The present book concentrates rather on investigating the contours and reliefs in the patterns that the Romans imposed on the time of the city and the empire. The systems under investigation include their calendar, which is still our calendar, with its near-total perfection in capturing the progress of natural time; the annual rhythm of consular government, with the accompanying annalistic frame of historical time; the plotting of sacred time onto sacred place; the forging of significant links across time so as to impose meaningful shapes on the past in the form of anniversary and era; above all, the experience of empire, by which the Romans took the temporal consciousness of a city-state and meshed it progressively with foreign time systems as their horizons expanded to embrace the entire Mediterranean, and beyond. This is a process that touched on practically every dimension of their experience, as they had to establish links and connections backwards and sideways, to fix themselves within a worldwide web of time. Since so much of this process was carried out in dialogue with Greek schemes of time, I have found myself once more returning to the problem of cross-cultural comparisons between Greece and Rome.[7] Indeed, comparison turns out to be the main theme of the investigation, for almost all the schemes I discuss have an element of comparison of like and unlike inherent in them—between Greece and Rome, myth and history, past and present, city and country, nature and culture.

I do not promise to find a unifying holism behind these topics. I do not aim to reconstruct a unitary Roman temporal worldview. Various schools, especially that associated with Lévi-Strauss, have advanced the idea that cultures do operate with incommensurable, wholly culturally determined worldviews, and by this model each culture will have its own unique and distinctive way of configuring time.[8] Since such approaches tend to share a holistic tendency, the society's distinct view of time will often be presented as a unitary one, and its quintessential expression will regularly be sought in a ritual context, held to embody the core of the society's beliefs. Yet the multiplicity of any group's possible constructions of time is more striking than its uniformity;[9] and ritual constructions of time are only one of many sets, not enjoying any necessary primacy over the others.[10]

An example of a supposedly distinctive cultural time-view that will be familiar to classicists is that of the Greek "circular" conception of time, as opposed to the "linear" or teleological conception of the Hebrew Bible. It has, however, been repeatedly demonstrated that this is a misconception as far as both the Greeks and the Jews are concerned, mistaking occasional or circumscribed or dialectical usages for some holistic mentality.[11] As A. Möller and N. Luraghi well put it, "We cannot label one culture cyclical, another linear, because most people perceive time in different ways according to their context or situation, with the result that any one culture is characterized by a range of different perceptions of time."[12] In any society individuals are liable to inhabit different frames of time, often simultaneously—cyclical or recurrent, linear, seasonal, social, historical.[13] The earliest study I know of that explores the experience of dwelling in such different frames of time is that of Le Goff (1960). Here we meet the bicameral mind of a medieval merchant, who occupies his own mercantile time horizon while still intermittently engaging with the Church's time horizons; he is engaged throughout in a dialectic between two different temporal calculi, of profit versus salvation, of time to be used as a commodity versus eternal time as the goal of his earthly existence.

If this interest in internal diversity and multiplicity is a challenge to the model of unitary and discrete worldviews, then so is the growing tendency to see more in common across different societies than was the case in past scholarship, as some anthropologists have become more and more interested in what human beings share after so many years of concentrating on what they do not share. A number of recent anthropological studies have argued that the human experience of time has more in common at fundamental levels of cognition than has generally been allowed.[14] Gell, for example, reacts against the claims that other people inhabit thought-worlds "where there is no past, present or future, where time stands still, or chases its own tail, or swings back and forth like a pendulum"; such claims mistake ritual stagings for universal and radical understandings.[15] Adam (1990) goes farther, seeking to ground the experience of time in the natural rhythmicity of humans as organic life-forms: we do, after all, have circadian rhythms built in to our biology, just as oysters and potatoes do.[16] But Adam herself argues that human conceptualizing of time is, as she puts it, "irreducibly social since human culture is a pre-requisite to the development of concepts."[17]

However this particular debate may develop in the future, it seems to me that we may resist the deep relativism of the Lévi-Straussian model while still allowing plenty of room for cultural specificity.[18] It still makes a difference whether you have clocks or not, or whether you have written calendars or not, or whether your main crop is rice in the plains of central India or sago in the forests of New Guinea, to take the example used by Gell to illustrate the different pressures of time facing cultivators in different parts of the world.[19] We shall be concentrating throughout, then, on what is distinctive about Roman representations of time, without attempting to reduce the complexity of their different strategies into a holistic view. In investigating the Romans' assumptions about the workings and constructions of time, it will also be important to keep facing the challenge of uncovering our own assumptions about time.[20] We "know" what a date is, or a year, or a calendar; it is all the more important to keep reminding ourselves of how often our understanding of such apparently obvious concepts will completely misrepresent the Roman equivalent—if indeed there is an equivalent. Studying Roman time becomes an exercise in trying better to understand our own.

The book follows the structure of the six lectures in being divided into three pairs of chapters, on three main topics. The first two chapters treat chronography, through the focus of synchronization. Without a universally accepted dating scheme, the societies of the ancient world had to chart past time by a complex system of correlation, lining up significant events in the distinct time-columns of different cities, each of which had their own calendars, dating systems, and eras. The historians of Greece had perfected a Panhellenic framework of cross-reference by the time the Romans came onto the stage of Mediterranean history. The first two chapters, then, analyze the mechanics and the implications of the Romans' past and present being charted onto these Panhellenic grids of time. In this story, as Erich Gruen kept reminding me, it is often impossible to tell what was happening at the initiative of the Greeks and what was happening at the initiative of the Romans. For Rome to become a world empire it was essential that the Romans become part of the time schemes of the Greeks, and the work that went on to make this happen was collaborative work. The project of synchronization was a technical challenge of a high order for them, and it provides us with a demanding test case in the history of Roman Hellenization, as the Romans and Greeks made sense of the contours of the Roman past and present through media that had been devised for Greek cities and empires. We shall be considering what was at stake in the choices that were made in these synchronistic patternings: how were the Romans mapped onto a Mediterranean past that had been surveyed by Greek chronography and historiography, and which distinctive patterns of Greek time were adapted for the Romans as their empire grew until it had physically embraced and subsumed all of the focal points for Greek chronology?

The topic of synchronism is a large one and could have engrossed all six lectures and chapters. In the first chapter I outline the issue and show why it matters, giving an outline of the main developments in ancient chronography insofar as they impinge on synchronism, with the chronological endpoint being the Christian chronicles of Eusebius and Jerome. The chapter concludes with an overview of the synchronistic essay of Aulus Gellius, from around 180 C.E. We have nothing but fragments surviving of the many large volumes Gellius was working with, and his four pages are the only intact sequence of writing devoted to the subject that survives from all the wreckage of pagan chronography. His snapshot synchronistic chapter, with its panorama of some seven hundred years of history, is the most economical introduction we have to this fascinating and indispensable aspect of the organization of time in the ancient world. It is valuable to some extent precisely because Gellius is not an especially original operator in this domain; his text shows just how much work this tool could do, even in the hands of someone who was not particularly exerting himself. After looking at the scholars and antiquarians in the first chapter, in the second chapter we shall look in more detail at the story of how the time schemes of the Greeks and Romans worked to accommodate the Romans' unprecedented rise to dominance over the whole world.

The second pair of chapters examines two crucial divisions in past time. Chapter 3 treats one of the most important of the ancient world's time divisions, between the time of myth and history. Here the test case is the foundation of the city of Rome, an event that is surprisingly mobile, and that becomes a focus of obsessive interest in the historiographical tradition. Even today there is dispute over what it means to speak of the beginning of Rome as a mythical or historical event, and in the ancient world there was even more at stake: the claims of the Romans to status as full participants in the civilized world were involved in their claims to a connection with Greek schemes of myth and history. Chapter 4 considers a related demarcation moment in time, the division between the times of the Gold and Iron ages, which could sometimes be seen as a kind of transition from myth to history. For the Romans, this is the point at which organized time comes into being along with the other appurtenances of civilization. Here we consider also the related topic of the Romans' long-standing fascination with the possibility of a return to the lost Age of Gold.

The final two chapters turn to the Romans' own distinctive indigenous charts of time, the schemes of organization seen in the consular lists and in the calendar. The lists of past consuls were the principal mechanism for charting the past time of the city and provided a base for the Romans' distinctive form of annalistic history. As Rome went through the traumatic transition from Republic to Principate, the presentation and function of the consular lists were transformed along with all other aspects of public life, and the norms of historiography were correspondingly redrawn in the process. The calendar likewise underwent radical changes as part of these transformations. Totally remade by Julius Caesar, the new calendar's power and reach were unrecognizably different from those of its Republican predecessor. We shall investigate the impact of the reformed calendar on the way the Romans conceived of time's recurrence, and of the mesh between the time of the imperial city and the time of the natural world. As the regulator of the city's festival life, the calendar had always provided a backdrop against which the Romans could reflect on the meaning of the festivals and commemorations inscribed there; as the meanings were transformed under the new regime, and especially as new festivals and commemorations were added, the calendar became a different kind of document in this regard as well. The calendar also provided a platform for connection between past and present in the form of anniversaries, linking significant days and events across time so as to throw into relief the question of the relationship between the past and the present. The discussion of the calendar in these last two chapters will complete a piece of intellectual ring-composition for me, since it was Ovid's calendar poem, the *Fasti*, that first hooked me, almost twenty years ago, on the subject of Roman time.

Greece and Rome

THE AXIS OF B.C./A.D.

It is a practically impossible mental exercise for readers of this book to imagine maneuvering themselves around historical time without the universalizing, supranational, and cross-cultural numerical axis of the dates in B.C. and A.D., or B.C.E. and C.E. These numerical dates seem to be written in nature, but they are based on a Christian era of year counting whose contingency and ideological significance are almost always invisible to virtually every European or American, except when we hesitate over whether to say B.C. or B.C.E.[1]

The axis of time along a B.C./A.D. line is not one that has been in common use for very long. It was sometime in the first half of the sixth century C.E. that the monk Dionysius Exiguus came up with our now standard linchpin of Christ's birth date, but his aim was to facilitate the calculation of Easter not to provide a convenient dating era, and the common use of the numerical dates generated by Dionysius's era is surprisingly recent, despite their apparently irresistible ease and utility.[2] It is true that the eighth-century Bede, for example, will provide A.D. dates, but they are not the backbone of his chronicling technique, which is fundamentally organized around regnal years. Bede's A.D. dates are still felt to be orientations in *divine* time, from the incarnation of Christ, and are accordingly used for "ecclesiastical events, such as the death of an archbishop, or astronomical events, such as an eclipse or a comet"; they still require to be synchronized with other mundane time schemes and are not an historical absolute in themselves.[3] Even for those who use an A.D. date, it is not necessarily natural, as it may appear to us, to use the reverse dimension of B.C. Sir Walter Raleigh's *History of the World* (1614) refers to the civil years of recent time with the familiar enumeration (though without the A.D. annotation); his history from the creation to 167 B.C.E., however, proceeds without a single B.C. date, using unspecific and relativizing dating schemes that are still essentially those of a universalizing pagan historian such as Pompeius Trogus.

Joseph Scaliger's great work on chronology, *De Emendatione Temporum* (1583), devoted much space to the question of when Christ was born, but the birth of Christ, so far from being the key benchmark in temporal calculation, is not even included among the historical eras he lays down in book 5.[4] As one sees from Scaliger's practice, a major reason that B.C./A.D. dates were not automatically used as historical markers was that scholars could not agree on when Christ was born. Scaliger's main predecessor in historical chronology, Paul Crusius, in his posthumously published *Liber de Epochis* of 1578, did not use B.C. and A.D. as his benchmark because he thought that the Gospels could not yield a verifiable date for Christ's birth; instead, he used the Passion as one of his determinative eras, which he "arbitrarily" fixed at the date of "midnight preceding January 1 A.D. 33."[5] The date of the incarnation was not simply a conventional peg in time to these Christian scholars, and the undecidability of the incarnation's position in time as an event overrode the utility that would emerge once the era could be regarded as a convention rather than as an actual count from a verifiable happening. Only in 1627 did Domenicus Petavius, in his *Opus De Doctrina Temporum*, expound the B.C./A.D. system as a basis for a universal time line for scholars and historians, on the understanding that the reference point of the birth of Christ represented "not the actual event but an agreed upon point from which all real events could be dated."[6] Even after Petavius's work, history continued to be written without the numerical grid until the eighteenth century.

One aim of the present book is to make this apparently bizarre recalcitrance understandable by bringing to light the power and significance of the dating mentality that was surrendered in the transition to the universal numerical grid. It has long been conventional to condole with the Greeks and Romans for never really coming up with a usable numerical dating system.[7] But this teleological view not only makes it hard for us to intuit how the ancients "coped," as it were, without a numerical dating system, but, more importantly, obscures the positive dimension to the issue—what were the advantages and insights that accrued to their visions of history as a result of the chronological systems they did inhabit?[8]

Our numerical C.E. dates are convenient enough in themselves, and they have generated other numerically derived conceptual instruments for us to manipulate, especially the century and the decade. These units are, again, surprisingly recent. We have been thinking in centuries for only three and a half centuries, and in decades for only seven decades.[9] Les Murray puts the century mentality a little late, but his wonderful poem on the subject, "The C19–20," cries out for quotation:

> The Nineteenth Century. The Twentieth Century.
> There were never any others. No centuries before these.
> Dante was not hailed in his time as an Authentic
> Fourteenth Century Voice. Nor did Cromwell thunder, *After all,*
> *in the bowels of Christ, this* is *the Seventeenth Century!*[10]

With all their attendant dangers of facile periodization, their refinements of "long" and "short," and their explanatory epithets of "German" or "American," these units have become indispensable to our apprehension of the rhythms of time.[11]

The centuries, decades, and individual numbered years make orientation in time so easy that we scarcely any more conceive of the process as orientation. The numerals provide a time line that appears independent of focalization. In addition, the Western calendar to which the numbered years are tied is likewise of such rigorous power that we consistently assume the existence of a comprehensive time grid whenever we are working with the past. The consequences have been well expressed by P.-J. Shaw:

> A date is the symbol of a moment rather than the moment itself, and a calendar is a device for identifying a day, month, sometimes a year, distinct from a system of reckoning, which is a tool for computing the passage of time. But because the modern (Christian) calendar acts also as the modern system of reckoning and is universally acknowledged as such, the correspondence between day and date, between a moment and its given symbol, is so close that the two tend to be treated as identical. One consequence of this is that the artificial nature of that date becomes obscured; it assumes the privilege . . . of a universal law.[12]

TIME WITHOUT B.C./A.D.

The situation was profoundly different for the Greeks and Romans, to a degree that is virtually impossible to recover in the imagination. In the ancient world each city had its own calendar and its own way of calibrating past time, usually through lists of local magistrates, just as they each had had their own currencies, their own weights and measures, and their own religions. As recent disputes over harmonizing currencies or weights and measures have demonstrated, utility is not the only consideration at work in such matters, and modern societies have likewise shown considerable resistance to the harmonizing of time and calendars, as we shall see in chapter 5.[13] Still, ancient societies did not face the uniquely modern challenges to time measurement that came with the ability to move quickly over space. Before rapid stage coaches and railways there was no need for anything but local time, and it was the squeezing of physical space by the increase of speed in connecting separate places that made the harmonization of time standards necessary, with the eventual apparatus of international time zones.[14]

In the atomized time world of the ancient Mediterranean, expressing dates in a format that would make sense to inhabitants of more than one city presented an intellectual and organizational challenge of a high order, one that it took ancient scholars centuries to meet. The first two chapters will bear this point out in detail, but for now two brief examples may serve to illustrate the practical difficulties. A calendrical date was hard enough. When Plutarch gives a date for the battle of Plataea he says, "They fought this battle on the fourth of Boëdromion, according to the Athenians, but according to the Boeotians, on the twenty-seventh of the month Panemus" (*Arist.* 19.7).[15] A year date presented its own problems of calibration. When Diodorus Siculus wishes to mark the beginning of "384 B.C.E." he says, "At the conclusion of the year, in Athens Diotrephes was archon and in Rome the consuls elected were Lucius Valerius and Aulus Mallius, and the Eleians celebrated the ninety-ninth Olympiad, that in which Dicon of Syracuse won the footrace" (15.14.1).[16] Comparable mechanisms are observable in all literate societies that have no universalizing numerical dating system but have chancelleries or historians who must make correlations outside the penumbra of their own state. A historian working in Asia who wanted to describe events in what we call 936 C.E. would be using the following synchronisms: "In China, Shi Jingtang destroyed the Latter Tang Dynasty and became Emperor Gaozu of the Latter Jin, inaugurating year one of the Tianfu ('Heavenly Felicity') Era. Meanwhile, Wang T'aejo unified the Korean peninsula under the Koryo Dynasty in his 19th regnal year. In Japan, in the sixth year of Jōhei ('Consenting in Peace') Era, under Emperor Suzaku, Kino Yoshihito and Fujiwara no Sumitomo fought pirates off the southwest coast of Japan. It was the 33rd year of the 60-year cycle of the zodiac: the Year of the Fiery Monkey."[17]

If you were a Greek or a Roman moving between the ambits of two or more states, it was impossible to have any kind of time frame in your head at all if you could not handily correlate disparate people and events. At the end of this chapter, in the synchronistic chapter from the *Attic Nights* of the late second-century c.e. writer Aulus Gellius we shall see a sustained example of the kind of correlating work required of a Roman or Greek maneuvering through the past. Here I may illustrate the difficulties with the story Gellius tells to open his chapter, as a justification for the work he undertook in compiling his essay on synchronism (*NA* 17.21.1):

> Ut conspectum quendam aetatum antiquissimarum, item uirorum inlustrium qui in his aetatibus nati fuissent haberemus, ne in sermonibus forte inconspectum aliquid super aetate atque uita clariorum hominum temere diceremus, sicuti sophista ille ἀπαίδευτος, qui publice nuper disserens Carneaden philosophum a rege Alexandro, Philippi filio, pecunia donatum et Panaetium Stoicum cum superiore Africano uixisse dixit . . .

> In order to have a kind of considered overview of very ancient eras, and correspondingly of the illustrious men who had been born in those eras, so as to avoid by chance blurting out in conversation some unconsidered remark about the era or life of men who are quite well known, as that uneducated sophist did who recently gave a public lecture in which he said that Carneades the philosopher had been given some money by king Alexander, the son of Philip, and that Panaetius the Stoic had been in the circle of the elder Africanus . . .

The elder Africanus in fact died when Panaetius was a baby, and it was Africanus Minor with whom Panaetius consorted, while Carneades visited Rome in what we call 155 b.c.e. Even a well-informed modern classicist might struggle to come up with this exact date for Carneades' embassy, but most will be able to straddle the decade, or at least to have him pegged in the right century, and so will handily avoid correlating him with Alexander, who died in what we call 323 b.c.e. I am sure all our hearts go out to that poor sophist, but his blunders bring home how very difficult it is to keep historical events in their correct relative order without our universalizing cross-cultural and supranational numerical dating, which makes it easy for us to maneuver our way around the past, working with larger or smaller spreads of pattern distribution. If users of the b.c.e./c.e. grid were in the habit of making systematic synchronistic comparisons with the Islamic or Jewish calendars, we would know what it was like for the Greeks and Romans; but not many people in the West habitually do that. That is something *they* have to do. The time imperialism works in the favor of the users of the Christian time grid.

The ease and apparent naturalness of our dating system conspire to beguile us into overlooking the fact that all of the dates it generates are themselves ultimately synchronisms. The centuries-long work on constructing a coherent historical chronology on an axis of B.C.E./C.E. time has been absorbed and naturalized so thoroughly by all of us that we can take it completely for granted, and forget just how much synchronistic work our predecessors going back to the Renaissance had to do in order for us to be able to say something like "Xerxes invaded Greece in 480 B.C.E."[18] This project of domestication has brought incalculable benefits in terms of convenience and transferability, but it is one that students of antiquity should be regularly defamiliarizing, because we lose as much in historical understanding as we gain in convenience when we cloak our discrepant ancient data with the apparently scientific unified weave of the Julian calendar and the B.C./A.D. system.[19]

EVERY DATE A SYNCHRONISM

Not just in terms of European history, but in terms of anything we call a "date," it is the case that "every chronological statement is, in a sense, a synchronism," grounded on the correlation of past events.[20] Indeed, relativity has made it clear that there is no absolute time to be sought in science any more than in history; just as in history, the apparent absoluteness of physicists' time is actually a matrix for connecting events: "Time and space . . . are not real extensions but only conceptual, mathematical devices that are used to situate events and measure the intervals between them."[21] The ability to synchronize, to construct relationships between events separated in time and space, underpins our apprehension of time at fundamental levels of cognition. Antonio Damasio, in his studies of brain function in patients with physical damage to various parts of the brain, has investigated patients who have lost their sense of past time, so that they have no sense of chronology: "How the brain assigns an event to a specific time and places that event in a chronological sequence—or in the case of my patient, fails to do so—is a mystery. We know only that both the memory of facts and the memory of spatial and temporal relationships between those facts are involved."[22] Marriages, bereavements, new jobs, new houses, births of children—these greeting-card moments appear to be the hooks by which we organize our apprehension of our lived "private" time, and these hooks are regularly attached to memorable events in the "public" sphere that provide comparatively fixed points of contact.[23] Mark Twain's comments on this dating function of the Civil War in the South are famous: "The war is what A.D is elsewhere they date from it. All day long you hear things 'placed' as having happened since the waw; or du'in' the waw; or befo' the waw; or right aftah the waw; or 'bout two yeahs or five yeahs or ten yeahs befo' the waw or aftah the waw."[24] One of my favorite modern examples is the ghastly moment in *Joy in the Morning* when Bertie Wooster comes within an ace of losing the brooch entrusted to him by Aunt Agatha to deliver to Florence Craye at Steeple Bumpleigh. If he had lost it, he says, "the thing would have marked an epoch. World-shaking events would have been referred to as having happened 'about the time Bertie lost that brooch' or 'just after Bertie made such an idiot of himself over Florence's birthday present.'"[25]

The examples of Damasio, Twain, and Wodehouse can serve to remind us that B.C.E. and C.E. dates do not speak for themselves, even if it usually feels as if they do. The numbers are not just numbers. We may feel as if we orientate ourselves in European history since archaic Greece on an axis of pure numerals, but those numbers are charged with event-laden significance, and the emptiness of a merely numerical time grid comes home to someone like me as soon as I read a history of a country about whose past I am relatively ignorant, such as premodern China. If I open a book on China before 1500 C.E. I am immediately adrift in an ocean of digits, for the events that have generated those numbers have no instinctive significance to me. The only way the time lines of Asian history can come to make sense to a novice like me is after a process of immersion in the events, so that the numbers are more than numbers, or else, as I find in my case, precisely through a process of synchronism: the date of an event in Asian history may stick in my head if I can find a link with a contemporary event in European history, so that the number thereby becomes meaningful, and memorable.

If modern Westerners operate in this way, then it is even more the case that within a society without our B.C./A.D. axis people will almost inevitably organize their perception of past time by relation to a striking event, involving well-known people, shared in the memory of the peer community. An excellent early example from Greece is in Xenophanes, who asks at dinner, "How many years do you have, my good man? How old were you when the Mede came?'" (in "546/5 B.C.E.").[26] What eventually comes to underpin the entire ancient project of organizing historical time is precisely the use of such canonical events as hooks from which intervals forwards or backwards could be counted; these intervals provided a way of dividing the past, giving a kind of map, making it possible to develop a sense of contours, large-scale and small-scale.[27] The backbone to the scheme of Eratosthenes' *Chronographiae* shows this very clearly. The first of Jacoby's fragments from this work shows a system of "x years from a to b" ("80 years from the fall of Troy to the return of the Heraclids," and so on), until we finally get to Alexander's death, roughly a hundred years before Eratosthenes; the death of Alexander is such a famous event that readers can construct their own links back to it, just as any reader of this book could construct his or her own links via family back to the time of the First World War.[28]

Any construction of the past that involved more than one community meant that you needed more than one column of events, and you needed a series of significant Aunt Agatha moments in each column, which could then be used as points of orientation for parallel synchronization. Cicero provides a fine example in a letter he wrote to Atticus on 19 March 45 B.C.E., requesting historical information, needed for background in his *Academica,* concerning the year "155 B.C.E." (*Att.* 12.23.2 = Shackleton Bailey [1965–70] 262.2):

> quibus consulibus Carneades et ea legatio Romam uenerit scriptum est in tuo annali. haec nunc quaero, quae causa fuerit—de Oropo, opinor, sed certum nescio; et, si ita est, quae controuersiae. praeterea, qui eo tempore nobilis Epicureus fuerit Athenisque praefuerit hortis, qui etiam Athenis πολιτικοὶ fuerint illustres. quae te etiam ex Apollodori puto posse inuenire.

> It is written in your Book of Annals in which consuls Carneades and that embassy came to Rome. What I now want to know is their business—Oropus I think it was, but I don't know for certain; and if that is it, what were the points at issue. Furthermore, tell me of a notable Epicurean of the period, head of the Garden at Athens; also who were the leading Athenian politicians of the period. I think you can get the information from Apollodorus' book among others.

First of all, it is worth pausing over the first two Latin words in this quotation, *quibus consulibus.* I have given the excellent translation of Shackleton Bailey, apart from the first sentence, where his version almost imperceptibly miscues Cicero's Latin by domesticating it into the equivalent of what an English speaker would have said. "Your Annals give the year in which Carneades and that embassy came to Rome" is Shackleton Bailey's version, and my own "in which consuls" definitely sounds unnatural in comparison, but this more literal phrasing brings out the way in which the Romans marked the year with the names of the two consuls, not with a number. Their phrasing is not straightforwardly a date, but an event—the holding of supreme power by so-and-so and so-and-so, in this case by

P. Cornelius Scipio Nasica and M. Claudius Marcellus, both for the second time.[29] The Roman side of this time event, then, is anchored in Cicero's mind with the names of the consuls, but at the end of the extract we see him asking for an Athenian equivalent, a prominent Epicurean and the leading Athenian politicians of the time, so that he can have a series of connecting points, bridges, to link up affairs at Athens with the names of the Roman consuls. For us, the bare "155" does virtually all the work of giving a sense of depth and relative location in time, but Cicero needs names to provide a peopled background that will give him some recognizable contours against which to measure the position of Carneades and his embassy.[30]

The argument so far produces an important result for our concern in the first two chapters, of investigating what is at stake in correlating dates in the time charts of Greece and the time charts of Rome. We are now in a position to see that correlating Greek and Roman *dates* means correlating Greek and Roman *events*. There is, in fact, no Greek or Latin word for "date." An ancient date is an event—or, to be more precise, any date is a relationship between two or more events. As inhabitants of the B.C.E./C.E. grid, we simply cannot help thinking of ancient writers as working with dates, which to us are numbers. But they are not connecting numbers; they are connecting significant events and people.[31] In so doing they are not placing events within a preexisting time frame; they are constructing a time frame within which the events have meaning.[32] Again, the *ultimate* foundation of our modern chronological system is, likewise, the connecting of events, but that event-based substratum is almost always hidden from us by the apparent abstraction of the numbers within their own coherent framework, and this "absolute time" has an autonomy that can all too easily exempt us from the difficult but rewarding work in which the ancients were inescapably involved, of apprehending past time as a set of relationships between events, people, and places, or as parallel series—discrete or interpenetrating—of such relationships.[33]

A number of important recent studies have shed light on the profound differences between our modern "absolute time" and their "relative time," from Hunter (1982) to Wilcox (1987) and Shaw (2003).[34] These scholars have made it easier for their successors to grasp the fact that ancient writers are not working with "dates" under another guise, but with relative frames of time that are always being reconstructed in each project, even if many of the anchoring points stay constant.[35] Nonetheless, it remains an imaginative challenge of the first order to attempt to intuit how the Romans and Greeks were able to move around in past time without numerical coordinates.[36] Once again, Cicero's correspondence with Atticus provides an invaluable thought-experiment for anyone trying to develop such a sense, in the form of the many letters he wrote to Atticus in May and June 45 B.C.E., crammed with prosopographical chronological questions about the ten legates who went to Corinth after its capture in 146 B.C.E.[37] As Cicero attempts to marshal the names with which Atticus supplies him, and to make sense of the relationships between them, we can see him using the mentality that a Roman aristocrat developed by growing up with the Leges Annales, the legislation that governed the minimum ages at which it was possible to stand for each of the magistracies. Cicero and his peers could monitor their position in time almost spatially—this is the sensation that Bettini has brought alive for us so memorably.[38] Romans of the governing class developed a layered sense of their peer group, with some a little bit ahead, and some a little bit behind. This mentality emerges very clearly from Cicero's *Brutus* and obviously provided a template for them to map back onto earlier generations, with an analogous sense of depth.[39] What to us is a matter of numbers is to Cicero a matter of personal relationships—fathers and sons, uncles and nephews, junior and senior friends.[40]

Without a universal, serial, and numerical system of chronology, then, hooked on a single agreed point, orientation was only possible with synchronization of different schemes of time, ones arranged by interval along vertebrae of significant events with their significant actors. As the examples from Cicero vividly illustrate, their historical consciousness is less abstracted than ours, for it is anchored in a series of connecting points that are marked by people and their deeds. Roman years did not have numbers; they had names, "taking their name from the consul" (*annos a consule nomen habentis*, Luc. 7. 441). The Romans' time horizons are not plotted out with numbered milestones in a series but dotted with clusters of people in significant relationships with each other through memorable events. We now turn to an account of the basic instruments by which these clusters were organized, before investigating what the entailments of these instruments of organization could be.

THE FIRST INSTRUMENTS
OF GREEK SYNCHRONISM

My focus is on the consequences of the Romans being fitted in to Greek time schemes, and a sketch of the Greek instruments of synchronism is therefore indispensable. The Greek networks to which the Romans were being accommodated were already old by the time the Romans encountered them. The Greek world itself had many diverse calendars and civil years, with each unite maintaining its own annual calendar, beginning at various points of the natural year, and marking the year in its own unique manner with the names of local officials.[41] It was a pressing need in historiography to find ways of producing a coherent narrative that could integrate the different time frames of the different participants.

Classicists regularly first encounter this issue when they get to the beginning of the second book of Thucydides, where the historian faces the problem of giving a Panhellenically comprehensible beginning point for the Archidamian War in "431 B.C.E."[42] This is a passage that no discussion of synchronism ever omits (2.2.1):

> Τέσσαρα μὲν γὰρ καὶ δέκα ἔτη ἐνέμειναν αἱ τριακοντούτεις σπονδαὶ αἳ ἐγένοντο μετ᾽ Εὐβοίας ἅλωσιν· τῷ δὲ πέμπτῳ καὶ δεκάτῳ ἔτει, ἐπὶ Χρυσίδος ἐν Ἄργει τότε πεντήκοντα δυοῖν δέοντα ἔτη ἱερωμένης καὶ Αἰνησίου ἐφόρου ἐν Σπάρτῃ καὶ Πυθοδώρου ἔτι δύο μῆνας ἄρχοντος Ἀθηναίοις, μετὰ τὴν ἐν Ποτειδαίᾳ μάχην μηνὶ ἕκτῳ καὶ ἅμα ἦρι ἀρχομένῳ Θηβαίων ἄνδρες ὀλίγῳ πλείους τριακοσίων (ἡγοῦντο δὲ αὐτῶν βοιωταρχοῦντες Πυθάγγελός τε ὁ Φυλείδου καὶ Διέμπορος ὁ Ὀνητορίδου) ἐσῆλθον περὶ πρῶτον ὕπνον ξὺν ὅπλοις ἐς Πλάταιαν τῆς Βοιωτίας οὖσαν Ἀθηναίων ξυμμαχίδα.

> The thirty years' truce that took place after the recapture of Euboea lasted for fourteen years. In the fifteenth year, when Chrysis was then in her forty-eighth year as priestess in Argos and Aenesias was ephor in Sparta and Pythodorus was archon for the Athenians with still two months to go, in the sixth month after the battle at Potidaea and just as spring was beginning, a little over three hundred men of Thebes under the command of the Boeotarchs Pythangelus son of Phylides and Diemporus son of Onetorides entered around first sleep with their weapons into Plataea, a city of Boeotia that was an ally of the Athenians.

Here Thucydides is no doubt using as his departure point the first Panhellenic work of synchrony in the Greek world, the work of Hellanicus of Lesbos on the priestesses of Hera at Argos. Hellanicus's work was not strictly or systematically synchronistic in the manner of the later chronological works we shall be examining shortly, in that he did not give parallel series of eponymous officials for each year but attached "facts and events to a certain name and a certain year in the list of the priestesses of Hera at Argos, and add[ed] for the sake of convenience synchronisms with, or relations to, a great epochal event."[43] It was Thucydides' initiative, in other words, to key in the names of the Spartan ephor and Athenian

archon to that of the Argive priestess.[44] These three names are not straightforwardly dates, but a vital way of reinforcing his theme that this is a war, and a history, of Panhellenic importance. And they are only one element of a panoply of
different time frames that Thucydides deploys here. The names are markers of an
event that happens "in the fifteenth year" after another key event, to form part of
a series that goes back to the Persian Wars; the incursion into Plataea is marked as
happening "six months after the battle at Potidaea," to form part of the small-scale
chain of events that lead directly to the outbreak of war; the beginning of the war
is given a framework within the phases of the natural year, so that the naturalness
of his beginning point is insensibly reinforced ("just as spring was beginning");
finally, the decisive instant of the incursion itself is marked as a time of the natural
day, keyed in to human rhythms ("around first sleep").[45]

One of the major problems for anyone wanting to use eponymous officials as the
organizing principle of a narrative is that archons at Athens and ephors at Sparta
did not take up office on the same day. Indeed, archons at Athens and ephors at
Sparta did not necessarily take up office one precise civil year after their predecessors, let alone one precise lunar year of 354 days, let alone one precise solar year of
365¼ days.[46] It is exactly this failure of civil demarcations and natural proceedings
to mesh that leads Thucydides later in his work to forswear counting off from
eponymous markers and to justify his practice of organizing his narrative by the
natural succession of summers and winters, counting year by year from the first
year of the war (5.20). In terms of an absolute chronology, of course, the sum-
mer/winter counting only works as a *dating* system if there is a fixed point provided as the departure, of the kind that Thucydides provides at the beginning of
book 2. After any lapse of time, it is no use saying, "It lasted exactly ten years," if
you do not say ten years "from *when*."

Our consideration of Thucydides brings home the fact that it was the writing of
history, of both Panhellenic history and its offshoots in local history, that provided
the original motivation for lining up the time schemes of the different states of
Greece.[47] The motivation did not come, as is sometimes claimed, from any "practical" need, such as dating documents, facilitating intercity diplomatic relations, or
harmonizing intercity festivals.[48] It is no coincidence, then, that the first person to
compose a systematically Panhellenic work of synchronistic chronography was
the historian Timaeus of Tauromenium (c. 350–c. 260 B.C.E.), who undertook this
labor in order to lay the basis for his comprehensive history of Sicily and the
Western Mediterranean.[49] This person will play an important role in the argument
of this book, for he is a major figure in the history of charting time in the Mediter-

ranean, as a flamboyant exponent of the significant synchronism, and as a crucial influence upon the development of the Roman historiographical tradition. His technical work of synchronistic chronology lined up Olympian victors, priestesses of Hera at Argos, Athenian archons, and Spartan kings and ephors;[50] he was, almost certainly, the man who made dating by Olympiads the norm in Greek historiography.[51]

The main synchronizing works of Greek chronography that became canonical in Hellenistic times were produced by the great Alexandrian scholars Eratosthenes and Apollodorus.[52] Eratosthenes, writing his *Chronographiae* toward the end of the third century B.C.E., with a terminus at the death of Alexander, roughly a century earlier, began his time lines with the fall of Troy, which he placed in "1184/3 B.C.E.," a date that eventually came close to being canonical.[53] He can only have established this mark by counting back in intervals from a fixed point in time, and this fixed point is most likely to have been the first celebration of the Olympic Games, which Eratosthenes placed in "776/5 B.C.E.," using a system he had laid out in a separate work on Olympian victors.[54] The evidence for the *Chronographiae* is so thin that we cannot securely recover his techniques or working assumptions.[55] It is certainly tempting to follow Wilcox and make a connection between the *Chronographiae* and Eratosthenes' interests in mathematics and geography, so that he would be pursuing the same interests in quantifying and measuring time as he had pursued in measuring space with his invention of the meridian or in measuring the circumference of the earth.[56] In chapter 3 we shall follow up the possibility that these demarcations in time, with Troy and the Olympic Games, had a significance in their own right, posting degrees of knowability about the past.

Apollodorus, writing about a century after Eratosthenes, composed his *Chronica* in four books, in iambic verse.[57] He followed Eratosthenes in beginning with the fall of Troy and extended his time frame down to his own time, in the 140s B.C.E. The possible significance of Troy as a starting point may be perceived in the book divisions Apollodorus imposed on the material of his first two books. His first book went from the fall of Troy to the Persian Wars, and the second book continued to the death of Alexander: the divisions themselves show an attempt to construct significant frames of time, in which the seesawing altercation between Greeks and barbarians could be discerned as the governing pattern of history. Apollodorus's purview did not restrict itself to kings and battles; he also charted the development of philosophical schools and poetic traditions.[58] He attempted to link succeeding generations, depending usually on his rule of thumb of the ἀκμή (peak), the idea that someone reaches their intellectual or creative peak at the age of forty.[59] Apollodorus, by birth an Athenian, used Athenian archonships as the backbone of his scheme, no doubt in large part because it was much easier to get an Athenian date of "in the archonship of so-and-so" into iambic verse than the cumbersome numerals of the Olympiads: anyone who has tried to write Greek iambics will know that "*epi/ep*' so-and-so [in the genitive]" scans a lot more easily than 'in the third year of the seventeenth Olympiad."[60] The Athenocentric backbone of the work, however, is not just a question of prosody; we shall follow the Athenocentric centripetal momentum of the Hellenistic chronographical tradition throughout the rest of this chapter, and in chapter 2, we shall see how much it matters that the real unifying thread in Apollodorus's work was Athens.

A number of other chronological works could claim our attention before we reach the transition point where the first Roman begins working in this tradition.[61] Here I note only one, the *Chronica* of Castor of Rhodes, written sometime soon after 61 B.C.E. This work appears immediately before the first Roman works of synchronistic chronography, and it is of special importance because it for the first time takes the crucial step of bringing the kingdoms of Asia into the synchronistic frame of the Hellenized world.[62]

THE FIRST INSTRUMENTS
OF ROMAN SYNCHRONISM

Synchronizations between Rome and Greece ultimately depend upon these intra-Hellenic systems of synchronization. As we shall see throughout, Roman-Greek synchronizations are inextricable from the Hellenized world's attempts to accommodate the Romans, and they form an indispensable part of Roman historical consciousness from the start. At the very beginning of the Roman historiographical tradition we find the Romans using parallelism in time as a mechanism for finding material when it was necessary to plug the gaps in reconstructing early Roman history. Pais first documented this favored technique a century ago, showing how, for example, the story of the catastrophe of the three hundred Fabii at the battle of the Cremera in 477 B.C.E. was calqued upon the catastrophe of the three hundred Spartans at Thermopylae in 480 B.C.E.[63] There is far more to such a procedure than merely casting around for handy stopgap material, for the first practitioners of this kind of synchronization must have been intent on demonstrating that early Roman history ranked in dignity with the history of Greece and was entitled to the venerability of proper historiographical treatment.[64]

It has long been debated whether any of these parallelisms may perhaps be rooted in actuality rather than in retrospective creation. The work of Wiseman shows an interesting movement from one pole to the other. In his recent paper on the ideology of Liber in the early and middle Republic, he no longer argues, as he did twenty years before, that the later Romans simply used synchronism to plug gaps in the stretches of early Roman history that they knew nothing about; rather, he argues that there may well have been in fact genuine links between the worlds of Greece and Rome at that time, specifically between the ideology of the early Republic and of contemporary democratic Athens.[65] According to tradition, the expulsion of the Athenian tyrants and the establishment of the Roman Republic happened at more or less the same time:[66] is the Roman ideology of freedom from tyranny in the Athenian mode an actual trace of contemporary interpretation or the creation of later retrospective historiography? In 1979 Wiseman would say that the connections are the result of retrospective gap-plugging, whereas in 2000 Wiseman would be much more inclined to the view that the connections represent a real link made by the Romans sometime around 500 B.C.E.[67] This example shows how hard it can be for us as well as them to draw the line between the significant link and the adventitious or coincidental. Both we and they must always be asking what actually makes synchronism not just technically useful or contingently convenient or thought-provokingly piquant, but historically or ideologically significant.

It is only in the age of Cicero that we meet the first Roman writer of chronography, the first person systematically to bring Roman events within the framework of Greek chronographic scholarship.[68] The man responsible was Cornelius Nepos, who is hailed by Catullus in his dedicatory poem as the one who "alone/first of Italians dared to unfold the whole of past time in three rolls, learned ones, by Jupiter, and full of hard work" (*ausus es unus Italorum/omne aeuum tribus explicare cartis/doctis, Iuppiter, et laboriosis*, 1.5–7).[69] The date of Nepos's *Chronica* will therefore fall somewhere in the mid-50s B.C.E.

Nepos synchronized events and persons in Greek and Roman history, lining up the Greek poet Archilochus, for example, with the reign of the Roman king Tullus Hostilius.[70] His project aimed at "a public perplexed by how Homer, Archilochus, and the Olympic Games might fit into a chronological scheme that they could themselves comprehend."[71] A key fixed point of reference for Nepos was the foundation of the city of Rome, which he followed Polybius in assigning to the second year of the seventh Olympiad, "751/0 B.C.E." Among the fragments of the work, we may see him using the foundation as an interval marker, giving an ἀκμή for Homer of 160 years before the foundation of the city, or marking the birth of Alexander the Great in the 385th year after the foundation of Rome, with the names of the consuls of the year.[72] The best way to get some idea of what the *Chronica* may have looked like is perhaps to read the first book of Velleius Paterculus.[73] Here one finds extensive use of all the paraphernalia of chronological scholarship: interval counting ("in the eightieth year after the capture of Troy," 1.2.1); positioning of important literary figures (Homer, 1.5; Hesiod, 1.7.1); the memorable digression on the clustering of talent at circumscribed periods (1.16–17); significant synchronisms (Carthage and the Macedonian monarchy founded at the same time, 1.6.4–5); counting back from the time of writing (1.8.1; 1.8.4; 1.12.5); dating by Olympiads (1.8.4).

The correlation of Greek and Roman years that Nepos is constructing is much harder to achieve than it looks, not least because the basic unit of the year is a variable one.[74] A Roman consular year looks as if it is a secure unit, running, like our year, from the beginning of January to the end of December, but in fact the consuls had only regularly taken up office on 1 January from 153 B.C.E.;[75] between that date and 222 B.C.E. they had taken up office on March 15, and before 222 the consuls took up and left office at any point in the seasonal year, depending on campaigning exigencies.[76] The consular year, then, is a fuzzy chronological unit, not corresponding necessarily with the civil calendrical year. Further, if Nepos is counting from the foundation of the city, he is strictly counting from 21 April, the anniversary of Romulus's founding of Rome on the feast of the Parilia, not from January, or March. When he turns to correlate any of these years with a Greek year, he is faced with problems that will now be familiar to the reader, for the years of the various Greek states did not overlap, beginning now in summer, for example, as in Athens, or in autumn, as in Macedonia or Achaea. The only Panhellenic chronological unit available to scholars or historians was the Olympian year, but this ran from midsummer to midsummer, bisecting the campaigning season together with the corresponding Roman consular year.[77] How aware Nepos was of the problems, and how successfully he solved them, we cannot now ascertain.

One can develop a sense of the problems facing ancient chronographers and historians by imagining how a modern Nepos might express a date if we lived in a counterfactual world without an internationally agreed calendar and numerical dating system. The D-day invasion would no longer be dated to 6 June 1944. First of all, the event would be marked as coming after an interval of so many years from an earlier important event, as part of the interval-spacing mechanism—let us say, thirty years after the outbreak of the previous war. The actual day would have a different notation in the different calendars of Britain, Germany, and the United

States, and the year might be expressed as the fifth year of the war (counting from the equivalent of 3 September 1939), the fifth year of the premiership of Winston Churchill (from 10 May 1940), the eighth year of King George VI (from 11 December 1936), the twelfth year of Adolf Hitler (from 30 January 1933), the fourth year of the third presidential term of Franklin D. Roosevelt (from 20 January 1941), the 168th year of the republic of the United States (from the Declaration of Independence in 1776).[78] This counterfactual example brings home, once again, how what for us are numerical expressions are for the Romans and Greeks patterns of intervals and clusters of individuals and institutions.

Some few years after Nepos's *Chronica*, at the end of the year 47 B.C.E., Cicero's friend Atticus published his *Liber Annalis* (Book of Years).[79] To correlate with the Roman consuls, Atticus (the nickname of course means "Athenian") used the archons of his adopted city of Athens as the backbone of his work, so that the real unifying thread of the Greek side of his comparison was Athens.[80] In this respect, he is a continuator of the Athenian Apollodorus, with similar interests in Athenian philosophical and literary history, and we shall see the importance of this Atheno-centric focus recurring as a theme later in this chapter, especially with Aulus Gellius, and in chapter 2.[81] For the composer of synchronisms, it is not a neutral process to choose which events and protagonists in one culture are going to be lined up against which events and protagonists in another culture; even more, as we see with Atticus, it is not a neutral process to choose which cultures are going to be lined up against each other in the first place. We may talk casually about synchronisms between Greece and Rome, but there is no Greek time against which to plot Roman time. Roman time is unified, as the time of one city, but Greek time is not: there is only Athenian time or Spartan time or Syracusan or Argive. It is always vital to ask which perspective on Greek time is being adopted at any moment, through which calendrical or historical tradition the idea of Greek time is being focalized, and what motivates the choice of the dates that are going to be used as hooks on either side. In the case of Atticus we see how his domicile and his cultural interests must be motivating the selection of Athens as the counterweight to Rome in the construction of a shared Greek and Roman past.

Atticus's book was soon superseded by what became the canonical Roman chronographic work, the *De Gente Populi Romani* of the polymath Varro, completed probably in 43 B.C.E.[82] It was Varro, very probably, who defined the date for the foundation of the city of Rome that came closer to canonical status than any other, the third year of the sixth Olympiad, "754/3 B.C.E."[83]

SIMILE, *SYNKRISIS,* AND SYNCHRONISM

As we observe these Roman authors making connections between Greek and Roman persons and events, it becomes clear that the project of Roman-Greek synchronism is part of the larger project of comparison between Rome and Greece— that immense exercise in comparison, or *synkrisis,* that we label as Roman Hellenization. It is telling that two of the first Roman chronographers, Nepos and Varro, also wrote biographical series of lives of famous Romans and Greeks, as a kind of an analogue to this synchronism project.[84] The urge to compare and contrast Roman and Greek finds expression in synchronistic chronography and in synkristic biography.[85] Nepos's arrangement of the *Lives* shows this most clearly. His lives were not paired one by one, as was Plutarch's way a century later; rather, in each category (generals, historians, and so on), a book of foreign lives came first, followed by a book of Roman ones. By chance, Nepos's words survive from the end of his book *On Famous Generals of Foreign Nations* (*De Excellentibus Ducibus Exterarum Gentium*). They make the comparative nature of the project quite explicit (*Hann.* 13.4):

> Sed nos tempus est huius libri facere finem et Romanorum explicare
> imperatores, quo facilius, collatis utrorumque factis, qui uiri praeferendi sint
> possit iudicari.

> But it is time to make an end of this book and to unfold the commanders of the
> Romans, so that, by comparing the deeds of each, judgment may more easily
> be passed on which men should be put first.

From this comparative perspective, "synchronisms are the application of similes to history."[86] As we shall see repeatedly, the simile-like nature of synchronism is one that repays taking very seriously. Just as a simile may stress difference as much as likeness, opening up areas of disjunction as much as closeness, so too the project of synchronism—as with any dimension of "Roman Hellenization"—may bring disparity and difference into focus as much as similiarity.[87] The instruments of synchronism are not simply helpful lists of scholarly fact. The chronographies are frames of exclusion as well as inclusion, with their own strategies and ideologies. It is very telling, for example, that neither Apollodorus nor Eratosthenes mentioned—that is, gave a synchronic date for—the foundation of Rome, and that they only started to take notice of Roman events at all when they arrived at the invasion of Italy by the Greek king Pyrrhus, when Roman affairs are directly in-volved with those of mainland Greece, in the person of a descendant of Achilles.[88] This is an example of, as it were, a "reverse simile," a simile that operates by focus-ing on difference and unlikeness. By this approach, the Romans are denied the "likeness" of synchronicity, not being allowed to be part of civilized time until the latest possible moment. They are stuck in what Fabian's study of anthropologists' constructions of time calls an "allochrony," an "other-time," a temporal space that is qualitatively unlike "ours," in being static, early, undeveloped.[89] From the per-spective of an Apollodorus, the Roman past is isolated and unintegrated, not involved with Greece's past, and not participating in the movement of progressive historical time.[90]

Once again, the modern Western digits can make it easier for us in many con-texts to conceive of dates as somehow "there," with time in different cultures being inherently shared in a sense, by virtue of being plottable on the same numerical axis. The ancients' mechanisms for synchronism, on the other hand, bring the pro-cess of selection to the fore, so that one may remain continually aware of whether the shared quality of time is being asserted or denied. If we had more evidence, it might be possible to be more confident that the synchronistic projects of Nepos, Atticus, and Varro were working against the Greek perspective of an Apollodorus, and striving to establish a pattern of "likeness," in response to the enormous pres-sure exerted by Hellenism, following the pattern whereby "a superior culture per-suades an inferior that to be significant its past must be interdependent with its own."[91] Certainly Nepos's biographical project is one that operates comparison on the "likeness" model, stressing that "Greek and Roman subjects are placed together on a level," as Rawson puts it;[92] his *Chronica* may well have worked in analogous fashion, showing that Greek and Roman events could likewise be "placed together on a level."

A CICERONIAN TEST CASE: FROM "LIKE" TO "UNLIKE"

The intellectual career of Cicero vividly illustrates how much difference could be made to a Roman's perception of the past by a refocalizing of synchronistic per-spective, one that in his case involves a movement from the mode of "like" to the mode of "unlike." His attitude to the chronological relationship between Roman and Greek culture undergoes a definite shift in 47/6 B.C.E., and at the beginning of the *Brutus* (13–16) he explicitly attributes his new interest in chronology and literary history to the experience of reading the *Liber Annalis* of his friend Atticus. It is by no means the case that his great dialogues before this date, *De Oratore* (55 B.C.E.) and *De Republica* (51 B.C.E.), are ill informed or unlearned—on the contrary, they reveal a remarkable level of scholarly knowledge about Greek and Roman history, embedded in a secure chronological framework.[93] Nor should we attribute all the changes we discern in the later dialogues, especially *Brutus* (46 B.C.E.), to the impact of reading one book; Cicero had been reading continuously in the intervening years, and even after reading Atticus's *Liber Annalis* he did not rely solely upon it for all chronological information.[94] Nonetheless, a new intellectual excitement about the issues of chronology reveals itself in the *Brutus;*[95] in particular, there is a new perspective on the question of how to synchronize the historical developments of Greek and Roman culture, and this new perspective is one that it makes sense to see coming from the experience of reading Atticus's book, as Cicero tells us it did.[96]

In the masterpieces of the 50s, Cicero's use of transcultural parallels between Greece and Rome is very different from what we see later in the *Brutus*. Cicero's main interest is in "likeness" across the cultures, rather than disjunction. In the earlier works there is a constant seeking of parallels between the cultural development of Greece and Rome, together with a use of chronological analogy that seems practically unhistorical in comparison with what we shall see in the *Brutus*.[97] One of the most striking cases in the *De Republica* can be seen in his discussion of the apotheosis of Romulus (2.18–19). Here the speaker, Scipio, argues that we should believe in the apotheosis as a fact, not a fable, since Romulus did not live in a rude age, but less than six hundred years earlier, at a time of letters, "when Greece was already full of poets and musicians, and there was less belief in fables unless they were about old events" (*cum iam plena Graecia poetarum et musicorum esset minorque fabulis nisi de ueteribus rebus haberetur fides*). As Zetzel puts it, "the argument is that even the earliest period of Roman history was contemporary with (and therefore took part in) a high level of culture in Greece."[98]

In the *Brutus*, a different sensibility is in view, one that is far more interested in the "unlikeness" that is generated by the act of comparing the chronologies of the two cultures. Looking at Atticus's synchronisms opened Cicero's eyes, it appears, and at the beginning of the *Brutus* he praises and acknowledges his friend's accomplishment (13–16). The comparison of the time schemes seems to have brought home in detail just how different the two societies were in their intellectual and literary development. In particular, Cicero is now very struck by the fact that Greece has a literature from the beginning, whereas Rome only develops one late, a mere two centuries before the date of Cicero's last dialogues.[99] This novel perspective is not one that Cicero finds it automatically convenient to work with, and there are some slightly confused passages in the *Brutus* that owe their complexity to Cicero's attempts to adapt familiar material to this new framework.[100]

Early in the *Brutus*, at the climax of his brief survey of Greek oratory, Cicero even goes so far as gracefully to act out the impact Atticus's book is having on him. The passage begins with Cicero carefully stressing the different comparative chronologies of Greece and Rome, in the manner he has been recently rethinking. Solon and Pisistratus are early by Roman chronology, he says, but late by Greek (or, as he vividly puts it, old men by Roman reckoning, just teenagers by Greek: *at hi quidem, ut populi Romani aetas est, senes, ut Atheniensium saecula numerantur, adulescentes debent uideri,* 39). After going back in time to Homer momentarily (40), Cicero returns to his chronology and mentions the key figure in the generation after Pisistratus, namely Themistocles. Here again he is at pains to stress his new apprehension of the difference in comparative chronologies, for Themistocles is a piece of hoary antiquity to the Romans, but not so very old to Athenians, living at a developed period of Greek history, and a primitive state of Roman (41): for, he says, the Volscian war in which Coriolanus was involved occurred at the same time as the Persian Wars. At this point, having made his careful disjunctive chronological point, Cicero swerves into a piece of adventitious synchronism of the "bad old" kind: Coriolanus and Themistocles did not just happen to live at the same time; they even had similar fortunes (*similisque fortuna clarorum uirorum,* 41). Cicero sketches the parallels of their careers, concluding with the claim that they both committed suicide, whereupon he turns to Atticus and acknowledges that this is not the version of Coriolanus's death to be found in Atticus's book (42). Atticus, the expert, proceeds to correct and mock the spurious parallelisms created by this kind of history, ending with a dig at Cicero's wish to make Coriolanus a second Themistocles (*alter Themistocles,* 43). Cicero accepts the correction (44) and promises to be more cautious in his historical treatment for the rest of the dialogue—as indeed he is, carefully avoiding such synchronistic parallels between Greece and Rome from then on. The implied compliment to Atticus's education of his friend is very striking, and Cicero has gone out of his way to stage this example of how he has been instructed in the use and abuse of parallelism and synchronization.[101]

What might it have been about Atticus's book that particularly seized Cicero's attention and brought home to him a different sense of the chronological relationship between the two cultures? Habinek suggests that Atticus's "work must have been more condensed and exhibited better layout than Nepos's did."[102] Cicero's language in praise of the book certainly stresses its utility and seems to do so in terms of its physical appearance. Atticus asks him, "What did that book have that could have been so new or so useful to you?" (*sed quid tandem habuit liber iste quod tibi aut nouum aut tanto usui posset esse? Brut.* 14). Cicero responds (15):

> Ille uero et noua, inquam, mihi quidem multa et eam utilitatem quam requirebam, ut explicatis ordinibus temporum uno in conspectu omnia uiderem.

> "It really had many things that were new to me," I replied, "and it gave me that usefulness that I was looking for, namely that, with the ranks of times deployed, with one overview I could see everything."

The utility resides in the way you could see everything at once, as a result of the fact that the "orders of the times" were "explicated" in one view (*explicatis ordinibus temporum*). My translation above ("with the ranks of times deployed") brings out one possible metaphor, a military one: instead of being in a single array, the "times" have been "deployed out into lines or columns."[103] Possibly, then, Atticus's book was arranged in parallel columns, with Greek events, organized around Athenian archons, on one side, and Roman, organized around consuls, on the other. It may have been this novel and useful physical layout that gripped Cicero, as it made the act of synchronous comparison so easy and brought home to him the disparate relationship in event and achievement between the two columns. One can imagine Cicero scanning the book for information about literary culture: on the Greek side, Archilochus—on the Roman side . . . a gap; on the Greek side, Demosthenes—on the Roman side . . . And so on, all the way down to 240 B.C.E., where finally there is a literary entry for the Roman column, for the first time, when a tragedy is staged in Rome, over 160 years after the deaths of Sophocles and Euripides. This possibility is a lot to conjure from the trace of a metaphor, but it would help explain the impact of the book on someone who already had a good acquaintance with synchronistic scholarship, in the form of Nepos's *Chronica*.

THE CHRISTIAN
SYNCHRONISTIC CHRONOGRAPHERS

If Atticus's book did have an arrangement in columns, it was almost certainly the first synchronistic work to do so.[104] But the book had little impact after Cicero, and the true credit for the columnar arrangement belongs to the Christian bishop Eusebius of Caesarea, whose *Chronicle* we may briefly consider here, as the culmination of the tradition I have been sketching, before we turn to the test case of Aulus Gellius.

The first edition of Eusebius's *Chronicle* appeared around 300 C.E., comprising a *Chronographia*, setting out "all his sources and the raw information that he derived from them," and the Chronological Tables (Χρονικοὶ κανόνες, *Chronici Canones*), "the synthesis and tabulation of the raw material in the *Chronographia*."[105] All of this has been lost, but we have surviving Jerome's *Chronicle*, completed in 381 C.E., in which he not only translated the second, major part, the *Chronici Canones*, from Greek into Latin but also continued the work down to the very recent past, ending with the battle of Adrianople in 378.[106] Jerome preserved the columnar layout very faithfully, and his work enables us to appreciate the extraordinary innovation in design represented by Eusebius's parallel time lines.

These works are part of a long-standing Christian project of synchronizing the new sacred history with the old profane history of the pagans and the old sacred history of the Jews so as to create a new truly universal human history, the plan of God for salvation, one that was regularly interpreted as part of various end-time obsessions.[107] In this tradition the pagan time lines confront and finally succumb to the much greater antiquity of the Hebrew and Eastern tradition, in a classic example of what Zerubavel calls "out-past-ing."[108] The greater antiquity of the East had been an issue for the Greeks ever since Hecataeus of Miletus, sometime around 500 B.C.E., had bragged to an Egyptian priest that his lineage went back a whole sixteen generations to Heracles, and the priest had beckoned him around the corner and shown him the statues of 345 successive high priests, going back 11,340 years.[109]

In Eusebius and Jerome you could see this out-past-ing graphically embodied, with pages of Hebrew and Asiatic history before any significant events in Greece, or any events at all in Italy. The reader could follow the teleological direction of human history in a series of parallel columns lined up in chronological unison across the page. These columns presented the major monarchies and civilizations of the world, and as you went through the book you would see their number collapsing and shrinking through the theme of the succession of empires. On an early page (see figure 1), you would see in parallel the time line of the Medes, the Hebrew kingdoms of Judah and Israel, the Athenians, the Romans (or, before the foundation of Rome, the Latins of Alba Longa), the Macedonians, the Lydians, and the Egyptians. To accommodate all these columns, a full double spread was necessary, covering both pages of the codex. Each column counts off regnal years of each individual monarchy; the far left-hand column gives the Olympiads, marking

Medorum	Hebraeorum Iuda		Hebraeorum Israhel	Atheniensium	
XVIIII	I		III	VI	
II·Olymp.					
XX	II		IIII	VII	
XXI	III		V	VIII	
XXII	IIII		VI	VIIII	5
XXIII	V	ᵃ Profetabant qui et supra	VII	X	
III·Olymp.					
XXIIII	VI		VIII	XI	
MCCL XXV	VII		VIIII	XII	
XXVI	VIII		X	XIII	10
XXVII	VIIII	ᵇ Profetabant	XI	XIIII	
IIII·Olxmp.	Osee				
XXVIII	X	Ioel	XII	XV	
XXVIIII	XI	Esaias	XIII	XVI	
XXX	XII	Oded	XIIII	XVII	15
Medorum · III ·					
Madydus · ann · XL ·					
I	XIII		XV	XVIII	
V·Olymp.					
II	XIIII	ᶜ Eumelus poeta, qui Bugoni-	XVI	XVIIII	20
III	XV	am et Europiam, et Arctinus,	XVII	XX	
IIII	XVI	qui Aethiopidam conposuit, et	XVIII	XXI	
	Hebraeorum	Ilii persis agnoscitur			
	Iuda · XIIII ·				
	Achaz · ann · XVI ·				25
MCCLX V	I		XVIIII	XXII	

FIGURE I.

Jerome's *Chronicle* for the years 773–757 B.C.E., showing eight time columns spreading over both pages of the codex. Helm 1956, 87.

them off every four years. The big underlined numbers in the left column, marked off every ten years, are the years from the birth of Abraham in "2016 B.C.E.," the Christianizing year that really counts as the anchor; accordingly, the second year of the third Olympiad for the Greeks is 1,250 years from the birth of Abraham. It goes without saying that the B.C.E. dates in the far right-hand column are the addition of the modern editor, Rudolf Helm.

As you made your way through the book of history, one column after another would disappear as it was absorbed by the power of another column. By the time Jerome arrives at 281 B.C.E., with Antiochus Soter taking over Syria and Asia, there are only four columns on each page, and Jerome can fit all of them onto one page of the codex, without a double spread. The last pages showing four columns cover the years 106–93 B.C.E. (see figure 2). On each of these pages, left and right, one

Latinorum	Macedonum		Τγ̣ηυραυ	Αεγγ̣ρtιορϋm	
XXIIII	I	*d* Remus et Romulus generantur Marte et Ilia	VI	VIII	773 a. Chr.
XXV	II		VII	VIIII	772
XXVI	III	*e* Athenis primum trieres nauigauit	VIII	X	771
5 XXVII	IIII	Aminocleo cursum dirigente	VIIII	XI	770
XXVIII	V		X	XII	769
XXVIIII	VI		XI	XIII	768
XXX	VII	*f* Hesiodus secundum quosdam clarus	XII	XIIII	767
10 XXXI	VIII	habetur	XIII	XV	766
XXXII	VIIII		XIIII	XVI	765
		g Cinaethon Lacedaemonius poeta,			
XXXIII	X	qui Telegoniam scripsit, agnoscitur	XV	XVII	764
XXXIIII	XI		XVI	XVIII	763
15 XXXV	XII		XVII	XVIIII	762
		h Theraei Cyrenen condiderunt oraculo sic iubente. Conditor ur-			
XXXVI	XIII	bis Battus, cuius proprium nomen Aristoteles	XVIII	XX	761
20 XXXVII	XIIII		XVIIII	XXI	760
XXXVIII	XV	*i* Aradus insula condita	XX	XXII	759
XXXVIIII	XVI		XXI	XXIII	758
		k In Lacedaemone primus Εφορος, quod magistratus nomen est, con-			
25		stituitur. Fuit autem sub regi-			
XL	XVII	bus Lacedaemon · ann · CCCL ·	XXII	XXIIII	757

sees the same four columns: (i) the kings of Alexandria, the Macedonian inheritors of the Egyptian pharaohs, (ii) the Romans, (iii) the Seleucid kings of Syria and Asia, the inheritors of the various Asiatic kingdoms, and (iv) the Jews. At the bottom right of the last page, under "93 B.C.E.," is the announcement of the end of the kingdom of the Seleucids: *Syriae et Asiae regnum defecit* ("The kingdom of Syria and Asia ended"). Accordingly, for the years 48–45 B.C.E. (see figure 3), there are only three time lines, those of the Romans, the Alexandrians, and the Jews. The year 48 B.C.E. is marked as the first regnal year of Julius Caesar, the first Roman emperor: *Romanorum primus Caius Iulius Caesar;* and from now on the Roman column is counted off in terms of the emperors' regnal years. In 30 B.C.E., the Alexandrian column disappears with Augustus's conquest of Ptolemaic Egpyt, leaving only two columns, those of the Romans and the Jews, as for the years 27–24 B.C.E.

	Alexandrinorum	Romanorum	Syriae et Asiae	Iudaeorum	
106 a. Chr.	X	*a* Cicero Arpini nascitur matre Heluia, patre equestris ordinis ex regio Vulscorum genere*	VII	XXV	
105	XI CLXVIIII·Olymp·	*b* Gn· Pompeius Magnus oritur*	VIII	XXVI Iudaeorum Aristo- bulus ·ann·I·	5
104	XII	*c* Aristobulus, filius Ionathae, rex pariter et pontifex primus aput Iudaeos diadematis sumpsit insigne post ·CCCCLXXXIIII· annos Babyloniae captiuitatis. Post quem regnauit Iannaeus cognomento Alexander, qui pontificatum quoque administrans crudelissime ciuibus praefuit	VIIII	I post quem Iannaeus, qui et Alexander, ann·XXVII·	10
		d Turpilius comicus senex admodum Sinuessae moritur*			15
103	XIII	*e* Gaius Lucilius satyrarum scriptor Neapoli moritur ac publico funere effertur anno aetatis ·XLVI·*	X	I	
		f M· Furius poeta cognomento Bibaculus Cremonae nascitur*			20
102	XIIII	*g* CC· milia Cimbrorum caesa et LXXX· milia capta per Marium cum duce Teutobodo*	XI	II	
101	XV	*h* Gaius Marius quinquies consul iuxta [h]Eridanum Cimbros superat et de his	XII	III	25

FIGURE 2.

Jerome's *Chronicle* for the years 106–93 B.C.E., with the four remaining time columns taking up one page of the codex. Helm 1956, 148–49.

(see figure 4). In 70 C.E. the Jewish column disappears with Titus's capture of Jerusalem, so that for the years 73–78 C.E. (see figure 5), there is only one column on each page, *Romanorum*, the column of Roman time. Now there is only one time line left for the whole of the known world, the time line of the Roman Empire, which was to be perfected into a Christian empire in the lifetime of the original author, Eusebius.[110] This is, as it were, a graphic inverse image of the way that the early Roman annalistic tradition mushrooms as it assimilates more and more of the world, so that the year-by-year history of a single city becomes a way of narrating the history of the entire world.

AULUS GELLIUS'S SYNCHRONISTIC CHAPTER: A PARADIGM CASE

These Christian developments would have astounded and dismayed our cheerful pedant Gellius, who would have heard of Christians and perhaps even seen some,

Alexandrinorum	Consules	Syriae et Asiae	Iudaeorum	
III.XX Olymp·	cum Catulo triumfat(∗)			
XVI	*a* Thraces a Romanis uicti	XIII	IIII	100 a. Chr.
	b Rursum in Sicilia bellum ser-			
XVII	uile consurgit	XIIII	V	99
Aegypti ·VIIII· Ptolemaeus, qui et Alexander, ann·X·				
I	*c* Expulso de regno Ptolemaeo	XV	VI	98
	Fyscone per matrem Cleopa-			
MDCC II	tram et in Cyprum secedente	XVI	VII	97
CCXX CLXXI·Olymp·				
III	*d* Aquilius in Sicilia bellum	XVII	VIII	96
	seruile conpescuit			
	e Ptolomaeus, rex Cyrenae, moriens Ro-			
	manos testamento reliquit heredes∗			
IIII	*f* Seleucus ab Antiocho, filio Cyzi-	XVIII	VIIII	95
	ceni, uiuus exuritur	Syriae Filip-		
		pus ·ann·II·		
V	*g* Titus Lucretius poeta nascitur.	I	X	94
	Qui postea amatorio poculo in fu-			
	rorem uersus, cum aliquot libros			
VI	per interualla insaniae conscripsis-	II	XI	93
	set, quos postea Cicero emendauit,	Syriae et Asiae		
	propria se manu interfecit anno	regnum defecit		
	aetatis ·XLIIII·∗	ꙅꙅꙅꙅꙅꙅꙅꙅꙅ		

but who could have had no conception that his world would be turned upside down by these people within five generations. I now turn finally to him, to pick out briefly some of the most important ways in which the synchronistic mentality could work for the pagans. Gellius's essay is sometimes derided as an inconsequential magpie jumble of disparate synchronisms, but he knows his traditions, and his collection shows a series of valuable intuitions about what is at stake in this apparently mechanical exercise.

At the very beginning of the essay, Gellius says that his subject is "the times when those Greeks and Romans flourished who were famous and conspicuous *either for talent or for political power* (*uel ingenio uel imperio nobiles insignesque*), between the founding of Rome and the Second Punic War" (*NA* 17.21.1).[111] We are reminded that the programme of Apollodorus and his followers included what we would call literary and intellectual history as well as political and military. It is this larger cultural dimension of the synchronism project that provides the main explanation for why Gellius stops where he does. He says he will stop with the Second

	Romanorum		Alexan-drinorum	Iudae-orum	
		a Gaius Iulius Caesar primus aput Romanos singulare optinuit imperium, a quo Caesares Romanorum principes appellati			
	Romanorum primus ·C· Iulius Caesar ·ann·IIII· mensib·VII·				5
	b Ab hoc loco I Antiocheni	*c* Pompeius proelio uictus et fugiens a spadonibus Alexandrini regis occiditur	III	XX	
48 a. Chr.	sua tempora computant	*d* M· Caelius praetor et Titus Annius Milo exul oppressi res nouas in Thuriano Bruttioque agro simul molientes*			10
47	MDCCCCLXX II	*e* Ptolomaei cadauer cum lorica aurea in Nilo inuentum*	IIII	XXI	
		f Caesar in Aegypto regnum Cleopatrae confirmat ob stupri gratiam			15
46	III	*g* Romae basilica Iulia dedicata*	V	XXII	
		h Decretum senatus et Atheniensium ad Iudaeos mittitur, qui per legationem amicitiam postularant			
		i Cleopatra regio comitatu urbem ingressa*			20
		k Prohibitae lecticis margaritisque uti quae nec uiros nec liberos haberent et minores essent annis ·XLV·*			
45	IIII	*l* Nigidius Figulus Pythagoricus et magus in exilio moritur*?	VI	XXIII	25

FIGURE 3.
Jerome's *Chronicle* for the years 48–45 B.C.E., showing three time columns.
Helm 1956, 156.

Punic War ("218–201 B.C.E."), but he carries on for a hundred years past this declared *terminus*, ending with the death of the poet Lucilius. It is in keeping with his usual carefully cultivated air of amateurism that he should meander on past his announced end point, just as he throws in the dates of Homer and Hesiod at the beginning with apparent artlessness (3), even though they predate his starting point of the foundation of Rome. But the transgression is very pointed, for, by carrying on to Lucilius, Gellius is able to end the essay with a catalogue of Roman literary figures (Cato, Plautus, Ennius, Caecilius, Terence, Pacuvius, Accius, and Lucilius, 46–49). He feels able to conclude the essay, in other words, only when he has reached a point in time where Rome has established some kind of record in the domain of literature, and this is plausible only a long time after the Hannibalic War.[112]

An insistent theme of the entire essay is the late arrival of literature, or of any kind of intellectual culture, in Rome. Gellius derives this perspective above all

Romanorum				Iudaeorum	
			et magus ab Augusto urbe Italia-		
			que pellitur∗		
			a M· Terentius Uarro filosofus pro-		
			pe nonagenarius moritur∗		
27 a. Chr.	MDCCCCXC	XVII	*b* Thebae Aegypti usque ad solum erutae	VII	5
			c Cornelius Gallus Foroiuliensis poe-		
			ta, a quo primum Aegyptum rectam su-		
			pra diximus, XLIII· aetatis suae anno		
			propria se manu interficit∗		
			d Trallis terrae motu consederunt		10
26		XVIII	*e* Indi ab Augusto per legatos amiciti-	VIII	
			am postularunt∗?		
			f Messala Coruinus primus praefec-		
			tus urbi factus sexto die magi-		
			stratu se abdicauit inciuilem po-		15
			testatem esse contestans∗		
25		XVIIII	*g* Augustus Calabriam et Gallos	VIIII	
			uectigales facit		
			h Munatius Plancus Ciceronis discipu-		
			lus orator habetur insignis. Qui		20
			cum Galliam comatam regeret,		
			Lugdunum condidit∗		
	CLXXXVIIII · Olymp ·				
24		XX	*i* M· Lollius Galatiam Romanam pro-	X	
			uinciam facit		25

FIGURE 4.
Jerome's *Chronicle* for the years 27–24 B.C.E., showing two time columns.
Helm 1956, 164.

from Cicero, who seems to have come to this recognition, never quite apprehended by him in this way before, via his perusal of Atticus's *Liber Annalis* in the winter of 47/6 B.C.E.[113] All the way through, Gellius subtly highlights a consistent disparity between the early entries on the Greek literary and cultural side and the gap on the Roman side. Early on (10), he tells us that at the time when Aeschylus was flourishing, the Romans were instituting the offices of tribune and aedile. When Empedocles was eminent in natural philosophy, the Romans were drawing up the Twelve Tables (15). The Greek period that boasted Sophocles, Euripides, Hippocrates, Democritus, and Socrates, has as a counterpart in Rome the good old Roman story of a father mercilessly executing his son for disobeying military orders (17–18). The synchronism of the philosophers Epicurus and Zeno with the stern censorship of Fabricius and Aemilius Papus (38–39) clearly plays to a traditional Roman pattern, whereby the Greeks rely on philosophers to tell them how to behave, while the Romans have authoritative father-figures who enforce the *mos*

Romanorum

CCXIII · Olymp ·

73 p. Chr.	V		*a* Uespasianus Capitolium aedificare or- sus	
			b In Alexandria facta seditio	
74 ĪĪLXXXX VI			*c* Achaia Lycia Rhodus Byzantium Sa- mus Thracia Cilicia Commagene, quae liberae antea et sub regibus amicis erant, in prouincias redactae∗	5
75	VII		*d* Colossus erectus habens altitudinis pedes ·CVII·	10
			e Q. Asconius Pedianus scriptor histori- cus clarus habetur. Qui ·LXXIII· aeta-	
76	VIII		tis suae anno captus luminibus duo- decim postea annis in summo omni- um honore consenescit∗	15
			f Gabinianus celeberrimi nominis rhe- tor in Gallia docuit∗	

CCXIIII · Olymp ·

77	VIIII		*g* Tres ciuitates Cypri terrae motu conruerunt	20
			h Lues ingens Romae facta ita ut per mul- tos dies in efemeridem decem milia fer- me mortuorum hominum referrentur	
78	X		*i* Uespasianus colonias deduxit et mor- tuus est profluuio uentris in uilla propria circa Sabinos	25

FIGURE 5.
Jerome's *Chronicle* for the years 73–78 C.E., showing the only time column left, that of Roman time. Helm 1956, 188.

maiorum. When Gellius, shortly afterwards (42), finally arrives at the beginning of Roman literature, in "240 B.C.E.," he puts enormous stress on how late this was in comparison to Greece:

> primus omnium L. Livius poeta fabulas docere Romae coepit post Sophoclis et Euripidis mortem annis plus fere centum et sexaginta, post Menandri annis circiter quinquaginta duobus.

> The poet Lucius Livius was the very first to produce plays at Rome, more than 160 years after the death of Sophocles and Euripides, and about 52 years after the death of Menander.

This dating is not a synchronism; it is an anti-synchronism, highlighting just how drastically the two cultures were not in harmony with each other. This is a text-book example of the phenomenon that Zerubavel calls "inflating the divide be-tween periods"—in 241 Rome has not got a literature; in 239, it has.[114] Gellius

might have stopped soon after, with the first literary figures of Rome, but it is significant that he carries on until he reaches Accius and Lucilius at the end of the
essay. Only with them is there not simply a literary tradition in Rome but a liter-
ary-critical tradition as well: Accius was, if anything, more famous as a scholar and
literary historian than as a tragic poet, and Lucilius is noted here by Gellius not just
as a poet, but as a critic of the poetry of his predecessors (*clarior . . . in poematis
eorum obtrectandis,* 49).[115] In other words, Gellius stops when the Romans have
established the foundations not only of a literature but of a literary history, with
the attendant apparatus of literary scholarship inherited from their contemporaries
and predecessors in Alexandria. This is the moment when it has achieved some
kind of parity with Greece in the realm of culture—or at least can be represented
by a partisan Roman, with some kind of plausibility, as having achieved parity.

It is this same cultural perspective that accounts for the fact that none of the
Romans mentioned after the end of the Second Punic War (46 to the close of the
essay) is mentioned in a political or imperial context: all of them are literary. Even
the great Cato figures in this list as an *orator* (47), that is, in his capacity as the
inventor of Latin prose, rather than as consul, censor, or imperator. This eclipse of
the political or imperial dimension in Gellius's scamper through people after the
end of the Second Punic War is most revealing. Throughout the essay he has been
charting the synchronism of Greek and Roman *political* and *imperial* developments, and now, once the war against Hannibal has been won, he stops doing this.
The one mention of a political nature is the embassy of Athenian philosophers to
Rome in 155 B.C.E. (48), where we see the Greek philosophical tradition at the disposal of the Roman state.[116] The key point, of course, is one that emerges obliquely
from this citation of the embassy of philosophers: Greece is now completely under
the thumb of Rome following Rome's destruction of Greek military strength after
the Hannibalic War, and Greek knowledge is now harnessed to Roman power.[117]
The project of synchronism carries with it implicitly the theme of *translatio
imperii,* the transference of empire; Gellius's choice of this cut-off date is a kind of
anticipation of Eusebius's visual demonstration of *translatio imperii* with his dwin-
dling columns.[118] At the end of Gellius's essay, the Greek "column," as it were,
drops off, and the Roman "column" is the only one remaining.

Before this climax, however, for much of the essay one has the impression that
Gellius's synchronisms are working to establish the idea that Rome was for centuries as belated and backward in the imperial realm as in the cultural. The synchronisms highlight the idea that while Greek states were performing heroic deeds
at the center of the world stage, the Romans were engaged in minor brawls in the

wings.[119] The mechanics of synchronism bring out this theme in a particularly effective way, because we are kept waiting for a long time before we actually see the worlds of Greece and Rome directly impinging on one another. Again, these dates are not "just" dates: they are events. Centuries of Greek and Roman events have to go by before they start overlapping in a more than merely temporal sense, before the parallelism of event dating becomes a genuine parallelism of events, overlapping in place as well as time. The key moment for Gellius is the war with Pyrrhus, which appears also to have been the moment when the Greek scholars Eratosthenes and Apollodorus started taking account of Roman events, or dates.[120] This is another of Zerubavel's moments of "inflated divide"—before Pyrrhus, no contact with Greece; after Pyrrhus, Greece and Rome in tandem.

The way that Gellius focalizes his synchronisms bears out the crucially significant power of the Pyrrhus intersection. The first major part of Gellius's essay, before the invasion of Pyrrhus (37), is, so to speak, focalized through Greece, whereas the second major part, starting with the invasion of Pyrrhus, is focalized through Rome.[121] By this I mean that the chapter begins with a pattern of mentioning Greek dates or events and then goes across to Rome: Gellius does not say, "When Romulus founded the city, what was happening in Greece?" but "When Solon was active in Greece, what was happening in Rome?" (4). But after the war with Pyrrhus he switches and starts giving Roman dates first, sometimes in both the *ab urbe condita* and consular form, and then goes across to Greece. This pattern is not absolutely watertight, since in the first part, before the war with Pyrrhus, there are strings of synchronisms that are formally tied to the *ab urbe condita* hook (9, 19, 28); but even in these sections, the focalization is heavily on Greek events, with glances across to Rome. After the war with Pyrrhus, the switch is complete: the Roman focalization becomes preponderant, the default mode of the comparison.

Before that crucial turning point with Pyrrhus, and as if to throw its stunningly unexpected outcome into relief, the Romans are consistently represented as small players in the great game of Mediterranean history. Just after mentioning "that famous battle of Marathon" (*pugnam illam inclutam Marathoniam*, 9), Gellius mentions Coriolanus, who, he says, "turned traitor to the Republic, and joined the Volscians, who were then our enemies" (*qui tum hostes erant*, 10). All the work here is done by the disjunction between the glamorous language surrounding Marathon and the bare "then" (*tum*) that marks the status of the Volsci as quondam enemies: the implication is that the Persian Wars were a world-historical clash of empires, whereas the Volsci, by implied contrast, were all the Romans then had to cope with, a day's ride away from the city of Rome. A little later Gellius sets up a similar contrast, between, on the one hand, the mighty Peloponnesian War on Greek soil, immortalized by Thucydides (*bellum . . . in terra Graecia maximum Peloponnensiacum, quod Thucydides memoriae mandauit*), and, on the other hand, the names of the now vanished peoples who were "at that time," *tunc*, the enemies of Rome, the Fidenates and the Aequi (16–17). Soon after the end of the Peloponnesian War, Rome comes within a whisker of being rubbed off the map altogether, before it has impinged on history at all, when the Gauls capture Rome apart from the Capitol (22).

The most interesting case is found in sections 32–33, where we get a developed discussion of Alexander—not *the* Alexander, Alexander the Great, but his namesake and uncle, Alexander Molossus, the king of Epirus. This "other" Alexander invades Italy at just the same time that his namesake and nephew is invading Asia, about fifty years before Pyrrhus, and here Gellius gives us a tantalizing glimpse of what might have been: if Alexander Molossus had not first been killed in a skirmish in South Italy, he might actually have been the one to bring Rome into the orbit of world history by carrying out his plan of attacking Rome, whose reputation was just then beginning to be known abroad (*iam enim fama uirtutis felicitatisque Romanae apud exteras gentes enitescere inceptabat*, 33). But before he could make this happen, *priusquam bellum faceret,* before he could make the events of Greece and Rome overlap for the first time, he just happened to die. The achievement of bringing the two time schemes together was left to another nephew of Alexander Molossus, Pyrrhus. But immediately before Gellius mentions *that* event, he reinforces once more his theme of Rome as a comparatively minor player in the world events of this period, by stressing that within two years of the death of Alexander the Great, Rome was still being forced into humiliating defeats by the Samnites (36).

Although synchronism would initially appear to be an exercise in correspondence, Gellius's chapter shows how it can be an exercise in disparity. The synchronism lens consistently brings into focus just how disparate and various the developments of these empires were. The synchronism lens may also create a heightened awareness of the contingency of historical developments and interactions. This is especially clear from the cases of the Gallic sack and the premature death of Alexander Molossus. The Romans could well never have recovered from the destruction of their city, in which case they would *never* have figured in what the Greeks considered world history;[122] likewise, we will never know what might have happened if Alexander Molossus had gone north and encountered the juvenile Roman Empire at the time that his namesake and relative was demolishing the

Persian empire. "What if?" history is relatively rare in the ancient world; the most famous example of it is precisely Livy's digression on what would have happened if the other, Great, Alexander had turned west after his conquest of the East (9.17–19).[123] Gellius's little essay offers its readers the opportunity to do some "What if?" thinking for themselves, and by reminding readers that the Romans were still being defeated by Samnites years after Alexander invaded Asia, he would appear to be going against Livy's verdict that the Romans would have beaten him if he had turned west.

So far in our analysis our emphasis has been on Gellius's interest in the mode of "unlikeness," but any act of comparison also highlights likeness, and it is clear that some of his synchronisms invite us to think about the *parallel* development of Rome and various of the Greek states, especially Athens. The focus on likeness is particularly clear in the area of constitutional and political matters, where developments in Roman and Greek constitutional history are sometimes linked. The first of these parallels is one still keenly discussed in modern scholarship, that between the end of tyranny in Athens and the establishment of the Roman Republic.[124] In fact, this parallel is so famous that Gellius doesn't explicitly mention the Roman half of it when he mentions the end of the tyranny at Athens (7); but it is very hard to believe that we are not meant to fill in the gap ourselves, when he has just mentioned the name of the last Roman king in the same sentence (6), and then moves on to the murder of Hipparchus by Harmodius and Aristogeiton with the words *isdemque temporibus* ("and at the same period"). A more overt parallel in constitutional history comes soon after, when extreme democracy in action ends the careers of both Militiades and Coriolanus (9–10). A vital epochal year in Mediterranean history comes when the year "404 B.C.E." shows the reintroduction of the military tribunate at Rome, the imposition of the thirty tyrants by Sparta upon Athens, and the beginning of the tyranny of Dionysius in Syracuse (19).[125]

In the next chapter we shall follow up the Sicilian and Athenian connection, for the mention of Syracuse here in connection with Rome and Athens is highly significant; it was from the Sicilians that the Romans first learned to play this game of establishing significant correspondences with the mainland of Greece proper. And, just as was the case with the Sicilians, we shall see that when the Romans concentrated on aligning themselves in a parallel column against Greece, the real comparandum was Athens. This tendency is strongly evident in Gellius, practically every one of whose artists or philosophers is Athenian or based in Athens, while the major Greek political and military events down to the battle of Chaeronea, when the Athenian empire was destroyed by Philip, are Athenian.[126] It is a telling illustration of Gellius's Athenian focalization that the battle of Chaeronea itself is described as the battle where Philip conquered the *Athenians* (30). This is scarcely an obvious way to describe the opposing sides—in leaving out the Thebans, this perspective is like describing El Alamein as the battle where Montgomery defeated the Italians. Gellius is careful to mark the end of the Spartan empire (26) and of the Persian empire (34), thus revealing his interest in the theme of succession of empires; but the dominant interest throughout is in the Athenians. The last Greeks mentioned in the whole essay are the heads of the philosophical schools at Athens sent by the people of Athens on an embassy to Rome (48).

Gellius's essay is the tip of a large Athenocentric iceberg, which the next chapter will explore in more detail. A history of synchronism in the Mediterranean from the invasion of Xerxes onwards must also be a history of Athenocentrism in the Mediterranean. Gellius's little essay alerts us to this point, as it alerts us to the importance of the Sicilian connection and to the theme of succession of empire. Above all, by illustrating how synchronization is a tool for thinking about cross-cultural interaction, highlighting difference as much as similarity in the process, Gellius's essay shows that working with synchronization is fundamental to the understanding of Roman Hellenization. It is not possible to think systematically about Roman Hellenization without some kind of picture of the differing historical development of the Greek and Roman cultures, and that is a picture that can be gained only by sustained attention to synchronization. Synchronism becomes another window onto the comparison mentality, and to its fundamental role in Roman culture.[127] Even in Greek culture this mentality eventually becomes inescapable, as we see most dramatically with Plutarch's *Parallel Lives*, a century before Gellius, in which the Greek past is presented "as half of a diptych, face-to-face with, and mirroring, the Roman past," creating a fictitious "partnership of equals" for the evolving Empire.[128] The fundamental mind-set of the synchronizer is a comparative one, operating on events as if constructing gigantic similes, manipulating tenors and vehicles on an enormous scale, using the comparison trope to highlight sameness or difference, not between Hector and a lion or Gorgythion and a poppy, but between Syracuse and Athens, Rome and Greece.

Even as Gellius's essay reminds us of the indispensable importance of the comparative exercise of synchronism, it brings home how much harder the operation of synchronism was for the ancients, and how much more out in the open the process of alignment was. While we can use our universal numerical dating system as a synchromesh to make the differentially whirling gears of all dating systems interlock without any graunching, their synchronistic gearboxes had no such smoothing devices.[129] The process of making the systems mesh together was one that the Romans and Greeks could never internalize as natural or overlook, and the work they had to do to make the systems mesh was such that it provoked many other kinds of work in addition to the merely chronological—although it is becoming clear that we can never talk about the *merely* chronological.

The Romans had to begin their side of this synchronistic project by making sense of the contours of the past through media that had been devised for Greek cities and empires. Eventually the Romans forced themselves into a position where they were partners in Greek time, sharers of a synchronized past history, one that conferred status on them as the only other full player on the Mediterranean stage, the only other culture that was really "like" Greece. Quite how they did this, how the comparison worked to maintain difference as well as likeness, and what was at stake for them at various stages in the developing story, will be the subject of the next chapter.

TWO · Synchronizing Times II

West and East, Sicily and the Orient

WHEN IS A SYNCHRONISM
JUST A COINCIDENCE?

In chapter 23 of the *Poetics* Aristotle begins his discussion of epic. The first point
he makes is that epic should be like tragedy in its plots and should be about one
whole and complete action. Epic should not be like history, he says, in which there
is no unity of action but only of time; historians have to mention whatever happened in their time period, and "each of these things may have a quite casual inter-
relation" (ὧν ἕκαστον ὡς ἔτυχεν ἔχει πρὸς ἄλληλα, 1459a24).[1] As an example of
the inconsequential random scatterings of events in time, Aristotle mentions two
crucial battles fought 500 miles apart in "480 B.C.E.," one near Athens and one in
northern Sicily: "If one thinks of the same time, we have the battle of Salamis
and the battle of Himera against the Carthaginians not directed to achieve any
identical purpose" (ὥσπερ γὰρ κατὰ τοὺς αὐτοὺς χρόνους ἥ τ' ἐν Σαλαμῖνι
ἐγένετο ναυμαχία καὶ ἡ ἐν Σικελίᾳ Καρχηδονίων μάχη οὐδὲν πρὸς τὸ αὐτὸ
συντείνουσαι τέλος, 1459a24–27). Aristotle is presumably relying on Herodotus
for this synchronism of Salamis and Himera, but he does not give the extra detail
reported by Herodotus, who tells us that the Sicilians said these two victories were
actually won on the same day (7.166).[2]

Aristotle displays his usual tough-mindedness in refusing to attribute any significance to the link in time between these two great battles.[3] He sees no causal link

and no joint purpose in the fact that the Greeks in Sicily happened to be defeating Carthaginians at the very same time that their cousins in mainland Greece were defeating Persians. Just as he does not approve of coincidence in tragic or epic plots, so he does not attach significance to coincidence in history. Most people in the ancient world were not so robust, and even now we can fnd ourselves mindlessly impressed by the striking chronological coincidences with which history is littered.[4] Many people's favorite extraordinary historical coincidence would be the simultaneous death of John Adams and Thomas Jefferson, who both died on 4 July 1826, fifty years to the day after signing the Declaration of Independence together in Philadelphia.[5] It would have been striking enough if they had died on the same day; the fact that it was 4 July is somehow more astounding, and the fact that it was the fiftieth 4 July makes it seem prodigious. The patterning would have been absolutely perfect if they had been the last two signers alive, but unfortunately Charles Carroll, the last signer to die, was still lingering on in Maryland and would survive for another six years.[6]

Our minds seem to be so structured that we seek pattern, and this is much easier to do if you are bad at statistical probability and do not understand the issues of coincidence. Most of us nowadays are still hopelessly bad at statistical probability (and I include myself); we continue to be amazed by striking coincidences, even when they are statistically likely.[7] In the ancient world, every single person was hopelessly bad at statistical probability, because they were born before that moment in the mid-seventeenth century when probability came into being. And so it took an Aristotle to refuse to be impressed by the accident that Himera and Salamis happened at the same time, while others continued to comment on it, together with the other striking coincidences that were perceived, or constructed, around the Persian Wars—the sea battle of Artemisium and the land battle of Thermopylae happening on the same day, or the simultaneous battles of Plataea and Mycale.[8]

SICILY AND MAINLAND GREECE:
THE "COMMON CAUSE"?

Aristotle's selection of Himera and Salamis out of all the other possible coincidences of history turns out to be a happy coincidence for me, since the first part of this chapter will focus on Sicily and Athens. The historian Ephorus, a contemporary of Aristotle, felt that he could meaningfully link the affairs of Athens and Sicily and give some purposive significance to the synchronism by saying that in fact the barbarians to the west and the east had been sharing intelligence and were working together to attack the Greek world from either side simultaneously.[9] But even without trying to force the two battles to be part of what Aristotle might have seen as a linked chain of events, one can readily see why the potential symbolic significance of this synchronism was enormous, and virtually irresistible: "It is a small step from the synchronisation of battles to a sense of 'common cause', and indeed of a common enemy: it seems fair to see here the roots of the generalized Greek/barbarian dichotomy in its developed form."[10] Indeed, the ideological point is even stronger if the synchronization is the product of the sense of common cause, rather than the other way around.[11]

This sense of "common cause" is exactly what we see Pindar working so hard to construct in his *First Pythian*, written in 470 B.C.E., only ten years after the two battles, to celebrate Hieron of Syracuse, who with his brother Gelon had been joint victor in the battle of Himera. Pindar does not mention the synchronization of Himera and Salamis, and there is every reason to think that it had not yet been established;[12] his main focus of attention (72–75) is the more recent battle of Cumae (474 B.C.E.), in which Hieron defeated a combined naval force of Carthaginians and Etruscans. Pindar does, however, mention Salamis, Plataea, and Himera as the crowning glory of, respectively, the Athenians, Spartans, and Syracusans (75–80), and it is clear that the whole project of the poem is to claim that the Sicilian victories over *their* barbarians are as important and significant as the mainland Greeks' victory over *their* barbarians, part of a universal Hellenism defended by both West and East Greeks. Saying that two of these great victories were fought on the same day, an extra flourish that almost certainly entered the tradition after Pindar, is an extremely powerful way of reinforcing this claim to a share in the burden of Hellenism against barbarism.

The synchronization of the victories over barbarians is one of the many strategies adopted by Sicily, and especially by Syracuse, as they try to elbow their way into the top league of Hellenism. Herodotus's extremely subtle narrative in book 7 of the buildup to the crucial battles allows us to get a glimpse of what was at stake. Herodotus's report of the synchronism of Himera and Salamis is part of a complex narrative about the rivalry between West and East Greece, and the key to his story is the argument over who should lead Hellas against the barbarians. When ambassadors from Athens and Sparta arrive in Syracuse to ask Gelon, tyrant of Syracuse, to join the alliance against the Persians, Gelon replies that he will contribute large forces and provision the Greek army so long as he is the supreme commander of all the Greek forces (7.157–59). As Gelon himself points out, Syracuse was easily the most powerful single Greek state of the day. His offer, however, is dismissed by the Spartans and Athenians with two pieces of Homeric one-upmanship: the Spartan ambassador paraphrases an Iliadic line in order to say that Agamemnon would turn in his grave if he heard that Spartans were under the command of a Syracusan;[13] the Athenian ambassador makes the usual snobbish claim to autochthony and backs it up with the usual Athenian Homeric quotation about the Athenian contingent in the catalogue in *Iliad* 2.[14] The cultural prestige of Homer can be harnessed by the descendants of the Iliadic heroes in order to trump the mere military might of the colonial upstarts.

This context of keen cultural and military rivalry is important to bear in mind when we read what Herodotus says shortly afterwards about the synchronism between Himera and Salamis (7.166). It is often casually said that Herodotus reports that the battles were fought on the same day, but the synchronism is all part of a report of "what the Sicilians say," with Herodotus not vouching explicitly for any of it. Only eight pages earlier, after all, comes the famous passage where he declares that his duty is to report what people say, not to believe it, and that this holds for the whole work (7.152.3); the context there is very similar, reporting the various stories about why the Argives did not join in the common defense against the Persians. When Herodotus, then, says that the Sicilians say that the battles of Himera and Salamis took place on the same day, we must remind ourselves that the synchronism comes in the middle of his report of the Sicilian version of why Gelon did not help the Greeks against the Persians. The mainland version may reflect badly on Gelon, making his vanity and colonial gaucheness the stumbling block, but the Sicilian version exculpates him by saying that he was threatened by the Carthaginians and had to concentrate on his self-defense; it is this context that motivates the discussion of his victory at Himera, and the synchronism of Himera and Salamis (165–166.1).

Here Herodotus is mediating a long-standing Sicilian project of integration together with competition. The synchronism of Himera and Salamis is a special case in its claim that the Sicilians are sharing the same anti-barbarian burden as the mainland Greeks, but it is part of a general attempt on the part of the colonists to make meaningful connections between their experience and that of the old home-land, attempting to put themselves on the map—in particular, on the map of shared historical time. Diodorus Siculus, for example, notes that "the Peloponnesian war in Greece and the first war between Dionysius and Carthage in Sicily ended roughly together."[15] The Sicilians are not alone in this, for we can see other western Greeks trying to ensure that they are plotted onto the time maps of Hellas.

For the year 338 B.C.E., for example, they engineered a significant synchronism between the battle of Chaeronea in mainland Greece and the battle between the Tarentines and Lucanians in southern Italy—these battles took place, it was alleged, not just on the same day but at the same hour.[16] The crucial importance of these West/East synchronisms comes through very clearly in Polybius's initial plotting of the time charts at the beginning of his history (1.6.1–2). Here he secures his ultimate starting point of "387/6 B.C.E." by means of key events as benchmarks at intervals of nineteen years earlier and sixteen years after. These benchmark events, the battles of Aegospotami and Leuctra, are as epoch-making in his audience's mind as the French Revolution for us, and about as far back in time. He goes on to itemize crucial events occurring in his epochal year, events that link together in sequence (i) the realms of Sparta and Asia, with the peace of Antalcidas, (ii) the realms of Sicily and southern Italy, with the siege of Rhegium by Dionysius of Syracuse, and (iii) central Italy, with the Gauls' capture of Rome.[17] In our analysis of Gellius's synchronistic chapter we noted the important theme of the two Alexanders simultaneously moving out from mainland Greece in opposite directions, to invade Asia and Italy; we can now put this into a wider context and see the synchronism of the two Alexanders as part of a long-standing Greek urge for comparison and contrast between West and East, grounded in what Purcell refers to as "the Greek conceptual division of the Mediterranean into two domains."[18]

PUTTING SICILY ON THE GREEK TIME CHART: TIMAEUS OF TAUROMENIUM

Sicily dominates the western Greek discourse of rivalry with the mainland, and the single most important representative of this discourse is Sicily's greatest historian, Timaeus of Tauromenium, whom we have already briefly met in the survey of Greek synchronism in chapter 1. He is a figure of crucial significance for the theme of synchronism, and for the history of charting time in the Mediterranean, not least because he was the first Greek historian to pay sustained and thoughtful attention to the new power of Rome.[19] The author of a technical work of synchronistic chronology as well as of a history of Sicily, he spent fifty years working in Athens and died aged over ninety shortly after the outbreak of the first war between Rome and Carthage in 264 B.C.E.[20] His "Sicilian History" was really a history of the western Mediterranean, going from the earliest times down to his own day, and it remained the fundamental historical work on the western Mediterranean for centuries.[21] A major part of his project was to boost Sicily and the West so as to make the western Greek world look like more of an equal partner in Hellas, and significant synchronisms between Sicily and Greece proper were an important part of this operation.[22]

It has long been a scholarly occupation to point out how many of Timaeus's synchronisms appear strained, inconsequential, and foolish. A favorite target has been Timaeus's claim that Euripides died on the day Dionysius became tyrant of Syracuse, so that as the man who wrote tragedies exited the stage the man who was the protagonist in tragic events entered.[23] It is "a kitschy metaphor devoid of any serious meaning," according to Asheri, although in the full version of Timaeus we might have seen a more serious link, between the advent of the tyranny of Dionysius in Syracuse and of the "thirty tyrants" in Athens in the same year.[24] Other synchronisms have a more obvious historical symbolism, as may be the case with the Polybian synchronism we saw above, between Dionysius's siege of Rhegium and the Gallic sack of Rome. This synchronism comes from Timaeus, and via Fabius Pictor and Polybius it becomes a grounding synchronism for the Roman historiographic tradition.[25] It is possible that Timaeus was already thinking along the same lines that Walbank suggests for Polybius: the victories of Dionysius were not just a useful synchronism for Sicilian readers to use for orientation, but "an example of how a strong power in Sicily or Italy would eventually cross the straits," and therefore "a pointer to the First Punic War."[26] As always with synchronisms, we face the problem of deciding when a coincidence in time has significance, and, if so, what kind of significance. The issue still faces historians today, especially with the recent fashion for universal global histories.[27]

Timaeus's synchronistic net could be thrown over Asia as well as Greece, since he had an interest in the career of Alexander the Great. The birth of Alexander generated one of his more notoriously portentous synchronisms, according to which Alexander was born on the day that the temple of Artemis at Ephesus burned down.[28] The sack of Tyre by Alexander likewise provoked a synchronism, but one of days, not of years. Timaeus says that a statue of Apollo was looted from Gela in Sicily by the Carthaginians (in 405 B.C.E.) and was sent to the Carthaginians' metropolis of Tyre. When Tyre was being besieged by Alexander seventy-three years later (in 332 B.C.E.), the people of Tyre abused the statue, but it did no good, because Alexander captured the city "on the same day with the same name and at the same hour on which the Carthaginians had seized the statue of Apollo at Gela."[29] Vattuone attractively suggests that the coincidence is meant to bring home the message that the impious barbarians of the West still remain unpunished and a threat, even though Alexander has finally and definitively removed the threat of their ancestors, the impious barbarians of the East.[30] Half of the work from Pindar's *First Pythian* remains to be done.

In Timaeus's eyes, however, the main counterweight to Sicily is Athens, the city where he spent fifty years working as a historian.[31] His pugnacious sense of defensiveness in the face of Athens' status has often been remarked upon;[32] his declaration that Syracuse was the largest of Greek cities and the most beautiful of all cities looks very pointed, coming from a resident of Athens.[33] It is important to remember that Timaeus started writing less than a hundred years after his mother city of Syracuse had totally annihilated the greatest overseas expedition Athens ever mounted, and it cannot have been easy for him to cope with what he will have seen as an Athenian assumption of superiority. One catches a similar atmosphere of resentment in the peevish cavils of Theopompus of Chios at the way the Athenians misrepresent the battle of Marathon "and all the other things that the city of the Athenians brags about and uses to dupe the Hellenes."[34] Parallels with modern experiences of colonials in the metropolis will be partially misleading, no doubt, but they afford some inkling of what will have been at stake.[35] After all, for the Athenians and the Athenian historiographic tradition, the Sicilians' role on the world stage was a very recent affair: "events in the West would not be considered as part of Hellenic history by Athenians until the West became involved in the Peloponnesian War."[36] This is exactly the mentality we detected in Eratosthenes, Apollodorus, and Aulus Gellius, in whose schemes events in the Roman sphere only properly become part of Hellenic history when a Greek king invades Italy. All of these cases are striking instances, once again, of what Irad Malkin meant when he said that "'snobbery' was a grossly underrated factor in history—'a superior culture persuades an inferior that to be significant its past must be interdependent with its own.'"[37]

This feeling of being patronized is part of what motivates Timaeus's desperate overcompensation as he tries to show that Sicily and Syracuse were just as venerable and significant as the mainland and Athens. He was, for example, the first person to place the rape of Persephone near Enna in Sicily, as part of an attempt to show that Demeter had blessed the Sicilians with the gift of agriculture first, and Athens second.[38] Again, he did everything he could to assert the claims of Sicily, not Athens, to be the cradle of oratory.[39] His attempts to boost the West at the expense of the East produced apopleptic reactions from the Achaean Polybius, writing a hundred years later. Polybius had a special need to put Timaeus in his place, for the Sicilian was his principal predecessor and competitor as a historian of the West; for all his hostility, Polybius paid Timaeus the compliment of being his continuator, beginning his narrative with the Romans' first crossing of the sea from Italy (264 B.C.E.), following straight on from where Timaeus stopped (1.5.1). A lot of what we know about Timaeus comes from Polybius's sustained polemic in book 12, in which he denounces Timaeus's parochial attempts to make Sicily look as important as Greece "proper." One of Polybius's most revealing passages attacks Timaeus's synchronistic comparison between Alexander the Great and the Sicilian hero Timoleon; here his acute understanding of Timaeus's comparative West/East mentality comes through very clearly (12.23.7):[40]

ἀλλά μοι δοκεῖ πεισθῆναι Τίμαιος ὡς, ἂν Τιμολέων, πεφιλοδοξηκὼς ἐν αὐτῇ Σικελίᾳ, καθάπερ ἐν ὀξυβάφῳ, σύγκριτος φανῇ τοῖς ἐπιφανεστάτοις τῶν ἡρώων, κἂν αὐτὸς ὑπὲρ Ἰταλίας μόνον καὶ Σικελίας πραγματευόμενος εἰκότως παραβολῆς ἀξιωθῆναι τοῖς ὑπὲρ τῆς οἰκουμένης καὶ τῶν καθόλου πράξεων πεποιημένοις τὰς συντάξεις.

But I think Timaeus was convinced that if Timoleon, who had sought fame just in Sicily, as if in a saucer, looked comparable to the most spectacular of heroes, then he himself, who dealt only with Italy and Sicily, could reasonably be thought worthy of comparison with those who composed comprehensive histories of the inhabited world and of deeds on a universal scale.

Another highly revealing passage contains Polybius's denunciation of how Timaeus treated the negotiations between Gelon and the Greeks before the invasion of Xerxes.[41] Here we return to the crucial events of 480 B.C.E. treated by Herodotus in book 7, with the dispute over who will be the supreme commander against the Persians. After praising the Greek coalition's stance on the issue of supreme command, Polybius once again ridicules the misuse of the comparative mode by Timaeus, once again explicitly drawing attention to the *synkrisis* form (12.26b.4–c.1): [42]

ἀλλ' ὅμως Τίμαιος εἰς ἕκαστα τῶν προειρημένων τοσούτους ἐκτείνει λόγους καὶ τοιαύτην ποιεῖται σπουδὴν περὶ τοῦ τὴν μὲν Σικελίαν μεγαλομερεστέραν ποιῆσαι τῆς συμπάσης Ἑλλάδος, τὰς δ' ἐν αὐτῇ πράξεις ἐπιφανεστέρας καὶ καλλίους τῶν κατὰ τὴν ἄλλην οἰκουμένην, τῶν δ' ἀνδρῶν τῶν μὲν σοφίᾳ διενηνοχότων σοφωτάτους τοὺς ἐν Σικελίᾳ, τῶν δὲ πραγματικῶν ἡγεμονικωτάτους καὶ θειοτάτους τοὺς ἐκ Συρακουσῶν, ὥστε μὴ καταλιπεῖν ὑπερβολὴν τοῖς μειρακίοις τοῖς ἐν ταῖς διατριβαῖς

καὶ τοῖς περιπάτοις πρὸς τὰς παραδόξοις ἐπιχειρήσεις, ὅταν ἢ Θερσίτου
λέγειν ἐγκώμιον ἢ Πηνελόπης πρόθωνται ψόγον ἤ τινος ἑτέρου τῶν
τοιούτων. Λοιπὸν ἐκ τούτων διὰ τὴν ὑπερβολὴν τῆς παραδοξολογίας
οὐκ εἰς σύγκρισιν, ἀλλ᾿ εἰς καταμώκησιν ἄγει καὶ τοὺς ἄνδρας καὶ
τὰς πράξεις ὧν βούλεται προΐστασθαι.

But Timaeus, on each of these points, is so long-winded and makes such a fuss
about making Sicily more important than the whole of Greece, with the deeds
in Sicily being more spectacular and fine than in the rest of the world, and the
wisest of the men distinguished for wisdom being those in Sicily, and the best
generals and most godlike men of action being from Syracuse, that he could
not possibly be overtaken in striving for paradox by the boys in the schools
when they are told to write an encomium of Thersites or an attack on
Penelope or anything else like that. As a result, because of his exaggeratedly
paradoxical way of talking, he exposes the men and deeds he wants to champion not to proper comparison but to ridicule.

In the Herodotean context of the negotiations of 480 B.C.E., it looks as if Timaeus
had his own distinctive spin on the crucial Sicilian synchronism of the battles of
Himera and Salamis. The fundamental point of the synchronism was that these
great Hellenic victories against barbarism were won on the very same day. This
makes a good story—but not, it seems, good enough for Timaeus. It is virtually
certain that in Timaeus's version the synchronism was not between Himera and
Salamis but between Himera and Thermopylae, a few days before. So now, instead
of the story showing that West Greece and East Greece are equal partners, the
story shows that the West is *superior* to the East: on the day that the Sicilians annihilated the Carthaginian hordes at Himera, the Greeks were being annihilated by
the Persians at Thermopylae; and when the Greeks managed to bounce back at
Salamis, they did so in emulation of what the Sicilians had already achieved in
Sicily under the leadership of Gelon.[43]

Timaeus's tactics are daring, but it would be a mistake simply to enjoy the jibes
of Polybius and not to take seriously the claims Timaeus advances for the status of
his mother city. Timaeus gives us a clear glimpse of the imperial pretensions of
Syracuse, which under Gelon and Hieron at the beginning of the fifth century, and
then under Dionysius, a century later, and then under Agathocles, a century later
still, repeatedly came close to being one of the great Mediterranean powers. Syracuse is indeed "a place with imperial stories to tell, stories of one empire giving

way to another."[44] Its pretensions to this status continue to be overlooked in modern scholarship,[45] but there are traces in the ancient historiographical tradition that enable us to see Syracuse as a contender for imperial status, in addition to being the place that destroyed Athens' claims.[46]

In this story, Syracuse, Athens, and Carthage are linked together as the Big Three of their day.[47] Plutarch says that many Athenians saw their attack on Syracuse in 415 B.C.E. as a preliminary for an attack on Carthage, so as to establish total hegemony over the Mediterranean.[48] This vision is discernible in Diodorus Siculus as well. When he describes the catastrophe of the Carthaginians at Himera in 480 B.C.E., with the reaction at Carthage (11.23), he models the whole sequence systematically on Thucydides' description of the catastrophe of the Athenian expedition against Syracuse; in this way he creates a pattern whereby the Syracusans do to the Carthaginians what they were later going to do to the Athenians, and what the Athenians planned to do to Carthage. The interwined destinies of the three great maritime cities are also brought into view by Livy and Plutarch, when they narrate the capture of Syracuse by Marcellus in 212 B.C.E.[49] They both describe the tears of the Roman commander as he looks at the conquered city, with Livy telling us that he was reflecting on Syracuse's destruction of the Athenian expedition and on its victories against Carthage; Plutarch adds the telling detail, to establish a parallelism with Carthage, that the amount of booty taken from Syracuse was no less than the amount taken from Carthage when it was sacked. Syracuse is a link in a chain of imperial destiny that connects Athens and Carthage. And Rome.

ROME, CARTHAGE, AND
THE SICILIAN PARADIGM

As the tears of Marcellus at Syracuse show, when the Romans are trying to chart their position on the map of Mediterranean time with its sequence of imperial succession, they do so in the first instance as the inheritors of the Sicilian tradition we have been investigating.[50] Before the Romans, it was the Syracusans who were the people in the middle, facing West and East, the only state successfully to fight both the barbarian Carthaginians and the Greeks of the mainland. It is not simply that the Romans scrabble around for significant coincidences and parallelisms in order to ratchet themselves up to become equals in Mediterranean power and inheritors in the succession of empires theme: it is crucial to recognize that they are using a preexisting West Greek paradigm in order to do so. Hanell was therefore right to point to Timaeus as the father of Roman historiography[51] —not just in the sense that he was the first to bring Rome "within the normal range of Greek knowledge,"[52] but in the sense that he showed the Romans what you had to do to maneuver your way into the larger matrix of Hellenic time frames from a starting position on the sidelines.

Timaeus even provided the Romans with a beginning point within the matrix of Greek time. He plotted the foundation of the city within his time grids, generating in the process his most famous synchronism of all, the synchronism between the foundations of Rome and Carthage. This was a radical intervention in terms of the accepted chronologies of the time, and one that we shall examine further in the next chapter. For now, we may note that Timaeus came up with the date for the foundation of Carthage that became canonical, thirty-eight years before Olympiad 1, "814/13 B.C.E."; and he also placed the foundation of Rome in the same year.[53] Jacoby believed that this heavily symbolic synchronized dating was completely unthinkable ("ganz undenkbar") before 264 B.C.E., the outbreak of the First Punic War;[54] accordingly, Timaeus will have glimpsed the possible future consequences of this clash and created his synchrony right at the end of his very long life (he died within a very few years of the outbreak of the war, and his history stopped in 264 B.C.E., before the Romans crossed into Sicily). There are other possibilities, however, since Rome and Carthage had long been allies, most recently and significantly during Rome's war against Pyrrhus, so that the linked origin of the two cities might have carried a more positive meaning.[55] The crucial point, as Momigliano so clearly saw, lay in the synchronism itself: "Timaeus recognized that Carthage and Rome were on the same level. The Greeks, accustomed to respecting Carthage, now had to attribute the same importance to Rome. Within the strange symbolism of a coincidence a historical discovery of the first importance was concealed: the rise of Rome to the position of a great power in the West."[56]

The implied symbolism of a linked destiny for Rome and Carthage was very potent. Rome and Carthage were the uncategorizable odd ones out for the Hellenistic Greeks, in that these complex imperial entities could not simply be relegated to the bald category of "barbarians." They seemed uniquely anomalous among their non-Greek neighbors in terms of civic development and level of organization—as Aubet puts it, "in the Greek sense, Carthage is the only Phoenician foundation to meet the criteria of a genuine city,"[57] while Rome had been described as a πόλις Ἑλληνίς, a "Greek city," by Heraclides Ponticus a generation before Timaeus.[58] Early on in the history of Greek observation of the two cities we find evidence for a number of ways of reflecting on the parallelism between them, often stressing their sameness. Eratosthenes, toward the end of the third century, asserted that Rome and Carthage were twinned in space, being located on the same meridian; he also mentioned the two cities as models of "admirably governed barbarians."[59] Polybius likewise produces a sustained comparison of the two cities in book 6 (51–56); in particular, he stresses the similarity between the constitutions, saying that Carthage had monarchical, aristocratic, and democratic elements, rather like Rome and Sparta (6.51.1–2). Such a perspective is perhaps to be expected from Greeks, trying to make sense of these two non-Greek rivals. But Cato the Elder apparently also stressed how much the constitutions of Rome and Carthage had in common, for he commented on how Carthage had a mixed constitution, with monarchical, aristocratic, and democratic elements.[60]

This interest in Carthage as a mirror of Rome is a major preoccupation for the Romans. Carthage is indeed the "Other" to the Romans—barbarian, mercantile, untrustworthy, cruel.[61] But this is no simple polarity, for the "Other" does not represent only alterity, as a collection bag for all of the differences between oneself and the other identity. Rather, the "Other" can be a screen on which to project the aspects of oneself that one would rather not think about on home ground. Cultural issues that are too vital to ignore but too painful or embarrassing to acknowledge as integral can be displaced onto another object for comparatively safer contemplation.[62] From this perspective, Carthage is a way of thinking about many aspects of Romanness that are disquieting, and that Romans would generally prefer not to recognize as germane to themselves—foreign ancestry, luxury, decadence, and barbarism. This orientalist catalogue represents qualities that the Romans spend a lot of time denouncing in the Carthaginians, but they are qualities that are central to Rome, or potentially central. Rome is indeed, as Ovid's Dido calls Aeneas's future foundation, "a city the equivalent of Carthage" (*instar Carthaginis urbem*, *Her.* 7.19).

The shared destinies of the two cities are nowhere more memorably evoked than in the reaction of Scipio to the sack of Carthage in 146 B.C.E., where he imitated the weeping Marcellus at Syracuse sixty-five years earlier.[63] The capture of Syracuse was remembered in the tradition as a crucial tipping point in Rome's imperial progress, marking a stage of no return in the encounter with the allures and decadence of Hellenism;[64] the capture of Carthage was another such defining moment in Roman memory, removing from the map the only power that had presented a mortal threat to the Romans, and accelerating irreversibly their movement toward the corruption of unthreatened power.[65] Our knowledge of the scene with Scipio comes from the report of Polybius, who was embedded in the Roman

North African Expeditionary Force (38.21–22), Polybius's actual text is lost at this point, and for a reconstruction we depend on three later sources, of which the version of Diodorus Siculus is probably closest to what Polybius originally wrote (32.24). Diodorus tells us that Scipio wept as he watched the city in flames; when Polybius asked him why, he replied that he was struck by the mutability of fortune, reflecting that some time a similar fate would overtake Rome. Scipio then quoted from Homer: ἔσσεται ἦμαρ ὅτ᾽ ἄν ποτ᾽ ὀλώλῃ Ἴλιος ἱρὴ/καὶ Πρίαμος καὶ λαός ("There will be a day when holy Troy shall perish, and Priam, and his people").

The lines that Scipio quotes occur twice in Homer, spoken both by Agamemnon (*Il.* 4.164–65) and by Hector (6.448–49). Scipio, as the inheritor of Rome's complex traditions, may be seen as quoting both of them: he is the conquering general of the West crushing Asiatics, and he is the descendant of Asiatics foretelling the doom of his own city. He sees the fate of Rome in the fate of Carthage, and Troy is the model for both.[66] There is much more to Scipio's whole utterance than the mere idea of the changeability of fortune, important though that is.[67] In Polybius's work, Scipio's words are part of a huge piece of ring composition, circling back to the beginning of the *Histories*, where Polybius had sketched the various empires treated by history so far, showing that the empires of the Persians, Spartans, and Macedonians had fallen short of the scope of the Roman Empire (1.2). At the beginning of the work the theme of succession is not explicitly present, but it certainly is toward the end, in book 29, when Polybius reflects on the catastrophe of the Macedonian kingdom after Pydna (168 B.C.E.). Here he quotes, with awe, the insight of Demetrius of Phalerum, who had written shortly after the Persian empire had been replaced by the Macedonian: Demetrius had pointed out how extraordinary it was that Macedonia should have taken over the power of Persia, and prophesied that one day the Macedonian primacy would likewise pass (29.21). A succession from Persia to Macedonia to Rome is clearly what Polybius sees as the pattern of history, and Scipio at Carthage is made to reflect, as had Demetrius, but with Troy as the prototype, that the primacy of the current occupant of hegemony cannot escape Fortune's changes.[68]

The Romans, then, could be twinned with Carthage, even by the Romans themselves, in a mode of comparison that could stress likeness in constitution and imperial fate. But for well over a hundred years the Romans were enemies of Carthage, and from this point of view they could be represented as following in the steps of Sicilian predecessors in the same role. It is highly likely that Timaeus had already represented them as taking over the anti-Carthaginian burden from Sicilian

Greeks, at the very end of his very long life, as he saw the Romans moving out of the peninsula and crossing over into his homeland of Sicily for the first time. Timaeus himself may have seen the Romans as stepping into the Syracusan part of the anti-barbarian paradigm, a paradigm originally constructed on the basis of a synchronistic analogy with mainland Hellas.[69]

We need to remind ourselves that it was not in the least inevitable that the Romans should configure their relationship with the Greeks in this way, as partners, and successors, in a battle of civilization against barbarism. In many ways, as we have seen, they could be represented as having more in common with the Carthaginians than with the Greeks. Our monolithic polarities between Greek and barbarian eclipse the complexity of the issues for contemporaries.[70] The main Greek historian of the First Punic War, after all, was a pro-Carthaginian Sicilian, Philinus of Acragas, and another Sicilian Greek historian, Silenus, accompanied Hannibal in the next war and wrote of his campaigns against the Romans.[71] There were many pro-Carthaginian Greek cities in Sicily at various times, and the whole Greek-versus-barbarian paradigm is far less monolithic in Sicily than Pindar and Timaeus and modern constructions of the "Other" would have us believe: Greeks and Phoenicians coexisted for the most part peacefully in Sicily for centuries.[72] For most readers it is quite a surprise to learn from Herodotus that Hamilcar, defeated by Gelon at Himera in 480, was the son of a Carthaginian man and a Syracusan woman (7.166).[73] In other words, the Sicilian Greek tradition allowed for a pro-barbarian as well as an anti-barbarian stance, and it was a clear statement of a particular kind of Hellenism when the Romans opted for the latter rather than the former—when they opted not to be represented as barbarians, in this particular paradigm, but as Greeks of a certain kind. The Romans will already have been practiced in playing such roles, or acceding to the attempts of others to cast them in such roles. From the time of the Roman conquest of central and southern Italy there is evidence for Greek communities casting the Romans in the role of victorious "Greeks" against vanquished Samnite "barbarians," and for competition between Romans and Samnites over who was going to get to play the part of "Greek victor."[74]

Naevius, in his poem on the First Punic War, may be our first just tangible evidence for the way that the Romans in Sicily insinuated themselves into the Syracusan half of the civilization/barbarian paradigm.[75] One of the most powerful Greek icons of anti-barbarian struggle was the Gigantomachy, in which the gods asserted order against chaos in mythical time, as their Greek counterparts in human time imposed order on the barbarian threat, whether it be Persian, Celt, or

Carthaginian. In Sicily, the temple of Zeus Olympius at Acragas had a famous Gigantomachy on its eastern pediment, and it has long been suggested that this representation motivated the description we find in Naevius's first book of a relief of a Gigantomachy.[76] Whether Naevius's description explicitly referred to this particular monument or not, his use of such a potent image at the beginning of the war between Rome and Carthage in Sicily cannot have been gratuitous and may well have depended on Sicilian configurations of order against barbarism, which he continued into the present, with different protagonists.

FROM SICILY TO THE *OECUMENE*

If the Romans can inveigle themselves into the Syracusan half of the paradigm in Sicily as they fight the Carthaginians, they still face the problem of what to do with the other half of what Purcell calls "the Greek conceptual division of the Mediterranean into two domains."[77] In other words, they face the problem of what to do with the Sicilian paradigm of inferiority and competition in relation to the Greeks of the homeland, "Greece proper," *germana Graecia,* as Plautus calls it (*Rud.* 737). The Romans were, after all, aligning themselves with that part of the Sicilian tradition that saw mainland Hellas, and Athens in particular, as the real focus of concentration. Rawson has clearly brought the main issues into focus in her important analysis of Roman Hellenization in the second century B.C.E.[78] In the early stages of overseas expansion Sicily is central for the formation of Roman attitudes to Hellenism, but Sicily gets sidelined as the Romans turn themselves, as it were, into the new Sicilians, occupying the Western part of the paradigm: now they find their attention focusing more and more on mainland Greece, with Athens above all becoming the principal comparandum. Sicily and the provinces lose status as cultural models as the "real" Greek world looms larger on the Roman horizon.[79] The momentum led Rome eventually to be the only state of the western Mediterranean to attain "true modernity, the latest in state management, going further even than Syracuse and Carthage in bringing to the west the new methods of the hellenistic age."[80]

The sidelining of Sicily did not happen overnight. Ennius's "minor" works, from around 200–180 B.C.E., are still all based on Sicilian models—Epicharmus, Archestratus, Euhemerus;[81] and when Scipio Africanus Maior was asked whom he thought to be the most accomplished men of affairs in terms of wisdom and courage, he replied, "Dionysius and Agathocles, the Sicilians."[82] But the tendency is clear, and the tendency of Athens to become the center of gravity in the *synkri-*

sis is also clear, for the focus on Athens was a vital part of the paradigm that the Romans had taken over from the Western Greeks. The Athenocentric tendency that we observed in Aulus Gellius is, then, not simply a function of the Athenocentrism of the Second Sophistic, but a long-standing feature of the intellectual world of the Hellenistic Mediterranean.[83] The chronographical tradition in particular shows a strong focus on Athens. The so-called Marmor Parium, anchored on the Athenian archon of 264/3 B.C.E., is principally organized around Athens; it uses archons as the real backbone, and it keeps Sparta on the sidelines, for example, even to the extent of describing Plataea as an Athenian victory.[84] Apollodorus's chronological work was organized by Athenian archons and concentrated heavily on the cultural life of the city.[85] In the lists of lucky and unlucky days discussed by Grafton and Swerdlow (1988), it is clear that the dates the historians and antiquarians manipulate are from the Athenian calendar, or adapted to the Athenian calendar; only the Athenian calendar could have had enough Panhellenic sway to make this kind of game possible. It is, further, highly significant that when the Romans get incorporated into this particular chronological framework, which kept track of which days are lucky or unlucky for Greeks or barbarians, the Romans go in the Greek column, not the barbarian one.[86]

For the synchronizing historian, Athens, however important, is but one piece of the jigsaw. The range of data needed to incorporate Rome into the time charts of the Hellenistic Mediterranean world can be seen fully deployed by Polybius.[87] Polybius's ability to cover the whole range of Greek time and to integrate its various components with Roman time is inextricably bound up with his vision of a Mediterranean world that has been united synoptically for the first time by Roman expansion.[88] The beginning of his work pins down his points of departure: first, the 140th Olympiad, "220–216 B.C.E.," where his narrative proper will begin (1.3.1); second, the 129th Olympiad, "264–260 B.C.E.," the starting point of his scene-setting first two books (1.5.1); third, the year "387/6 B.C.E.," the earliest agreed-upon era that can provide a starting point for the introductory sketch of Rome's rise to dominion in Italy (1.6.1). The first and third of these dates are marked with careful synchronisms, which bring under one view the spheres of audiences in West Greece, Greece proper, and Italy. These synchronisms record events that embody Polybius's theme, that the whole world is now united under one power, for these diverse regions are now part of one whole. He can claim that from the 140th Olympiad on, with the Hannibalic War, history is for the first time an organic whole (1.3.4), "and the events of Italy and Libya have been interwoven with those of Greece and Asia, all leading up to one end," as if finally answering

Aristotle's objection that the events of history are not "directed to achieve any identical purpose."[89]

Such synchronistic views of the interrelated nature of the new Mediterranean order are not just the apparatus of scholarship, if Purcell (1995) is right, as I believe he is, to argue that the Romans deliberately engineered the simultaneous destruction of Corinth and Carthage in 146 B.C.E. as a spectacular demonstration of the reach of their power into the two halves of the world. The "two domains" of the "Greek conceptual division of the Mediterranean" had always resisted integration until now, but from this point on events in both domains would be linked by an unprecedented power.[90] A new unity of time and place is emerging, in dialogue with a developing sense of integration in the Hellenistic world itself. A Greek predisposition to conceive of the *oecumene* in integrated terms is forced to redefine itself in order to accommodate the new power of Rome.[91]

INCORPORATING ASIA

There is still one major episode in our story, the last significant act in the synchronistic project before the advent of Christianity. The "West" and "East" of this chapter's title have been referring so far to the western and eastern halves of the Greek Mediterranean. The more normal reference of West and East would be to Europe and Asia, and we need now to mark the incorporation of the Asian chronologies into the Mediterranean ones, along with the full incorporation into the Roman *imperium* of the seaboard and hinterland of the Eastern Mediterranean. For it is plain that despite Polybius's talk of Asia in his initial programmatic synchronism (1.3.2), he is aspiring to a universalism that does not correspond to realities on the ground in the second century B.C.E.[92] This universalism did not come until the conquests of Pompey the Great. It was not until the late 60s B.C.E. that the Roman *imperium* could lay claim to a genuinely pan-Mediterranean reach; it is only then that we see the appearance of the first synchronistic work that integrates the time charts of Asia with the time charts of Greece and Rome, and only then that we see the emergence of the first genuinely universal histories.[93] The new realities of the Eastern Mediterranean elicited new constructions of time, which were not only broader in their synchronic range but deeper in their diachronic reach.[94]

It is all too easy to overlook the impact of Pompey's achievements in the 60s B.C.E., especially with his Eastern command.[95] As Millar reminds us, "in the early first century B.C., after all, Rome directly ruled (i.e., raised taxes from) no more than Italy itself, with Sicily, Sardinia, and Corsica; part of Spain and the route to it through southern Gaul; a small island of territory in North Africa; and, in the east, Macedonia, Greece, and the province of 'Asia' (the western coast of Turkey and its hinterland)."[96] Gruen has shown in detail just how attenuated and hands-off Roman involvement in the East had continued to be for more than a century after the battle of Magnesia in 189 B.C.E., when the Scipios broke the back of the Seleucids.[97] This entire situation was transformed by Pompey, who divided up territories, organized kingdoms, and incorporated provinces throughout the Eastern world, redrawing the map of the Roman Empire in the process and increasing provincial tax revenues by 70 percent.[98] Above all, he brought the East home to Rome in a way that had never happened before, as Kuttner has shown in her fine study of Pompey's theater complex, dedicated in 55 B.C.E., and stuffed with art objects, jewels, animals, plants, and trees from the Orient.[99] According to the elder Pliny, Pompey told the people in a *contio* that he had assumed command of the province of Asia when it was on the outside edge of the Roman world, and handed it back to his fatherland as a central part of it (*Asiam ultimam prouinciarum accepisse eandemque mediam patriae reddidisse, HN* 7.99).[100] The most compelling explicit testimony to this frame of mind comes at the end of Appian's *Mithridatic Wars* (114–18), where Appian spells out in great detail the incorporation of the East into the *imperium* for the first time.

Appian also calls attention to the universal reach of Pompey's power in the 60s, from Spain to Syria, above all with his unparalleled command against the pirates, which gave him *imperium* over the whole Mediterranean.[101] Pliny likewise alludes to this universalism, not least with his reference to Alexander the Great as the prototype, and also to Hercules and Dionysus, the paradigms for "the two options for world conquest" in West or East.[102] As Clarke puts it, in her comprehensive discussion of the universalism of the 60s, "it was with Pompey that the idea of Roman rule stretching right across the known world took on a coherent form."[103] Similarly, Gruen has pointed out that with Pompey we see for the first time a Roman imperator boasting about extending the territory of the Roman Empire, as he claimed to have "pushed the frontiers of the empire to the boundaries of the earth."[104]

When Pliny refers to Pompey's role as a world conqueror, he reveals that it was not possible to speak of Pompey in this role without also speaking of Caesar (*HN* 7.99):

> si quis e contrario simili modo uelit percensere Caesaris res, qui maior illo apparuit, totum profecto terrarum orbem enumeret, quod infinitum esse conueniet.

If anyone on the other side wishes to catalogue in similar fashion the achievements of Caesar, who appeared greater than he, he would indeed count off the
entire globe, and it will be agreed that this is a task without limit.

Both men embody the emulation of Alexander the Great in pushing the boundaries
of Roman civilization to the edge of the world.[105]
Catullus 11 is priceless contemporary evidence for how these massive conquests
on either side of the world were received in their time.[106] We can see the repercussions of this style of speech throughout the poem and document how the implications were immediately felt:[107]

Furi et Aureli, comites Catulli,
siue in extremos penetrabit Indos,
litus ut longe resonante Eoa
    tunditur unda,

siue in Hyrcanos Arabasue molles,   5
seu Sagas sagittiferosue Parthos,
siue quae septemgeminus colorat
    aequora Nilus,

siue trans altas gradietur Alpes,
Caesaris uisens monimenta magni,   10
Gallicum Rhenum, horribiles uitro ulti-
    mosque Britannos,

omnia haec, quacumque feret uoluntas
caelitum, temptare simul parati,
pauca nuntiate meae puellae   15
    non bona dicta:

cum suis uiuat ualeatque moechis,
quos complex simul tenet trecentos,
nullum amans uere sed identidem omnium
    ilia rumpens,   20

nec meum respectet ut ante amorem,
qui illius culpa cecidit uelut prati
ultimi flos praetereunte postquam
    tactus aratrost.   24

Furius and Aurelius, who will accompany Catullus,
whether he will penetrate to the Indians at the outside limit,
where the beach is beaten by the wave
    of the far-resounding Dawn,

or to the Hyrcani and the soft Arabs,   5
or the Sagae or the arrow-bearing Parthians,
or the plains dyed
    by the sevenfold Nile,

or whether he will march across the high Alps,
inspecting the monuments of Caesar the Great,   10
the Gallic Rhine, the Britons, horrible with woad
    and on the edge,

prepared to try along with me all these things,
wherever the heavenly ones' wish will tend,
give my girl a brief message,   15
    not a kind one:

good-bye and good luck to her, along with her adulterers,
whom she holds three hundred at a time in her embrace,
loving none of them truly, but again and again
    rupturing the loins of all of them;   20

nor should she look back, as before, on my love,
which by her fault has fallen like a flower
on the edge of a meadow, after it has been nicked
    by a passing plow.   24

The language of extremities and borders controls the whole poem, as Catullus plays with the idea that he will emulate Pompey and Caesar in their emulation of Alexander the Great, going to the edge of his world with the end of his love, where the vulnerable flower of his love will go under to the civilizing plow of Lesbia (22–24). Pompey had bragged of taking over the province of Asia when it was *ultimam*, on the outside edge, and making it *mediam*, in the middle (Pliny *HN* 7.99). In Catullus's poem, this language of extremity is vital: ends, boundaries, extremities of all kinds, are what makes this poem of termination work. The word *ultimos* is in the middle of the poem (10–11), and it recurs at one of the edges of the poem, in the second-to-last line (23), while its synonym, *extremos*, is at the other edge of the poem, its beginning, in line 2. Catullus is responding to the notion that the limits of the Roman world are being redefined, and he works into this apprehension the idea that his own world is having its limits redefined as well. In line 2 Catullus implicitly reinforces Pompey's message that Asia is no longer the edge of the Roman world; the *extremi*, the men on the outside limit, are now the Indians, beside Ocean, where Alexander the Great dreamed of going, and never did. Other unincorporated peoples who now mark the new borders follow in the second stanza, before he turns to Caesar, the Western Alexander, who has wickedly filched the epithet *magnus* from his son-in-law (10)—not Pompey the Great but Caesar the Great.[108] In Catullus, Caesar deserves the epithet more than Pompey, because he has actually crossed Ocean, to encounter the ghastly Britons, on the Western edge of the world (11–12).[109] The Alps used to be the boundary of that part of the Roman world—now the limit is the natural boundary of Ocean, and the Rhine, which is now the limit of the Roman province of Gallia, *Gallicum Rhenum* (11). In crossing the Alps, Catullus and his companions will see the monuments of Caesar the Great (10); these are another attribute of Pompey's appropriated by Caesar, for they are territory-enhancing markers of the novel kind that Pompey erected to stake out his enlargement of the *imperium*.[110]

These colossal achievements in West and East provide the context for the new wave of universal histories, which we shall consider shortly. But it is Pompey's expansion of the *imperium* in the East that provides the focus for a crucial innovation in the charting of Roman and Greek time, as we see the timescales of the Asian monarchies brought into synchronous harmony with the timescales of Hellenism for the first time. The Greeks had been aware ever since Hecataeus of how the Asian timescales dwarfed their own, definitively "out-past-ing" them, to use Zerubavel's phrase; but for the most part they had defensively or neurotically or chauvinistically managed somehow to keep this knowledge off to the side of their consciousness.[111] In this period, however, we see the appearance of the chronological work of Castor of Rhodes, a figure for whom we have no solid biographical information. His *Chronica* for the first time incorporates the Eastern King lists into the synchronistic Greek schemes, and even mentions the figure of Moses.[112] He started with Ninus of Assyria, in "2123/2122 B.C.E.," and managed to link him to a Greek contemporary, King Aegialeus of Sicyon, the oldest Greek king he could come up with.[113] Part of his motivation, no doubt, was to ennoble Greek civilization by tracing it back even beyond the Trojan War, to show that it was no less venerable than the Assyrians, whom he took as his beginning point; by a kind of jujitsu flip, this attempt to give the Greek past more depth brought the Greeks crashing down when the chronographic tradition was eventually co-opted by the

Christians, for they could claim that the Greeks were mere Johnny-come-latelies in comparison with the Jews, whom the Christians were able to annex as their predecessors in God's story, taking the range of chronography back to the very moment of creation.[114]

It was not by accident that Castor was described as Φιλορώμαιος, "Roman-lover."[115] He was intent on linking up important Greek and Roman events in the way with which we are now familiar. He chose a crucial epochal year, for example, for the end of his first book—754 B.C.E. This was the year in which the life archonship at Athens was ended, the unlimited powers of the kings at Sparta were curtailed, and the year before the foundation of Rome—the event, presumably, with which his second book began.[116] Far more telling than his opening, however, is his ending, for he carried his chronology down all the way to the year 61 B.C.E., the year of Pompey's triumph after his Eastern conquests.[117] From the perspective of Castor, who is systematically harmonizing Eastern and Greek and Roman time frames for the first time, the triumph of Pompey is the ideal end point, since only now has the Eastern world finally been made part of the Roman power and brought into order by Pompey.[118] Pompey's settlement at last incorporates the realms of Mithridates and the Seleucids, and the settlement of the Eastern Mediterranean as a whole brings to an end that confusion and bewilderment that had been engendered up till now by Rome's refusal to behave like a proper hegemon.[119]

Castor's *Chronica* had a substantial impact at Rome in the following generations, on Varro's chronological researches, for example, and even on such amateurs of history as Horace.[120] It is in the years immediately after Castor's work appeared that we find the first Roman works of synchronistic scholarship, with Nepos's *Chronica* sometime in the early or mid-50s, and Atticus's *Liber Annalis* in 47/6 B.C.E. It is likely, however, that the impulse for these first Roman works of synchronism did not come from Castor directly, for they appear not to synchronize West and East, but Rome and Greece, just as we see Varro and Nepos doing with their pairs of Greek and Roman lives. Rather, we should conceive of these first Roman scholars of synchronism responding to the same universalizing atmosphere as Castor, and providing for their readers a guide to the development of the past events that had led in their lifetimes to an unprecedented involvement of times and places. If these developments had taken place under Augustus, we could all spin the usual tales about the centralization of the *imperium* and the creation of a single gaze under the unifying figure of the emperor, and the case we are discussing is a useful caution against reading the age of Augustus in too teleological a way: it looks as if the age of Cicero, the age of the late Republic, anticipates the intellectual environment of the Principate in this respect as in so many others.[121]

INCORPORATING THE WORLD

Intimately related to these movements in chronography are the universal histories that flourish in these decades, covering history from beginning to end.[122] Even Livy's history is also really a universal history or at least has the teleological tendencies of one. Its annalistic, urbi-centric form may appear to militate against its universal nature, but Livy could plausibly represent the history of the city and the world eventually becoming coextensive, with the city's rhythm of annual magistracies becoming a pulse for the whole world.[123] Once again, the phenomenon of universal history has its beginnings in the age of Cicero, Pompey, and Caesar, rather than Augustus.[124] Diodorus Siculus begins where Castor begins, with Ninus of Assyria, and he fixed the end point of his universal history as the start of Caesar's Gallic campaigns (1.4.7), in which Caesar carried the boundaries of the Empire to Ocean: his termination is, as it were, a Western counterpoint to the Eastern closural point of Castor. Diodorus may have completed his work around 30 B.C.E., but he started around 60 B.C.E.; his case provides a good example of the "Walter Raleigh" trap of facile periodization, for even though we tend to pigeonhole Diodorus as an Augustan author, the conception of the work is late Republican (not that he "knew" it was "late Republican").[125] Nonetheless, Augustus's reign sees the universal histories flourish, as they consolidate the insights and achievements of the previous generation, and as they react to his decisive last act in the drama of incorporating the ancient time lines, for Augustus had brought into the Empire the last remaining unincorporated element of the Mediterranean fringe, the primeval kingdom of Egypt. In 30 B.C.E. the circle around the sea's rim was finally made complete.[126]

If a universal history begins with the earliest ascertainable times, then one of the most interesting problems facing the writer of such a history is where to stop. The universal history of Pompeius Trogus took the same beginning point as Castor of Rhodes, starting with Ninus of Assyria. He went down to the ultimate closural end point, of the apparent final domination of the world by Augustus, with the submission of Spain in the West in 19 B.C.E., and the treaty with the Parthians in the East in 20 B.C.E.[127] This is the same Eastern end point as Castor's, but forty years later on. Castor had represented Pompey's settlement of the East as a definitive moment of closure, but we can see from Pompeius Trogus that the job kept having to be revisited, and he makes it clear that the Parthians in fact remained unconquered.[128] The mirage of definitive victory over the desert dwellers of Mesopotamia kept tantalizing the Western imperialists, deluding successive generations into thinking that they had managed to effect a final closure.

Here we confront the whole problem of an ending in time, of how you can impose a definitive closural shape on the unstoppable and indivisible onward flow of time.[129] Triumphal moments are particularly alluring in their deceptively definitive appeal. Ennius planned the first edition of his *Annales* to conclude with the triumph of Fulvius Nobilior in 187 B.C.E.;[130] but he found himself adding another three books.[131] Polybius began his project in the belief that the battle of Pydna and the destruction of the kingdom of Macedonia in 168/7 B.C.E. was a definitive end point, the moment at which Rome took over its role as the latest imperial power;[132] the refusal of events to stand still drew him on to 146 B.C.E., with the destructions of Carthage and Corinth.[133] If a writer evades the issue of closure by simply writing down to his own time, like Livy, then he faces the Tristram Shandy problem, whereby the more you live, the more you have to write.[134]

A universal history written under the Roman Empire is one that may aspire to cover all of space as well as all of time. In keeping with our theme of continuity in this area between the late Republic and early Principate, it is debated whether the first author of a truly universal geography of the whole (Roman) world is Cornelius Nepos in the 50s B.C.E. or Strabo in the 20s.[135] Once again, however, the unification of the world under the single undisputed political leadership of one man provides a new momentum to a drive that was already under way.[136] The places as well as the times of the Mediterranean are now bound up in each other, through Rome, and the resulting sense of geographical cohesion is caught in the map of Agrippa just as the sense of temporal cohesion is caught in the synchronistic chronographies and the universal histories.[137]

These newly refined grids of time and space worked to create an imperial sense of identity, enabling the inhabitants of the Empire to develop a lateral sense of localization in a shared time and a shared space; in chapter 6 we shall investigate the role that the Roman calendar likewise had to play in this function. Whatever this imperial sense of identity may have been for different people in different times and places, it was not a modern nationalism. Nonetheless, Anderson's account of modern nationalism is strikingly suggestive in its evocation of how important to nationalism is this sense of simultaneity in a shared time and participation in a parallel space: "For this sense of parallelism or simultaneity not merely to arise, but also to have vast political consequences, it was necessary that the distance between the parallel groups be large, and that the newer of them be substantial in size and permanently settled, as well as firmly subordinated to the older."[138] The newer members of the Roman Empire were indeed "substantial in size and permanently settled, as well as firmly subordinated to the older"; but these newer members, the inhabitants of the Hellenized East, thought of themselves as belonging to a far older and more prestigious culture than their new masters. The stakes were therefore very high in the operation of collating the times of Greece and Rome, and the process saw the whole gamut of possible interactions between the cultures being played out: snobbery, deference, competition, self-assertion, enlightenment. Both Greeks and Romans worked at the task, attempting to create a mesh of past time that would make sense of the present—a present that for centuries was ceaselessly revolutionary and unpredictable and did not settle into anything like an equilibrium until the early Principate. By that time something like a shared Roman and Greek past had been forged, at least to a degree, with the Romans established as the only non-Greeks who would be allowed, however grudgingly, to participate fully in the Hellenistic web of time that shaped the Mediterranean.

In the next chapter we shall go farther back in time, to investigate the way the Romans and Greeks coped with the problem of how to graft the Romans into the deep past of the Mediterranean's time webs, and how to negotiate their transition from that deep past into the time dimension of history.

THREE

· Transitions from
Myth into History I

The Foundations of the City

THE MYTH/HISTORY EVENT HORIZON

We move now to a different focus on time, and a different kind of horizon. The synchronistic charts of time that have been our subject so far enable the observer to construct webs of connection that are primarily lateral or horizontal. Of course the synchronism charts play a vital part in constructing a sensation of historical depth as well, since the whole of past time is mapped out through an expanding series of lateral synchronisms, and the construction of synchronism is tightly bound up with the apprehension of empires following each other in succession. But the fundamental mind-set of the synchronizer is a sideways comparative one, and the next two chapters will be concentrating on a rather different comparative perspective, one that directs the gaze not sideways but forwards and backwards, with the pivot being the contentious horizon between myth and history. How could that horizon be plotted by the Greeks and Romans, and what was at stake in making this demarcation? How does the working of time differ on either side of the divide, wherever one imposes it? And what kind of similes become necessary when one is comparing and contrasting across this time divide?

In the present chapter we shall consider the transition from myth to history in the Greek and Roman historiographical tradition, and our main test case, in the second half of the chapter, will be the foundation of the city of Rome. This is an event, or perhaps I should say a concept, that acts as a magnet for ancient and modern investigators alike. The foundation of the city generated for the ancients an important cluster of questions about what counts as history, questions that still exercise historians of the early period of Rome. How can historical time be defined and mapped out? What can and cannot be plotted in historical time? What is at stake in claiming that a particular event is part of historical time or not? How does the historian define the limits of historical knowledge? And how does the historian cope at the limits of historical knowledge? Further, we shall consider the problem of whether the transition from myth to history can be definitive: the founding of the city may look like a once-and-for-all event, but the movement of history can eddy backwards to the foundational moment, making refoundation necessary, again and again, threatening to breach once more the divide between myth and history. The next chapter in this pairing will examine a rather different way of conceiving of this transition from myth to history, with the myth of the Gold and Iron ages. Here we shall be concentrating more on the poetic tradition, and especially on the very moment of demarcation between the Ages of Gold and Iron, to see how the passage from myth to history warps the net of time that covers the transition. Once again, the problem of a return will engage us, with the possibility of a return to the Golden Age providing a powerful magnet at many periods.

It is a diverting, though demoralizing, exercise to type in the keywords "myth and history" in a library catalogue search. Even in studies of Greece and Rome there is an overwhelming body of material to deal with, and it would be very easy to get totally bogged down in the swamps of *spatium historicum* and *spatium mythicum*, of *illud tempus* and "temps des dieux, temps des hommes"—to mention only the most imposing of the phrases that have been coined by students of this problem. It looks in fact as if the pendulum is swinging, in the way it does; perhaps partly in reaction to the vacuity and portentousness of much of the discussion, more and more scholars nowadays are inclined to deny that there is much value in the language of "mythical time" and "historical time," holding that these distinctions are not current in the ancient world.[1] I would like to push back on the pendulum before it gathers too much momentum, but I do not want to make it swing back all the way. The received wisdom on the dichotomy certainly deserves to be questioned, but both its proponents and opponents have tended to run together issues that ought to be kept distinct. I shall argue that the activity of demarcating between myth and history mattered in the ancient historiographical tradition, though not necessarily in ways that might correspond closely to any of our current modern divisions between myth and history;[2] and I shall argue that the chronological dimension to this demarcation between myth and history is one that is worth retaining for investigation. The mass of inherited material in the historio-graphical tradition could be sliced up in various ways, but one of the razors you could bring to it was a chronological one. The chronological razor could also be used to slice up different *degrees* of historicity, as we shall see; we are very seldom talking about a single line of demarcation.

STRATIFYING TIME:
HOMER, HESIOD, ATHENS

The general idea of demarcations within past time, and of a gulf between the pres-ent and a past time of gods and heroes, is well established from the very first Greek texts. In their different but related ways, Homer and Hesiod each clearly have an intuition of different time dimensions in the past, with different strata going back, discontinuously, from the present. In Homer, Troy is unbridgeably distant in time, accessible only to the inspired poet (*Il.* 2.485–86). Homer's attitude to the past is grounded in a powerful feeling that the heroic action of the poems is taking place long ago, at a time from which the current audience, οἷοι νῦν βροτοί εἰσιν, "such as mortals are now," is irrevocably cut off, a time to which the audience has access only when the past is revivified in the poet's song.[3] A sense of an estrangement from an earlier, different time is palpable even in the *Iliad* itself. Both of the oldest characters on each side, Nestor and Priam, can remember an earlier age when con-ditions were markedly different: Priam remembers fighting against Amazons (3.188–89), while Nestor remembers fighting against Centaurs, beside men far greater than any alive today (1.261–72).[4] Hesiod, too, works with a cognate con-ception of layers of time, moving from a primeval past of cosmogonic time toward the time of the Olympian gods, and then via the age of the heroes toward the pres-ent of the contemporary audience.[5] These layered time schemes are closely paral-lel to those underpinning the Akkadian "cycle" of narratives, from the cosmogo-nic *Enuma elis* to the heroic *Gilgamesh,* and beyond.[6]

The subject matter of Attic tragedy is likewise clearly localized in some other time, one that can have tangible links with contemporary time through aetiology in a way that Homer's epoch can never have, but a time that nevertheless is removed and discrete, a self-contained category.[7] Hall has shown how the mythi-cization of the Persian Wars depends precisely on an understood dialectic between the far distant past and the very recent past, or near present, in the three tragedies that treated the Persian Wars (two by Phrynicus, one by Aeschylus).[8] Since her book appeared we have had the great good fortune to have discovered the "New

Simonides," in which the distant events of Troy are a template for the heroism of the contemporary Greeks in their battle against the Asiatics at Plataea.[9] Again, the Athenian tradition of funeral orations shows a heightened self-consciousness about the relationship between the status of the recently dead and the great heroes of the mythic past.[10] The author of the funeral speech preserved in the Demosthenic corpus reflects on the different levels of commemoration represented by the different levels of time that the dead inhabit (Dem. 60.8–10). The old Athenians (at the time of the Amazons, Heraclids, and Seven against Thebes) are celebrated in recited and sung poetry and in histories; the speaker then goes on to mention the Athenians who fought in the Persian Wars, whose deeds, he says, have not yet reached the same status: "things which, in terms of evaluation of achievement, are no lesser than the ones I've mentioned, but through being closer in time have not yet been mythologized nor lifted up to heroic rank" (ἃ δὲ τῇ μὲν ἀξίᾳ τῶν ἔργων οὐδέν ἐστι τούτων ἐλάττω, τῷ δ᾽ ὑπογυώτερ᾽ εἶναι τοῖς χρόνοις οὔπω μεμυθολόγηται οὐδ᾽ εἰς τὴν ἡρωϊκὴν ἐπανῆκται τάξιν, Dem. 60.9).[11]

The public monuments of classical times work with a similar dialectic between events of a stratified mythic past and a contemporary present. A highly complex monument such as the Athenian Parthenon shows an intuition of multitiered layers of past time.[12] The earliest event depicted in the programme is the birth of Athena on the east pediment, part of the beginning of the current cosmic order. Directly underneath this pediment the metopes show the Gigantomachy, from primordial mythic time, and this is the next phase in chronological order, for Athena participated in the Gigantomachy to protect the new divine cosmos against this threat. The next items in chronological order are on the western side, showing exactly the same pattern of establishment of order on the pediment with a threat to it on the metopes underneath. On the west pediment we see the birth of the city; here is the contest of Athena and Poseidon for the honor of being the city's patron god, at the very beginning of the city's time. Directly underneath this western pediment, in the metopes, we see a crisis in the life of the now established city in the form of the Amazonomachy, a mortal threat to the city's existence from the time of King Theseus. Likewise from the lifetime of Theseus is the Centauromachy, depicted on the metopes of the south side. The metopes on the north side show the sack of Troy, which took place after the death of Theseus (to anticipate this chapter's main focus on Rome, it is worth pausing here to note that one of these metopes showed Aeneas escaping from the doomed city, with his father and son).[13] Finally, whatever we may decide about the question of the identity of the horsemen in the frieze itself, they are either in the idealized contemporary world or else from only two generations earlier, if Boardman is right to identify them as the dead of Marathon.[14]

STRATIFYING TIME: HERODOTUS

At the beginning of the historiographical tradition, it is often claimed, Herodotus first formulates a conception of two different expanses of time, the time of myth and the time of history, often referred to as *spatium historicum* and *spatium mythicum*.[15] Discussion inevitably focuses on three key passages in which Herodotus has often been seen as distinguishing between two phases of time. In the first, at the beginning of his work, Herodotus relates what the Persians have to say about who started the series of injustices that resulted in the Persian Wars (1.1.1–5.2). After telling us the Persian version of Io, Europa, Medea, and Helen and the Trojan War, with a little footnote on what the Phoenicians say about Io, Herodotus declares (1.5.3):

> ταῦτα μέν νυν Πέρσαι τε καὶ Φοίνικες λέγουσι. ἐγὼ δὲ περὶ μὲν
> τούτων οὐκ ἔρχομαι ἐρέων ὡς οὕτως ἢ ἄλλως κως ταῦτα ἐγένετο,
> τὸν δὲ οἶδα αὐτὸς πρῶτον ὑπάρξαντα ἀδίκων ἔργων ἐς τοὺς Ἕλληνας,
> τοῦτον σημήνας προβήσομαι ἐς τὸ πρόσω τοῦ λόγου.

> Well, that's what the Persians and Phoenicians say. But as far as these things are concerned I am not proceeding to say that they happened like this or maybe some other way, but the one whom I myself know first to have begun unjust deeds against the Greeks, him I shall point out and then I shall proceed to the rest of my account.

He then begins with Croesus, the king of Lydia some hundred years before the time of writing.

In his "second preface," introducing the actual invasion of Xerxes, Herodotus deploys the same antithesis between what is said about ancient events and what he actually knows (7.20.2–21.1):

> στόλων γὰρ τῶν ἡμεῖς ἴδμεν πολλῷ δὴ μέγιστος οὗτος ἐγένετο, ὥστε
> μήτε τὸν Δαρείου τὸν ἐπὶ Σκύθας παρὰ τοῦτον μηδένα φαίνεσθαι μήτε
> τὸν Σκυθικόν ... μήτε κατὰ τὰ λεγόμενα τὸν Ἀτρειδέων ἐς Ἴλιον ...
> αὗται αἱ πᾶσαι οὐδ' ἕτεραι πρὸς ταύτῃσι γενόμεναι στρατηλασίαι μιῆς
> τῆσδε οὐκ ἄξιαι.

Of the expeditions which we know of, this was much the greatest, so that neither Darius' against the Scythians seems an expedition by comparison with this
one . . . nor the Scythian one . . . nor the one (according to what is said) of the
Atreidae against Troy . . . All these campaigns and others which happened like
them are not worthy of this single one.[16]

Finally, in book 3, Herodotus uses a very similar turn of phrase to introduce a distinction between the thalassocrats Minos and Polycrates—Minos from sometime
before the Trojan War, and Polycrates from the generation of Herodotus's grandfather (3.122.2):

Πολυκράτης γάρ ἐστι πρῶτος τῶν ἡμεῖς ἴδμεν Ἑλλήνων ὃς
θαλασσοκρατέειν ἐπενοήθη, πάρεξ Μίνω τε τοῦ Κνωσσίου καὶ
εἰ δή τις ἄλλος πρότερος τούτου ἦρξε τῆς θαλάσσης· τῆς δὲ ἀνθρωπηίης
λεγομένης γενεῆς Πολυκράτης πρῶτος.

For Polycrates is the first of the Greeks of whom we know who had the plan of
ruling the sea, apart from Minos the Cretan and any other person before him
who ruled the sea—of the so-called human race Polycrates was first.

Now, it is tolerably clear that when Herodotus points to Croesus and Polycrates as
the first of whom he knows in their various contexts, he is not saying that there is
some ineradicable line positioned about a hundred years in the past that separates
off real history from myth—whatever "myth" might mean to Herodotus, or "history" for that matter. Scholars have sometimes taken Herodotus to be drawing
some such line; his pronouncement about Croesus in particular has been taken to
be an opening programmatic statement about a time distinction that is operative
for the whole of the rest of the work.[17] This view cannot be right in its blunt form,
since Herodotus does vouch for a great deal of material that he narrates from
before this period, and he even gives a number of different "firsts of which we
know" from before the time of Croesus and Polycrates, such as the first dithyramb
(1.23–24), or the first barbarian dedications at Delphi (1.14.2).[18] Nonetheless, at
the start of his work he definitely is making a distinction between the stories of the
Persians about Io and his own account of Croesus; if you really want to know how
the cycle of aggression and revenge between Europe and Asia began, you look to
Croesus, not to those other stories.[19] Herodotus can certainly go back in time
before Croesus to set the scene for that narrative, but this does not invalidate the
fact that Croesus is a crucial demarcation line.[20] Above all, Herodotus makes a dis-

tinction between the value of the stories about Io and her like and the value of what he is going to tell us about Croesus, the one whom he himself "knows first to have begun," just as in his second preface he makes a distinction between "what is said" about the Trojan War and the expeditions "about which we know."[21] If this distinction is not one of time alone, it is still a distinction that has an important time dimension to it, since it is a distinction based on knowledge, and Herodotus knows that knowledge and time are linked.[22] This is one of the many things he learned from Homer.[23]

Herodotus is playing off a Homeric conception of the deep past as a time inaccessible to normal human knowledge, a conception most crisply formulated by Homer when he invokes the Muses in *Iliad* 2.485–86.[24] Here Homer says that the Muses do have knowledge (ἴστε) about this heroic past, whereas we hear only report (κλέος οἶον ἀκούομεν) and do not know anything (οὐδέ τι ἴδμεν). Much of the force of this Homeric passage comes from the fact that the Greek word "know" is cognate with the word "see," while the word κλέος, "report," is cognate with the word "hear." This is an antithesis of wide importance in Homer, one referred to by characters as well: seeing something and knowing it for yourself is incomparably superior to merely hearing about it from another source.[25] When Herodotus rejects the Persian version of Io and turns to Croesus, he is playing on precisely this Homeric antithesis, for he uses Homer's verb of knowledge, but positively. "We do not know anything," Homer had said; "I know" (οἶδα), says Herodotus, without a negative, of his own sure knowledge, not of his ignorance. Homer cannot know for himself about the distant past and has to rely on the Muses to tell him; Herodotus cannot know for himself about the distant past either, and so he will tell about the things that he *can* know for himself—αὐτός, he says, "myself."[26]

Throughout his history Herodotus is extremely scrupulous in marking what he will vouch for and what he will not, on the basis of his claims to knowledge, maintaining systematically the distinction of his second preface "between the myths that are 'said' and what 'we can know.'"[27] This issue is regularly misunderstood by scholars, especially those who wish to deny Herodotus a developed interest in demarcating between his new "history" and the old stories. Harrison, for example, claims that Herodotus treats "Minos straightforwardly as a historical figure" in his account of Cretan participation in the Trojan War, without any reference to the fact that the entire section is in reported speech, explaining the reference of a Delphic oracle, and is not focalized by the narrator.[28] Again, scholars think that they can undo Herodotus's tension between myth and history by pointing to cases where Herodotus says god intervenes.[29] This, however, is a category mistake, confusing "myth" with "religion." Herodotus can perfectly well think that he can use evidence to discern patterns of divine action in recent or contemporary history;[30] this is very different from his thinking that he can get information of the kind he wants from the material of myth, which had been, as we have seen, long since precipitated out by his culture as occupying its own discrete and internally layered time dimension.

A very important part, then, of what Herodotus will claim as knowledge is bound up with an apprehension of time. This apprehension of time will of course vary depending on what part of his world he is talking about at any given moment, so that it is a mistake to imagine Herodotus working with some single yardstick he may lay across diverse times in order to form one line of demarcation.[31] After our first two chapters it should be plain that no one in the ancient world, let alone the first person to write history, could conceive of time as an absolute and continuous essence in which all parts of the world seamlessly participate. Thanks in particular to his Egyptian informants, Herodotus thinks he is in a better position to say authoritative things about very distant events and persons in Egypt than in Greece.[32] The difference between Egyptian and Greek time is one of quantity, in terms of depth, but this quantitative difference is so great that it translates into qualitative terms, giving Egyptian time a plotted-out texture that is incomparably superior to that of Greek time in its reach.[33]

The epistemological criterion is by no means the only one that matters to Herodotus as he grapples with demarcating his material from the material of myth. A highly revealing moment comes in the passage we have already quoted, in which he says that "Polycrates is the first of the Greeks of whom we know who had the plan of ruling the sea, apart from Minos the Cretan" (3.122.2). In his last book, *Truth and Truthfulness*, in the course of a bracing chapter on the concept of the historic past in Herodotus and Thucydides, Bernard Williams demolishes the structure of "time of gods" and "time of men" that has sometimes been built upon mistranslations of the phrase Herodotus uses to describe Polycrates. He is "the first of the Greeks of whom we know," says Herodotus, "apart from Minos the Cretan and any other person before him who ruled the sea—of the so-called human race Polycrates was first." The phrase translated here as "so-called human race," τῆς ἀνθρωπηΐης λεγομένης γενεῆς, has often been mistranslated as "human time" or "human epoch" or something of the kind, meanings it cannot bear, as Williams shows.[34] Williams finely demonstrates that Herodotus knows there is "something wrong with Minos," but he is not exactly sure what. He has not fully distinguished the categories he needs in order to be able to formulate what *is* wrong with Minos: is it our ignorance or is it Minos's status as a real human being that is at issue?[35]

Herodotus would incline to frame his answer in terms of knowledge and ignorance if pressed, since he does tend to see human time, or history, as being continuous as far back as one can go, in the sense that people and events even in the distant past were not qualitatively different from "now."[36] Still, Williams's fine teasing out of Herodotus's problems with Minos highlights the variety of ways in which demarcations could be made between "history" and "myth." I have been concentrating on the problem of what may be *known* about myth, but the question of Minos's status shows that another issue is the potentially destabilizing discrepancy between the nature of experience now and then, when demigods are said to have walked the earth. As we shall see throughout this chapter and the next, the sense of difference is what marks the boundary between history and myth, and that sense of difference is a mobile one, depending on what is at stake for any particular observer at any particular moment in stressing either likeness or unlikeness. Just as the synchronism operates laterally like a simile to create a sense of identity or of difference, so "the boundary between 'history' and the 'fabulous' can be taken to be the point where simile breaks down and categorical *un*likeness sets in."[37]

NEW KNOWLEDGE CLAIMS
FOR A NEW *TECHNĒ*

It is important to see Herodotus's knowledge claims for what they are, and for what they are not. In the twenty-first century we can monitor fairly well what Herodotus could in fact know or hope to know. From our vantage point at least there is a well-defined *spatium historicum,* since Herodotus knows some things worth knowing as far back as about 650 B.C.E., and for the period before that he knows, in effect, nothing.[38] But much of what Herodotus asserts even about Croesus or Cyrus, only a hundred years before his own time, does not count as knowledge in our terms. The situation is very close indeed to what we can observe in the contemporary worlds of medicine and science, so memorably evoked in the work of Geoffrey Lloyd.[39] What we have in the new discourse of history, as in the new discourses of medicine and science, which were evolving at the same time, is not necessarily an increase in knowledge—what Lloyd calls an improvement in "technological control"[40]—but a new kind of rhetoric, one founded in intellectual demarcation disputes, where victory depended on skill in presenting "plausible arguments and evidence" in a persuasive way.[41] Much of what Lloyd says about science and philosophy could be copied over verbatim for history. He highlights the importance to the new scientific discourses of "the habit of scrutiny, and . . . the expectation of justification—of giving an account—and the premium set on rational methods of doing so";[42] "the questions once posed, the answers given were sometimes not just schematic, but contained . . . elements of pure bluff. Yet while the Greeks' confidence in the rightness of their methods often outran their actual scientific performance . . . those methodological ideals not only permitted, but positively promoted the further growth of the enquiry."[43] Modern parallels readily suggest themselves—psychoanalysis, most obviously. The following features of Greek medical and scientific writings that Lloyd picks out as particularly distinctive are also directly transferable to Herodotus and Thucydides and their descendants: "the prominence of the authorial ego, the prizing of innovation both theoretical and practical, the possibility of engaging in explicit criticism of earlier authorities, even in the wholesale rejection (at times) of custom and tradition."[44]

The implications for Herodotus and Thucydides are obvious. What Herodotus begins is a project of carving out a new kind of discourse about the past that has powerful affinities in rhetorical method and authorial self-presentation with the new kinds of discourse about medicine and nature. His new discourse will enable him to compete not only with the body of inherited mythic story, but also, even more importantly, with the other discourses that had already evolved to compete with myth, above all the rationalizing and cataloguing of Hecataeus and the other mythographers. A crucial part of this new project is the ability to stake out credible and authoritative knowledge claims; and a crucial part of that ability is the claim—however arbitrarily grounded—to be able to demarcate what can be known in this *technē* and what cannot be known.[45]

DIVIDING UP THE PAST

Where the time dimensions of the past are concerned, the issue of knowledge continues to carry a lot of weight in the later tradition. The chronographic tradition's most explicit surviving example of the historical stratification of time is predicated on the degrees of knowledge that it is possible to reach concerning the different strata of time. We return shortly to Censorinus's important report of Varro's divisions of the past, but for now we may note that, even from the introduction to this passage, it is clear that the divisions of time are fundamentally divisions of knowledge: "If the origin of the world had come into humans' range of knowledge," says Censorinus, explaining why his divisions do not go back farther than the mythical origins of humans, "then that is where we would start from" (*et si origo mundi in hominum notitiam uenisset, inde exordium sumeremus*, *DN* 20.12).[46] The Christian chronographic tradition, of course, as we have already seen, *would* ultimately claim to have access to knowledge about the origin of the world.

Historians in particular continue to engage regularly in the demarcation of their subject matter from "the times of myth," as Dionysius of Halicarnassus calls them, when he says that the Assyrian empire reaches back εἰς τοὺς μυθικοὺς ... χρόνους (*Ant. Rom.* 1.2.2). Because the origin of this historiographical trope of demarcation was not a technological or methodological advance but a new kind of rhetoric, the demarcation of these times of myth could be mobile.[47] As we shall see, the Trojan War was regularly the chosen cut-off point, but for Ephorus, writing a Panhellenic history in the middle of the fourth century, the demarcation line was the return of the Heracleidae, eighty years after the Trojan War. Ephorus deliberately proclaims that he will not begin with the events of myth;[48] in a very Thucydidean passage he says that you cannot give an accurate account of ancient events, as opposed to contemporary ones, since deeds and speeches of the distant past cannot be remembered through such a long time.[49] One of the fullest discussions of this topic comes in Plutarch's preface to the paired lives of Theseus and Romulus, which has recently been the subject of a fine analysis by Pelling: in working on Theseus, Plutarch says, he has gone through that time "which can be reached by reasonable inference or where factual history can find a firm foothold," and has now reached a point where he might "say of those remoter ages, 'All that lies beyond are fables and tragic stories.'"[50]

Inevitably, these are broad generalizations about a very long, varied, and contentious tradition, one including historians who narrated the exploits of Dionysus in India or Heracles in the West as prototypes of later Hellenic arrivals, or who invented charter myths for Greek colonies.[51] Still, it seems to me that Marincola is fundamentally correct to say that the historians ended up with three options when dealing with myth: leave it out, rationalize it, or report it noncommittally, leaving judgment up to the reader.[52] The moments when historians confront the problem of myth can provide some of their most interesting moments of self-definition, as they maneuver on the boundaries of poetry or drama in order to define their projects in the same way that epic or elegiac poets maneuver on *their* intergeneric boundaries in order to define *their* projects.[53] Livy's preface, as we shall see shortly, is an important case in point, where he brushes against history's limits and acknowledges that much of the tradition concerning the foundation of the city is "more appropriate to the myths of poetry than to uncorrupted monuments of things that happened" (*poeticis magis decora fabulis quam incorruptis rerum gestarum monumentis, Pref.* 6). Here he is setting up a strategy of skirmishing with opposing genres that will carry on strongly into the first book.[54]

One of the factors that make this topic so difficult is that ancient writers intelligently anticipate such moderns as Hayden White by systematically running together "content" and "form."[55] Μῦθος and *fabula* ("myth" and "fable") are terms that apply both to subject matter and to genre, so that any ancient discussion of these topics keeps sliding—productively, but to the eyes of many moderns, confusingly—from one category to another.[56] If you are distinguishing between "history" and μῦθος or *fabula,* you are distinguishing not just between the historically verifiable and the fabulous, or nonverifiable, but also between what belongs in historiography and what does not: you are negotiating a generic as well as an epistemological boundary. Censorinus's account of Varro's divisions of time is once again highly revealing. The second epoch is called "mythical" in terms of what we might call "form," "because in it many fabulous things are *reported*" (*quia in eo multa fabulosa referuntur*); but he describes the historical period in terms of both content and form, without tilting the balance definitively either way: this period is "historical," he says, "because the things that were *done* in that period are *contained in true histories*" (*quia res in eo gestae ueris historiis continentur, DN* 21.1).

Historians, then, fenced off myth from their work in various ways, and one of their reasons for doing this—or perhaps we should say one of their strategies for doing this—was based on the idea that the times of myth were beyond the pale in terms of chronology. For the historians there is no chronology of myth, no set of interlocking synchronistic data that make a system; there is no "canon," as they put it.[57] "Mythical time had neither depth nor breadth," says Veyne: "One might as well ask whether the adventures of Tom Thumb took place before or after Cinderella's ball."[58] This is—rather typically—overstated: Veyne himself immediately concedes that the heroes had genealogies, which give both depth and breadth. At least for the historical tradition, however, his large statement is broadly true. Diodorus Siculus states the principle very explicitly, saying that he "cannot securely divide up the times before the Trojan War because of the fact that no reliable chronological system has been transmitted" (τοὺς μὲν πρὸ τῶν Τρωικῶν οὐ διοριζόμεθα βεβαίως διὰ τὸ μηδὲν παράπηγμα παρειληφέναι περὶ τούτων πιστευόμενον, 1.5.1).[59] The fundamental attitude is there from the start of historiography. Finley is right to claim that Herodotus already had a chronological scheme that he "refused to ruin . . . by incorporating the mythical events"; he "made no effort to assign dates to the undatable myths."[60] Sellar and Yeatman taught us in *1066 and All That* that history "*is what you can remember,*" and that is certainly true; but history is also what you can date.[61]

On the question of the datability of myth, the historiographical tradition must be distinguished from other traditions, especially those of the chronographers, mythographers, antiquarians, and local historians.[62] The first mythographers in the fifth century left their mythical genealogies floating, unmeasured, without any time hooks to the present.[63] But soon enough the task began of weaving a continuous mesh, one that would ultimately tie the present into a matrix that reached back beyond the measured time of Herodotus to before the Trojan War and the foundation of the first Greek cities, to link up with the genealogies of myth.[64] The Marmor Parium, for example, from the middle of the third century B.C.E., counts the years from "264 B.C.E." back to the time when Cecrops ruled Athens ("1581/0 B.C.E."), when Ares and Poseidon squabbled over the Areopagus ("1531/0"), when Demeter came to Athens and taught Triptolemus agriculture ("1409/8"), or when Theseus fought the Amazons ("1256/5").[65] It remains significant that even this document does not purport to go back farther than the foundation of the city of Athens. Deep cosmogonic time still remains beyond the pale.

This urge for chronological comprehensiveness is rather like what the geographers were aiming at throughout the Hellenistic period. When Polybius, for example, talks about the increasing success in mapping space, he says that in the old days authors could be forgiven for peddling fabulous yarns about the far reaches of the earth, since no one knew any better; but now that virtually all the world is accessible there is no excuse for not gaining a better and truer knowledge (3.58–59).[66] For the far reaches of time, as well, many felt the need to fill in the vacuum that inspired such horror, and to create the nets of connections between the present and the past that could mean so much to cities and to monarchs.[67] Not all chronographers succumbed to this compulsion to fill in the blanks. The great Hellenistic scholars, Eratosthenes and Apollodorus, as we shall see shortly, were reluctant to pin very much on dates before the first Olympiad, and certainly before the Trojan War. But especially after Castor of Rhodes published his chronography lining up Greek affairs with the deep reaches of Eastern time, the pressure to fill in the gaps systematically grew ever stronger. The issue comes clearly into focus when the Christian chronographers, especially Julius Africanus (c. 160–240 C.E.), get to work. They do not want any "uncertain" periods at all, as Adler explains; they want to fill it *all* in, to connect every dot, all the way back to creation.[68] Even among the Christian chronographers, however, there was room for dissension on the question of when knowledge gave out: Eusebius aroused the rage of George

Syncellus for saying that events were uncertain and undatable before the birth of Abraham.[69]

Scholars often represent the kind of continuous time map we see in the Marmor Parium as a constant feature of the ancient world;[70] but it is a map that the historians, and even some chronographers, ostentatiously refused to navigate by.[71] Sacks persuasively suggests that Diodorus's scrupulosity in avoiding a chronology for his mythic material may be a reaction precisely against the just-published *Chronica* of Castor of Rhodes, with its spurious precision in dating.[72] Historians, together with some chronographers, did not wish to envisage all past time as mapped out with equal precision, or as stretching back in some kind of continuity; they tended to work with a stratified past, with more or less agreed-upon marks in time that posted an increasing security of knowledge in the tradition as one approached the present.[73]

The two key markers that recur in the Greek tradition are the Trojan War and the first Olympiad, markers that writers in the Roman historiographical tradition picked up and transformed creatively for their own purposes. No single text bearing on this kind of stratification is canonical, but it is worth quoting here the fullest and clearest we have surviving, from Censorinus's report of Varro's demarcations of past time (*DN* 20.12–21.2):[74]

et si origo mundi in hominum notitiam uenisset, inde exordium sumeremus. nunc uero id interuallum temporis tractabo quod ἱστορικὸν Varro appellat. hic enim tria discrimina temporum esse tradit, primum ab hominum principio ad cataclysmum priorem, quod propter ignorantiam uocatur ἄδηλον, secundum a cataclysmo priore ad olympiadem primam, quod, quia in eo multa fabulosa referuntur, μυθικὸν nominatur, tertium a prima olympiade ad nos, quod dicitur ἱστορικόν, quia res in eo gestae ueris historiis continentur. primum enim tempus, siue habuit initium seu semper fuit, certe quot annorum sit non potest comprehendi.

And if the origin of the world had come into humans' range of knowledge, then that is where we would start from; but as it is I shall treat that interval of time that Varro calls ἱστορικόν ("historical"). For he gives three divisions of time epochs: first from the beginning of mankind to the first flood, which because of our ignorance of it is called ἄδηλον ("unclear"), second from the first flood to the first Olympiad, which, because many fabulous things are reported in it, is named μυθικόν ("mythical"), third from the first Olympiad to us, which is called ἱστορικόν ("historical"), because the events that happened in it are contained in true histories. For the first epoch of time, whether it had a beginning or whether it always existed, it is certainly not possible to comprehend its number of years.

We shall examine the Trojan War in the next chapter, for it is of crucial significance in the poetic traditions as a huge break in the relations between gods and mortals, a profound rupture after which there is no more mingling of human and divine. But in the historiographical and chronological traditions as well there is a tendency to locate a strong marker here, fixing the Trojan War as pivotal or transitional, with myth lying on the other side of it.[75] Even the Marmor Parium, which can tell you when Demeter or Poseidon visited Athens, and which in general has no investment in demarcating between mythical and historical time, has a significant feature in its layout when it comes to the Trojan War. There are only two places in the whole tablet that are marked with punctuation, a gap of a few letter spaces: the first is immediately after the prefatory material, and the other is immediately before the Trojan War, as if to bracket off that entire section.[76] Eratosthenes began his chronographical work with Troy's fall, implying that the mythical period before Troy was beyond chronology.[77] This decision would parallel his refusal, when wearing his geographer's hat, to put any store by the information about Mediterranean geography that was supposedly preserved in Homer: "You'd find where Odysseus wandered," he said, "when you found the cobbler who stitched together the bag of winds" (as reported by Strabo, 1.2.15). It was Eratosthenes who fixed the fall of Troy in "1184/3 B.C.E.," and this was the date that became dominant in the tradition.[78] One of the main reasons that the Trojan War is so important in the chronological canon is that it is "the first conflict between the continents";[79] as we have seen, synchronistic chronology is inextricable from the theme of *translatio imperii*, and the fall of Troy inaugurates this theme for the classical period and, even more significantly, for the epoch of Alexander. Apollodorus's book divisions show what is at issue. His *Chronica* was in four books, with book 1 going from the fall of Troy (the same starting point as Eratosthenes) to the Persian Wars, and book 2 going from there to the death of Alexander.[80]

In the Roman tradition the fall of Troy is likewise of the highest importance, with the added reason that the fall of Troy provides the impetus for the beginning of Rome. Livy's history of Rome begins, after the preface, with the aftermath of the fall of Troy, and the language with which he picks up the narrative at this point signals the primacy of the moment: *Iam primum omnium satis constat Troia capta* ("First of all it is generally agreed that when Troy was captured," 1.1.1). Varro made the fall of Troy a crucial watershed within his "mythical" period, "as the last of a series of events staggered at 400-year intervals between Ogygus' flood and the first Olympiad"; the fall of Troy closed off the second book of his *De Gente Populi Romani*.[81] Jerome's *Chronicle* represents the fall of Troy as being, in a sense, the beginning of Roman history. When he supplements Eusebius's *Chronicle* and translates it into Latin, he says that he will add more Roman material to it;[82] he translates straight from the Greek down as far as the fall of Troy, and that is where he starts adding the material that he has described as Roman.[83] The layout of the page devoted to the fall of Troy vividly symbolizes the status of the event as an epoch-making watershed, for "Troia Capta" spreads over the whole of the double page—no other event takes up a double spread in this way. The pivotal chronological significance of the Trojan War is clear from the opening of Virgil's *Aeneid*, which depends upon the idea that the Trojan War is a gigantic hinge between myth and history. Virgil shows Juno as driven by one mythical and one historical motivation, with her hatred of the Trojans reaching back into mythical, Homeric, time, and her partisanship for Carthage reaching forward into historical time.[84] As it progresses, Virgil's epic puts these apparently perspicuous categories under a lot of strain: a radical contamination of the categories of history and myth is one of the things the *Aeneid* is interested in, not least because the poet and his audience are now living in a new age of demigods and miracles, and, in a sense, returning to an age of myth. Aeneas was the last of the old demigods, and now Julius Caesar and Augustus are the first of a new breed.[85]

In Lucretius and Horace, in rather different ways, Troy is a crucial demarcation line for what may be known as human history. When Lucretius is arguing that time is not a *per se* existent, but the product of the interaction of body and space (1.459–63), he immediately turns to the related problem of whether historical events are *per se* existents or not (1.464–77). His illustrative examples come from the beginning and the end of the Trojan War (Paris and Helen, the wooden horse), and it is no accident that Troy should provide the nucleus around which cluster questions of the status of time and history, for Troy is the farthest back one can go in order to find examples of human beings doing verifiable things. Time does not exist in itself, nor do past historical events exist in themselves: both are accidents of body and space, which are the only real *per se* entities. The body and space existed and still exist that gave rise to the accidents we call "the time in which the Trojan war happened" and "the events of the Trojan War."[86] Beyond that point it is not possible to go. Lucretius believes that our knowledge gives out at Troy because the world is comparatively new. The earliest poetic tradition does not preserve "deeds of men" from before

Troy and Thebes because there were none to record (5.324–29). What happened before those events our age cannot see, unless by process of reason (*propterea quid sit prius actum respicere aetas/nostra nequit, nisi qua ratio uestigia monstrat*, 5.1446–47). Horace, on the other hand, would have it that there were many heroes before Agamemnon, but we do not know about them because there was no poetic tradition to record their deeds (*Carm.* 4.9.25–28). Either way, Troy is the event horizon.

The other epochal demarcation, one with even more canonical power, the anchor for the closest approximation to a universal dating system in the ancient world, was the first Olympiad, corresponding to "776 B.C.E."[87] Scholars regularly attribute the establishment of the "date" of the first Olympiad to Hippias of Elis or to Eratosthenes, but Jacoby was almost certainly right to argue that Eratosthenes followed in Timaeus's footsteps, with Timaeus first establishing this date as a peg from which historians could count in spaced intervals.[88] At least fifty years before Eratosthenes' *Chronographiae* Timaeus had already published his *Olympionicae*, of which nothing directly survives, but which must have used Olympic victors in a chronographic scheme of synchronism.[89] Möller is right to point out that we have no direct attestation of Timaeus using numbered Olympiads in the manner that later became normative; but the first evidence we have of ordinal numbers for Olympiads falls in the first half of the third century B.C.E., between Timaeus's and Eratosthenes' chronographic works, and the likelihood remains that Timaeus established the first Olympiad as a fixed point in time, together with the counting of intervals forwards and backwards from it.[90]

Nonetheless, Eratosthenes may well have made more of the first Olympiad as a watershed than had Timaeus. Jacoby makes a strong claim that, despite beginning his *Chronographiae* with Troy, Eratosthenes established the first Olympiad as the pivot where properly credible history began.[91] In other words, the fall of Troy may be a demarcation from myth, but the first Olympiad is a demarcation into history. This opens up an interesting 400-year-long grey area: if everything on the other side of Troy is mythical, but history begins with the first Olympiad, then what is the status of the material between these two markers—between "1184" and "776"?[92] Eratosthenes' own attitude to this intermediate period is quite impossible to recover, but I think it is likely that he was presenting some kind of stratified demarcation of historicity or knowability. Ultimately, this would be a development of the kind of distinctions Thucydides works with in his Archaeology, where he operates on the basis that it is possible to know the contemporary world with some kind of precision, the preceding generation with much less certainty, and the time before that only on the basis of hearsay and likely conjecture (1.1.3; 1.21.1). In the case of Eratosthenes we would then have a classic and overarching example of what Mazzarino has called the "diastematic" system of dating, which sets up major events as posts to establish time intervals.[93]

Part of the reason that discussion of the first Olympiad is so vexed is that scholars since Scaliger have tended to have a misguided reverence for the supposed historical sense and scientific rigor of the act of demarcating the first Olympiad as the beginning of proper history.[94] It really is very curious how many modern historians respond to this move of Eratosthenes by admiring the apparent historical precision and discrimination of their distant "colleague," and also how many of them can show a touching faith in the idea that Greek history somehow does get more secure or more "historical" around 776, whereas, as we have already seen, the Greek historical tradition actually knew nothing worth knowing about the early eighth century. Timaeus's and Eratosthenes' watershed of the first Olympiad is not a finding on the basis of research, any more than was the Hippocratics' discovery of the wandering womb or Freud's discovery of the id, ego, and superego. Timaeus and Eratosthenes did not use actual archival records to discover as a new matter of fact that "776" was when the first victory occurred, because there *were* no actual archival records, and the lists they were working with were not descendants of memorized lists, as many still wish to believe.[95] Nor is it the case that Greek history actually somehow in fact becomes more illuminated or accessible for Timaeus and Eratosthenes around the 770s. The establishment of the first Olympiad as a staging post between Troy and the contemporary world is a rhetorical move, another gambit in the ongoing scholarly exercise of looking more scientific, authoritative, and discriminatory, less naïve and credulous. The apparent precision of surveying differing degrees of historicity is part of this exercise. The real scholarly value of the first Olympiad was of course synchronistic. If we frame the question as "Why were the Olympic Games chosen as the backbone of Panhellenic history?" then the answer is obvious—because the Olympic Games could be plausibly represented as the oldest Panhellenic institution and therefore provided the farthest point back into time that you could push a universal synchronism hook.[96]

Let me sum up before we turn explicitly to Rome. I have tried to reassert that historiography did operate with a distinction between myth and history, even though it was never universal or clear-cut and could serve many different purposes; I have also argued that this distinction could often have a chronological dimension. There were no universally agreed hard-and-fast divisions between myth and history, but, equally, the act of making a division or the realization that there was an issue was always liable to come into play. The divide in ancient historiography between mythic and historic time is not like the blue line in ice hockey, static and highly visible, but more like the offside rule in soccer, in which an imaginary line can be activated anywhere in one half of the pitch by the relative—often highly disputed—movements of the players.[97] What ancient scholars were doing with their demarcations between myth and history is not what a modern historian might be doing, even if it has some apparent overlaps. Ancient scholars use this way of talking partly as a generic marker, and also as a source of authority, to show that they know how their tradition works and that they can manipulate these authoritative markers in independent ways. Most importantly, as we shall now see in our discussion of the foundation of Rome, the fact that this interface between myth and history was a live issue enabled them to do creative work at the various extremities where myth and history could be said to meet, or to diverge.

THE FOUNDATION OF ROME: MYTH OR HISTORY?

The fundamental question of whether to say that the city was founded in mythical or historical time immediately presents itself.[98] When the Greeks, in the fourth century B.C.E., first started writing about the foundation of the city of Rome, the inhabitants of the city themselves must have had no idea whatever of the age of their city.[99] And even if, unimaginably, they had had some tradition about how old their city was, the Greeks would not have paid it any attention. Scholars often write as if the Greek tradition on early Rome shows the Greeks helpfully reporting their occasional glimpses of what the Romans were really thinking, but this is very far from being the case.[100] The Greeks took matters into their own hands and placed the foundation of the city in the age of heroes, occasionally before the Trojan War, but usually at the time of the *nostoi*, the homecomings from the Trojan War.[101] Down into the third century, the same theme was played with different variations: Rome got its name from a granddaughter of Aeneas called Rhome, or else the city was founded by a son of Aeneas called Rhomos or a grandson of Aeneas called Rhomos or a son of Odysseus and Circe called Rhomos or a grandson of Aeneas called Romulus.[102] There were all kinds of notional dates for the fall of Troy before Eratosthenes managed to impose something like a canonical date in the form of "1184 B.C.E.," but whatever time frame was being used in any given case, these authors are positing a Roman foundation epoch on the borderlands of mythical time, a generation or two after Troy.

This time period, however, is of course three or four or five hundred years before the foundation date for Rome that every schoolboy used to know, 753—or, if you prefer, 751 or 748, but at any rate, somewhere in the middle of the eighth century, many generations after the fall of Troy. Only in the late third century B.C.E. did writers begin to home in on this newly canonical time zone for the city's foundation. As we have just seen in our discussion of Eratosthenes, a date some-time around "750" would have been recognizable as "historical" in the late third century. Many scholars have commented on this connection, remarking that it must have been very attractive to envisage the foundation of the city as falling just this side of "history," just this side of the first Olympiad.[103] The beginning of the city is thereby linked, though not with exact precision, to the beginning of history. We have to wait a long time until we meet a historian who goes all the way and says that Rome was actually founded in "776," to make the equation fit perfectly. This is Asinius Quadratus, writing in the third century C.E.; he composed a work in Greek tracing the history of the city for 1,000 years from the foundation in the first Olympiad up to his own time.[104]

Apart from being overly Grecizing, Asinius Quadratus was making it all too obviously trim and symmetrical.[105] Authors preferred to capitalize on the fact that the city's canonical foundation epoch was just inside where history began, because this made the historicity of the events surrounding the foundation the topic of fruitful debate.[106] Both Cicero and Livy are able to associate their narratives of Romulus with the hoary glamor of the *fabulae* of his divine parentage, while main-taining a nuanced distance from a pose of credulous assent.[107] In the case of Livy, this tactic is closely bound up with his subtle generic demarcations, as he creates a distinction between his own work and the mingling of divine and human to be found in poetic epic (*Pref.* 6–7). He deftly tilts the balance of credibility against the idea that Mars really was the twins' parent (1.4.2), while still allowing the story its place at the head of the Roman story, where it is inextricably part of the mind game of dominance that the Romans play over their imperial subjects (*Pref.* 7).[108] Here one is reminded that in Roman culture myth often comes already marked as "Greek," so that a new beginning of Roman history may be felt to demand a demarcation from *fabulae*, with belief in such things remaining the characteristic of the Greek inhabitants of Rome's empire. In the *De Republica*, Cicero's speaker, Scipio, is prepared to go farther down the road of assent to the divinity of Romu-lus, stressing in the process that Roman society at the time of Romulus's death and apotheosis was not rudely backward but in the full light of history (2.18–19).

Romulus is a good example of the value of the soccer offside analogy, for his case reveals the way that "776" or "753" are not rigid boundaries but mobile mark-

ers. Romulus is on a fascinating borderland, right on the fringe of what is susceptible to historical treatment. As Pelling observes, to Plutarch Numa lies "just this
side, Romulus just the other side of the boundary."[109] You can nudge Romulus farther back into the mist or bring him farther out into the sunlight, and the decision
as to whether he goes one way or the other will vary according to the agenda and
genre of each author.[110] Livy and Plutarch are not operating on the basis of
different data sets, and it is not as if one of them is better informed about the
"facts" than the other: they both have the same tradition, one that has a built-in
plasticity concerning this epoch. This does not mean that any of the authors who
treat this period is a fraud, or that any of them is more "correct." Romulus is there
in the tradition and remained there until the nineteenth century, when his status as
a historical figure was doubted for the first time.[111] He has to be dealt with, one way
or the other, and the very mobility of the various traditions about his epoch gives
an edge to whatever treatment an author brings to bear.

DOWN-DATING FROM
MYTH TO HISTORY

At this point we need to retrace our steps, since we have not yet properly investigated the change from a mythic era for the foundation of the city to this new incip-
iently historical era. In the early third century everyone is agreed that the city was
founded in the aftermath of the fall of Troy, but in the late third century we can
see a new consensus starting to emerge, which eventually places the foundation
somewhere in what we call the mid-eighth century. The canonical version we all
know from Virgil and Livy is an amalgam of these two stories, which preserves
and synchronizes the two chronologies. Aeneas, according to the eventually orthodox synthesis, came to Italy in heroic time but did not found Rome itself; instead,
he or his son founded Alba Longa, which was ruled by a long line of Trojan-
descended kings, and it was from Alba Longa, many years later, that Rome was
founded by Romulus, in historical time.[112] We must not, however, allow the success of this eventual synthesizing orthodoxy to distract us from remarking on the
very remarkable chronological relocation that made it necessary in the first place.
Sometime in the third century B.C.E. we have an extraordinary shift in the epoch of
the city's foundation, a down-dating of hundreds of years from the time of Troy
to the era of incipient history.[113] Why the move from myth to history?

As far as I can see, almost all scholars take it for granted that the new down-
dating was the result of new information from the Roman side. What scholars

seem to assume is that on one side you have all the Greeks telling their foundation stories from the Trojan era, while on the other side you have the Romans telling themselves an internal version about Romulus, a version with some kind of chronology, one that fixed Romulus somewhere in "the eighth century"; what happens then, so the assumption appears to go, is that suddenly people notice the discrepancy and have to come up with some way of papering over the cracks—hence the Alban king list.[114] But this way of looking at things obscures two crucial issues. First of all, as we shall see, it was Greek historians who first presented a historical date for the foundation of the city, not Roman historians or Roman tradition, and there is no reason to think that the Greek historians, after centuries of happily playing their own game, suddenly started paying deferential attention to what the Romans were saying.[115] These Greeks must have had their own reasons for downdating; they did not do it because they had learned a new truth from the Romans, or from the Latins.[116] And here we meet the second important question that the orthodoxy begs—did the Romans have a date for the foundation of the city anyway before they got one from the Greeks? What kind of format could have generated and preserved such knowledge—or "knowledge"—in third-century Rome?

Here we are materially assisted by the important paper of Purcell (2003), arguing for a historical sense in Rome already in the fifth century, before the development of a literary historiographical tradition in the late third century. One of his strongest pieces of evidence for preliterary Roman historical thinking helps the point I am trying to establish, that any historical sense the Romans had in the third century is unlikely to have included an indigenous date for the foundation of the city. Purcell rightly highlights the remarkable aedileship of Cn. Flavius, in 304 B.C.E., when Flavius dedicated, and dated, a sanctuary of Concordia. The dating convention he used fixed his dedication of Concordia in the 204th year *post Capitolinam aedem dedicatam*, "the 204th year after the dedication of the Capitoline temple [of Jupiter]" (Pliny *HN* 33.19). The year of the dedication of the Capitoline temple is also remembered in later tradition as the year of the foundation of the Republic; so we have here an important foundational moment as an era marker.[117] As Purcell points out, Flavius "did not employ the era of the foundation of the city."[118] Now, Purcell comments that at the time of Flavius, around 300 B.C.E., someone could well have "synchronize[d] a date for the foundation with an internal or an external chronological system," but I think we should draw the opposite conclusion, that an era based on the dedication of the temple is what had to be used by anyone wanting to do dating before an era was agreed upon for the foundation of the city.[119]

If you went to Rome in 300 B.C.E., in other words, they had some way of telling you how long ago the kings were expelled and the Republic established,[120] but I very much doubt that they had any measured way of telling you when the city was founded. It is, then, virtually certain that the Romans themselves at this time had no foundation date for the city of Rome, not least because around 300 B.C.E. the Greeks did not yet have one—the foundations in the time of the *nostoi* are not datable events. When the historical foundation dates did come into play, as we shall see shortly, they were based on calculations from the fall of Troy, and no one in Rome in 300 B.C.E. could have given you a date for the fall of Troy that did not come out of a Greek book.

It seems to be taken for granted that the Romans had an idea of how long the kings had reigned, and that all they had to do was add this figure to the year of the expulsion of the kings in order to go back in time to the foundation.[121] It seems to me much more likely that they originally had no coherent story about how long they had been ruled by kings, and that they only started to work on this issue once a tradition of historiography had started to develop in the city and they had to come up with a continuous historical-looking narrative from the foundation on-wards. As De Cazanove points out in an important discussion, it is highly significant that the first historical foundation dates vary widely and presuppose, accordingly, widely differing lengths for the regal period;[122] the eventually canonical time frame for the kings of between 240 and 244 years is not a given in the tradition from the start but a "fact" that had to be worked out in relation to other signposts and that took a good while to pin down in orthodoxy. The span of the monarchy is the result of counting forward from a fall of Troy date rather than backward from a beginning of Republic date: "The length of the regal period was deduced from the date assigned to the foundation, and not the other way around."[123] They did not figure out when the city was founded by counting back from the foundation of the Republic the number of years the kings had reigned; they figured out how many years the kings had reigned by counting forward from an independent Trojan-derived city foundation date to the foundation of the Republic. Walbank sums up well: "If in fact the foundation was fixed by calculations based on the fall of Troy, and the foundation of the republic by the *fasti*, discrepancies would naturally arise, which could be adjusted only by changing the number of regnal years."[124]

None of this argument is meant to imply that the Romans did not have their own indigenous foundation story. I am not claiming, as others have done, that the story of Romulus and Remus was made up by a Greek and that the Romans took it over from them.[125] For what it is worth, I am sure the Romans had been telling the story of Romulus and Remus for a good long time before the brothers Ogulnii, in the year 295 B.C.E., put a statue of the wolf at the base of the Palatine hill where the twins had been found (Livy 10.23.12). My sole concern here is the chronological dimension to this story, and I see no reason to doubt that the story of the founders will have been free floating in time until it needed to be meshed with Greek historiographical norms, either by a Greek or by a Roman. What kind of form the story had before it became part of Grecizing historiography is another issue. The story as we have it in Livy or Dionysius of Halicarnassus is organized like the plot of a Greek drama of exposure and recognition, and that plot form is due either to the adaptation of the story for the Roman stage or to the artistry of the first person to write the story up for history—and that first person was almost certainly a Greek, as we shall shortly see.[126]

If it is unlikely that the new down-dating from a "mythical" to a "historical" foundation date was the result of new indigenous information from the Romans, we are left still looking for an explanation of the shift. A number of modern scholars appear to think that the new mid-eighth-century dating somehow got it right after centuries of error, as if tradition was capable of preserving a chronological structure until it could be fixed in historiographical format.[127] But such views are fundamentally misconceived. For a start, Rome was not *founded* anyway. The whole issue is a mirage. Large-scale processes over long periods of time eventually led to what we could call a civic organization on the hills beside the Tiber, but this is not a "foundation," certainly not in the terms preserved in the literary tradition.[128] Still, some modern historians, such as Carandini (1997) and Grandazzi (1997), would have it that the mid-eighth-century date is "right" in some sense. Scholars such as these seem to be mesmerized by the overlap between the eventual canonical date in the literary tradition and the Iron Age huts on the summit of the Palatine or remains of a wall or a "palace" at its base.[129] The situation, however, is exactly the same as that so brilliantly described by Burkert in the case of Troy. Because the "1184" date that the Greeks in the third century eventually settled on for the fall of Troy happens to overlap with the remains of Troy VIIA, many people feel that the date is somehow "right."[130] But the Greek dates for the fall of Troy, as Burkert showed, are pure guesses, founded on air, and wildly discrepant for centuries; the apparent historical fit of the overlap between the eventual Roman tradition and a hypothesized true Roman settlement date is likewise complete and total coincidence, since the tradition about the foundation of the city is likewise founded on air, and likewise very discrepant in the beginning, as we have just seen.[131] If the ancient tradition had fixed on 1000 as the "real" date, then these scholars would all be focusing on the exiguous human remains at Rome from around 1000 as "corroboration."[132] It is not only ancient scholars who cannot abide a vacuum.

THE INTERVENTION OF TIMAEUS

We are left with the basic questions: who first down-dated the foundation from the heroic period, and what was at stake in doing this? What kind of levers did this new dating give the ancient writers, what did it enable them to allege or deny or construct? On the basis of the surviving evidence, the man who first down-dated the foundation of Rome from the mythical period was the first Greek historian to tackle the subject of Rome on any substantial scale—Timaeus of Tauromenium.[133] Strictly, this is an argument from silence, since someone else theoretically could have done this before him without leaving any trace in the record. But on our available evidence there is no one before him.[134] He is, as Herodotus would have put it, the first man of whom we know, and Timaeus is the right man, in the right time, and *from* the right place, even if not exactly *in* the right place—he is actually writing in Athens, but he comes from Sicily. We cannot pin down when he wrote or published this radically new version of when the city of Rome came into existence, since he was writing actively for fifty years before he died sometime in the late 260s B.C.E. Sometime in the first third of the third century B.C.E. will serve as a peg to orientate our investigation.

Timaeus, however, did not bring the foundation date all the way down into the eighth century. He fixed on a moment in time that is reported by Dionysius of Halicarnassus as thirty-eight years before the first Olympiad, "814/3 B.C.E."[135] Timaeus, then, is actually the first person to give a year date for the foundation of Rome, since all the earlier stories from the Trojan period were undated and undatable. Now, this is a shift of unmistakable significance. Unlike everyone before him, he says that the city of Rome was not founded in the heroic period of the *nostoi*, but hundreds of years later, over five hundred years later, by the date of "1334" that he used as the era of the fall of Troy.[136] He did not perform this down-dating for Rome alone. In the last chapter we saw that his Roman foundation date is a symbolically charged synchronism with Carthage, and he did to Carthage exactly what he did to Rome, breaking radically with tradition here as well. Before him, everyone had dated Carthage to the heroic period of the *nostoi*, but Timaeus moves its foundation date hundreds of years closer to history, bringing it to lodge on the same time line as Rome, in "814/3."[137] What kind of "evidence" he controlled or contrived in the case of either Rome or Carthage is beyond recovery, even though the most attractive hypothesis is that he had Carthaginian informants who gave him this date for the foundation of their city, and that he moved the Roman date to fit accordingly.[138]

What was Timaeus up to with his synchronized down-dating of the foundation of the two great rival cities? Secure answers are impossible because of the state of the evidence. It is disturbing that Dionysius of Halicarnassus had no idea what procedure Timaeus was following, and he knew a great deal more about Roman chronology and about Timaeus than we do.[139] But it is possible to make some suggestions as to what may have been at stake in his innovation.

First of all, fixing a foundation date at all is a significant statement, because it makes Rome look like a proper city in Greek terms, and not simply like a place that just evolved in a bumbling kind of way. Corroboration of this hypothesis comes in the next century, for Apollodorus's *Chronica* contained no date for the foundation of Rome, despite the fact that the book was published decades after the conquest of Greece by the Romans. Gabba first pointed out an important implication of this omission: it "carried the implication that the beginnings of the city were humble and obscure and could not be given a firm date."[140] From our perspective we can see that Apollodorus was absolutely right, even if for the wrong reasons; but this helps put in perspective the fact that Timaeus was making a significant claim in for the first time giving the city of Rome a fixed year of foundation at all. In shifting the foundation from fable toward history, Timaeus is denying that Rome is "unlike" a proper city, as it is if its origins are fabulous; he is making it "like" by granting it a real beginning, one with participation in significant, charted, dated time— time shared with Greece.

Timaeus's Sicilian origins are likely to have played an important part in how he conceived of the city's place in time. The earlier versions are mainly looking west from Greece "proper," but Timaeus is a Sicilian, with his eye on Carthage, especially Carthage in Sicily, and also with his eye on Rome's closeness to Sicily in the light of its assumption of control over Magna Graecia, a process that the Romans completed in a scant fifteen years, from 285 to 272 B.C.E. The Greek tradition had always been that when they got to the Western Mediterranean the Phoenicians and Romans were already there.[141] Timaeus is working with mid- to late-eighth-century dates for Greek colonization in the West, and it looks as if he wants to link Rome and Carthage as the two really important non-Greek powers of the West, peoples who were already there, though not by very much, when the Greeks arrived.

Although he down-dated the foundation of Rome from the time of Troy to almost within touching distance of Western Greek historical time, Timaeus by no means jettisoned the Trojan connection simply to jump down to the late ninth century. We do not know how he made the connection between the Trojan origin and the new date of "814/3," but somehow he did, because we know that he was very interested in the Trojan ancestry of the Romans.[142] He had learned from the inhabitants of Lavinium themselves, so he says, what the Trojan holy objects in Lavinium were, including a Trojan earthenware vessel.[143] Polybius tells us that Timaeus interpreted the Roman festival of the Equus October as being the Romans' way of commemorating the fall of Troy. It is clear from Polybius's reference that Timaeus is extremely well informed, for he actually gives the Latin name for the Campus Martius—ἐν τῷ Κάμπῳ καλουμένῳ, "in what is called the Kampos."[144] His reference to the calendrical date, incidentally, sheds fascinating light on another time issue. He says the festival is held ἐν ἡμέρᾳ τινί, "on a certain day," a phrase that reminds us of the problems posed by the jumble of calendars. A Syracusan based in Athens in the third century could not, it seems, comprehensibly translate a Roman date such as the Ides of October into another calendar, and transliterating "the Ides of October" into Greek, as Plutarch, for example, later does, would have been meaningless outside Italy in 270 B.C.E.

Even if the details of how Timaeus made the connection between Troy and Rome are lost, we can still see him performing the same operation that he performs in the case of the Greeks in the West. He used the first part of his *Histories* to set up one half of a double focus, between mythic precursors and historical followers. His vision of the Western Mediterranean is that the Greek claims go a long way back before their arrival in the eighth century—as a Sicilian he cannot simply say, as Thucydides had, "There is nothing to say about anything Greek in Sicily until the first colonies." He had to use a lot of free invention, since the data bank of myth for the Western Mediterranean was more or less empty. What he needed to do was to invent an "instant tradition" in order to endow the Greeks of the West with a glamorous and prestigious mythic inheritance.[145] To this end, he presented myths showing Greek heroes such as Heracles, Diomedes, and the Argonauts going through Italy and Sicily, providing a series of charters that could be cashed in by the later Greek colonists when they arrived.[146] Although the pattern that he follows is very familiar from Pindar, for example, Timaeus was exerting much originality here, since before him there is no evidence for any post-Trojan *nostoi* tales in the West involving any of the Greek heroes apart from Odysseus.[147] Antiochus of Syracuse, for example, Thucydides' source for the Sicilian colonies, had no "legendary" dates for precolonial precursors.[148] What Timaeus's narrative mode was for these stories, and how he discriminated between these earlier myths and his later material, is no longer recoverable. Did he adopt the pose of reporting "what people say," or did he engage in rationalizing in the manner of Dionysius of Halicarnassus?[149] If he had survived entire, he would certainly have provided a challenging and intriguing test case of the dialectic between myth and history.

Timaeus's system of relations between the heroic and historical periods looks like the right kind of place for an explanation of his down-dating of Rome. He is fitting both Rome and Carthage into his time map of the Western Mediterranean, and this is a Greek time map in which mythical precursors in heroic time plant footsteps in their travels for others to follow, establishing links that their inheritors will join up into chains between mythic and historical time when they come west to found the Greek colonies in the eighth century.[150] The Aeneas myth already gives him a set of mythical precursors for the Romans, but he does not want their city to have been there continuously ever since the time of Aeneas. Rather, he wants to have the same template for the Romans as for the Western Greeks, and what he therefore needs is a historical follow-up, some kind of retracing or reenacting or refoundation in historical time.[151] And by having the historical foundation date of Rome come just before the Greek colonies, he preserves a sense of the Roman priority in the area, and also a sense of their special link with Carthage, which is also already there before the Greek colonies. Carthage, however, is unanchored in mythic time, so far as we can tell from what survives of Timaeus, with no precursors to anticipate the later historical founding. Carthage is parachuted down into the desert with no links to a Libya of myth, whereas Rome's historical beginnings as a city somehow reactivate a link to Panhellenic myth from centuries before. Rome manages to share in the Greek template, while Carthage does not.[152]

REFINING THE "HISTORICAL"

Timaeus, then, has boldly brought the foundation of the city down from the time of Troy to within sight of the first Greek colonies in the West. This is a crucial departure from tradition, but it is not definitive. His date does not stick. Someone took it upon himself to say that Timaeus's version was not good enough, and gave instead a date within the boundary of the first Olympiad, somewhere around "750 B.C.E.," in a way that started a trend that eventually hardened into orthodoxy. The first concrete evidence we have is that Fabius Pictor, writing a history of Rome in Greek sometime toward the end of the Hannibalic War, around 210–205 B.C.E., used an Olympiad date to fix the foundation in "the first year of the eighth

Olympiad," "748/7 B.C.E."[153] Fabius presents what eventually became the canonical way of reconciling the old Trojan-era version and the new historical date, by saying that the Trojans in the time of the *nostoi* did not found the city of Rome directly but founded Alba Longa, of which Rome was eventually the offshoot.[154] According to Plutarch, Fabius's main source for his early material was one Diocles of Peparethus, and it is entirely possible that Diocles invented the whole Alban solution to the problem of resolving the mythic and historical chronologies, and also that he came up with the date that Fabius used.[155] We cannot be certain, but Diocles had a list of Alban kings, which means that he had a foundation in historical times, which almost inevitably means that he had a date, an Olympiad date.

What might have been at stake for the Greek Diocles and the Greek-writing Roman Fabius in presenting this new foundation date, even farther down-dated than Timaeus's? It is plausible to assume that the Roman aristocrat Fabius, at any rate, will not have wanted to follow Timaeus in having a synchronism with the great enemy Carthage; he may have been receptive, then, to the different—but still unmythical—date that he found in Diocles. This newly historical date of the first year of the eighth Olympiad brings the foundation firmly this side of the first Olympiad, and thus into what the new programme of Eratosthenes may have recently established as properly historical times.[156] Timaeus may have been the first to come up with the canonical date of "776" for the beginning of the Olympic Games, but he is very unlikely to have made a great deal of the date as the demarcation of history, in the way that Eratosthenes is thought by many scholars to have done.[157] It is, then, important in itself that Timaeus's date now looks too far back in time after the work of Eratosthenes and has to be brought down even farther. More surely, the very use of the Olympiad dating system is itself crucially symbolic. The very fact that the foundation of Rome is now to be located within the Panhellenic grid of the Olympiad system helps Fabius in his larger thematic plan of showing that Rome is not a barbarian outsider but an equal participant in the Greek cultural world of Italy, Sicily, and Greece "proper."[158] The very fact that his *History* is in Greek strengthens this claim to status as a cultural equal.

If we focus on this issue of Rome's relationship to the Greeks, we can see that the new down-dating also changes the relationship in time between Rome and the first Greek settlements in the West. Timaeus had possibly chosen his date of "814/3" as a way of deliberately putting the Romans on a West Mediterranean time map prior to the arrival of the Greeks, eighty years—two forty-year generations, for those who are inclined to think that way—before the foundation of his own mother city of Syracuse.[159] The new dating of Diocles and/or Fabius, in

"748/7," locates Rome only a dozen years before the first Sicilian colonies, and, tantalizingly, right at the very beginning of the Greek colonization movement in Italy.[160]

Now, the data here are very hard to work with, because the crucial question is obviously not when as a matter of fact do we now think the Greek colonies were founded in Italy and Sicily, but when might historians in the late third century have thought (or been able plausibly to assert) they were founded. The ancient traditions about these dates are all over the map, and the data in Eusebius, for example, make no distinction whatever between the first Greek colonies in Italy and the Ionian settlements, which modern scholars date to three hundred years earlier.[161] Eusebius lumps together in the eleventh century B.C.E. a cluster of Greek colonies in Ionia and in the West, along with Punic colonies.[162] The tradition on the Sicilian colonies tends to be fuller and more uniform than on the Italian ones, and Eusebius's eighth-century dates on the first Sicilian colonies closely track those given by Thucydides.[163] The Roman tradition on these Sicilian colony dates is a Sicilian one, surely mediated to them by Timaeus, who had them from Antiochus, the source for Thucydides in book 6.[164]

It is harder to know about the Italian dates in this tradition, since the data for the Italian colony foundation dates are much more sparse. If the Athenians had attacked Taras/Tarentum instead of Syracuse in 415 B.C.E., then we would know a lot more than we do about the tradition concerning the Greek colonies in Italy, since Thucydides' book 6 would have opened with a survey of what Antiochus had to say about the colonies of Magna Graecia. We know, however, that Antiochus wrote on Italy as well as on Sicily, and one of his Italian colony foundation dates survives, namely, that for Croton: Antiochus said that Croton was founded in the same year as Syracuse, that is, "733."[165] Our source, Strabo, says that Croton was founded after Sybaris, so that Sybaris is sometime before "733" in this tradition. Strabo also says that Cumae is the oldest of the Italian or Sicilian colonies, although he gives no date.[166] In other words, Croton dates to "733," Sybaris is older than that, and Cumae is older than that again. It is very likely, then, that this tradition had a foundation date for Cumae, the first Greek colony in the West, in the high "740s." I cannot produce an exact synchronism, but if I had to back one Greek colony as a synchronistic hook for Diocles and/or Fabius in their dating of Rome's foundation to "748/7," I would back Cumae, the very first Greek colony in the West. It would be no accident, accordingly, that Virgil's Aeneas should make his first landfall in Italy at Cumae, and that he should do so, as Barchiesi puts it, "in the guise of a Greek settler looking for a colonization oracle."[167]

Whatever the force of such speculation about a precise synchronism with a particular Greek colony, the crucial point remains that Rome now has a foundation date that can make it plausible to see Rome as part of real—that is, Greek—history, so as to defend it against the kind of aspersions that someone like Apollodorus might want to throw at it.[168] The very use of an Olympiad date furthers this design,[169] as would the time links with the Greek colonies in the West. These links would present Rome as not just a historical foundation but as a civilized *polis* from the start of civilization in Italy. Synchronisms are always more than simple dates, and this synchronism, contrived during the Hannibalic War, would say, "We Romans are partners in civilization with you Greeks against Carthage; we Romans and you Greeks were founding civilization in Italy at the same time, unlike those barbarians the Samnites and the Opici, who inhabit a timeless zone, an 'allochrony'[170]—and unlike those barbarians the Carthaginians, who remain stuck out on a time limb, stuck where Timaeus put them, in the age before Western civilization."[171] This tactic would be, as it were, an "out-modernizing," the reverse of the "out-pasting" of Zerubavel (2003). Instead of trying to annex venerability by claiming the most extended past possible and pushing the origins farther back in time than the competition's, the claim of a properly historical origin would be trumping the competition in terms of civilization and modernity.

Here we see the real power of the way of thinking of these synchronistic projects within a model of comparison. The greatest work done on the subject of comparison is by Jonathan Z. Smith, who observes that "x resembles y" really means "x resembles y more than z with respect to . . ." or "x resembles y more than w resembles z with respect to . . ."[172] Diocles and/or Fabius, then, could be seen as claiming not simply that "Rome resembles Greece," but that "Rome resembles Greece more than the other Italians and more than Carthage with respect to civilization." The late third century is a good context for such representations. The aftermath of the conquest of Sicily, and the threat that Hannibal posed to the nexus of alliances in Magna Graecia, will have been a good time for West Greeks and Romans to synchronize their colonial pasts, on the basis of similar stories of historical foundations picking up the traces of mythical pasts.[173] The developed Fabian story of the foundation of Rome is, after all, a colony story, with all the usual trappings—apparently humble origins of founder, rape, foundational act of murder.[174] It is highly significant that all the versions that have a "historical" date "make Rome a colony of Alba Longa."[175]

The new Fabian version of a historical foundation picking up traces from the time of myth via the metropolis of Alba Longa did not become orthodoxy immediately, or even soon. Some Greeks continued to tell the old story of the mythic era foundation;[176] It may appear initially more surprising that Rome's first epic poets, Naevius and Ennius, continued to adhere to the old version, with Romulus as the grandson of Aeneas.[177] Naevius was probably writing his *Bellum Punicum* immediately after the appearance of Fabius Pictor's *History*:[178] he was not to know that Fabius's new version would one day become the orthodoxy. By the time Ennius was writing the *Annales,* however, Fabius's book was about thirty years old, and Ennius could also have read the history in Greek written by Cincius Alimentus, which followed essentially the same story, although moving the foundation date down a further twenty years, to "728 B.C.E.," the fourth year of the twelfth Olympiad.[179] Nonetheless, Ennius wanted to keep to the mainstream Hellenistic foundation stories that associated Rome's beginnings directly with the heroic age.[180] He, like Naevius, must have conceived of the question as being whether to place the foundation of the city in heroic time or in historical time, and once the question is put like that the answer is obvious for a Hellenistic epic poet.[181] Further, Naevius and Ennius could now restate these origins as being directly linked to the beginning of universal history, with the fall of Troy leading to the rise of Rome.

By keeping to the older Hellenistic versions, recently validated by Eratosthenes, who still kept Romulus as Aeneas's grandson, Naevius and Ennius are behaving like Greeks rather than like Romans such as Fabius and Cincius—but, then, they *were* Greeks, or at least "semi-Greeks," as Suetonius puts it.[182] It would take a fully Roman poet, in a genuinely historical age, to canonize the Roman historians' version of the city's foundation in epic.[183] Well before Virgil's time, within decades of the appearance of Fabius's *History,* the balance of power in the Greek and Roman historiographical tradition had shifted, so that the focalizing time frames were now Roman, rather than Greek. As we have seen, it had been crucial to Fabius, very probably following Diocles, to use Olympiad dating as a way of fixing Rome within a Panhellenic chronological framework. In this he had been followed by his immediate successor, Cincius Alimentus, who likewise wrote in Greek. Cincius is, however, the last of the Roman historians to use this Panhellenic dating system.[184] Cato began writing his *Origines* some three decades after Fabius, and his was the first Roman historical work to be written in Latin prose.[185] With the shift in language went a shift in chronological representation. Dionysius of Halicarnassus explicitly tells us that Cato "does not make Greek time divisions" (Ἑλληνικὸν μὲν οὐχ ὁρίζει χρόνον), and Cato's date for Rome's foundation is accordingly not an Olympiad date, but "four hundred and thirty-two years after the Trojan War."[186] The Trojan War, not a Greek athletic festival, is the reference point for dating the beginning of Rome, since the Trojan War, according to Cato's way of doing things, is an event in universal, or Roman, history, not Greek, an *origo* in a profounder sense than simply marking the start of ascertainable history.[187] From now on, the Roman historians will use indigenous time frames, which we shall investigate in chapter 6.

REFOUNDING THE CITY:
ENNIUS, LIVY, AND VIRGIL

The city of Rome has now been successfully founded in historical time—whether that time is focalized as Greek or Roman—but we have not yet reached the end of the story. As everyone knows, the city of Rome kept having to be *re*-founded, and the patterns of refoundation drastically reconfigure the trajectory of movement from myth to history that we have been following so far.[188]

Ennius's most explicit surviving allusion to the date of the foundation of the city in fact comes at the moment when the city had just been virtually destroyed, and was on the verge of vanishing from history, after the sack by the Gauls in 387/6 B.C.E.[189] The context is a speech in which Camillus persuades the Senate not to move to Veii, but to refound the city instead (154–55 Skutsch):

Septingenti sunt paulo plus aut minus anni
augusto augurio postquam incluta condita Roma est.

It is seven hundred years, a little more or a little less,
since famous Rome was founded by august augury.

How this seven-hundred-year period between Romulus's foundation and the sack of Rome by the Gauls actually worked remains a mystery, at least to me.[190] Still, we should not overlook the symbolic significance of this number in its own right. The importance of the seven-hundred-year period has been very well illustrated in the fascinating book *Die rhetorische Zahl*, written by a scholar with the gloriously apt name of Dreizehnter.[191] Dreizehnter does not mention this passage of Ennius, but he collects a great deal of interesting material about seven hundred years as the life span of a city or an empire from foundation to extinction, or from foundation to virtual extinction or only just-escaped extinction. In various traditions that he examines there were seven hundred years from the foundation to the destruction of Melos, Carthage, and Macedonia, or from the foundation to the virtual extinction of Sparta.[192] What we see in the Ennius passage, in other words, is that the city was virtually destroyed and came within an ace of fulfilling the seven-hundred-year doom. The point will have been accentuated by Ennius's book divisions. Camillus's speech comes at the end of book 4, and the regal period ended with book 3, so that up to this point in the *Annales* we have had only one self-contained volume of Republican history, and if things had gone differently that might have been all we had.[193]

Livy activates the power of this Ennian symbolic numeral, even as he corrects Ennius's dating, with his allusion to the seven hundred years of Rome (*Pref.* 4):

Res est praeterea et immensi operis, ut quae supra septingentesimum annum repetatur et quae ab exiguis profecta initiis eo creuerit ut iam magnitudine laboret sua.

In addition, the matter is of immeasurable scope, in that it must be taken back past the seven hundredth year, and having started from small beginnings has grown to the stage that it is now laboring under its own size.[194]

Chaplin has argued that Livy's preface is constructing recent Roman history as a death, with a possible rebirth to come:[195] the Republic has been destroyed, and the Romans of Livy's time are like the Romans of Camillus's time, faced with the task of refounding the city after it has only just escaped its seven-hundred-year doom.

In Livy's treatment of the Roman response to the sack of the city by the Gauls, we can see him returning to the Ennian theme of rebirth from destruction, although this time using different significant numbers. Having exploited the numinous associations of Ennius's seven hundred years in his preface, Livy now produces another numinous numeral for the span from foundation to sack, one that conforms with the modern orthodox chronology. Livy has Camillus deliver a mighty speech to convince his fellow citizens not to abandon Rome for the site of Veii (5.51–54).[196] When Livy's Camillus echoes Ennius's by counting off the years since the foundation, it appears that some kind of great year has gone by. From Romulus's foundation down to the sack by the Gauls there have been as many years as there are days in a year: *Trecentensimus sexagensimus quintus annus urbis, Quirites, agitur* ("This is the 365th year of the city, Quirites," 5.54.5). This is of course a calculation that fully resonates only after Caesar's reform of the calendar, when a Roman year for the first time had 365 days.[197] This counting places Camillus's refounding of the city at a pivotal point in time, precisely halfway between the first founding of the city, in 753, and the refounding that faces Livy and his contemporaries 365 years after Camillus, in the 20s B.C.E.[198] Exactly the same structuring appears to underpin the panorama of Roman history on Virgil's Shield of Aeneas, where the barely averted destruction of Rome by the Gauls (*Aen.* 8.652–62) comes midway in time between the foundation of the city (8.635) and the barely averted destruction of Rome by Antonius and Cleopatra (8.671–713).[199]

In all of these authors, city destruction, whether achieved or barely averted, leads to refoundation and consequent reconfiguring of identity, in a process that begins with Troy and continues through the fates of Alba Longa, Veii, and Rome itself.[200] As Kraus has shown, when Livy begins his next book after the Gallic sack, he refounds his narrative along with the city, capitalizing on the annalistic tradition's identification of the city and history.[201] In an extraordinary moment, the opening sentences of book 6 tell us that only now is real history beginning. All of the material in the first five books, Livy now declares, has been "obscure because of its excessive antiquity" (*uetustate nimia obscuras*), and because there were few written records in those early days, while the ones that did exist "for the most part were destroyed when the city was burnt" (*incensa urbe pleraeque interiere*, 6.1.2). Everything up until this point, from Troy to the Gallic sack, is suddenly reconfigured as prior, prefoundational. In his preface Livy had drawn a line between myth and history around the time of the Romulean foundation of the city (*ante conditam condendamue urbem*, 6), but "the fresh start in 390 redraws the limits of the historically verifiable."[202] We now have a new entry into history, with a newly rebuilt city and a newly solid evidential base for its written commemoration (6.1.3):

> Clariora deinceps certioraque ab secunda origine uelut ab stirpibus laetius feraciusque renatae urbis gesta domi militiaeque exponentur.

> From here there will be a more clear and definite exposition of the domestic and military history of the city, reborn from a second origin, as if from the old roots, with a more fertile and fruitful growth.[203]

Livy here is picking up on the annalistic history of Claudius Quadrigarius, who had written about fifty years earlier. We know that Claudius began his history with the sack of Rome by the Gauls, no doubt on the grounds we see alluded to in Livy, that no history was possible before then, thanks to the destruction of monuments and archives.[204]

We have already seen how the Roman tradition picks up demarcations that are crucial from the Greek tradition—Troy and the first Olympiad—and recasts them as transitions into a new, Roman, phase of history. The Gallic sack is a vital addition to this series of watersheds. The first key fixed synchronistic point in Timaeus and Polybius that makes it possible for Roman history to be properly connected with Greek history, the Gallic sack is itself made to serve as the "beginning of history" in Claudius Quadrigarius and Livy book 6.[205] The very event that almost expunged Rome altogether is the one that put the city on the world stage—just as the destruction of Troy led to the city's existence in the first place.[206]

Ovid intuited the power of these associated watersheds of foundation and Gallic sack, and his subtle deployment of them in the *Metamorphoses* is proof of their understood significance. Before he arrives at the foundation of Rome in book 14, he has a very small number of proleptic references to the as yet nonexistent city. Book 1 contains two forward references to his own day, with the poem's first simile referring to the reign of Augustus (1.199–205), and the story of Apollo and Daphne likewise anticipating the reign of Augustus, as Apollo prophesies the use of his sacred laurel to grace Roman triumphs and adorn Augustus's house (1.560–63). His only other proleptic references to the city before the foundation in book 14 occur in book 2, and they are both references to the city only just escaping total catastrophe, catastrophes that would have ensured the city was never part of world history. One is in a cosmic setting, when the natural site of the city is almost expunged, as the Tiber is dried up along with other rivers by Phaethon's chariot (2.254–59); the other is an allusion to the geese that "were to save the Capitol with their wakeful cry" (*seruaturis uigili Capitolia uoce/ . . . anseribus*, 2.538–39).[207] Again, in the *Fasti*, when the gods meet in council to deliberate how to save Rome from the Gauls, Ovid takes as his template the Ennian council that deliberated over the foundation of the city: in both cases, Mars expostulates with his father, Jupiter, and is assured that all will be well.[208]

It is highly significant that these two events, the city's foundation and near destruction by the Gauls, are the only "historical" events commemorated on the Republican calendar, the Fasti Antiates.[209] Calendrical *fasti* from the Principate mention all kinds of events, but the Fasti Antiates, the only calendar we have surviving from the Republic, mark only two historical events: 21 April, the Parilia and the foundation of the city, and 18 July, the *dies Alliensis*, the day of the battle of the Allia, when the Roman army was scattered by the advancing Gauls on their way to the city, which they entered on the next day.[210]

The foundation of the city and its near extinction by the Gauls are symbolically joined events, linked by significant numbers, either 700 or 365, linked by themes of refoundation and rebirth. The history of the city keeps getting restarted at such crucial transition moments, when repetitive patterns of quasi-cyclical destruction and refoundation replay themselves, in a fascinating interplay between a drive for onward narrative continuity and the threat of eddying, repetitious, circularity.[211] It is poignant to observe the power of this theme still persisting in the fifth century C.E., when Rutilius Namatianus, six years after the sack of Rome by the Visigoths in 410 C.E., can hail Rome's potential to bounce back from disaster, citing its eventual defeat of Brennus, who led the Gauls to the sack of Rome, and of the Samnites, Pyrrhus, and Hannibal:[212] "You, Rome, are built up," he claims, "by the very thing that undoes other powers: the pattern of your rebirth is the ability to grow from your calamities" (*illud te reparat quod cetera regna resoluit:/ordo renascendi est crescere posse malis*, 139–40). Each of these key marker moments in time may become a new opportunity for the community to reimagine itself, as the epochal moment produces a new beginning point from which the community may imagine its progress forward into time, measured against its backward extension into time.[213]

REPUBLIC AND EMPIRE

A final epochal moment for us to plot into this sequence is the foundation of the Republic, traditionally dated to 509 B.C.E., and linked to the inauguration of the temple of Jupiter Optimus Maximus, as we have seen.[214] Livy makes it plain at the beginning of his second book, which inaugurates the new Republic after the first self-contained book of regal history, that this is another "origin," the origin of liberty (2.1.7):

> Libertatis autem originem inde magis quia annuum imperium consulare factum est quam quod deminutum quicquam sit ex regia potestate numeres.

> Moreover you may reckon the origin of liberty as coming more from the fact that the consuls' power was made annual than from any subtraction made from the king's authority.[215]

Kraus has finely demonstrated how this new origin of liberty under the Republic is tied in to the same nexus of rebirth after catastrophe as Livy describes at the beginning of book 6. She shows the close verbal links between the openings of books 2 and 6 and remarks, "The same relationship obtains between the near-destruction of Rome by the Gauls and its rebirth under Camillus as between Books

1 and 2, the end of monarchy and the start of the republic . . . Both the start of the republic and the *origo* in 390 in turn look back to the original foundation, establishing a historical continuity even across such cataclysmic events as the birth of *libertas* and the near-death of Rome."[216] The fall of Troy, the foundation of the city by Romulus, the foundation of the Republic by Brutus, the refoundation of the city by Camillus—such are the great staging posts picked out by Livy's narrative as it heads toward the now lost end point of Augustus's attempt to negotiate the Roman state's latest transition, from the Republic established by Brutus to a *nouus status*.[217]

Tacitus makes a great deal of these demarcation points. He brings a number of the key periodizations into play with the first sentence of the *Annales,* mentioning the foundation of the city and of the Republic: *Urbem Romam a principio reges habuere: libertatem et consulatum L. Brutus instituit* ("*The city of Rome* was *held* from the beginning by kings: liberty and the consulate were instituted by L. Brutus"). Here he is alluding to, quoting, and correcting Sallust, who had defied long-standing orthodoxy by moving the foundation of Rome back into the heroic age: *Urbem Romam, sicuti ego accepi, condidere atque habuere initio Troiani* ("*The city of Rome,* according to my sources, was founded and *held* from the start by Trojans," *Cat.* 6.1). According to Tacitus, then, real Roman history, proper constitutional history, begins not with the Trojans but with the historical foundation and the rule of the kings, and another watershed in history comes with the crucial chronographical marker of the expulsion of the kings.[218] This move from "Trojan" or "monarchical" myth to "Roman" history does not work, however, as Rome's history becomes circular: despite Tacitus's efforts, Roman history goes back into the realms of myth. With the monarchy of Nero, the last of the Aeneadae, as Dio Cassius calls him (62.18.3–4), Roman history reverts to the Trojan fairy stories peddled by the Julii.[219] On Nero's first appearance in the *Annales,* when he is nine years old, stories are being told about snakes looking over him as a baby, "the stuff of fables, modeled on foreign marvels" (*fabulosa et externis miraculis adsimilata*); Nero himself said there was only one (11.11.3). In his first public speech, delivered at the age of sixteen, before his accession, Nero spoke on behalf of the people of Ilium, speaking eloquently "on the Roman descent from Troy and Aeneas the founder of the Julian stock and other things close to fable" (*Romanum Troia demissum et Iuliae stirpis auctorem Aenean aliaque haud procul fabulis,* 12.58.1).

Roman categories of time are distorted by Nero along with everything else that is Roman, as we shall see in chapter 6; when it comes to the temporal distinctions between myth and history that the Roman tradition had been working on so hard for centuries, Tacitus shows that Nero blurs and subverts them too. Nowhere is this more clear than in the extended description of yet another destruction of the city, in the great fire of 64 c.e. (*Ann.* 15.38–41). Tacitus links together the fire of 64 and the burning of Rome by the Gauls;[220] both fires began on 19 July, the day following the *dies Alliensis,* and extravagant numerological calculations create a speciously meaningful association between the two fires (*Ann.* 15.41.2):

> fuere qui adnotarent XIIII Kal. Sextilis principium incendii huius ortum, et quo Senones captam urbem inflammauerint. alii eo usque cura progressi sunt ut totidem annos mensisque et dies inter utraque incendia numerent.

> There were people who noted that the beginning of this fire arose on July 19 [fourteen days before the Kalends of Sextilis][221], the day on which the Senones captured the city and burnt it. Others took their pains so far as to count a total between the two fires of equal numbers of years, months, and days.

The total works out at 418 years, plus 418 months, plus 418 days, to equal the 454 years between the two fires.[222]

Tacitus's tongue is no doubt deep in his cheek when he reports this portentous arithmetic, but he is completely serious in his reworking of the watershed of the Gallic sack.[223] His own account of the fire and rebuilding closely tracks Livy's, but the Livian opportunity to refound the city and move forward into a new phase of history is lost. Instead, the city loses to the fire the great monuments both of the first foundation, from the regal period, and of the second foundation, from the Republic (15.41.1).[224] No forward movement into a newly historical time frame is possible under Nero. Instead of the Camillan or Augustan title of being a *new founder* of the city, Nero, getting the emphasis seriously wrong, transfers the epithet and wants the glory of being the founder of a *new city* (*condendae urbis nouae . . . gloriam,* 15.40.2). To the deranged emperor, living in his never-never land of mythic fantasy, the burning of the city is not the historical Gallic sack, to be outstripped and redeemed, but the fall of Troy, all over again (15.39.3):

> peruaserat rumor ipso tempore flagrantis urbis inisse eum domesticam scaenam et cecinisse Troianum excidium, praesentia mala uetustis cladibus adsimulantem.

> A rumor had spread that at the very time of the fire he had gone on to the private stage in his house and sung the fall of Troy, making present evils look like disasters of the past.

This is a highly self-referential moment, for Tacitus's whole description of the fire is modeled extensively on Virgil's description of the fall of Troy.[225] Aeneas could escape from Troy and initiate a drive toward a new future; but now, Roman forward progress into the development that is possible in constructive history is always being blocked by an endless return to prototypical mythic patterns of action from which, it appears, there is no escape.[226]

We are back, then, with Troy, where this chapter began. The dialectic between myth and history often begins with Troy, even if the templates evolved for discriminating between myth and history can be brought to bear productively on any period, from the age of heroes to the recent past, or the present. In the next chapter we shall return to Troy, and to another way of configuring rupture and continuity, as we investigate the myths of the Fall, in the transition from the Age of Gold.

FOUR · Transitions from
Myth into History II

Ages of Gold and Iron

ACROSS THE DIVIDE

The last chapter closed with Nero singing as Rome burned, singing of the fall of
Troy, "making present evils look like disasters of the past" (*praesentia mala uetustis
cladibus adsimulantem, Ann.* 15.39.3). The question of how "like" are the present
and the distant past is one that will preoccupy us in this chapter as well, and the fall
of Troy will once again be an important focus. We have seen repeatedly how
important the fall of Troy was as a mark in time. On the other side of that demarcation live the heroes, who converse with gods and lift rocks it would take twelve
men now to lift; on this side of the demarcation begins the movement into current
human history. In the previous chapter we saw that the movement into human history could be represented by the historiographical tradition as a movement into
an increasingly ascertainable realm of knowledge, with an increasing security of
chronological emplotment, and we saw how much could be at stake in denying or
asserting the associated categories of historicity and datability. In this chapter we
shall investigate the transition from myth into history from a rather different angle,
with a data bank made up mainly of poetic, rather than historiographical, texts. We
shall investigate the most important transition in myth, at once the most important
beginning and ending moment in myth—the transition from the Golden to the
Iron Age. This is a moment when the human race enters a historical space, not just
in terms of coming over a horizon of historically ascertainable time, but in larger

terms—this is when humans enter upon patterns of life that are still current, and begin living a knowable and familiar life, continuous with ours. The terms of this currently lived experience are radically different from those imagined before the tipping point. As we shall see, according to this way of thinking the movement of historical time has taken human beings out of a state of harmony with nature and locked them into a place in nature unlike that of any other animal.[1]

Troy is not the only moment of rupture in this tradition, and for the Romans it is not even the single most significant one. The placing of the demarcation line itself could vary widely, but wherever it fell, it created a traumatic fault line in experience.[2] On the other side of that divide everything is different, "unlike," and fundamentally unknowable. Not the least significant of the categories of unlikeness are the very contours and reliefs of time, and we shall pursue the question of how differently time behaves on either side of that divide. What role do the various representations of time play in the function of discriminating between the experience of prehistory and the experience of history? Further, what happens to time right on that moment of divide? What kind of temporal net can be thrown over that transition? Other forms of temporality come into play here, differing from the quotidian flow of ordered time; especially when we come to consider the possibility of a return to the previous state, the fantasy of turning back time will call into question the basic structures of Roman time.

BEFORE THE FALL

The idea of a formerly happy time, when life was simpler and freer, before civilization, before the decline, is one deeply embedded in ancient thinking, as it still is in modern.[3] It is a variety of the myth of the fall from innocence, which appears to be more or less universal, even if it can take on all kinds of forms in different specific contexts. In the contemporary West the most prevalent form of the myth involves the loss of community, after our supposed fall into the fractured and atomized modernity of globalization.[4] Each modern subcommunity may have its own variation on this basic theme. Within the discipline of classics, the commonest variation is closely related to the myth of the loss of community, for it involves lamenting the transition from the oral to the literate, the fall from a natural state of orality into an estranged world of writing.[5]

In such models of fall from innocence, the quality and nature of the experience of time itself is regularly claimed to be different on the other side of the divide between innocence and contemporaneity. Anthropologists are still working through the impact of Lévi-Strauss's vision of "hot" and "cold" societies, according to which modern "hot" societies are fully immersed in the vicissitudes of historicity, whereas "cold" societies are by contrast in a history-free zone of unprogressive and circular time.[6] The Lévi-Straussian model is only one example of the common technique of displacing the diachronic perspective of "then/now" onto a synchronic one of "there/here," so that contemporary "primitive" societies are seen as persisting in a prelapsarian state: the geographically remote in the present comes to be equivalent to the chronologically remote in the past.[7] According to this same model, visions of lost bliss can be displaced in geography as well as in time, so that the Utopia in its location elsewhere distant in space becomes the correlative for the Golden Age in its location somewhere in the past.[8]

The conception that "primitive" societies actually have a history is deeply upsetting to the view that they have merely persisted unchanged in an earlier mode of life. A salutary shock to such a model of simple continuance is given by recent research on the Mlabri, hunter-gatherers in northern Thailand, which suggests that these people "came into existence in the relatively recent past, and are descended from farmers."[9] Similarly, the Yanomamo and other Amazonian Indians, it has been argued, do not embody a timeless "natural" life in the wilderness but are fragments of a historical catastrophe, exiled from their farms and villages in the seventeenth and eighteenth centuries by European diseases and depredations.[10] The quality of time for those living in a supposedly prelapsarian state is, however, not usually held to be part of history and is instead viewed as radically "unlike." Such people are held to be fragments, preserved as if in amber, of a past time before time, unregulated by the modern conditions that enmesh our experience within modernity's Gulliver-on-the-beach-of-Lilliput set of time constraints. We shall see that the ancient world has its own correlatives for such nostalgia, and for the notion that the experience of time was different "then" from "now"; as in the last chapter, we cannot get away from the issue of how society copes with its incorporation into the onward movement of history. At the same time as acknowledging the concept of a different experience of time "then," however, Roman authors may put it under severe pressure, as they question the possibility of an atemporal human existence, of imagining human beings in a time before, or without, time.

FROM BLISS TO MISERY

Modern scholarship has assembled a battery of evidence concerning the "real" Golden Age, to be located in the hunter-gatherer stage before the time about

13,000 years ago when the Iron Age of agriculture, animal domestication, and organized sedentary life started to take root in the Fertile Crescent. This agricultural revolution was itself not as swift or total as it is often painted, even though modern investigators tend to be as attracted as their ancient counterparts by the concept of a sudden revolution in lifestyle. The process of grinding cereal grains for human consumption goes back at least 12,000 years before organized farming in the Fertile Crescent.[11] And the hunter-gatherer lifestyle still endures (whether or not as a continuously persisting one), even if, according to Jared Diamond, it will die out forever in our lifetimes.[12] That really will be the end of the Golden Age. Still, even if agriculture and its discontents did not arrive overnight, the new agriculture-based life, once entrenched, observably shortened people's heights and life expectancies with the introduction of new diseases and stresses.[13] A modern historian frames the dilemmas in a manner that an ancient one would have recognized:

> Hunter-gatherers or gatherer-hunters . . . were not saved by the advent of agriculture from the immemorial threat of extinction. On the contrary, they enjoyed many millennia of "unending leisure and affluence." . . . The big question about the hunter-gatherers, therefore, does not seem to be "How did they progress towards the higher level of an agricultural and politicised society?" but "What persuaded them to abandon the secure, well-provided and psychologically liberating advantages of their primordial lifestyle?"[14]

So much for modern science, and its own nostalgias. In the ancient tradition, we see variations on the fundamental concept in our first extant source, Hesiod, who gives us a range of ways of thinking about this falling-off from primal bliss into the conditions of pain and toil that humans now inhabit. One complex set of stories meshes the culpability of Prometheus, who alienated Zeus and divided humans from gods with his trickery over the sacrifice at Mecone, together with the culpability of his brother Epimetheus; Epimetheus acted the part of Adam to the Eve of Pandora, who was destined to let loose misery upon humankind by unsealing her jar after she had been sent to deceive Epimetheus by the vengeful Zeus (*Theog.* 535–612; *Op.* 42–105). In addition, Hesiod has an alternative aetiology for the harshness of the current human condition, one with a far more potent afterlife, evidently taken over from a Near Eastern source (*Op.* 106–201).[15] In this story, contemporary humans are the fifth in a sequence of "Races," at the head of which is a Golden Race, whose members lived a life of ease and peace under Cronus, free from hard work and pain (109–26). Next comes a Silver Race, whose members were much worse and not like the Golden Race in nature or mind (127–39); after them comes a Bronze Race, unlike the Silver, terrible and powerful, devoted to violence (140–55). At this point the pattern of degeneration is reversed as Hesiod incorporates the Greek Race of Heroes into the paradigm: its members were better, and more just, and now live a life untouched by sorrow in the far-distant Islands of the Blessed, conforming to the pattern whereby the geographically and chronologically removed may overlap (156–73). Finally comes the Race of Iron, contemporary humans, "who do not cease from hard work and pain by day, or from perishing by night" (οὐδέ ποτ᾽ ἦμαρ/παύονται καμάτου καὶ οἰζύος, οὐδέ τι νύκτωρ/φθειρόμενοι, 176–78).

A cognate myth of former happy simplicity and subsequent decline into the complexities and miseries of contemporary life, or of modernity, is certainly pervasive among the Romans.[16] Indeed, it is clear that such a paradigm is more widespread and more powerful among the Romans than among the Greeks, so much so that the myth of a fall from a Golden Age to an Iron Age comes to be *the* great Roman myth.[17] In origin, as we have seen, the myth is Near Eastern, mediated to the Greeks by Hesiod; after him, and especially after the fifth century B.C.E., despite various noteworthy contributions we shall observe, the Greeks made surprisingly little of it.[18] Cole, in his study of the concept of human progress in the ancient world, describes a struggle in the fifth century B.C.E. between the myth of the Golden Age and the myth of human progress, between, as he puts it, "Hesiodic fantasy and Ionian science." In this struggle Hesiodic fantasy lost, and Ionian science won. Instead of believing that things were once much better and have since become worse, the Greeks were persuaded by science that things were once much worse and have since become better. Further, according to Cole, "these opinions went almost unchallenged from the beginning of the fourth century until such time as the Judaeo-Christian doctrine of the Fall began to colour ancient preconceptions of prehistory."[19] Cole's generalization, however true it may be for the Greeks, by no means holds for the Romans, where we find a powerful tradition of representing the past as fundamentally more free, desirable, and easy than the present, and of representing the present as radically worse than the past, in a decline from the state of nature.

Such a view is not by any means the preserve of the direct poetical heirs of Hesiod. A crucial role of the ideology of the Ages of Gold and Iron under the Principate of Augustus was precisely to play upon the idea of a fall in order to further the atmosphere of on-going crisis that made Augustus seem indispensable. As Wallace-Hadrill well puts it, "while for the Greeks the function of the Fall myth was to explain the present state of humanity, for the Augustans its function is to put the emperor at the centre of the scheme of things."[20] General historiographical conceptions are also informed by the concept of a lost early state of freedom and happiness. A prominent example is the account Tacitus gives in *Annals* 3 of the burgeoning of law that accompanies humans' decline from their pristine state of innocence. He presents a sequential picture, with successive phases of corruption and legislation going hand in hand.[21] A similar view informs the picture of the human past given by Varro, in his *De Re Rustica* (2.1.3–5). Here Varro is indebted to the work of Dicaearchus, one of the comparatively few Greek thinkers to pay serious attention to the paradigm.[22] Sometime around 300 B.C.E. Dicaearchus wrote a "biography of Greece," the *Bios Hellados,* in which he charted human falling-off from an initial state of harmony with nature, a rationalized Golden Age of self-sufficient contentment rather than of fantastic plenty, down to pastoralism (a kind of hunter-gatherer existence), and finally into agriculturalism.[23] Varro believes that he can date the onset of the last stage of progressive decline, because it is—significantly—linked to the founding of the first city in the Greek world, Thebes, 2,100 years before his time (3.1.2).[24] He further believes that even the last stage of life in the agricultural phase is better than life in the city: *neque solum antiquior cultura agri, sed etiam melior* ("Field cultivation is not only more ancient, but even superior," 3.1.4).[25]

It is striking that Varro's strong preference for rural over urban life appears to have no precedent in his Dicaearchan model.[26] With Varro's departure here from Dicaearchus we see a typical example of the crucial part that rural nostalgia plays in Roman thought, as the Romans digest their supposed estrangement from rural life and their incorporation into the modern alienations of urbanism. This is an attitude that easily accommodates itself to the view we noted earlier, in which the supposedly simple life of noncivilized contemporaries is a remnant of an earlier life now lost to "us"; the city, representing modernity and history, is in a different groove of time from the country, which is still somehow in touch with a more simple and virtuous past.[27] As Raymond Williams has shown in his study of the concepts of "country" and "city" in modern England, such templates have been phenomenally persistent in their appeal.[28]

The example of Varro highlights the complexity and ambivalence of such views of decline, for he follows Dicaearchus in seeing agriculturalism as the last phase of falling-off from an original state of nature, but he expounds the point in a work whose main purpose is to celebrate agriculture in Italy as a balance against contemporary corruption.[29] In particular, ever since the work of Lovejoy and Boas

(1935) we have been familiar with the complex dialectic between primitivist and progressive views of human history. The overtly pessimistic view of decline is often accompanied by an admiring acknowledgment of the remarkable technological and cultural achievements of human civilization; from this perspective, the Golden Age is not idyllic bliss but sloth, or savagery.[30] In fact the concepts of decline and of progress are inextricably linked, not only in the sense that all such contradictory oppositional pairs depend on each other for mutual definition, but in the larger sense that both progress and decline depend upon a cognate conception of "the nature and meaning of time."[31] Both templates ultimately depend upon a dynamic conception of the movement of the society forwards in successive phases through time, in which any "advance" is simultaneously open to being represented as a sacrificial "loss" of what previously existed; further, this apprehension of successive phases makes it always possible to envisage a recurrence, or return, whether in a positive or negative sense.

Lucretius book 5 is a fine example of how these two competing yet inextricably linked views of the human past can coexist very fruitfully in a single text; he creates a vision of human experience as having been always already in progress, and always already in decline.[32] Virgil's conception, particularly in the *Georgics,* is in dialogue with this Lucretian picture and is likewise closely related to the complex of ideas we see in Varro.[33] Virgil presents a transition moment early in *Georgics* 1 as Jupiter marks the shift to the Iron Age, away from a preagricultural life of common plenty toward the conditions of modernity, with the introduction of the arts of technology that enable and enforce the life of toil: fire, sailing, navigation, hunting, animal domestication, metallurgy, and plowing (1.122–49). The move from the pre-Jovian to the Jovian state looks like a moment of fall, however compelling the appurtenances of civilization may appear, and the grim necessities of wresting a living from a recalcitrant nature are given full treatment in the poem.[34] But the resulting life of agricultural labor is one that the poem regularly appears to celebrate, most conspicuously at the end of book 2, where the life of contemporary farmers is wistfully idealized as superior to the life of the city, so much so that it appears still prelapsarian: among the farmers Justice left her last trace as she departed from the earth to mark the onset of the Iron Age (2.458–74), and their current life preserves a living remnant of a life once lived by Golden Saturn (513–40).[35] These and other contradictory elements in the poem are variously read as self-consciously fractured or else as ultimately susceptible to a unified reading, whether "optimistic" or "pessimistic." However individual readers may wish to choose on this score, it is important to see Virgil working with a larger cultural template in which this kind of schiz-

ophrenia on the subject of progress and decline is radical. A Roman sense of accelerating departure from a revered and simpler national past into an unmanageably
complex present is blended with a philosophical and poetic tradition that sees contemporary life as a condition of estrangement from a natural state, and these combined themes are always liable to be in competition with an apprehension of tri-
umphalist forward movement toward greater control of the natural and political
world. Similar issues present themselves in the *Aeneid*'s representation of Italy,
which blends a "hard primitivism" model of progress from savagery toward civilization with a "soft primitivism" model of decline from a natural state toward
decadence, while adding in a cyclical pattern of recurrence.[36]

Even Tacitus is by no means fully committed to a global view of decline (in part,
perhaps, as a function of sheer Tacitean perversity in refusing to commit himself
to a global view of anything). It is not at all the case that he presents the contemporary Roman world as universally inferior to the past. In *Annals* 3, some fourteen
pages after the passage we have already noted on the growth of law as a result of
progressive decline from a state of nature, he has another passage on the movement of societal norms, in which he discusses the waxing and waning of personal
luxury at Rome (3.55). In accordance with the familiar model, an improvement in
this respect inside the city is the result of the arrival of new senators from outside
the city. These new senators represent a kind of return to the past, bringing with
them attitudes that have persisted in the different time groove of the Italian towns,
the colonies, and the provinces. Vespasian symbolizes the phenomenon, and his
personal lifestyle is marked as *antiquus*. Tacitus further speculates that the change
in habits might be part of a "cyclical pattern to all human affairs, so that as the
changing seasons come around again, so do fashions in customs" (*nisi forte rebus
cunctis inest quidam uelut orbis, ut quem ad modum temporum uices ita morum uertan-
tur*, 3.55.5).[37] Since the new senators themselves represent a fragment of the past
returning to the city, Tacitus's two explanations for an improvement in Roman
attitudes toward luxury are not as opposed as they have sometimes been taken to
be. The concept of a return is inextricably part of the construction of a nostalgia
for the past, as we shall see throughout.

TIME BEFORE THE FALL

One key Roman text after another deals with what is now no longer a concept of a
Golden *Race*, but of a Golden *Age*.[38] This time when human beings lived the simple
life, in a state of nature, before the Fall, is often described through a series of omis-

sions, as a life lacking all the defining characteristics of normal human life. In *Weltalter, goldene Zeit und sinnverwandte Vorstellungen*, the standard modern work on ancient conceptions of the Golden Age, Gatz collects in an index passages that deal with *absentia* of various things in the Golden Age.[39] It is quite a list: "absence of ships, war, private property, disease, slaves" (*absentia navium, belli, rerum privatarum, morbi, servorum*). We could add more "absences" to the list from other sources: fire, metallurgy, weaving, plowing, marriage, law, government, cities.[40] If we place such a list of absences beside Lucretius's snapshot list of the features of modern civilization (*nauigia atque agri culturas moenia leges / arma uias uestis et cetera de genere horum*, "ships and agriculture, walls, laws, weapons, land travel, woven clothing, etc. etc.," 5.1448–49), then it becomes plain that the fundamental point of these myths has endured through their transference to Rome or to the modern world. Now, as then, such myths bring "our" own current condition into focus by holding up as a counterexample a set of ideas embodying what "we" are not.[41]

For our present purposes, the crucial "absence" that is absent from Gatz's list is "time"—both ordered civic time and progressive historical time. As Prometheus says in his tragedy, before his invention of the necessities of civilization (numbers, writing, animal domestication, and sailing, 459–68), humans had no way of marking the progress of time ([Aesch.] *PV* 454–58):

ἦν δ' οὐδὲν αὐτοῖς οὔτε χείματος τέκμαρ
οὔτ' ἀνθεμώδους ἦρος οὔτε καρπίμου
θέρους βέβαιον, ἀλλ' ἄτερ γνώμης τὸ πᾶν
ἔπρασσον, ἔστε δή σφιν ἀντολὰς ἐγὼ
ἄστρων ἔδειξα τάς τε δυσκρίτους δύσεις.

They had no secure demarcation either of winter or of flowery spring or
of fruit-bearing summer, but they acted completely without judgment, until
I showed them the risings of the stars and their settings, indistinguishable
[before].[42]

In Lucretius's portrayal of the development of human civilization, the invention of the calendar (5.1436–39) comes at the crucial turning point just before the fortification of cities, the division of land for agriculture, sailing for trade in precious goods, developed political alliances, and poetry and writing (1440–45).[43] One of Plautus's characters, from his lost *Boeotia*, illustrates the pivotal importance of time marking with brilliant clarity, showing how constructions of time are determinative for the wretched modern condition. A starving parasite grumbles against the man who first "invented the hours" (*primus qui horas repperit*), the one who first set up a sundial *(solarium)*, when he was a boy, says the parasite, he followed natural time, for his belly was his one true sundial, but now the sun, as measured by the sundials all over town, dictates when he, and everyone else, can eat.[44] The ordering of time is a foundational element of what it takes to live in the Iron Age. It is not just an appurtenance, but a basic enabling constraint of civilization, and its absence is therefore a defining characteristic of the previous age.

Such a picture of a pre-Promethean time before time dovetails with the views of mythic time we examined in the previous chapter. In the time of myth the application of chronology cannot get any traction: in the age of heroes there are no wall charts that really work. In the Greek tradition in particular, the fall of Troy was the most important of the possible moments of rupture, when a qualitatively human time began to emerge from the twilight zone of the earlier chronology of gods and heroes. Hesiod memorably expresses the conception that once upon a time humans and gods dined and sat together (fr. 1.6–7). The notion that in the ancient times people were somehow nearer to the gods persisted strongly: Dicaearchus, for example, held that originally men were close to the gods, and the Stoics also maintained that in the beginning men were more intimate with divinity, having a consequently more intimate knowledge of divine things.[45] It is generally the Trojan War that brings an end to this phase of human existence, because that is when the gods stop mingling with humans, and, above all, that is when they stop mating with them: it is here that the race of demigods ceases.[46] The gods of myth have genealogies and progressions, but they all stop with the Trojan War demarcation. This is where the onward narrative of the gods stops, where narrative time ends for them, right where the narrative of human historical time begins.

The other main divine plot stops here too. The overarching theogonic superplot of the gods is essentially a story of recurrence, in which succession is followed by succession, with sons overthrowing fathers only to be overthrown in their own turn by their own sons. The gods embody a plot of potentially endless recurrence and repetition, and this fundamental narrative momentum is halted only by Jupiter's refusal to mate with Thetis, in the generation before the Trojan War, to stop the possibility of repetition of the divine plot.[47] Jupiter coveted the sea nymph Thetis, but Themis's prophecy said that the son of Thetis would be mightier than his father, so with a unique act of self-control Jupiter managed to restrain himself and married Thetis off to Peleus, who could afford to have a son stronger than himself, Achilles.[48]

Once Jupiter stops the plot of succession coming around yet again, and once the beginning of history takes the gods away from mating with mortals, the gods are stuck in a timeless zone, one that throws into relief by contrast the new entrapment of humans in time.[49] After the chronological divorce between humans and gods, it is now only human narratives that go on, forward-moving, deriving meaning from death: the gods, without death and without progeny, are by comparison fixed in an undynamic temporal zone. To be in human history is to be in narrative, and the only way out of this forward progression is through death; as we shall see repeatedly, it is not possible to arrest the flow of this narrative time or to swim back up against its current. As for their relations with the gods, in the Iron Age humans can only struggle to accommodate the timelessness of the gods into their mundane civic time frames, by means of their annually repeating festival calendars, just as they struggle to accommodate the gods' lack of physical presence by means of fixed temples and statues.[50]

AN INSTANT OF RUPTURE

The Trojan War, then, is a key marker of a transition from a period of myth to a period of history, as the first beginning of scientific historical chronology, and as the moment of passage from a more blessed time of heroes and gods to the continuous time of history. Yet Troy is only one of a number of possible moments of rupture, many of which share the same property of instantaneous demarcation between before and after. It is significant that the transition from a previous idyllic state is so often configured as an instant in time, in which the idyllic life is somehow lost in a single moment of catastrophe, with one bite of the apple.[51] This concept is one favored especially in the poetic tradition, and less marked in other discourses. Instead of a gradual shift of the kind we see in Tacitus—even one punctuated by significant moments of transition—the Roman poetic tradition loves to concentrate on a single moment. As we shall see, the possibility of focusing on that single moment can be called into question, but its allure persists. One moment in particular commands attention, from a generation before the Trojan War. This is the sailing of the first ship, regularly identified as the Argo, carrying the Argonauts to the edge of the world to collect the golden fleece.

The Roman interest in the first ship is very striking, as is the fondness for casting the Argo in this role. It is well known that in Euripides' *Medea* or Apollonius's *Argonautica* there is no real interest in the idea that the Argo is the first ship.[52] If you forced a Greek to name the first ship he would probably tell you it was the ship in which Danaus sailed from Egypt to Argos, but in general the question of first sailing did not intrigue the Greeks very much.[53] Yet already in Ennius's adaptation of the prologue to Euripides' *Medea* there is a huge emphasis on the Argo's primacy. Euripides has no word of "first" or "beginning" when he has his nurse wish that the Argo had never sailed, whereas in Ennius pleonastic language piles up as he describes the construction of the ship: *neue inde nauis inchoandi exordium/cepisset:* "if only from that point the ship had not taken the first step of beginning" (*Medea Exul*, fr. 1.3–4).[54] We cannot be sure that Ennius spoke specifically of the Argo as the first ship ever to sail, but certainly when we reach Catullus 64, a key text for this subject and this chapter, the firstness of the Argo is established and proclaimed early on: *illa rudem cursu prima imbuit Amphitreten* ("That ship *first* imbued inexperienced Amphitrite with her course," 11).[55]

One of the reasons why the first ship is such an attractive idea is precisely that it elides all of Hesiod's gradations into one moment of split. The gradualist view is very widespread—we have observed it in Dicaearchus, Varro, and Tacitus, and Roman poets can themselves at times exploit the concept of a series of successive stages of decline.[56] Regularly, however, the poets focus on a single transition from Gold to Iron, with all the other metals eclipsed.[57] The conception of the first ship enables them to represent this single transition as instantaneous—when a tree, grown in the earth, is cut down by iron and first hits the water to carry human beings to another piece of earth, that is an irrevocable moment of rupture, one that launches humans into a new phase of civilization.[58] The first cutting of the earth by a plow does not have the same degree of dramatic impact, even though plowing and sailing are regularly conflated, as joint harbingers of the Iron Age: when Catullus's Argo *plows* the windy plain with her beak (*quae simul ac rostro uentosum proscidit aequor*, 12), the verb used does not denote simply "to plow," but "to plow unbroken or fallow land."[59] The end of the Golden Age, then, not only violates old boundaries as the ship sails from one piece of land to another, but also creates new ones, by demarcating land in the form of farming, and by splitting gods and humans, who had mixed in each other's company before.

Catullus's interest in the instantaneous nature of the rupture is such that the beginning of the poem introduces a novel stress on the traditional concept of the Fall marking an end to the mingling of gods and humans. Men had never seen *sea* nymphs before, says Catullus, and the instant they did, it was the last instant: *illa atque haud alia uiderunt luce marinas/mortales oculis ... Nymphas* ("On that day and on no other mortals saw marine nymphs with their eyes," 16).[60] Beginning and end moments are compressed into one, with Catullus acknowledging the fact that the transition from Gold to Iron cannot be exclusively isolated as either a beginning or an end; as Fitzgerald well puts it, "the voyage of the Argo is both the moment of supreme cooperation and mingling between gods and mortals and the beginning of their separation."[61]

Again, this cluster of concerns is far to seek in the Greek sources. The distinctiveness of the Roman interest in the sailing of the first ship is very striking and deserves a brief discussion before we return to Catullus's Argo, and to the pressures the first ship puts upon the structures of time.

THE CORRUPTING SEA

The Romans are not simply more interested than the Greeks in the sailing of the first ship as a dramatic focus;[62] they also show a far greater interest in the wicked ship as a token of a divorce from a state of nature.[63] Hesiod expresses a landlubber's suspicion of sailing (*Op.* 618–94), and he claims that in a just society people get enough from the land without needing to sail (236–37)[64]—this is as close as he comes to moral condemnation of sailing, or to the concept that the Golden Age was free of seafaring. The Greeks were certainly impressed by the ship as an emblem of technology, as well they might be, considering that until the eighteenth century, with the invention of the industrial steam engine, the ocean-going ship was the largest and most complex and powerful single machine that human beings could make. Accordingly, when Odysseus and his men vindicate human crafty intelligence by blinding the Cyclops, the first simile describing their action compares them to a team of men making a ship (*Od.* 9.383–88).[65] In the famous ode in Sophocles' *Antigone* about the extraordinary nature of human beings, seafaring is the first example of their phenomenal and disquieting resourcefulness—and plowing is the second (332–41).[66] More strongly yet, Solon and Euripides relate the restless urge to sail the sea for profit to a morally dubious drive, one bordering on infatuation (ἄτη).[67]

To the Romans, however, the ship was always liable to be more than an emblem, however morally unsettling, of human audaciousness and technology. The ship was cast in the far more sinister role of embodying an estrangement from a natural state, since the ship enables humans to transcend, or rather violate, natural boundaries, as it goes in search of loot, trade, and empire. For the Romans, more truly than for the Greeks, "the Golden Age ended with the opening up of the Corrupting Sea."[68] The Greeks might happily think of themselves as living around the sea like ants or frogs living around a pond,[69] but the Romans idealized the land-based self-sufficient Italian days before their expansion outside the peninsula, and their collision with Carthage over Sicily was commemorated as the defining moment when they finally had to learn to sail: according to Polybius's already heavily idealizing account, before the First Punic War the Romans had no maritime resources at all and had never had a thought for the sea.[70] The standard modern authority on ships in the ancient world has subscribed to this dominant Roman ideology and speaks of "Romans being by nature little interested in the sea,"[71] but the real energy of the Roman debate over seafaring comes precisely from their guilty cognitive dissonance on the subject. They knew perfectly well that they were a mighty thalassocracy and that their city was the center of global maritime trade,[72] while simultaneously they were in thrall to a landowning value system that went so far as to ban senators from engaging in trade or owning their own commercial cargo ships.[73] The concept of the wickedness of the ship, as the marker of a divorce from a happier primal state, derives much of its energy from this guilty consciousness of double-think.[74]

The far-reaching ramifications of the ship's transgressiveness are expressed with unmatched compression in Horace's third ode. This poem is addressed to Virgil, the poet of the *Georgics*, and it addresses the main theme of the *Georgics*, the paradoxical place of human beings in nature, as simultaneously guilty violators of nature and upholders of the apparently natural order of agriculture.[75] Virgil in the *Georgics* had said very little about sailing, because the *Georgics* concentrate even more relentlessly on farming than Hesiod's *Works and Days*. Virgil does little more than mention the ship as one of the tokens of the Iron Age, along with fire, hunting, domestication of animals, fishing, ironworking, and agriculture (*G.* 1.134–48); he passes from riverine craft (136), "early experiments in navigation," to the astronomical skill needed for maritime navigation (137–38).[76] When Horace writes a poem to the poet of the *Georgics* about the themes of the *Georgics*, however, he ignores agriculture and concentrates on what lyric poets know about—sailing.[77]

The occasion is a sea voyage Virgil is undertaking, and Horace prays for his safe arrival, before turning to denounce the *first* man to sail, the first to undertake the paradoxical human mission of using fragile technology to impose his will on a stronger nature, "entrusting a breakable ship to the cruel sea" (*qui fragilem truci/ commisit pelago ratem/primus, Carm.* 1.3.10–12). The audacity of Virgil's embarking upon martial epic is part of what Horace is catching here, as his friend leaves the *Georgics* and sets course for the *Aeneid;* he is exploiting a Hesiodic paradigm whereby working the land and composing poetry about working the land are both safer enterprises than the more perilous alternatives of sailing and of "grandiose heroic poetry."[78] Horace's scope keeps broadening, however, as he proceeds to revivify the notion that sailing is a transgression of divine boundaries (*Carm.* 1.3.21–24):

> nequiquam deus abscidit
> prudens Oceano dissociabili
>   terras, si tamen impiae
> non tangenda rates transiliunt uada.

> In vain in his wise foresight did God cut off
> the lands of the earth by means of the dividing sea
>   if impious ships yet leap
> across waters which they should not touch.[79]

The last two words in this extract are particularly telling in their evocation of the difference between "then" and "now." Of the many Latin words for "sea," Horace has chosen *uada*, which is cognate with the English "wade." Before the ship, this word reminds us, the only bits of sea human beings could cross were the bits they could wade through; or else, if the section of sea was deep but narrow, it might be possible to jump across it—*transiliunt*. Horace's wicked ships are almost aware of how impious they are, as they try to jump across the water without touching it.

The ship as the sign of human transgressiveness in general then leads in to mention of Prometheus's theft of fire (27–28), simultaneously "the end of the Golden Age" and "the beginning of human civilization."[80] More outrageous symbols of transgression outside human bounds follow, with Daedalus breaking the boundary between earth and sky (34–35),[81] and Hercules breaking the boundary between earth and underworld: *perrupit Acheronta Herculeus labor,* "The labor of Hercules burst through Acheron" (36). As Hercules expends immense effort on his labor, Horace uses the license of lengthening the final vowel of the verb *perrupit* to mimic the exertion;[82] and as Hercules smashes the boundary between earth and underworld, Horace breaks across the diaeresis in the middle of the line, producing in the elision between *Acheronta* and *Herculeus* the single instance in the poem where the Asclepiad verse does not have a clean word break after the sixth syllable.[83] Human beings' inherent capacity to confound natural norms with their technology and with their audacious restlessness is the factor that determines the conditions of modern life, and it all began with the ship.[84]

In his third *Ode* Horace does not name the first man to sail, the *primus* of line 12, or give the name of his ship. As we have seen, when Romans did name the first ship it was the Argo, and we may now return to Catullus's launching of the Argo at the beginning of poem 64.[85] The inherently transgressive nature of Catullus's ship's invasion of the sea is wonderfully captured in line 15, when the sea nymphs come up from the water to look at it, *monstrum . . . admirantes,* "in astonishment at the monstrosity." Here the "monstrosity" feels misapplied, for the nymphs ought to be the extraordinary thing rather than the ship, but on this day of first sailing it is the ship that is the freakish one, the unnatural portent.[86] For this is the moment of rupture when the technology and ingenuity of human civilization first definitively smash the boundaries of nature ordained by God, and in this poem other boundaries go down as a consequence—the boundary between land and sea, since Thetis is a sea creature and Peleus is a human; the boundary between Greek and barbarian, since the captain of the Argo is going to marry Medea.[87]

The poem presents itself as a marriage poem, but it is really a divorce poem, and not just with Theseus and Ariadne on the tapestry.[88] The marriage of Peleus and Thetis, which provides such narrative connection as the poem bothers to have, is indeed a very famous marriage, but, just as with Jason and Medea, it is the divorce of Peleus and Thetis that makes their name.[89] From the start their union is a union of irreconcilables, as Catullus hints in line 20, *Thetis humanos non despexit hymenaeos,* "Thetis did not look down on marriage with a human." In Latin the word *humanus,* "human," was thought to come from *humus,* "earth," since that is where humans are from, and where they are buried.[90] The marriage of the sea nymph with this earth creature is anomalous, as is the presence of the earth creature out of his element, on the sea. Their wedding culminates with an epithalamium (323–81), and in the light of what we know is going to happen to this couple we are reminded of what a strange genre the epithalamium is, since any wedding is an act of hope, a kind of unilateral "optimistic reading" in the face of the knowledge that even long and happy marriages are not a continuation of the wedding mood. It is fitting that the poem should begin with the meeting of two individuals who are doomed to a very long estrangement, since estrangement is at the core of the myth of the Fall.

With all these violated boundaries the poem creates an atmosphere of anomie, of chaotic instability.[91] In accordance with this atmosphere, one of the categories put under intense pressure in the poem is the category of time. The poem destabilizes chronologies in such a systematic way that its chronological inconsistencies have become notorious.[92] There are two main crises of mythical chronology activated by Catullus.

First, Catullus shows us Peleus and Thetis falling in love on the first day of the Argo's voyage, when according to the usual story Peleus and Thetis were already married—and already divorced—before the Argo sailed.[93] This is the point of Catullus's anaphora of *tum* early on in the poem, repeated at the beginning of three consecutive lines (19–21): it was *then, then, then* that they fell in love, not earlier, as in the usual version. It matters very much to Catullus that the sailing of the Argo and the meeting of Peleus and Thetis should be simultaneous, whatever the accepted chronology. He wants the sailing of the first ship and the meeting of the earth creature and the sea creature to happen at one and the same time. These joinings of opposites, and their consequences, are so momentous that he yokes them together, smashing at once as many boundaries as he can.

The second problem—a more complicated one—arises from the fact that the story of Ariadne and Theseus on the coverlet, together with the whole chronology of the Theseus myth, is incompatible with the concept of the Argo as the first ship. If Peleus is one of the crew on the first ship, how can one of his wedding presents be a tapestry showing an earlier story about a famous sea voyage, with Theseus sailing to Crete, picking up Ariadne, and leaving her behind on the island of Naxos as he sails back home to Athens? Further, it is clear that Catullus alludes prominently to the usual version of the Theseus myth, especially the one to be found in Callimachus's *Hecale,* according to which Theseus did not go to Athens and meet his father and then go to Crete until quite a few years *after* the return of the Argo from its maiden voyage.[94] After Medea comes to Greece with Jason on the Argo, according to this usual story, she kills her children and then runs away from Corinth to Athens, where she marries King Aegeus, father of Theseus; she then tries to trick Aegeus into killing Theseus when he turns up from Troezen as a teenager to claim his inheritance. So if Theseus was a child in Troezen and had not even met his father when the Argo sailed to get Medea in the first place, how could he have sailed to Crete before the Argo sailed?

Catullus carefully highlights the collision of these two temporal frames—the sailing of the Argo and of Theseus—with his redundant use of two time expressions to describe Theseus's arrival in Crete: "from that moment, that time when defiant Theseus . . ." (*illa ex tempestate ferox quo tempore Theseus,* 73).[95] He reminds us of the "other" "first time" that his primal Argo is supplanting when he has Ariadne wish that "Athenian ships had never touched Cretan shores *in the first* time" (*utinam ne tempore primo/Cnosia Cecropiae tetigissent litora puppes*, 171, diamy ingly, his language here exploits the diction used by Ennius to describe what now feels like the "other" other first time, the original sailing of the Argo).[96] One may detect yet another "first time" lurking in the allusions to King Minos. His status as the first thalassocrat, the first ruler to exercise command of the Aegean Sea, is an important issue in the tradition and in Catullus's poem and is not casually introduced: the penalty of human sacrifice that Theseus sails to halt is one that was imposed on Athens by Minos during an imperial punitive expedition (76–79).[97] Here we have an allusion to another important demarcation moment in human history, anchored not on the first sailing of a ship but on imperial command of the sea, and this moment is one that might be more important than the sailing of the Argo or of Theseus.

The sailing of Catullus's ship looks like the divide between the chaos of unchartable events and the clear light of scientific day, but it is not an event that can be pinned down. It is an alluringly self-assured single and definitive moment, slicing through the chop and surge of myth, but it is a moment that turns out to be not only unverifiable but also in competition with other primary moments.[98] Here we see Catullus enacting the phenomenal difficulty of reaching back to a definitively originary moment. Such moments can appear definitive and sharp, but they are always blurred on closer inspection, and less primary than they appear at first.[99] The illusory clarity of that first and last day is described in natural terms as a "light" (*illa atque haud alia . . . luce*, 16), and this alluring image of the definitively bright light of day recurs throughout the poem. The day of the wedding itself is described as *optatae luces*, the "longed-for lights" (31); the day after the wedding is described as *oriente luce*, the "rising light" (376). The very last words of the poem are *lumine claro*, "bright light," but this is now a lost light, describing the bright light of day in which humans used to see the gods face to face, the bright light from which the gods now withhold themselves (*nec se contingi patiuntur lumine claro*).

The poem's beginning moments multiply, and each of them is also an ending moment. As the poem evokes the lost time of the past, it deploys many words of time to mark the end of diverse time frames within the poem, each of which is the loss of what went before. The heroes are described as born in "the excessively longed-for time of ages" (*nimis optato saeclorum tempore nati*, 22); *saeclorum*, "ages," is strictly redundant and is there to highlight the theme of successive epochs that have been lost.[100] Shortly thereafter, the moment of the wedding of Peleus and Thetis is described with an odd phrase that calls attention to the wedding as an ending moment in time: *quae simul optatae finito tempore luces/aduenere*

("When at the appointed time the longed-for lights/day arrived," 31). Commentators tell us that *finito tempore* = *definito tempore* according to the *simplex pro compo-sito* usage, meaning "to mark off a time so as to make an appointment," and *finire* is certainly used in this way.[101] But the verb carries also its primary meaning of establishing a limit or end, so that the phrase also means "when the time was ended" and marks the end of a time frame. In this clause, *optatae finito tempore* (31) occupies exactly the same position in the line as the phrase used ten lines before to describe the time of the heroes, *optato saeclorum tempore* (22). Catullus here puts his finger on one of the evasions of historical nostalgia, by which people look back enviously to a former glamorous time, forgetting that for the people in that former time it was nothing but the present, with its own glamorous past and its own potentially glamorous future. Catullus's readers are looking back with excessive desire at the time of Peleus when an era ended, but in his own time Peleus was looking forward with desire to another kind of end of time, the end of his time of waiting. Nor is Peleus the only one in the poem with a time's end confronting him. Ariadne describes Theseus's moment of crisis in the labyrinth as his "last time," as it potentially was (*supremo tempore*, 151). Her own crisis of abandonment on the beach is her "edge of time" (*extremo tempore*, 169), immediately followed in her thoughts by that "first time" when Theseus came to Crete, *tempore primo* (171); her fantasy of her death closes with the image of her "last hour" (*postrema . . . hora*, 191).

Instead of delivering on its apparent initial promise of recovering the clear day on which everything irretrievably changed, the poem keeps showing a range of different demarcations, different beginning and ending moments, in a welter of irretrievably inconsistent chronologies. A number of crucial demarcations are in play—the sailing of the Argo, the rule of the first empire of the sea under Minos, Prometheus the culture hero.[102] Finally, the war of Troy becomes the poem's climactic demarcation moment, with the savagery of the Trojan War evoked by the song of the Parcae (343–70), as the age of heroes degenerates into wholesale mundane carnage, continuous with our own depravities. The poem leaves us with the problem of wondering not just "What was that time of partition like?" but also "When was that time?" The urge to chart a definitive rupture in the human status, an entry into the current condition, so alluring in its appeal, finally comes to be seen as a mirage. None of the apparently pivotal moments can be definitively fixed; it proves harder and harder to isolate a moment, or even an epoch, when conditions turned.[103] Wherever he tries to make the cut, Catullus finds himself, as an author, enmeshed in time schemes that show humans to be always already enmeshed in time schemes, inextricably entangled in webs of time. At the end of the poem he even imagines calendars in operation at the epoch when gods still mingled with humans, even though, as we saw above, the usual tradition had it that organized time was not a feature of the pre-Iron ages, and that the Golden Age did not need such accommodations in engaging with the divine.[104] Jupiter in person, says Catullus, often saw sacrifice offered before his temple "when the annual rites had come on the festival days" (*annua cum festis uenissent sacra diebus,* 388). Here Catullus reinforces how hard it is, from our current perspectives, to recover a time before our implication in time.

If the urge to contemplate the instant of the Fall itself ends in a mirage, then the urge to communicate with that lost state before the Fall turns out to be a mirage as well. The poem embodies and evokes an *excess* of yearning (*nimis optato . . . tempore,* 22) for that lost past time, a piercing nostalgia that is conjured up by the glamorous and romantic atmosphere of so much of the poem.[105] Many other of Catullus's poems demonstrate the same obsession with a hiatus between the present and a past that is now unreachable, just beyond his recoverable grasp.[106] His "Peleus and Thetis" makes this obsession global.

SENECA'S ROMAN IRON AGE

Catullus's main heir in the deployment of the ship as the agent of the Fall is Seneca, above all in his *Medea.* In general, Seneca's work shows a highly developed use of the Golden/Iron Age matrix to focus on the ensnarements of human technology and denaturalization.[107] As a Stoic, he brings a new battery of preoccupations to the issues, for he is intrigued by the intractability of following the Stoic injunction to "live in agreement with nature" (ὁμολογουμένως τῇ φύσει ζῆν) now that humans have, according to the template we have been investigating, irrevocably left the natural state behind.[108]

In his *Medea,* Seneca focuses, like Catullus and Horace, on the vital moment of rupture represented by the sailing of the first ship, when humans left the state of nature and entered the definitively human state. He does not involve himself in Catullus's eddying temporal confusions but concentrates obsessively on the divorce between humans and nature as actualized through the ship's embodiment of transgressive technology.[109] The sailing of the Argo is emblematic of human beings' attempt to press the natural world into service, violating ordered patterns in order to try to impose their own patterns, as part of "civilization's paradoxical dislocation of the world to produce order."[110] A brilliant moment in the *Medea*'s second choral ode encapsulates this perspective and represents a true leap of imagination, as Seneca attempts the impossible task of projecting oneself back into the period before the Iron Age of sailing and agriculture: *nondum quisquam sidera norat,/stellisque quibus pingitur aether,/non erat usus* ("Not yet did anyone know the constellations, and there was no use made of the stars with which the aether is painted," 309–11).[111] The night sky is "painted" with stars, but then this painted panorama was not an object of use, but only the opportunity for aesthetic contemplation; the individual stars *(stellae)* remained individual and were not arranged into constellations *(sidera)*.[112] What, then, did the night sky look like in the Golden Age, when it was not pressed into time-marking service and its dots were as yet unconnected by navigators or farmers? What did the constellation of the Plow look like before there were any plows?

The radically paradoxical status of humans, in nature but not of it, receives sustained attention in the *Phaedra*, which becomes a meditation on the Iron Age condition, and the impossibility of escape from it.[113] Hippolytus believes that he can live according to nature by living in nature, as men did in the Golden Age (483–564), yet the futility of his dream has been exposed already in the first scene (1–84), where his irruption into the natural scene with his hunt shows that even in his supposedly edenic life in the woods he is still inescapably a modern human—invasive, destructive, cataloguing, dominating, artful, and technological.[114] After all, hunting is one of the *artes* that mark the fall into the Iron Age in Virgil's *Georgics* (1.139–40). The nurse's address to Hippolytus (435–82), urging him to follow the "natural" life for humans by living in the city, is richly ironic on many levels, especially when she totally misjudges her listener by using sustained metaphors from agriculture and arboriculture (454–60); yet her whole speech exposes the way in which the apparent naturalness of modern life is taken for granted by almost everyone.[115] The nurse's complacency and Hippolytus's delusion together provide the parameters for exploring what it could mean in the contemporary world to enact the Stoic tenet of living in agreement with nature.

In the end, the play offers no answer to the problem of what is natural for humans, except to claim that it is natural, inevitable, for humans to be out of place in nature, as the only animals to have perverted sex, animal domestication, and agriculture.[116] We cannot, according to the play's argument, extricate ourselves from the estranging matrix of civilization, history, and technology. Hippolytus thinks he can, by living a one-man Golden Age, but this is impossible—not just because it is utopian, but because he cannot remove himself from the river of time or swim back up against its current. Together with its master intertext, Virgil's *Georgics,* the play goes disconcertingly deep in its stripping away of the usual equation of the agricultural with the natural life. A telling quotation from a modern historian, Ernest Gellner, illustrates how instinctive this equation can still be: "Agrarian man can be compared with a natural species which can survive in the natural environment. Industrial man can be compared with an artificially produced or bred species which can no longer breathe effectively in the nature-given atmosphere, but can only function effectively and survive in a new, specially blended and artificially sustained air or medium."[117] Varro would have agreed with this observation (substituting "urban" for "industrial");[118] but it would have shocked Virgil and Seneca. The modern scholar has naturalized the agricultural state as being indeed a natural one, but Virgil and Seneca are wiser in seeing that this phase should be pushed one step farther back, since Gellner's "agrarian man" is himself already inextricably in the phase of estrangement from a natural environment.

A final key Senecan text to consider is *Epistle* 90, in which Seneca grapples with the Stoic problem of how close early man was to god and to nature, and how far the progress of human civilization is the work of philosophers.[119] Seneca agrees with his Stoic sources, in particular Posidonius, on many important points (4–6): early humans lived in harmony with nature, under the natural leadership of the wise men of the time, until the introduction of vice led to tyranny and the need for law. But he dissents very strongly in the rest of the letter on the question of the relationship of philosophy and technology, with far-reaching consequences for his views on the timing and nature of the Fall. In comparison with Posidonius, for whom those early wise men were philosophers who devised means of improving the conditions of life, Seneca firmly denigrates the *artes*, and he regularly quotes from the crucial Iron Age section of Virgil's first *Georgic* as his master text on the subject.[120] All the crafts that his Roman tradition marks as defining products of the Iron Age—architecture, hunting, metallurgy, weaving, agriculture, baking (9–23)—these are things he strenuously wishes to exempt from the realm of the philosopher.[121] The role of philosophy is not to discover these appurtenances of the Iron Age, as his Greek tradition claimed, but to compensate for them.

Seneca waits carefully to play the trump card of the Roman Iron Age tradition, the ship. In the Greek tradition from which he is working here, it is *agriculture* that is "the technological art *par excellence*";[122] but for Seneca the ship must be the emblem of technology. As he builds his case by listing the offending *artes*, a connoisseur of his work and of the Roman tradition will be waiting to hear about the ship, so crucial to the Romans as the quintessential emblem of technology's denaturalizing force. When Seneca comes to sum up, the ship is still left unmentioned: "All these things . . . are the discoveries of a human being, not of a philosopher," (*omnia ista . . . hominis . . . non sapientis inuenta sunt*, 24), he says—at which point he does at last produce his swerve into the long-awaited topic, with "just as the ships with which we cross rivers and seas" (*tam mehercules quam nauigia quibus amnes quibusque maria transimus*).[123] The ship inserts itself irresistibly, and it may be that it is indeed an addition to the list of land-based *artes* treated by Posidonius, to which Seneca has been responding so far.

However that may be, the whole attitude toward technology and toward the cause of the Fall from the primal state is profoundly different in Seneca from what he will have read in Posidonius. If we hold Seneca's letter up against what can be reconstructed of his Greek model, the cultural power of the Roman template we have been investigating emerges very clearly. In Posidonius, the original state of humans may well not have been described as a "Golden Age" at all, while it very clearly is in Seneca (*illo . . . saeculo quod aureum perhibent*, 5; cf. *fortunata tempora*, 36).[124] Further, in Posidonius it was not the introduction of the *artes* of technology that tipped human life toward decline, because in his scheme that stage came later, with tyrannies and law, while it was the first philosophers who oversaw the introduction of *artes*;[125] in Seneca, as befits a student of Catullus, Horace, and Virgil, the *artes* are themselves the tipping point, irrevocably pitching humans into the fallen state. Where Posidonius projects an early time ruled over by philosophers who introduce useful technological innovations until moral decay sets in with developed societies and their apparatus of law, Seneca follows his Roman predecessors in having a Golden Age that is lost with the advent of the morally flawed technology that enabled humans to dominate nature—or deluded them into thinking that they could.

At the end of the letter, Seneca introduces his own distinctively paradoxical twist on the complexities of interlinked decline and progress that we have observed as part of the Golden and Iron Age model throughout. For Seneca, philosophy is not an original condition, as Posidonius claimed. Those natural leaders and wise men in the earliest days, high-minded and close to divinity as they may have been, were not true wise men, in the sense of being philosophers, as Posidonius had it (44; cf. 35–36). Rather, for Seneca, philosophy is the product of civilization, a necessary remedy for our fallen state. For someone who relishes philosophy as much as Seneca does, this brings him very close to a kind of fortunate fall position, since without the fall into the Iron Age, we would not have had the art of philosophy at all.[126] The natural goodness of a primal natural state has no appeal for Seneca, for it involves no knowledge, no choice, and no struggle (44–46). He sharpens the paradox by rehabilitating the crucial word that has attracted so much scorn in the letter so far: *non enim dat natura uirtutem; ars est bonum fieri* ("For nature doesn't just give virtue; it is an art to become a good man," 44). The decline into civilization is regularly regarded ambivalently by our authors, who after all would not have been exercising their prized skills in prose or verse without it. Seneca seizes the opportunity to take the paradox as far as possible, since he removes the supreme good of philosophy from the natural state and converts it into the ultimate art, the only one of value that the degradation of civilization has to offer.

RETURNING TO THE GOLDEN AGE

Seneca did not just write about the Golden Age; he lived through one, in the form of the emperor Nero's reborn Golden Age, which was itself a return to Augustus's return to a Golden Age. Although Nero's and Augustus's returning Golden Ages are the best known, many such ages are documented under the Empire.[127] The frequent recycling of this ideology throughout the imperial period is itself ironic commentary both on the repetitive periodicity that is potentially part of the concept of return and also on the inherent tendency of patterns of imperial power and succession to repeat themselves.[128] The idea of a return is partly enabled by the profound shift in emphasis that comes with the change from the Greek concept of a Golden "Race" (γένος) to the Roman one of an "Age" (*aetas, saeculum*).[129] A qualitatively different "race" is gone forever, even if it may be hearkened back to as a point of comparison, but an "age" is easier to imagine returning, or being returned to, especially once a distinctive sense of imperial history has solidified, with its own periodizations.[130]

We are so accustomed to this aspect of the Golden Age ideology that it can be a surprise to learn how long it took to be first deployed. Although there are earlier examples of life in particular periods being compared to life under Cronus, the first text to speak of an actual return to the Age of Gold is Virgil's fourth *Eclogue*.[131] Here Virgil expresses the fantasy that the rupture in human experience can be repaired, so that an Age of Saturn will return (6): humans and gods will mingle together once more (15–16); eventually the emblematic machine of the Iron Age, the ship, will disappear (38–39); the agricultural technology of the Iron Age will likewise disappear as the earth returns to its former spontaneous bounty (39–41). Before this Saturnian Age can be reached again, however, the process of rolling back the lapse of time since the Fall will involve rerunning the heroic age as well (31–36).[132] In Hesiod's scheme the heroes complicate the descent from Gold to Iron by representing a movement "upwards"; in Virgil's, the heroes complicate the ascent from Iron to Gold by representing a movement "downwards." The repetition backwards of this progression through time involves Virgil in a repetition of Catullus 64. In lines 34–35 we see Catullus's poem beginning again, for a second time: *alter erit tum Tiphys et altera quae uehat Argo/delectos heroas* ("There will then be a second Tiphys, and a second Argo to carry the picked heroes"); in lines 35–36 we see the same consequences of this sailing as in Catullus, with second wars and with great Achilles being dispatched to Troy again (*erunt etiam altera bella/atque iterum ad Troiam magnus mittetur Achilles*). The chronological and ethical puzzles of the Catullan model are rerun with this new, second, beginning. Just as in Catullus the heroes occupy a middle ground between glamor and grubbiness, and between innocence and the Fall, eddying in their chronological and moral no-man's-land, so too in Virgil the second Argo and second Trojan War are a chronological and moral interruption, disturbing the apparent trajectory of the poem's attempt to regain the lost time before time. Virgil also picks up on Catullus's collapsing of certainties of time at the pivotal moment of transition. Virgil's poem creates great difficulties for readers in trying to assess when the new Golden Age is actually beginning (now?—after the second heroic age?);[133] this dilemma reactivates the Catullan problem of when the Golden Age actually ended. Virgil's whole poem, in sum, depends intimately on Catullus 64, especially in its development of Catullus's sense of desire to recapture a lost state. Catullus had mobilized nostalgia in order to construct a "longing for a return";[134] Virgil is accentuating that feeling of nostalgia by showing how his own longing for a return has to be mediated through Catullus's.

The fourth *Eclogue* illustrates vividly the special appeal such models have at times of crisis and instability between eras, as they respond to the threatened collapse of social order with the attempt to conjure up a "deep legitimacy."[135] A similarly escapist response to the same social crisis is to be found in Horace's *Epode* 16, where the dream of an escape to the "Blessed Isles" in the far West is the geographical correlative of Virgil's chronological regression. Horace's vision, however, is far bleaker than Virgil's. He responds to Virgil's supposed Sibylline prophecy of release by alluding to another Sibylline prophecy in which Rome's destruction is foretold.[136] Horace's first line "corrects" Virgil's proclamation of the "*last* age" (*ultima . . . aetas*, 4). "No, not the last age" is the implication of Horace's opening—instead, "A *second/other* age is being worn away by civil war" (*Altera iam teritur bellis ciuilibus aetas*).[137] Virgil's language of repetition (*alter Tiphys, altera Argo, altera bella*), intended to be a looping back with a trajectory to a point beyond war, is turned back on him by Horace, so that the repetitions are now merely repeated, with cycles of civil war, instead of potentially glamorous Trojan wars, cycles that can never escape from their circularity.

The idea of the Golden Age is particularly associated with the Age of Augustus, and Augustus's promotion of a new Golden Age is the subject of numerous studies.[138] As often with studies of ideology, work on the Augustan Golden Age can create the impression of a very homogeneous system; especially in the fundamental work of Zanker (1988) the reader is introduced to a uniform programme, one reflected with little variation in the poems of Horace and Virgil and in the buildings and iconography of Augustus himself. Such an impression of uniformity does not do justice to what was "a highly differentiated concept."[139] In particular, the division we have already noted between Virgil and Horace carries on past the triumviral years, and one of the points on which they differ is precisely that of the possibility or desirability of a returning Age of Gold.[140] As Barker (1996) well argues, Virgil's conception of a returning Golden Age is distinctly idiosyncratic, and not just a reflection of a homogeneous ideology; as Barker further demonstrates, Horace continues to have serious misgivings about this Virgilian conception and is intent on correcting it in his later poetry, especially in the *Carmen Saeculare* of 17 B.C.E.

The *Carmen*'s performance at the Ludi Saeculares comes less than two years after Virgil's death and the posthumous publication of the *Aeneid*. In the sixth book of the epic, Horace and his peers will have read Anchises prophesying to his son Aeneas in the underworld that Augustus would "again found the golden ages in Latium, through the fields once ruled by Saturn" (*aurea condet/saecula qui rursus Latio regnata per arua/Saturno quondam, Aen.* 6.792–94). These words appear to be doing more than announcing a general conception of the return of *aurea saecula,* since planning for the Ludi Saeculares will have been already well under way before Virgil's death at the age of only fifty on 21 September 19 B.C.E.[141] Especially if we take note of the language Anchises uses at the end of this speech, where he speaks to his son in words translated from the Sibylline oracle that laid out the formula for the rituals of the Ludi, it looks to me as if Anchises' speech was written by a man with a commission: if Virgil had lived, he would have composed the *Carmen Saeculare.*[142] However that may be, and whatever Virgil might have written if he had been the one to compose the *Carmen,* there is no doubt that Horace's *Carmen,* despite its many debts to the *Aeneid,* refrains from endorsing the fantastic and mystical Virgilian conceptions of a returning Age of Gold.[143] Horace's deep misgivings about the moral associations of gold have a great deal to do with his reluctance to endorse Virgil's returning Age of Gold. As Barker argues, Horace had spent a lot of his career discoursing on the moral problems of gold in its literal, physical sense, and it is perhaps no surprise that he did not find it attractive to shift gear into endorsing the value of gold, even if it was warped towards a metaphorical register.[144]

METAPHOR OR BULLION?

Readers of the *Aeneid* may well remark that Virgil is himself already one step ahead of Horace, for it is possible to detect a typical Virgilian equivocation over goldenness built into the *Aeneid* in advance. The qualifications that Virgil introduces are not so much in Anchises' prophecy itself, but two books later, when Virgil shows us Aeneas on the future site of Rome in book 8, being led to the humble home of Evander. Evander informs his guest of the "first" Golden Age in Latium under Saturn, in language that should remind Aeneas, and certainly reminds the reader, of Anchises' earlier prophecy of Augustus's refounding of the Golden Age of Saturn: *aurea quae perhibent illo sub rege fuere/saecula* ("Under that king were the ages that they call golden," 324–25). This metaphorical goldenness is already being undone two lines later in Evander's history lesson, when he says that the next, "off-color," age (*decolor aetas*) brought in "love of possession" (*amor . . . habendi*, 326–27).[145] But the real cap to Evander's words comes twenty lines later, when the pair pass the Capitoline hill, described by the poet as "golden now, but at a remote point in time bristling with woody thickets" (*aurea nunc, olim siluestribus horrida dumis*, 348). The contemporary Age of Gold is marked by the physical material, blazing forth from the golden roof of the Capitoline temple of Jupiter, and it is inevitable that we ask how, and whether, the moral values of Saturn's metaphorical gold can be left unthreatened by the modern world's physical gold. The chronological disjunction between Evander's Rome and Augustus's, over a thousand years later, opens up a potential disjunction in values, captured in the two-edged references of "golden."[146] The opposed chronological and symbolic poles define each other: the more splendid the physical goldenness of the modern city, the more keenly the contrast with the time of origins is felt, and the more creative effort is poured into covering over, or prising open, the fissures.[147]

Ovid, predictably, is more interested in the prising open, and he plays up the tension between the literal and metaphorical reference of "gold" with great zest.[148] As so often, what look like finely discriminated nuances in Virgil look like shabby equivocations once Ovid has gone to work on them. For the modern Ovidian lover, the splendid wealth of Rome guarantees its sophistication, and the former state was one for bumpkins: *simplicitas rudis ante fuit; nunc aurea Roma est* ("Uncultured simplicity existed formerly; now there is golden Rome," *Ars Am.* 3.112; cf. 2.277–78: *aurea sunt uere nunc saecula: plurimus auro/uenit honos: auro conciliatur amor,* "Now truly are the ages of gold; the greatest number of honors are sold for gold; by gold is love procured"). Twin-headed Janus, who has seen both Golden Ages, of Saturn and of Augustus, is able to give Ovid valuable two-sided information in the *Fasti.* When Ovid asks him why he is given coins as well as honey on his feast day, Janus laughingly remarks that Ovid has been taken in by the ideologies of the current age if he thinks that honey is sweeter than cash (*risit et "o quam te fallunt tua saecula" dixit,/"qui stipe mel sumpta dulcius esse putas!"* *Fast.* 1.191–92). When Saturn was reigning, says Janus, he hardly saw a single person who was not fond of profit (193–94).[149] Janus agrees that the "love of possession" has grown (*amor . . . habendi,* 195, quoting *Aen.* 8.327), and gold has now ousted the old bronze (221), but there never was a time when the literal presence of money was not felt.[150] The gods like golden temples, however much they speak up for the old ones (223–24).[151] As the god who can see both sides of everything, Janus concludes, *laudamus ueteres, sed nostris utimur annis;/mos tamen est aeque dignus uterque coli* ("We praise the old days, but our own are the ones we live in; still, each custom is equally worth maintaining," 225–26).[152] Crucially, as Barchiesi remarks, there is no word in any of these Ovidian passages of the myth of an Augustan *return* to an Age of Gold;[153] instead, Ovid's Augustus is firmly associated with the Age of Iron, and with its presiding deity of Jupiter.[154]

Seneca likewise delivers himself of some mordant reflections on the degrading literalization of the metaphorical apparatus of the Golden Age, together with its new Neronian instantiation as an age of the golden Sun.[155] He draws on Ovid's picture of the golden palace and chariot of the Sun in order to shed oblique scorn on Nero's building projects, chariot racing, and glorification of the Sun;[156] he sums up, "Finally, the age they want to look the best they call 'Golden'" (*denique quod optimum uideri uolunt saeculum aureum appellant, Ep.* 115.13). As Champlin well remarks, "This passage shows startlingly open contempt for the new Golden Age. . . . The concept of a new Golden Age is turned upside down, not sublime but ignoble."[157]

The most savage comment on the pretentious hypocrisies that always threaten to topple the whole ideology comes from Tacitus, in his account of Nero's reign. He seizes on an opportunity to work with the friction between the various associations of gold when he opens *Annals* 16. Here he recounts the mania of a deluded Carthaginian, one Caesellius Bassus, who had a dream revealing to him the presence on his property of a vast cave stuffed with bullion (16.1.1). In accordance with his usual strategy of associating Nero with the spurious allure of the Virgilian myths, Tacitus makes this crackpot a second Dido, for she too had a significant dream about treasure in the earth, and it is supposedly her trove that lies beneath Bassus's land.[158] Nero's dream of a new Golden Age is wickedly made literal with this vision of physical hunks of unworked bullion lying underground, and the impossibility of Nero's fantasies is made real when Bassus's fantasies are dispelled. The absurdity of the yearning to return to the Golden Age of myth is further underlined with Tacitus's mocking report of how the bards and orators at Nero's quinquennial games latch on to the treasure hunt to make topical their references to the hackneyed themes of the Golden Age (16.2.4). The language of fruitfulness that usually allows goldenness a metaphorical reference is now grotesquely concretized, since these flatterers are talking of the earth bringing forth literal lumps of gold.[159]

AN UNBRIDGEABLE DIVIDE

An author who is often cited as evidence for Nero's renewed Golden Age is Calpurnius Siculus, a pastoral poet whose bucolics regularly allude to leitmotifs of the Neronian renaissance. His status as contemporary evidence, however, has been the subject of animated discussion since Champlin (1978) revived the formerly accepted but long abandoned view that Calpurnius belonged in the third century C.E. and not in the time of Nero. The weight of authority would now appear to be against a Neronian date;[160] pending further developments in the debate, and provisionally accepting Calpurnius as post-Neronian, we are left with the question of why someone in a later period would want to return to the Neronian era in this way, apparently going to considerable lengths to create the impression of a dramatic date in Nero's reign. The bizarre appeal of Nero's posthumous reputation must play some part, for rumors of his return swept the Eastern empire at periodic intervals.[161] Yet the strange nature of the yearning for a Golden Age acquires a new perspective if Calpurnius Siculus is indeed recreating such an atmosphere many years after Nero's death. This belated poet, whoever, and whenever, he was, appears to have penetrated to the heart of the whole ideology. He has intuited that at the core of these evocations of a Golden Age is the agony of nostalgia, the knowledge that the Golden Age is irretrievably lost and was—as Catullus in particular suggests—perhaps never something that human beings could reach a hand out to and grasp. Calpurnius Siculus, writing in an age even more fallen than Nero's, has given a cruel extra twist to this apprehension of nostalgia, which here becomes a kind of metanostalgia. In his postdated bucolics we may see not simply a nostalgia for a lost mythical Golden Age, but a nostalgia for a lost historical age in which you could still feel a nostalgia for a lost mythical Golden Age.

FIVE

· Years, Months, and Days I

Eras and Anniversaries

STARTING POINTS

In the first four chapters we investigated the ways in which Romans and Greeks worked together to construct significant temporal patterns as Roman horizons moved out to embrace the Mediterranean. The horizons of Roman time were progressively extended, reaching backwards to Troy and sideways to assimilate the synchronistic time systems that the Greeks had devised as an indispensable part of their own contentious historical sensibilities; further, key transitional moments in Greek mythology became a tool for the Romans to use in order to reflect on their status as an imperial people, guilty masters of nature and of technology. The final pair of chapters will adopt a more Romanocentric focus, concentrating on the time machines of the city itself. Here we shall consider distinctively Roman modalities for shaping time—their cult of the anniversary, their internal dating systems, and their molding of the temporal patterns of the year, especially in the form of that great Roman monument that we still inescapably inhabit, the Julian calendar.

We begin with eras, which mark off watersheds from which time may be counted, and with anniversaries, which link points in time. Often, anniversaries make their connections between points in time through symbolic totals of years (twenty, one hundred, and so on), but what most Roman anniversaries connect are significant days, so that already in this chapter we shall consider the beguiling intricacies of the mechanisms of the Roman calendar, in order to understand what is at stake in the recurrence of days. In the next, and final, chapter, we continue to investigate the power of the Roman Fasti, the monuments by which the city's time is organized and memorialized.

ERAS

The contemporary world takes the use of a particular era in dating so much for granted that surprisingly many people can be startled when they are reminded that the date "2007" is precisely the product of an era, a count from the watershed of the birth of Jesus Christ.[1] A less secularized Islam can less readily overlook the fact that the Muslim tally of years goes back to a specific event, the Hegira, or "departure," of the Prophet from Mecca in 622 C.E. Modern B.C./A.D. dates are so "natural" to us in all their utility and convenience, allowing projection forward into the future as easily as tracking back into the past, that it may seem automatic to assume that the Greeks and Romans would use the mechanism of orienting themselves in time by counting from an agreed mark in past time. As we have already seen in the first two chapters, however, eras hardly figured even in historiography, where the Olympiad system might appear tailor-made to assist historians, and outside these learned circles even the Olympiad system had no impact.[2] In general, the concept of the era had a circumscribed role to play in the life of the societies of the pre-Christian Greco-Roman Mediterranean.

There were certainly a great number of eras deployed by individual cities, provinces, and kingdoms.[3] Yet the only era that broke out of the commemorative or scholarly domain to impose itself on official practice and daily life was the Seleucid era.[4] This era was used as a dating system by the inheritors of Alexander's Persian domains, taking as year one the year we call 312/11 B.C.E., the year that Seleucus I reconquered Babylon. Strictly this only became an era (rather than simply a traditional regnal year count) when Seleucus's son Antiochus I succeeded him and continued the enumeration instead of beginning anew for his own reign.[5] The Seleucid era was a prominent feature of their empire, regularly used for official purposes of all kinds, and forming an integral part of their coercive apparatus.[6] The era was very tenacious, continuing in use by the Arabs after the Arab conquest—they called it the "era of the Romans," the "era of Alexander," or the "era of the two-horned one [Alexander]."[7]

With this sole, if important, exception, the eras are not really dating systems in any significant sense. The eras supplement, rather than replace, existing dating systems, and their status is honorific, so that often the only evidence for them is numismatic.[8] I do not mean to imply that the system of honorific exchange is not worth the serious attention of any historian, and it is obviously very important that the construction of time was part of the system of honorific exchange; yet we need always to remind ourselves that the eras were not dating systems, as they so inevitably appear to be. Eras could be invented for all kinds of purposes. Even Cicero could invent an era off the cuff, with some irony dating with a new era of "the battle of Bovillae" the brawl in which his archenemy Clodius was killed (18 January 52 B.C.E.): he arrived at Ephesus, he tells Atticus, 559 days after the battle of Bovillae.[9] "Real" battles were in fact regularly used as the anchor for eras. It has been argued that the so-called Macedonian era (148/7 B.C.E.) marked the victory in that year of Metellus over Andriscus.[10] Caesarian eras were used in the Greek East, counting from the battle of Pharsalus, and the battle of Actium likewise generated eras all over the region.[11] Pompey is an important figure in the history of Greek eras in the East, blazing a trail in this regard as in so many others, and we find numerous cities marking eras from the date when he liberated them from the Seleucids.[12]

If honorific eras of this kind are common in the Greek East, often prompted by actions of Roman generals or emperors, the Romans themselves showed very little interest in the eras of this part of their empire.[13] Correspondingly, it is very difficult to find eras in use in the Latin West. As Knapp points out in his important discussion of the *era consularis* in Cantabria, the Latin West shows only three eras actually in use, with the eras of Patavium and Mauretania the only other ones apart from the Cantabrian.[14] In Knapp's argument, the Cantabrian era emerges as a genuinely interesting case of a local piece of ad hoc identity construction. The Cantabrians took year one to be Vespasian's granting of Latinity to the region somewhere around 75 C.E., and they did this centuries after Vespasian, at a time of increasing chaos in Spain, as a way of grounding their identity in the face of the collapse of Roman authority and the encroachment of peoples from outside Spain.[15]

What of eras in the city of Rome itself? Unwary students can sometimes get the impression that the Romans in general used an era "A.U.C.," *ab urbe condita*, "from the foundation of the city." In fact, this is not the case, not least because agreement was never reached on a precise foundation date.[16] Only one coin survives that gives a date A.U.C., a Hadrianic coin from 121 C.E., marked as minted in the "874th birth year of the city" (*ann[o] DCCCLXXIIII nat[ali] urbis*).[17] This appears to be the only imperial coin that bears any date other than a regnal year.[18] Roman historians will sometimes say that something happened so many years after the foundation of the city, but their motive in each case is always something more than just providing a date, and they do not deploy this phraseology as part of an agreed system for chronographic organization. Livy uses this language in a symbolic fashion to create a sense of significant demarcation posts in the trajectory of the city's fate, with the Gallic sack coming 365 years after the foundation (5.54.5); or else he marks crucial constitutional innovations in this way, as if to chart the developmental phases in the life of the city, telling us that the Decemvirate was instituted 302 years (3.33.1) or the consular tribunes 310 years after the foundation of the city (4.7.1).[19] Here he is following the early Latin annalists, who likewise marked vital staging posts in the city's history in this way.[20] Cassius Hemina identifies the religious recuperation after the Gallic sack as taking place in the 363rd year from the foundation of the city,[21] while the first Greek doctor arrived in the 535th;[22] Calpurnius Piso noted the beginning of Rome's seventh *saeculum* in the 600th year.[23] Modern observers can scarcely help feeling that it would have been highly useful to employ A.U.C. as a dating mechanism, since it so closely resembles our own era dating, and when we see such a reference in Livy many will inevitably, but erroneously, take him to be supplying a date.[24] These apparent era dates are not, however, part of an understood dating system that exists independently outside the text, but rather symbolic exploitations of the pervasive interval-based chronographic systems we discussed in chapter 1.[25] As we shall see in the next chapter, the real temporal backbone for Roman historiography is not any era system, but the list of consuls, the Fasti Consulares.

A more likely candidate for a Roman era is the year of the simultaneous expulsion of the kings, foundation of the Republic, and dedication of Tarquin's long-planned Capitoline temple of Jupiter, a year regularly used as a time reference by writers in the late Republic.[26] Especially if there is a grounding to the tenacious story about the consuls banging a nail into the doorposts of the temple of Jupiter Optimus Maximus on the Ides of September every year, then the tradition that the Republic is coextensive in time with the temple will have corroborated the power of this foundational era.[27] The first attested date from a Roman source refers to this era, as Purcell (2003) has recently reminded us in the course of a fine evocation of the time machine embodied in the Capitoline hill in the mid-Republic. As we have already seen in chapter 3, the aedile Cn. Flavius dedicated a sanctuary of Concordia at the base of the Capitoline at the end of his turbulent term of office, in the year we call 304 B.C.E., and the sanctuary bore an inscription testifying that it had been dedicated in the 204th year *post Capitolinam aedem dedicatam*, "the 204th year after the dedication of the Capitoline temple [of Jupiter]" (Pliny *HN* 33.19).[28]

There is much debate about Flavius's method and purpose, and even about whether with this terminology he was referring to an agreed method of dating;[29] his technique may have been idiosyncratic, a way of avoiding the regular dating by the names of the consuls, with whom he had been feuding throughout his office, and a way of linking his dedication with the most prestigious of all religious monuments in the city.[30] As always, what look like dates are never just dates. Nonetheless, as Purcell has shown, the complex of the Capitoline is central to the consciousness of time in the middle Republic: the temple of Jupiter is acknowledged as coextensive in time with the Republic itself, standing as a visible embodiment of the duration and durability of the Republic; the annual eponymous consuls are closely linked with the cult of Jupiter; nearby stands the temple of Juno Moneta, "Remembrancer," a center for the preservation of memory.[31] In the next chapter we shall investigate what happens to this Republican era when the Republic is replaced by the new Principate.

ANNIVERSARIES OF YEARS

At the beginning of the Roman historiographical tradition, as we have already seen in chapter 3, the fall of Troy served to mark an important era. The first Latin history, that of Cato, fixed the foundation of the city by counting 432 years from the fall of Troy rather than by using Olympiads, as his predecessors Fabius Pictor and Cincius Alimentus had done in their Greek histories of the city.[32] Cato was capitalizing on, and transforming, the crucial importance of Troy in Greek time schemes. Troy's function in era counting helped it serve also as an anchor for anniversaries, and we move now to this different, though related, topic.

The use of Troy in anniversary contexts has been the subject of a splendid study by David Asheri (1983) that collects much fascinating evidence for the role of Troy in the construction of symbolically significant anniversaries, especially millenarian anniversaries. The canonical date for the fall of Troy after Eratosthenes came to be accepted as "1184/3 B.C.E.," but Duris of Samos and Timaeus, both writing before Eratosthenes, had a far earlier date, "1335/4 B.C.E."[33] A modern reader can look at this date and in a flash see the significance that comes from removing the first digit—334 is the year that Alexander the Great invaded Asia. Duris and Timaeus reveal that this invasion occurred exactly 1,000 years after the comrades of Alexander's ancestor Achilles sacked the prototypical Asiatic city. Alexander's invasion becomes part of a chain of significance, linking the historical present with the mythic past, and showing Greek history to be a long series of confrontations between the East and the West, culminating, as it began, in Greek victory.[34] Such historiographical constructions reflect and enhance Alexander's own cultivation of the resonances between his actions and those of his mythical forebears, from his sacrifices at the site of Troy to his fighting the initial battle of the Granicus in the same month as that of the fall of Troy.[35]

The most impressive Roman example of this millenarian use of the Trojan anniversary is not an absolutely certain one, although it is very tantalizing. The possibility was detected by Gratwick, who made an inspired suggestion about the frame of the first fifteen books of Ennius's *Annales*.[36] Ennius's initial plan was to go from the fall of Troy, in "1184/3 B.C.E.," the canonical date by his time, established by Eratosthenes, all the way down to his own time. When exactly in his own time did he stop? Gratwick suggests the year 184 B.C.E., the 1,000th anniversary of the fall of Troy. This year was important in various ways, bringing together crucial preoccupations of the poem as a whole.

First of all, the year was important to Ennius himself, since it was the year he became a Roman citizen, on the grounds of being enrolled as a member of a colony established in Pisaurum by Q. Fulvius Nobilior, the son of his patron at the time, M. Fulvius.[37] It is very attractive to think of the autobiographically inclined epic poet mentioning this fact in the culminating portion of the poem: the poet who has been celebrating the deeds of the *populus Romanus* actually becomes a member of the *populus Romanus* himself. He certainly mentioned this crucial event in his life at some point in the epic: *nos sumus Romani qui fuimus ante Rudini* ("I am now a Roman who was before a Rudian," fr. 525). The final book of the original fifteen-book edition is one of the most plausible locations for this proud assertion. The theme of the expansion and evolution of the Roman citizenship, marking the key turning points of Roman expansion, was clearly an important one for the poem as a whole. We have a mention of the granting of the *civitas sine suffragio* to the Campanians: *ciues Romani tunc facti sunt Campani* ("The Campanians were then made Roman citizens," fr. 157). Cornell compellingly suggests that this key moment marked the climax of the first pentad, with the end of the Latin War of 340–338 B.C.E.[38]

If the year 184 was important to Ennius, it was also important to Ennius's first patron, Cato, since it was the year that Cato was censor.[39] The year was likewise important to Ennius's current patron, M. Fulvius Nobilior, since, on Gratwick's hypothesis, this was the year that Fulvius dedicated, *ex manubiis* from his triumph over Aetolia in 187, the temple of Hercules Musarum, "Hercules of the Muses."[40] We return in the next chapter to the temporal power of this temple, which was a major Roman time machine, for it almost certainly housed, and almost certainly for the first time, both kinds of Roman Fasti, a list of consuls and a set of calendrical *fasti*. In addition, the temple of Hercules Musarum provided for the first time a physical home in Rome for the Greek Muses. The city had not had a cult of the Muses before, but the new temple housed the statues of the Muses that were looted from the city of Ambracia, the old capital of Rome's first overseas enemy, King Pyrrhus. These Muses were very much Pyrrhus's Muses, for the statues had been in Pyrrhus's old palace.[41] The Muses now have a physical home in Rome, just as Ennius's *Annales* provide them for the first time with a poetic home in Rome; this massive piece of ring composition carries us back to the beginning of the poem, which opened with the word *Musae*, as the first Roman poet to invoke the Greek Muses began his unprecedented task.[42] The fall of Ambracia, commemorated in the triumph of 187 and the temple of *(ex hypothesi)* 184, "must have seemed a culminating point in history."[43]

Ennius's fifteen books, then, will have contained a thousand-year span of Roman history, from apparent total destruction by the Greeks to military and cultural triumph over the Greeks. And this significant span of Roman time is being constructed using a millenarian calculation from the fall of Troy of the kind that had originally been constructed by Greeks, to demonstrate Greek triumphalism over Asia. Now, however, the tables are turned, and the thousand-year span is being used to demonstrate Roman triumphalism over Greece as the Romans rise from the ashes of Troy. Ennius's Hellenistic cultural inheritance is the ideal environment to locate this kind of searching out of significant patterns of reciprocity and reversal in history, structured around symbolic numbers.[44] If the Alexander cult claimed that the descendant of Achilles had finally laid the Asiatic threat to rest after a thousand years, then Ennius claims that the descendants of the defeated Asiatics have looped back to conquer the homeland of another descendant of Achilles, the would-be Alexander, Pyrrhus.

Millenarian numbers continued to exercise their fascination, with Troy's fall regularly being superseded by the foundation of the city as the epoch for calculation. In the third century C.E. the historian Asinius Quadratus found it opportune to place the foundation of the city in "776 B.C.E.," partly so that he could have a thousand-year span of time from then down to his own time: his history was entitled Ῥωμαικὴ Χιλιετηρίς, "Rome's Thousand Years."[45] Not very long after Asinius Quadratus, Philip the Arab staged celebratory games in 248 C.E. to fall on the 1,000th anniversary of the foundation of the city, using the foundation date of "753 B.C.E."[46] The appeal of ten units of one hundred years was strong, and Christianity produced many variations of significant multiples of the talismanic "1,000."[47] Other groupings of units of one hundred were also popular in constructing pre-Christian anniversaries. Claudius celebrated games in 47 C.E. to mark the 800th anniversary of the city's foundation, and Antoninus Pius celebrated the 900th anniversary in 147 C.E.[48] It is just about possible that contemporaries descried the same significance in the year 117 C.E. as Syme, who calculates 1,300 years from the fall of Troy to this portentous year, the year of Hadrian's accession.[49]

As these examples show, the century of one hundred years was a crucial link in the chains of significance that were forged between past and present. Sometimes the bare century carried its own symbolic power.[50] The African fate of the Scipios is a probable example: P. Cornelius Scipio Aemilianus Africanus conquered Carthage in 146 B.C.E., while another Scipio, Q. Caecilius Metellus Pius Scipio, was defeated in Libya by Caesar in the civil wars exactly one hundred years later.[51] In 44 B.C.E. Caesar started to rebuild Carthage as a Roman colony, and likewise Corinth, which had been destroyed along with Carthage in 146 B.C.E.; Diodorus Siculus comments that Corinth's rebuilding took place "nearly one hundred years" after its destruction (32.27.1–3), and Dio Cassius reports that Caesar deliberately planned the simultaneous rebuilding of the cities that had been simultaneously destroyed (43.50.4–51.1). The one hundred years could be further broken down, for anniversaries of imperial accession and so on, into tens and fives.[52]

THE *SAECULUM*

We are all very familiar with the century in our own experience, and it is deceptively easy to read our century into the Roman time unit of the *saeculum*. Eventually the *saeculum* did come regularly to denote our "century" of one hundred years, but originally and for long it did not have this sole meaning.[53] Even when it did, it referred not to a preexisting grid of time but was used as part of the interval-spacing era mentality, being mobilized from any ad hoc point of departure. Rather than a "century" in the modern sense, then, *saeculum* denoted a "generation," particularly a generation measured as the life span of the longest-lived individual in the community.[54] Accordingly, as is pointed out by our best source, Censorinus, mediating Varro, the actual span of a Roman *saeculum* is elastic (*modus Romani saeculi est incertus, DN* 17.7), even though the Roman state has fixed the *saeculum* at one hundred years (17.13). Censorinus is here working from the normal Varronian distinction between the "civil" and the "natural" (17.1).[55] This distinction, as usual, cannot escape deconstruction for very long. Censorinus links the *saeculum* of nature to the moment of city foundation, so that the natural is indissolubly associated with the civil: according to Etruscan lore, which ultimately lies behind these Roman obsessions, the end of a city's first *saeculum* comes with the death of the last person who was born on the day of the city's foundation, at which point another *saeculum* begins, to terminate in its turn with the death of the last member of the second cohort (17.5). The Etruscan *saecula* of this tradition, then, vary in length, with the first four lasting 100 years, the fifth 123, the sixth and seventh 119: at the time of Varro, whom Censorinus is using here, the eighth was now in progress, and the end of the Etruscan name would come with the end of the tenth (17.6).

The eschatological power of this secular scheme is very clear. It must have emerged from some Etruscans' contemplation of their impending cultural obliteration after their absorption into the Roman commonwealth, a contemplation given new focus especially after the definitive annihilation of their military capacity in the Social and Sullan wars.[56] This environment, so hospitable to eschatological speculation, produced the memorable moment in 88 B.C.E. when a celestial trumpet blast and other portents were interpreted by Etruscan specialists summoned by the Senate as announcing "a change to another generation and a change in condition" (μεταβολὴν ἑτέρου γένους ... καὶ μετακόσμησιν, Plut. *Sull.* 7.3). As Plutarch goes on to explain, the Etruscans believed that there were eight ages (not ten, as in the reports of Varro and Censorinus), differing in quality, whose ends were announced by a wonderful sign from earth or heaven.[57]

The same period and environment have regularly been seen as the most likely general setting for the "prophecy of Vegoia," an intriguing text that most scholars have taken to be an early first-century B.C.E. translation from Etruscan into Latin.[58] The "prophecy" displays knowledge of the Etruscan secular scheme, opening with cosmogony and speaking of "the greed of the eighth *saeculum* now almost at its end."[59] J. N. Adams, however, does not believe that the "prophecy" is a first-century translation, concluding that "the piece on linguistic grounds appears to be imperial, and has no place in a discussion of Latin-Etruscan bilingualism."[60] On the assumption that Adams is right, the text still remains important as confirmation of the Romans' abiding fascination with the Etruscan secular schemes. Roman interest in this secular eschatology was activated especially in the crisis-ridden atmosphere of the collapsing Republic. In 44 B.C.E. another spectacular sign from heaven, the comet following Caesar's death, was interpreted by an Etruscan haruspex as portending the end of the ninth *saeculum* and the beginning of the tenth.[61]

He promptly died, confirming the Etruscan definition of *saeculum*: "he died because he was the last member of his generation, of the past *saeculum*."[62] A ninth *saeculum* ending in 44 does not consort with an eighth ending in 88, and it is clear that the Etruscan experts, like all such, were adept at juggling their frames to suit the contemporary demands.[63] Varro, as we have already seen, showed an interest in the Etruscan *saecula*, transmitting to us, via Censorinus, the ten-*saecula* format (*DN* 17.6). He was able to adapt the scheme to Roman needs as well. Censorinus relates from Varro's *Antiquitates* the engaging story in which Varro tells how he heard one Vettius, an expert in augury, interpret the twelve vultures of Romulus according to a secular formula (*DN* 17.15): the vultures cannot have stood for decades, since the Roman people had safely got past the 120-year milestone, so they must have symbolized centuries, guaranteeing 1,200 years for Rome from the time of Romulus's foundation.[64]

The Roman state institutionalized the *saeculum* in the ceremony of the Ludi Saeculares, a religious ritual that marked the end of one *saeculum* and the beginning of the next.[65] The Ludi Saeculares are a most impressive and subtle tool for working with time, focusing on the discrepancy between the life span of the individual and of the community, between "natural" and "civil" time, as Varro would put it: even though the longest-lived individual in the city may see only one celebration of the Ludi, the state still continues, outstripping the fate of the singletons who make up the collective.[66] The rite, at least in its Augustan incarnation, the only one for which we have adequate evidence, provides a pivot for looking backwards and forwards in time, invoking the gods to help the city in the future, as they have in the past. It is a symbolic rupture of great power when the first Christian emperor breaks this continuity and refrains from celebrating the Ludi Saeculares on schedule in 314 C.E.[67] The new dispensation would have its own way of ensuring that it endured *per saecula saeculorum*.

All of these schemes—eras, millennial and centennial anniversaries, epochs and *saecula*—are attempts to impose meaningful shape on the flux of past time, and to create a sensation of monitored progress through time. They are of particular importance in a setting where there was no one common grid of chronology, but a medley of diverse tools for orientation in time. Patterns were not picked out of a preexisting frame of decades and centuries grounded on an unshakable foundation, as may so readily be done now, but manufactured anew on many occasions. It is perhaps easy to regard the various calculations with condescension as misguided numerology, and to patronize the attempts to seek significance in what are after all mere contingent digits. Readers who lived through the hysteria of Y2K will be able to remind themselves that, on occasion, mere numbers become talismanic to any audience.[68]

ANNIVERSARIES OF DAYS

The anniversaries we have been considering so far all fall under the heading of what Grant calls "anniversary years."[69] We turn now to the kind of anniversary that links days. Any given day can acquire meaning or resonance by being the anniversary of another day on which something memorable took place, and any society with a calendar pays some attention to marking the recurrence of days that bear the stamp of important past events.[70] The Greeks certainly had an interest in significant days and their commemoration;[71] but the Roman fascination with anniversary days goes deeper, a reflex of their deeper investment in the annual calendar as a unifying grid for their culture.[72] The impact of the calendar with its annually recurring opportunities for anniversary commemorations made itself felt both in everyday life and in public contexts.[73] Tombs were important venues for anniversary sacrifices, and Virgil devotes the fifth book of the *Aeneid* to the games commemorating the anniversary of Anchises' death.[74] Temples had their dedication days, to be celebrated with care every year: very significantly, the Romans called this day the temple's "birthday," *dies natalis*.[75] As individuals, too, the Romans devoted great attention to the observing of annual birthdays, unlike the Greeks, who regularly had no anniversary at all, and marked only the day of the month.[76] If you were a Greek and were born on the twelfth day of the month, then each month on the twelfth day you might have an extra bowl of wine and pour a libation; but if you were a Roman you celebrated an annual birthday, just as we do. Centered for men around the cult of their *genius* and for women around the cult of their *iuno,* the birthday was a significant moment in the year for any free individual, and friends likewise joined in honoring the occasion.[77]

Romans were alert to the potential symbolic power of birthdays in many contexts. Cicero and the people of Brundisium dwelt on the apparently significant concatenation of birthdays that clustered on the day he arrived there on his return from exile. The birthday of the colony of Brundisium itself was 5 August; it was founded on that day in 244 B.C.E.; it was likewise the birthday of Cicero's daughter Tullia, who welcomed him there, and of the temple of Salus.[78] Pompey carefully planned his triumph in 61 B.C.E. to coincide with his forty-fifth birthday on 29 September, waiting seven months after his return from the East before entering the city.[79] Observers could not resist dwelling on the apparent irony that he was murdered either the day before his birthday or the day after or—ideally—on the very day itself.[80] The dramatic crises of the civil war produced other such striking birthday stories for historians and biographers to savor. Cicero relished the coincidence whereby news of D. Brutus's victory at Mutina on 21 April 43 B.C.E. was announced in Rome on the very day of Brutus's birthday.[81] It was on his birthday that Cassius suffered defeat at Philippi and committed suicide.[82] According to Plutarch and Appian, M. Brutus was celebrating his birthday when he suddenly shouted out a line from Homer: ἀλλά με μοῖρ' ὀλοὴ καὶ Λητοῦς ἔκτανεν υἱός ("But destructive fate and Apollo the son of Leto have killed me," Il. 16.849).[83] There was no rationale to this (ἀλόγως), says Appian; "for no reason" (ἀπ' οὐδεμιᾶς προφάσεως), says Plutarch: but Brutus is very likely to have been alluding to the birthday status of his enemy Octavian, for it was highly important to Octavian, as we shall see shortly, that he shared a birthday with Apollo.[84]

The anniversary mentality is surprisingly rich and far-reaching. Any day can turn into a significant day and have its date charged with meaning, unpredictably—7 December, 11 September, 6 June. Days that are significant for one thing can fortuitously become significant for something else altogether, since there is no rhyme or reason to the accumulated sedimentation of events clustered on a contingent daily basis. As Beard (1987) demonstrated for the Roman calendar, taking as her test case the Parilia, the birthday of Rome on 21 April, the new associations of a particular day can overlap or compete with, or contradict, the old ones.[85] A. Barchiesi (1997) has explored the implications for Ovid's Fasti, with a telling example from the Ides of March. For centuries, this was the date for the popular picnic feast of Anna Perenna, but then it became famous for another reason altogether, the death of Caesar and, in Ovid's treatment in Fasti 3 (705–10), the revenge of Caesar's heir. As Barchiesi puts it, "Which would you prefer, a jolly picnic in the open air, complete with food, wine, and lovemaking, or the slaughter of the conspirators? The calendar guarantees that the two options will always be open, on every new 15 March."[86] Again, Horace opens Carm. 3.8 with a question from Maecenas, asking why Horace, a bachelor, should be celebrating the first day of March, the festival of the matrons of Rome (Martiis caelebs quid agam Kalendis, 3.8.1). It is indeed bizarre that he should be sacrificing on the Matronalia, which has a corporate meaning that would appear to exclude a bachelor such as himself; but the contingency of the calendar is radical, for this just happened to be the day that he was almost killed by the falling tree, and he must now give thanks for his deliverance each year on 1 March (Carm. 3.8.6–9).

THE MECHANICS OF
ANNIVERSARY CALCULATION

Before exploring the theme further, it is worth pausing to reflect on what exactly an anniversary is. What does it actually mean to say that "today" is the anniversary of another day? The issue is not so hard if we are talking about dates since the Gregorian reform of Julius Caesar's calendar of 45 B.C.E., which means since 1582 in most of Europe, since 1752 in Britain and the North American colonies (Britain always lags behind European initiatives), 1918 in Russia, 1923 in Greece. Since the reform, anniversaries have some kind of logic, for the calendar is the same, but anniversaries across the divide, including those reaching back to the ancient world, are factitious. In 1582 ten days were dropped to allow for the uncorrected shifts since Caesar's time: "Adjustment was necessary because the Julian year, consisting of 365 days, with a 366th day added every fourth year, has an average length of 365 days 6 hours, which is some 11 minutes 12 seconds too long, causing Julian dates to fall progressively further behind the sun."[87] This was done in such a way that 4 October was immediately followed by 15 October—Virgil's birthday, as it happens.[88] If you wish to celebrate an anniversary across that divide, then, you cannot claim that a precise number of years has passed since the corresponding day in the original year, whether you use a sidereal year, with the planet facing precisely the same spot in space, having revolved a given number of times every 365 days, 6 hours, 9 minutes, and 9.5 seconds, or a tropical year, calculating from spring equinox to spring equinox, a slightly different year of 365 days, 5 hours, 48 minutes, and 45.2 seconds.[89]

Anyone raising a glass of wine in Virgil's honor on 15 October is performing a commemoration but cannot strictly be said to be observing an anniversary, a turning of the year to the same place. In fact, the chaotic state of the pre-Julian Republican calendar means that we do not know when in plottable time Virgil was born: 15 October 70 B.C.E. certainly did not fall on what an astronomer would call 15 October. Dates from the Republican period, unless they can be controlled by astronomical data, are not precise indicators of time, but conventional expressions: "historical dates, even in modern authors, should be understood as pertaining to the Republican, not the retrojected Julian calendar: the statement that Cicero was born on 3 January 106 B.C. refers to *a.d. III Nonas Ianuarias Q. Servilio Caepione C. Atilio Serrano coss. [= consulibus]*, not to 3 January in the 106th Julian year before the Christian era."[90] As a result of these difficulties, historians of Republican Rome and of the modern period use a makeshift for chronology, simply sticking to

Republican dates before the Caesarian reforms, as in the example of Cicero's birth-day just quoted, and to Julian dates for events between the Caesarian and Gregor-ian reforms.

Anniversaries across these divides, then, are not strictly anniversaries. You have to take your dates extremely seriously to think this is not good enough. You have to take your dates as seriously as the Protestants of Northern Ireland, who observe the battle of the Boyne on 12 July every year. The battle, hallowed in their tradi-tion as the victory of Protestantism over Catholicism in Ireland, was fought in 1690, on 1 July in the Julian calendar, which was then still in force in Britain, but the Loyalists faced a problem when the Gregorian calendar was introduced in Britain in 1752, 170 years after the rest of Europe, because eleven days had to be dropped.[91] The "new" 1 July was simply not acceptable as the anniversary of the Boyne, because it would not really be *the same day* in exact calculation of years and days. The Protestants therefore kept the skipped eleven days of the 1752 reform, on the calculation that even if the date was different—12 July, not 1 July—the *day* remained the same. Nowadays the twelfth is canonical in its own right, and they have not kept adding an extra day roughly every century to track the original 1 July, as they strictly should: the power of the date trumps the power of the day in the end.

In the United States people usually first meet this issue with George Washing-ton's birthday. He was born on 11 February 1732, when Britain and its colonies were still using the old Julian calendar. Washington turned twenty on 11 February 1752, and then faced the question of when to celebrate his twenty-first birthday after the eleven days were dropped between 2 and 14 September later in the year. In the event, Washington did not celebrate his next birthday on 11 February 1753, because that would not have been 365 days after 11 February 1752, thanks to the missing eleven days; logically enough, he celebrated his next birthday 365 days after his previous one, and that was on 22 February. For quite a while in the early Republic people kept celebrating 11 February as Washington's birthday, because that, after all, had been the name of the day he was actually born on; but eventu-ally the nation adopted 22 February as his "real" birthday.[92]

CALIBRATING ACROSS
THE JULIAN REFORM

Issues rather similar to those facing Washington and his peers also confronted the Romans when they were keeping track of birthdays and religious festivals after the

Julian reform, and their solutions are highly revealing of their attitudes to the identity of days and dates.[93] Caesar's reform took effect from 1 January 45 B.C.E.—though "reform" is a misleading word for what he did, as we shall see in more detail in the final chapter, for "Caesar did not reform the Roman calendar, but abandoned it and instituted the solar calendar of 365¼ days which was stable and agreed with the seasons."[94] In order to understand the implications of the reform for anniversaries across the divide, a brief introduction to the workings of the Roman Republican calendar is necessary; those who have these facts already at their fingertips may skip over the next two paragraphs.[95]

Roman calculation of the date was very different from the calculation we use. We start at the beginning of the month and count forward: January 1, 2, 3, and so on.[96] The Romans did not do this forward counting. They had three fixed points in each month, and they counted down, "backwards," to whichever of these points was coming up next. Each month is split in half by the Ides (*Idus*), a name that the Romans thought came from an Etruscan word meaning "to divide."[97] In the Republican calendar, four months are long months of 31 days, in which case the Ides split them in the middle on the fifteenth day; the rest are short months of 29 days, or 28 in the case of February, in which case the Ides split them in the middle on the thirteenth day. Nine days before the Ides comes another marker day. The Latin word for "ninth" is *nonus*, so the ninth day before the Ides is called the Nones (*Nonae*).[98] The only catch here is that the Romans counted inclusively, counting both pegs at the end of a sequence instead of only one as we do, so that nine days before the Ides for them is eight days before the Ides for us. In a long month, by Roman counting, the Nones will be on what we call the seventh day of the month, nine inclusive days before the fifteenth day; in a short month, the Nones will be on the fifth day, nine inclusive days before the thirteenth. The Ides, then, split the month, and nine inclusive days before the Ides come the Nones. The third of the three fixed points in the month is the first day, the Kalends (*Kalendae*).[99]

The fixed markers of Kalends, Nones, and Ides serve as orientation as the month progresses, but you count down to the next marker coming (always inclusively), and not forward from the last one. The Ides of March, to take the most famous Roman date as an example for orientation, is on the fifteenth day of the month, splitting in half the long, 31-day, month of March. Once we are past the Nones (our "seventh" day of March), we are counting down (always inclusively) toward the Ides. Accordingly, our "thirteenth," two days before the Ides, as we would see it, is for the inclusively counting Romans *three* days before and so is called "the third day before the Ides," *ante diem tertium Idus*.[100] Our "fourteenth," the day before the Ides of March, is called, very simply, "the day before the Ides," *pridie Idus*. Then come the Ides themselves, and after they are passed we are counting down to the next marker, the Kalends of the next month, April. What we think of as the sixteenth day of March, the day after the Ides, is for the Romans seventeen (inclusive) days before the next Kalends: *ante diem septimum decimum Kalendas Aprilis*. We keep counting down (sixteen days before the Kalends, fifteen days before, and so on) until we hit the Kalends of April, and once we have arrived at the Kalends of April we start counting down until we hit the Nones of April, then the Ides, and then we count down to the next Kalends, the Kalends of May, and so on through the year.

The Republican calendar had four long months with 31 days—March, July, October, May.[101] The other months were all short, with 29 days, apart from February, with 28. Even the mathematically challenged can see that $(31 \times 4) + (29 \times 7) + 28$ adds up to only 355.[102] Caesar had to add ten days to get the 365 he needed.[103] He left the long months and February alone, and added these ten extra days, the *dies additi*, to the seven short 29-day months, to make them up to 30 or 31, creating the month lengths we still use. The extra one or two days went at the end of the month in each case.[104] The position of the Nones and Ides was therefore totally unaffected, and the dating of any festivals counting down to the Nones and Ides was likewise totally unaffected.[105] In the second half of the month, however, after the Ides, as we have just seen, the Romans counted down to the beginning of the next month, the Kalends, and having one or two extra days at the end of a month is going to change this counting. When a festival (or a birthday) fell between the Ides and the following Kalends in a month whose length had changed, Caesar notionally had a choice, rather similar to the one facing the Ulster Loyalists or George Washington. He could leave the festival on the same date, or he could leave it on the same day. In other words, if the festival had fallen so many days before the next Kalends in the old calendar, he could leave it the same number of days before the next Kalends in the new calendar, even if the Kalends had "moved" one or two days farther away. Leaving the festival with the same "date" in this way, however, would mean that the "day" would change, for the festival would now be further removed from the Ides, tugged toward the end of the now longer month by the attraction of the now more distant Kalends, to which it was inextricably tied for dating. The wish to keep the festivals where it felt as if they had always been was too strong to allow for this possibility. What Caesar did was to leave the festivals on the same "day," the same number of days after the Ides, even though this meant changing their "date," the notation that marked their position relative to the following Kalends.[106]

The festival of Apollo may serve as an example. The anniversary of the foundation of his temple in 431 B.C.E. fell, in the Republican calendar, on what we call 23 September. Since the Republican September had 29 days, the Romans' equivalent of 23 September was "the eighth day [by inclusive counting] before the Kalends of October," *ante diem octavum Kalendas Octobris*. Caesar's reform, however, added one more day to September to make it a 30-day month. If Apollo's day had stayed on the Republican date, "the eighth day before the Kalends of October," then it would have moved one day away from its old spot, since there was now one more day to go before reaching the Kalends. Caesar's formula instead leaves Apollo's festival on the same "day," the same number of days after the Ides, but it now needs a different date: it is now no longer eight but nine days before the Kalends of October: *ante diem nonum Kalendas Octobris*.

I have not selected the example of the festival of Apollo at random, because "23 September" is of course also the birthday of Augustus, and we may use this day to return to the Roman birthday.[107] Suetonius records that the future Augustus was born on "the ninth day before the Kalends of October" (*Aug.* 5); since he was born in the year 63 B.C.E., under the Republican calendar, the question immediately arises of whether Suetonius is giving a Republican date (corresponding to 22 September, in a 29-day September) or a Julian one (corresponding to 23 September, in the new 30-day September). I am sure that Suerbaum is correct to argue that Augustus was born on the festival of Apollo, twenty-three days into the month, and that the same thing happened to his birthday as happened to the festival: between 63 and 46 B.C.E. his birthday and the festival were both described as "the eighth (inclusive) day before the Kalends of October," and from 45 B.C.E. on birthday and festival were both described as "the ninth (inclusive) day before the Kalends of October."[108] The coincidence of his birth on the day of Apollo must have mattered greatly to Augustus, who cultivated this god all his life: the last thing he will have wanted to do in September of 45 B.C.E. was to celebrate his eighteenth birthday on a day that for the first time was not the feast day of Apollo. Still, his recalibration of the date of his birthday obviously generated a degree of confusion, and some keen, or cautious, cities celebrated his birthday on both the eighth and the ninth day before the Kalends of October just to be absolutely sure.[109]

Others recalibrated their birthdays as well. Some birthdays, of course, just as some festivals, were left unaffected by Caesar's reform. If your birthday fell in the first half of the month, between the Kalends and the Ides, there was no problem, since there were no extra days inserted except at the end of the month; only if your birthday fell between Ides and Kalends was there an issue. Augustus is not the only observable case of a person in this situation who treated his or her birthday as Caesar treated the festivals, keeping the same "day," but changing the notation. This could have highly bizarre results, as Suerbaum has finely demonstrated in the case of M. Antonius.[110]

Antonius was born in 83 B.C.E. on the day after the Ides of January (not that he would have described the day in that way).[111] By the Republican calendar then in operation, January is a short, 29-day, month, with the Ides falling on the thirteenth day: according to our system, then, he was born on the fourteenth day of January. To find the Roman date for this, since he is born after the Ides, Antonius must count down (inclusively) to the next marker, the Kalends; since January has 29 days, his Republican birthday is "the seventeenth (inclusive) day before the Kalends of February," *ante diem septimum decimum Kalendas Februarias*. On 1 January 45 B.C.E., however, January acquires two extra days, to become a 31-day month, so that Antonius faces a choice when he prepares to celebrate his thirty-eighth birthday in that same month, his first birthday under the new Julian calendar. Should he celebrate his birthday on the seventeenth day before the Kalends of February, as he always had? In that case, however, he would be celebrating his birthday two days later, on the third day after the Ides, not the day after the Ides. What he did was to keep celebrating his birthday on the day after the Ides, and the notation changes accordingly, in just the same way as we observed for the festival of Apollo and the birthday of Augustus. The day after the Ides of January is no longer seventeen (inclusive) days before the first day of February, but nineteen: *ante diem nonum decimum Kalendas Februarias*.

This new Julian date, however, produces a bizarre result, for it is not a possible date in the Republican calendar. When Antonius was born there was no such date as "the nineteenth day before the Kalends of February," since the farthest back you can count from the next Kalends in a 29-day month before you bump into the Ides is seventeen days: in the Republican calendar, nineteen days before the first day of February is actually the day before the Ides of January. Antonius's new Julian birthday, then, is an anniversary of the *day* he was born in some sense, but it is not actually the *date* on which he was born, because when he was born this date could not exist. This piquant but inconsequential result of the recalculation suddenly acquired a potent weight of significance after Antonius's death, when his memory was damned. As commemorated on the Fasti Verulani, the Senate voted to mark the calendar for "nineteen days before the Kalends of February" as a *dies uitiosus*, "a defective day," unfit for public business, and the reason is given: *Antoni natalis*, "the birthday of Antonius." Except that, in a sense, it is not—because when he was born that date did not exist. As Suerbaum well puts it, it is as if the Senate is saying not simply, "It would have been better for Rome if Antonius had never been born," but somehow almost "Antonius never *was* born."[112] The deprivation of the birthday brutally reinforces Antonius's nonexistence.

If Augustus and Antony are examples of people who kept their birthday on the same day even if it meant a different—in Antony's case, a "nonexistent"—date, then Augustus's wife Livia is an example of a person who kept her birthday on the same date even if it meant a different, "non-existent," day.[113] Livia's Julian birthday under Augustus was "the third (inclusive) day before the Kalends of February," *ante diem tertium Kalendas Februarias;*[114] since January in the Julian calendar has 31 days, this translates into 30 January. Now Livia cannot conceivably have been born thirty days into the month of January, since when she was born, in 58 B.C.E., under the Republican calendar, January was a short month of 29 days. In 58 B.C.E. Livia must have been born on "the third (inclusive) day before the Kalends of February," *ante diem tertium Kalendas Februarias*, on the twenty-eighth day of January as it then was; when the Julian reform came she simply went on celebrating her birthday on "the third day before the Kalends" as before, except that now the identical "date" denoted a different day. If she had done what Antonius and Augustus did, then she would have celebrated her birthday on "the fifth day before the Kalends of February" instead, keeping to the original "day," twenty-eight days into the month, sixteen days after the Ides, and redescribing it according to the new calendar.

THE BIRTHDAY AS AN ANNIVERSARY

It has been claimed that the Romans recalibrated their birthdays wholesale after the Julian reform to take systematic account of the 445 days of the year 46 B.C.E., rather as George Washington and his peers recalibrated theirs to take account of the 11 days dropped from 1752.[115] In fact, the Romans did not do so.[116] One reason they did not go to this trouble is no doubt that until the Julian calendar had a chance to sink in and become part of their mental equipment they did not have any fixed conception that there had to be an absolutely regular span of time from one birthday to the next, or indeed from any date in the year until the corresponding date in the next year.[117] George Washington knew in his bones that his birthday each year ought to be 365 days after the preceding one, or occasionally 366, just as we do;[118] but for a Roman under the Republican calendar a year could be anything from 355 days to 378 days long, because every other year the priests were supposed to add 22 or 23 days by inserting an intercalary month at the end of a truncated February.[119] The Republican year, then, is a flexible unit, and it is hard to see how they could have a highly developed sense of an invariably fixed span between one birthday and the next, or from any one date in the year to the next.

From this point of view it perhaps looks more sensible to celebrate just the day each month, in the Greek way, rather than an anniversary, as the Romans had done for centuries under the Republic. But the Republican calendar's system of notation itself must have encouraged the feeling that the day you were born on was one that was the same every year, and not the same every month. After all, if you are a Greek then you can say the tenth of the month is the same every month, but it does not work like that for the Romans. Cicero was born on what we would call the third day of January, and what a Greek would call the third day of January, which is what a Roman calls the third (inclusive) day before the Nones of January. In the next month, February, the third day of the month is also the third day before the Nones, but in March the third day of the month is the *fifth* day before the Nones, because March is a long month with Nones on the seventh day, not the fifth. Your birthday, then, was not necessarily the same day every month, but it *was* the same day every year. The name of the day was enough to create the identity, without the feeling that the anniversary marked the passage of an inflexible unit of time since the last day of that name.

One of the first consequences of Caesar's reform, however, must have been to change this apprehension of anniversary time, since it was now possible to conceive of an anniversary not just as the recurrence of a day but as the recurrence of a day after an identical interval every year. Hinds points out how Ovid highlights the impact of the new system in the way he describes his birthday in his autobiographical poem, *Tristia* (4.10). Here Ovid tells us that he had an older brother, who had been born "three times four months" before him—and on exactly the same day (*qui tribus ante quater mensibus ortus erat./Lucifer amborum natalibus affuit idem*, 10–12). Ovid's brother, then, was born on 20 March 44 B.C.E., only fifteen months after the reform, and Ovid himself on 20 March 43 B.C.E.; as Hinds well puts it, "the 365-day coincidence of birthdays between Ovid and his brother . . . constitutes one of the first true Roman anniversaries (in the modern sense) ever documented. . . . Behind the special case of the two Ovidian brothers lies the larger truth that, given the systemic irregularity in the computation of the year before 45

B.C.E., *no* individual older than the Julian reform could ever be in a position to share Ovid's birth-anniversary, in the post-Julian sense, *or indeed to have any continuous possession of his own.*"[120]

It is plausible to see the impact of the Julian reform making itself felt also in the sudden new Augustan interest in the genre of the birthday poem. There are no birthday poems in Catullus, interestingly, and Philodemus's invitation to Piso to join him on the morrow for the celebration of Epicurus's "Twentieth," certainly pre-Julian in date, "does not qualify as a birthday poem."[121] After the calendar reform, however, Roman poets show a sustained and pointed interest in writing poems on their own and on friends' birthdays.[122] Tellingly, it is only under Augustus that we first see Greeks writing in the tradition of the *genethliacon*, "birthday poem."[123] The first recorded practitioner, Crinagoras of Mytilene, was a frequent sojourner in the city of Rome and mixed intimately with the highest circles there; three of his surviving epigrams, addressed to Greeks and Romans, accompany, or ventriloquize as, birthday gifts, although they do not lay stress on the return of the day in the way the Roman poems so often do.[124] It has been suggested that Crinagoras's initiative lies behind the Roman interest in the form;[125] it is far more likely that this visitor was struck by the Roman interest in the anniversary and adapted the form to his knowledge of "dedication" poems.

THE "SAME" DAY

The long-standing Roman interest in anniversaries gains new force, then, after Caesar's reform. In particular, the already strong Republican sense of the identity of the day from year to year is now given new edge by the intuition that the same identical span of time is linking the recurring day in every manifestation. This conception of each particular day remaining the same day, whatever the year, is certainly one of the most striking features of the Roman anniversary mentality. I first became properly aware of it over twenty years ago when I was marking a piece of prose composition.[126] I had set my students the close of Ronald Syme's *Roman Revolution*, the obituary notice of Augustus. One sentence in particular gave my students trouble: "He died on the anniversary of the day when he assumed his first consulate after the march on Rome."[127] Dissatisfied with their solutions, and uncertain how to do it myself, I was saved by the thought that Syme was artistically grafting the end of the *Roman Revolution* onto the beginning of Tacitus's *Annals*, making his masterpiece the prequel to Tacitus's by writing the history of Augustus that Tacitus had said he would write if he lived long enough (*Ann.* 3.24.3).

Turning, then, to the competing obituary notices of Augustus that come early in the first book of Tacitus's *Annals*, I discovered that one of the things some people were amazed at was the fact that *idem dies accepti quondam imperii princeps et uitae supremus* (1.9.1). Syme introduces the more natural "anniversary" in his English adaptation; but Tacitus's Latin simply says that the first day Augustus received *imperium* and the last day of his life were the same day, *idem dies*. And so they are, the same day on the grid of the *fasti*, although fifty-six years removed in time, the fifty-six years between what we call 43 B.C.E. and 14 C.E., between a nineteen-year-old and a seventy-five-year-old.

Horace similarly activates the identity of days separated by years when he congratulates Augustus on the fact that Tiberius and Drusus gained the decisive victory in their German campaign on the very day (*quo die*) on which Alexandria had surrendered fifteen years earlier (*Carm.* 4.14.34–38).[128] This is a mentality we perhaps find easier to understand when it is keyed in to sacred time. When Ovid describes 1 January in the *Fasti*, he says that "the fathers dedicated two temples on this day" (*sacrauere patres hac duo templa die*, 1.290). He does not mean that the two temples were dedicated within the same twenty-four-hour period, for the temple of Aesculapius was dedicated in 291 B.C.E. and that of Vediovis almost a century later, in 194 B.C.E.; yet it is, for all that, still "the same day."[129] This is very close to the kind of feeling that Zerubavel describes in the case of the Sabbath: "Jews have traditionally referred to their holiest of days as '*the* Sabbath.' Whether it fell in April 1716 or September 1379, it has nevertheless always been regarded as one and the same entity."[130]

The Roman apprehension of the identity of the day is particularly strong because their calendar has the same pattern every year, undisturbed by the contingencies introduced by our system of the week. For us, 12 January might be a Tuesday this year and a Friday next; but the Romans of this period did not have a week, so that there is not even this degree of fluctuation to distract from the feeling of the identity of the day. We need to buy a new calendar every year solely because of the variations introduced by the week. If the modern world ever adopts one of the proposed World Calendars, in which the days of the week would be constant from year to year, then we would be much closer to the Romans' apprehension that the day does not change from year to year.[131]

As we have repeatedly seen, however, the assertion of identity and the very exercise of comparison are inextricably tied up with an apprehension of difference. The identity of the same day from year to year is always capable of being called into question, in just the same way as the asserted identity of Roman and Greek time or culture, or the asserted "likeness" of any two elements in simile. Recent studies of Ovid's *Fasti* have concentrated productively on this issue, analyzing the many different effects Ovid achieves as he compares and contrasts the "same" day in contemporary Rome *and* back in whatever past time frame it links up with through aetiological connection.[132] As these scholars suggest, if Augustus may often be read as trying to assert an identity and continuity of values across the gulf of centuries between the Roman past and present, then Ovid regularly opens up the fissures and reveals the gaps between the two sides of the comparison. A telling example comes on the first day of May, when Ovid is looking for the old Lares Praestites, whose day this is.[133] He can no longer securely identify their images, however, so worn are they by the lapse of time (*Fast.* 5.131–32, 143–44). Instead, Ovid finds, the old Lares have been ousted by the new Lares Augusti, so that the day, with its cult, are no longer the same: what Augustus might construe as a restoration of a link is presented by Ovid as an obstruction of access to the past.[134] In Ovid's case, the pressure on the issue of continuity and discontinuity is very strong, since it is an issue inextricable from his key concern, aetiology, whose linking of the past and present always causes as many explanatory problems as it solves.[135] Yet the question acquires extra power in a calendrical context, where the supposed identity of the day in each recurrent year is presented as a plain fact by the very format of the inscription.

Apart from Ovid's *Fasti*, the most powerful laboratory for testing the "sameness" of Roman anniversary days is Virgil's *Aeneid* 8, in which Aeneas arrives at the site of (future) Rome. This book is Virgil's most sophisticated time machine, and the anniversary is the best way to begin investigating the rich effects he produces as he works with the two opposite poles of mythical and contemporary time, structured by the book's recurrent antitheses of "now" and "then/once."[136] The poem as a whole is interested in forging links between these time perspectives, explaining how this present was generated out of that past, and how that past is to be understood in the light of this present; at the same time, the poem constructs powerful discontinuities between the past and the present, as it opens up the perhaps unbridgeable disjunctions between the modern empire and the rustic roots to which it nostalgically harks back.[137] In book 8, when Aeneas is on the site of Rome, the reader is juggling these two time perspectives all the way through, working on the problems of identity and difference in the process; at times the two perspectives are collapsed together, as we see Aeneas walking on the same significant ground as Augustus, and doing so on days that continue to be the "same"; for on the site of the city the significance of time and of space prove to be mutually self-defining.

When Aeneas rows up the Tiber and comes to the site of Rome, he sees the locals sacrificing to Hercules in what will be/has become the Forum Boarium (*Aen.* 8.102–4):

> Forte die sollemnem illo rex Arcas honorem
> Amphitryoniadae magno diuisque ferebat
> ante urbem in luco.

> By chance on that day the Arcadian king was performing sacrifice to the great son of Amphitryon and the gods, in front of the city, in a grove.

Just by chance, on that day, says Virgil. Now, nothing really happens by chance in the mapped-out and claustrophobic world of the *Aeneid,* and Aeneas's arrival on this day is no exception.

The day of sacrifice to Hercules Invictus at the Ara Maxima in the Forum Boarium is what we call 12 August. In Virgil's lifetime the month was not yet called August, and it would not acquire the name until 8 B.C.E., when Virgil had been dead for over ten years;[138] to him this day would have been *pridie Idus Sextilis,* the day before the Ides of Sextilis. As many scholars have noted, in the year 29 B.C.E. this was a very significant date for Augustus (although he was not to be called "Augustus" for another seventeen months).[139] It was on this day that he took up station outside the city of Rome on his return from the East, having defeated Antonius and Cleopatra, ready to begin celebrating his triple triumph on the next day.[140] The compressed layering of time provided by the identity of days reinforces the feeling that this is the "same" day: Virgil insinuates that Aeneas is arriving before the city on the very day that Octavian/Augustus will later arrive, on the very day that Hercules is honored for his killing of the monster Cacus. There is evidence that the coincidence is not simply one that appealed to Virgil, but was designed by Octavian. Aiming to trump Antonius's long-standing cultivation of Hercules, and to associate himself with Hercules' ideology of victory, Octavian will have arranged for his arrival outside the city to coincide with the major feast day of Hercules Invictus.[141]

Virgil's chronological flattening is a corollary to the typological parallels between Hercules, Aeneas, and Augustus: the prototypical actions of deliverance that Hercules and Aeneas undertake in mythical time prefigure the actions of deliverance that Augustus will perform in historical—contemporary—time.[142] All this is made possible by the calendar's generation of a sense of identity of the "same" day, which connects the present with the distant past. Thanks to the Roman Fasti you can travel between time zones through a version of what the space-time physicists call a wormhole.[143] Through the superimposed layers of the *fasti*, 12 August 1177 B.C.E. can take you tumbling down to 12 August 29 B.C.E.[144] The repetitive "sameness" of this numinous day through Roman history is marked by the unique device of repeating the line-ending *quae maxima semper* from line 271 to 272 in the description of the institution of the cult.[145] The calendrical resonances continue as the book goes on. The "next" day, after Aeneas has passed the night in Evander's hut, is 13 August, the first of the three days of Octavian's triple triumph; on this day Aeneas will receive from his mother the shield of Vulcan, whose description will culminate in Octavian's triumph, likewise taking place on the "same" day.

Aeneas's arrival puts the site of Rome into the heart of meaningful time, locating the city at the intersection point of a number of matrices, with the anniversary doing most of the work of creating the significant links. Here we see Aeneas, the last demigod, the survivor of the Trojan War, who brings world history in his person to intersect with the site of Rome for the first time; the arrival of Jupiter's favored Trojans definitively marks the end of the local Golden Age.[146] The Roman calendar, dotted with wormholes of anniversary that connect disparate epochs through the identity of the day, is here brought into history for the first time through its proleptic reach down into future time, linking the fates of Aeneas and Augustus. Only at the site of Rome is the Roman calendar operative in this poem, and on the shield at the end of the book there is a battery of events that will all have triggered calendrical associations for the reader: 25 August, the Consualia, with the rape of the Sabine women (635–36); 15 February, the Lupercalia, with 19 March and 19 October, the processions of the Salii (663); the glorious Nones, 5 December, 63 B.C.E., with Cato giving judgment on Catiline (668–70); 2 September 31 B.C.E., the battle of Actium (671–708); 13, 14, and 15 August 29 B.C.E., the triple triumph of Augustus (714–29).

It is pleasing that the anniversary power of the Roman calendar is first brought into effect on the feast day of Hercules, when Aeneas meets Evander, because Evander is an Arcadian, and traditionally the acorn-munching Arcadians were the first of men, born before the moon—which is to say, for people who use lunar calendars, born before time.[147] But on the site of Rome Evander's Arcadians have a calendar, even if it might have only one day on it, the day of Hercules, 12 August: "it is Hercules' deliverance of the Arcadians from the threat of Cacus that starts their historical (and aetiological) clock; he and his rites mark the turning-point of Arcadian history."[148]

What happens when time hits space, as Katherine Clarke has shown us in her studies of history and geography, is that space becomes place: mere area becomes significant locality once it becomes a historical venue for agents moving in plotted time.[149] When Aeneas meets Evander, Rome becomes a true "place" for the first time as it is fixed in a grid of meaningful time, and the anchoring of time and place in the ritual calendar intensifies the effect, since the annotations for the festivals on the calendar prescribe a day and almost always a place as well (usually a temple).[150] The two poles of time and place meet at the Altar of Hercules. Here Evander tells Aeneas how they instituted the cult of Hercules: they have kept the day (*seruauere diem*, 269), and the first priest of Hercules has fixed the altar in a place, a grove (*hanc aram luco statuit*, 271).[151] These words refer back to the first glimpse of the cult, when Aeneas first arrives, for these two key words of time and place are already present there, *die* (102) and *luco* (104): the place word *luco* is carefully placed in exactly the same place in the line on each occasion.[152] The festival's evocative sense of contiguity in time, providing a link across great lapses of time, is powerfully reinforced by the persistence of the monument in its immovable location: "*periodic fusion with the past*" provided by anniversaries "is even more evocative when synchrony is combined with constancy of place."[153] Historical time and mythical time are fused in the recurrent time of the festivals, and given a grounding in the sacred places of the city.

REVOLUTIONS OF TIME

As Aeneas surveys the city's landscape he is able to catch glimpses of the past Golden Age of Saturn, seeing the wreckage of Saturn's city (8.355–57). At the same time, he is providing a focus for Virgil's readers to contemplate the nature of their own Age of Gold, and to envision the unknowable but inescapable future patterns of imperial succession. For Virgil's way of representing the layering of time has a vertiginous dimension to it. The calendar allows for connections between widely separated epochs, but the identity of the day always allows for thinking of the gap between the days, and the massive gaps between past and present are insistently making themselves felt all through the book. Further, in *Aeneid* 8 another way of reaching the past is presented as well, in the form of a return to the Golden Age.[154] If you can conceive of a revolution of time, you can potentially conceive of a revolution that keeps on revolving, not just back up to the Golden Age, but back down again. The future of Rome may not be locked in a perpetual Golden Age but may be susceptible to the same vicissitudes undergone by the preceding empires.

Virgil opens up this possibility as Aeneas and Evander walk down what is later, in the time of Virgil's audience, to be the Roman Forum, proleptically described as such by the poet, before the space has become that place: *passim . . . armenta uide-bant/Romanoque foro et lautis mugire Carinis* ("They saw cattle everywhere, moo-ing in the Roman Forum and the chic Carinae," 8.360–61).[155] From our perspec-tive it is easy enough to relish an abysmal irony in these words, since any modern reader can reflect on the fact that the Roman Forum in medieval times returned to the time of Evander and was for centuries yet again a place for cows to graze, "Campo Vaccino."[156] The irony does not work only for modern readers, however. The site of Evander's settlement is already littered with ruins, after all, in the form of the fallen walls of the foundations of Janus and Saturn, which are pointed out to Aeneas by his guide Evander (356–58): one of the many strange effects of the book's time compression is that we see the demigod Aeneas as a "modern" tourist, indulging himself in the fashionable pursuit of visiting famous ruins, the "monu-ments of men of earlier times" (*uirum monimenta priorum*, 312).[157] When Aeneas and Evander take a right turn out of the "Forum" at the top of the "Sacra Via" to go up to Evander's hut on the Palatine, they would go through one of the old gates of the Palatine, the Porta Mugonia.[158] Virgil does not name the gate, but with *mugire* in 361, he alludes to its name, "Moo-Gate," reminding us of its obvious ety-mology. He is also alluding to a Greek play on words that stands out in a group of epigrams on scenes of the once great Greek cities of Argos and Mycenae, whose day is gone, leaving them as haunts of herdsmen with their cows and goats.[159] The gold of these cities has now gone (*Anth. Pal.* 9.101.5; 103.1); their devastation is the revenge of Troy (9.103.7–8; 104.5). In one of these poems one also sees the pun on mooing. Mycenae is now "pasture for sheep and cattle," and "of all my greatness I have only my *name*" (103.5–6): Mycenae (Μυκῆναι) shares the opening letters of the Greek verb "to moo" (μυκάομαι), so that the imperial city really has become "Moo-town," with only its significant name left as a sign of its abandonment.[160]

The cows wandering over the site of Rome, then, are at once a romantic image of primal pastoral innocence and an emblem of postimperial desolation.[161] Aeneas encounters ruins where we might expect him to find a clear ground. An eerie par-allel is available in the journey of Lewis and Clark.[162] As they pole their way up the Missouri River, the first white men apart from a handful of trappers ever to go that far, it seems to them that they are entering an Eden, an unspoiled paradise with unheard-of animals in unheard-of quantity, and natives living in a state of grace. But the horse riding Sioux they pass by have been living that nomadic horseback life for no more than a hundred years, having only then domesticated the horse imported by Spaniards from the Old World; and this new lifestyle is a modern intrusion into that landscape. Colonizers are always prone to think that the natives they meet are inhabiting a timeless zone, but the Sioux were not inhabiting a timeless zone. As the expedition gets farther up the Missouri they pass by abandoned villages of the Mandan, deserted by the few survivors of the whites' measles and smallpox.

The vertiginous sensations conjured up by these views forwards and backwards, or up and down the cycle, are condensed in the adverb Virgil deploys in his description of the "now" golden Capitoline, "once *(olim)* bristling with woody thickets" *(aurea nunc, olim siluestribus horrida dumis,* 348). As Zetzel has pointed out, *olim* ("at some indefinite point in past or future time") can point in either direction, either to the distant past of Evander's day or to the distant future, when the Capitol will once again resemble its then state.[163] Further, when the survivor of the fall of Troy finds himself on the site of the future Rome, the theme of imperial succession needs little pressure to be activated.[164] As the tears of the Homer-quoting Scipio at the fall of Carthage showed, the transition of empire to Rome inevitably carries with it the future prospect of Rome itself suffering the fate of all previous holders of the *imperium*.[165] This is no idiosyncratic Virgilian subversion, but the fruit of a powerfully informed historical and philosophical imagination reflecting on a long-standing debate among his predecessors.[166] In Virgil's case, there is a characteristic wrestling between the apprehension that mutability cannot be arrested and the urge to impose a definitive closure, with an end to time's patterns of change and succession in an eternally existing Roman Empire.[167] As usual, Virgil's reception is reductive, fixing him as the advocate only of closure. Lucan sends Caesar to the site of Troy in a parody of Aeneas's tour, mocking Virgil's pretensions to finality and permanence by showing that the "old" Troy is an emblem of what the "new" Troy will one day be (9.961–99); yet the passage aims to puncture a Virgilian illusion that is not actually there.[168] The speech of Ovid's Pythagoras, in the final book of the *Metamorphoses*, is more open-ended, and readable within this suggested Virgilian frame; Pythagoras prophesies the rise of Rome, without spelling out the lesson to be drawn from the fates of all the other great imperial cities he has listed just before (15.424–52).[169]

The sense of chronological displacement generated in *Aeneid* 8 is very disturbing. Virgil takes us back to the site of Rome hundreds of years before Romulus, and it is already littered with ruins. Evander, almost within reach of Saturn, is the immediately postlapsarian man; Virgil's audience, living in their own supposed Golden Age, are thereby brought to imagine the time when it too will leave its own traces and ruins. As indeed it did; as indeed it has.

SIX · Years, Months, and Days II

The Grids of the Fasti

TIME'S ARROW AND TIME'S CYCLE

In this final chapter we continue to explore the charts of the Roman Fasti, investigating their role in placing the city and its empire in time, and analyzing in particular the revealing transformations the *fasti* underwent as they were revolutionized along with the rest of Roman life by Julius Caesar and his heir. Although in the previous chapter we discussed the *fasti* in the form of the calendar, the term *fasti* embraces two principal kinds of time chart for us to consider. The word denotes not only the annual calendar but also the list of eponymous chief magistrates, the elected officials (usually consuls) who gave their names to the year and enabled orientation in past time. We shall also briefly consider the so-called—and misnamed—Fasti Triumphales, a list of those who had celebrated triumphs; these are much the rarest of the three categories under discussion, with the only substantial remains coming from the list put up by Augustus at a site in the east end of the Forum to accompany the list of consuls he had already installed there.[1]

The term Fasti Triumphales, together with Fasti Anni and Fasti Consulares to describe the calendar and list of chief magistrates respectively, has been popularized by Attilio Degrassi in his superb editions of the surviving inscriptions of the various *fasti*. I shall make use of these terms, reluctantly, together with the equivalent designations of "calendrical," "consular," or "triumphal" *fasti*, but it is important to bear in mind that all of these expressions are modern helpmates, which can obscure important divisions and connections in the original.[2] The calendrical and consular *fasti* are both called simply *fasti* in ancient sources, without qualification, so that it can sometimes be difficult to know to which category a Latin text is referring.[3] It was, unsurprisingly, Mommsen who first drew attention to the significance of this shared nomenclature and gave an explanation for it: both documents are part of a shared calendrical system.[4] Any developed calendrical system needs to fix both the day and the year, and at Rome the day was fixed by the Fasti Anni and the year by the Fasti Consulares—or rather, since both those terms are modern usages, not Roman, we should say that day and year were fixed by the *fasti*.[5] This crucial point was systematically developed by Hanell (1946). Even if one does not accept his whole origin story about the introduction of a new calendar with a new principle of eponymity at the time of the establishment of the Capitoline cult of Jupiter at the end of the sixth century B.C.E., his study remains a compelling account of the symbiosis of the two kinds of *fasti* as part of a calendar, revealing their interdependence as the means of fixing a mark in Roman time.[6] The principal of eponymity was so strong that the use of the consuls' names to identify the year continued up to the time of the emperor Justinian, who introduced dating by regnal years in 537 C.E.[7] What modern scholars regularly call Fasti Triumphales, on the other hand, are not *fasti* at all. They are not part of the calendar; the triumphs they record may fall on any day in the year and do not occur on an annual basis; the individuals who celebrate them are not necessarily eponymous magistrates. Nor is the term *fasti* meaningful when applied to lists of other noneponymous magistrates, as so often occurs in modern scholarship.[8] Properly speaking, then, however useful the various modern terminologies may be, the Roman Fasti are the annual calendar and the list of eponymous magistrates, and nothing else.

In the light of their joint calendrical force it is not surprising that both charts, of eponymous magistrates and of the days and months of the year, share the same name. Nor is it surprising that the two kinds of *fasti* are so regularly found together, in monumental contexts or in books, since charting the city's time required this dualistic pairing.[9] Especially after the reform of 153 B.C.E., when the consuls began to take up office every year on 1 January, the god Janus provided a key link between the two *fasti*, as the god of the first month and the recipient of the consuls' first sacrifices on the occasion of their first day in office.[10] It is always worth entertaining the hypothesis that when we know one kind of *fasti* existed in a certain place, the other may have been there as well. In Fulvius Nobilior's temple of Hercules Musarum, for example, we know that calendrical *fasti* were exhibited, and scholars have suggested that consular *fasti* were also present;[11] conversely, it has been sug-

gested that Augustus's temporal complex in the Forum included now lost calundri-
cal *fasti* to accompany the surviving consular and "triumphal" *fasti*, to make a
complete representation of civil time.[12] However these cases may be, there is no
doubt that our first surviving *fasti*, found at Anzio (Antium) and dating to around
55 B.C.E., are a doublet, with a consular list and a calendar displayed together on the
walls of a private house: the term Fasti Antiates refers to both. This pattern continues well into the Empire, all the way to the Codex-Calendar of 354 C.E.[13]

The pairing of these two kinds of *fasti* is one to which modern readers may
readily respond, through the common modern conception of time as either an
arrow or a cycle.[14] The onward linear progress of time's arrow is visible in the
Fasti Consulares, the list of the executive magistrates of the state, laid out in
sequence back to the beginning of the Republic; the recurring patterns of the city's
life, time's cycle, are laid out in the Fasti Anni, with its grid of invariable days and
months. Ovid capitalizes on these two perspectives in his two overlapping masterpieces on time, the *Metamorphoses* and the *Fasti*. In his proem to the *Metamorphoses*
he announces that the poem will go all the way from the origin of the world down
to *mea tempora*, "my times" (1.3–4); Barchiesi first noticed the crucial point that
tempora is the first word of the *Fasti*, so that the arrow of Ovid's hexametric time
in the *Metamorphoses* carries on down until it hits the circle of his elegiac time in
the calendrical *Fasti*.[15] These two categories are not watertight in separation, since
time's arrow and time's cycle are never completely independent in the apprehension of time. The serried ranks of the consuls are themselves a part of a cyclical
pattern, with every year yielding another pair, so as to reinforce the feeling that the
official life of the city is an orderly cycle as well as a forward movement through
time; while the calendar of the Romans is an embodiment of history's movement
in various ways, showing the successive temple dedications of the Roman people,
and eventually, as we shall see, under the Empire, incorporating the historical
deeds of the imperial family, their assumptions of power, and their deaths.[16] Again,
Ovid is perfectly alive to these issues, as he lays out the historical force of the
imperial *fasti* and reveals the onward progress of time's arrow even in his circular
Fasti: the death of Augustus in 14 C.E. moves the initial dedication from the first to
the second book, and the new dedication to book 1 focuses on Germanicus, who
now occupies the inherently anticipatory position of heir to the current emperor.[17]

The pairing of calendrical and consular *fasti* very probably goes back to Fulvius
Nobilior's temple of Hercules Musarum, dedicated sometime after his Ambracian
triumph of 187 B.C.E., perhaps, as suggested in the last chapter, in 184 B.C.E.[18] Certainly the temple contained calendrical *fasti*, most likely in the form of painted

inscriptions on the walls.[19] These *fasti* did not, like earlier *fasti*, simply identify the festivals or give a note for the legal status of particular days, marking whether it was possible to conduct business on that day or hold assemblies. Fulvius's display seems to have set a precedent for subsequent monumental *fasti* in starting the practice of annotating the *fasti* with exegetical material; we are told, for example, that Fulvius's *fasti* had a learned discussion of the etymologies of the names of various months.[20] Fulvius may have controlled such material from his own resources, but a more likely candidate as the learned source is the poet Ennius, who had traveled with Fulvius on the Ambracia campaign and had celebrated his victory in a *fabula praetexta*.[21] Ennius may also have assisted Fulvius in the construction of a set of consular *fasti*, for he was engaged at the time on his *Annales*, for which he will have needed a data bank of his own.[22] There is no direct evidence that Fulvius's temple contained consular as well as calendrical *fasti*, yet the likelihood is increased by the clear later popularity of the paired format, and especially by the paired consular and calendrical format of the only *fasti* to survive from the Republic, the Fasti Antiates.[23] The best case for the coexistence of both kinds of *fasti* in Fulvius's complex is that of Gildenhard, who suggests a Fulvian "conception of time that combined the sacral (calendar) with the historical (names and dates of magistrates)," together with "the representation of a historical continuum, sketched out year by year through the names of former consuls and censors."[24] As Gildenhard goes on to argue, such a conception of time and of history's movement to an end point through the actions of great individuals is precisely what one finds in Ennius's *Annales*, a fitting poetic counterpart to the complex of Fulvius's temple, with both the epic and the temple combining "a linear chronology with a sacral conception of time and military success."[25]

THE CONSULS' YEARS

The purpose and function of the consular *fasti* are not as easy to grasp as may appear at first. Their symbolic and commemorative power is vast, as they embody the Republican principles of collegiality and succession, record the names of a phenomenally tenacious and successful set of families, and identify the elapsed time of the Roman people with an eponymous office of immense prestige: "historical time was represented for the Romans by the annual rhythm of consulships; they symbolised, in the temporal dimension, the Republic."[26] Such is the mentality underpinning Lucan's despairing characterization of the lost Republic as "the times of laws, years taking their name from the consul" (*tempora legum/ . . . annos a consule nomen habentis*, 7.440–41). The utilitarian dimension of the *fasti* is less clear.[27] Certainly the combined calendrical and consular *fasti* work as a calendar to identify days, months, and years, and the regular association of the two kinds of *fasti* shows that they were used for these calendrical purposes. A calendar, however, is "distinct from a system of reckoning, which is a tool for computing the passage of time."[28] Scholars ancient and modern have so regularly used the lists as chronographic guides that it is easy to forget that the original purpose of the *fasti* was not to facilitate chronological reckoning: for that purpose, further synchronization is necessary.[29] As Cornell well puts it, "the important thing to remember about Roman dates is that events were associated in the first instance with the names of the consuls of the year in which they took place. Locating that year in any general scheme of chronology, whether Olympiads or years after the founding of the city, or years before or after Christ, is a secondary and necessarily somewhat artificial process."[30] This point is hard to assimilate because our familiarity with our own virtually absolute dating system runs so deep. One finds, accordingly, statements such as the following, which reveal an unconscious intuition that an absolute time underlies the consular names: "Linear time at Rome was expressed through the annual magistracy of the consulships of individuals from the elite. This was not the easiest system to handle, since one needed to remember who were the two or more consuls for any particular year."[31] But the consuls *were* the particular year; it is not as if there is an independent year in its own sphere with the consuls in another, waiting to be matched up. Livy and Tacitus will sometimes even put the "consuls" and the "year" in apposition, creating a unity between the time period and its designation.[32]

We must be precise and circumspect, then, in conceiving of a pair of consular names as a "date." The paired consulship is an office that makes orientation in time possible when part of a series, but we should be careful about the implications of saying that Quintus Fabius Rullianus and Publius Decius Mus *equals* 297 B.C.E., to pick an example at random out of the *fasti*. Further, the year we are talking about in the consular *fasti* is, for much of Republican history, not coextensive with the calendar year. The year of the consuls' office and the year of the civil and religious cycle is not the same unit until surprisingly late in Republican history.[33] Only in 153 B.C.E. did the consuls begin taking up office on 1 January every year, synchronizing their term of office with the start of the calendrical *fasti*;[34] before then, back until 222 B.C.E., they regularly took up office on 15 March, and before 222 B.C.E. they could and did enter and leave office on any day.[35] The Republican consulate was primarily a military office, and as long as the consuls were in post at the beginning of the campaigning season, that was all that mattered. The adoption of 1 January as the start of the consular year in 153 B.C.E. is in large part due to the exigencies of fighting guerrilla warfare in Spain: if you are fighting a war in southern Italy you can have the consuls come into office in March in time for the campaigning season, but if one of the consuls is going to fight in Spain virtually every year then he and any men he is taking with him will need to start walking in January.[36]

The parade of paired consular names on the Republican *fasti* is most imposing, then, but the very fact that each pair of names does not necessarily correspond to a calendar year shows that the names originally represent "dates" as we understand them only in a limited sense. In time, however, the consular names did come to stand for "dates" in a more rigorous sense; in part this is a development from the synchronization of the consular and calendrical year from 153 B.C.E. on, but it is no accident that this process is most distinctly visible when the power of the office as an *office* is compromised, under the pressure of Augustus's Principate. We now turn to the fate of the *fasti* under Augustus, to see how his and his father's revolution produced this transformation, along with many others of equal, or greater, significance.[37]

AUGUSTUS'S CONSULAR YEARS

The fullest and most imposing surviving consular *fasti* are the so-called Fasti Capitolini, erected by Augustus in some kind of proximity to his father's temple at the east end of the Forum Romanum.[38] Together with Augustus's so-called Fasti Triumphales, they take up an entire wall of a room in the Palazzo dei Conservatori on the Capitoline, and they are beautifully on display in Degrassi (1947) in photographic and transcribed form.[39] Figure 6 shows a photograph of the section covering the years 260–154 B.C.E.;[40] figure 7 is Degrassi's drawing of one portion of this section, covering the years 173–154 B.C.E., and figure 8 is Degrassi's transcription in modern conventions of that same portion of text. Each line gives the names of the two consuls of the year, or of the *tribuni militum* during the years in the fifth and fourth centuries B.C.E. when they were the eponymous magistrates. If one of the consuls died or vacated office, then underneath his name is written the name of his successor, the so-called suffect consul, indented by about three letter spaces: this may be seen in the penultimate lines of figures 7 and 8, where the name of M.' Acilius Glabrio, suffect consul for 154 B.C.E., is indented beneath the name of his predecessor, L. Postumius Albinus, who died in office.[41] At increasingly regular intervals, ideally every five years, come the names of the two censors, indented by about one letter space, as in the last lines of figures 7 and 8, where one may see the names of the censors for 154 B.C.E. The *fasti* mark turning points of note in the

FIGURE 6.

The Capitoline Fasti for the years 260–154 B.C.E., showing two ranks of paired names of consuls. Degrassi 1947, Tab. XXXV.

history of the college: the *decemuiri* of 451 B.C.E. are listed; at 309 and 301 B.C.E. it is noted that the dictator and master of horse were in a year without consuls; the consuls of 367 B.C.E. are followed by the notice *consules e plebe primum creari coepti* ("Consuls first began to be elected from the plebs"); and after the consuls of 172 B.C.E. (fig. 7, line 4; fig. 8, line 3), we read *ambo primi de plebe* ("the first both to come from the plebs").[42] The first year of a few major wars is marked, the earliest of which is *Bellum Punicum Primum,* in the center of the line above the names of the consuls of 264 B.C.E.; in figures 7 and 8, above the names of the consuls of 171 B.C.E. is written *Bellum Persicum,* marking the beginning of the war against King Perseus of Macedon in that year (fig. 7, line 5; fig. 8, line 4).

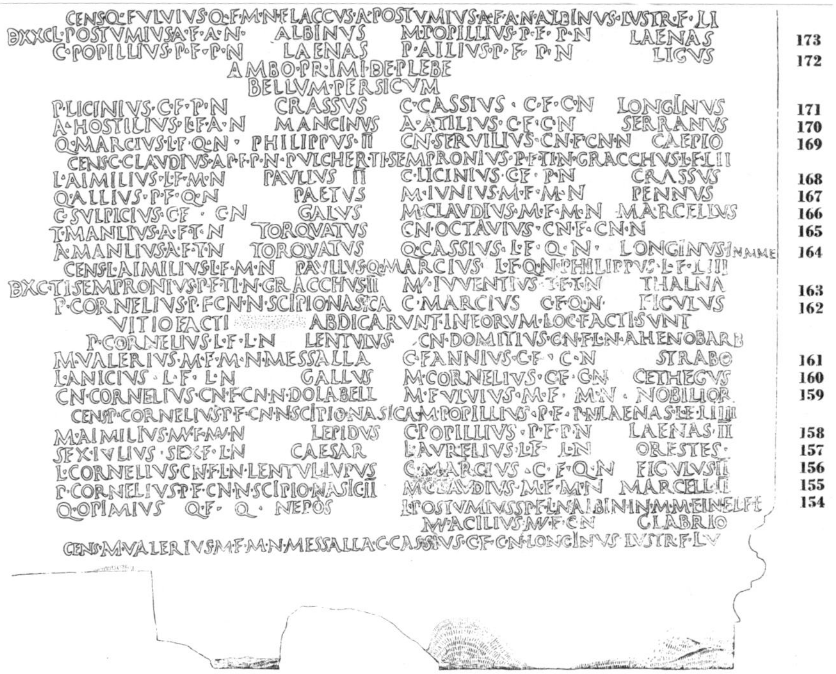

FIGURE 7.

The Capitoline Fasti for the years 173–154 B.C.E., a drawing of a portion of figure 6.
Degrassi 1947, 50.

What we see on the consular *fasti* erected by Augustus are a number of subtle
but profound realignments of how the viewer is meant to apprehend the lists. They
look like Republican *fasti*, but they are Augustan, imperial, *fasti*.[43] One apparently
small innovation, with far-reaching repercussions, is the addition of years from the
foundation of the city in the left-hand margin. Every ten years a numeral stands
for the number of years that have elapsed since a foundation date of "752 B.C.E.":
beside the names of the consuls for 173 B.C.E., then, one sees DXXC, counting the
580th year since the foundation (fig. 7, line 2; fig. 8, line 1). For a start, this innovation compromises the independent character of the list of eponyms as an instrument of time reckoning, for the numbering system is at the very least competing
with, and at worst supplanting, the list of names for the purposes of charting past
time.[44] Further, since the city was founded by Romulus on 21 April, a count of
years from the foundation of the city goes from 21 April to 20 April, not from 1
January to 31 December.[45] As a result, there are actually two concepts of the year

Year	Left consul	Right consul
173	ÞXXC L. Postumius A. f. A. n. Albinus	M. Popillius P. f. P. n. Laenas
172	C. Popillius P. f. P. n. Laenas	P. Aelius P. f. P. n. Ligus

Ambo primi de plebe
Bellum Persicum

171	P. Licinius C. f. P. n. Crassus	C. Cassius C. f. C. n. Longinus
170	A. Hostilius L. f. A. n. Mancinus	A. Atilius C. f. C. n. Serranus
169	Q. Marcius L. f. Q. n. Philippus II	Cn. Servilius Cn. f. Cn. n. Caepio

cens(ores) C. Claudius Ap. f. P. n. Pulcher, Ti. Sempronius P. f. Ti. n. Gracchus l(ustrum) f(ecerunt) LII

168	L. Aimilius L. f. M. n. Paullus II	C. Licinius C. f. P. n. Crassus
167	Q. Ailius P. f. Q. n. Paetus	M. Iunius M. f. M. n. Pennus
166	C. Sulpicius C. f. C. n. Galus	M. Claudius M. f. M. n. Marcellus
165	T. Manlius A. f. T. n. Torquatus	Cn. Octavius Cn. f. Cn. n.
164	A. Manlius A. f. T. n. Torquatus	Q. Cassius L. f. Q. n. Longinus in m(agistratu) m(or-

tuus) e(st)

cens(ores) L. Aimilius L. f. M. n. Paullus. Q. Marcius L. f. Q. n. Philippus l(ustrum) f(ecerunt) LIII

163	DXC Ti. Sempronius P. f. Ti. n. Gracchus II	M.' Iuventius T. f. T. n. Thalna
162	P. Cornelius P. f. Cn. n. Scipio Nasica	C. Marcius C. f. Q. n. Figulus

vitio facti abdicarunt. In eorum loc(um) facti sunt

	P. Cornelius L. f. L. n. Lentulus	Cn. Domitius Cn. f. L. n. Ahenobarb(us)
161	M. Valerius M. f. M. n. Messalla	C. Fannius C. f. C. n. Strabo
160	L. Anicius L. f. L. n. Gallus	M. Cornelius C. f. C. n. Cethegus
159	Cn. Cornelius Cn. f. Cn. n. Dolabell(a)	M. Fulvius M. f. M. n. Nobilior

cens(ores) P. Cornelius P. f. Cn. n. Scipio Nasica, M. Popillius P. f. P. n. Laenas l(ustrum) f(ecerunt) LIIII

158	M. Aimilius M.' f. M.' n. Lepidus	C. Popillius P. f. P. n. Laenas II
157	Sex. Iulius Sex. f. L. n. Caesar	L. Aurelius L. f. L. n. Orestes
156	L. Cornelius Cn. f. L. n. Lentul(us) Lupus	C. Marcius C. f. Q. n. Figulus II
155	P. Cornelius P. f. Cn. n. Scipio Nasic(a) II	M. Claudius M. f. M. n. Marcell(us) II
154	Q. Opimius Q. f. Q. nepos	L. Postumius Sp. f. L. n. Albin(us) in m(agistratu)

m(ortuus) e(st). In e(ius) l(ocum) f(actus) e(st)
M.' Acilius M.' f. C. n. Glabrio

cens(ores) M. Valerius M. f. M. n. Messalla, C. Cassius C. f. C. n. Longinus lustr(um) f(ecerunt) LV

FIGURE 8.

The Capitoline Fasti for the years 173–154 B.C.E., a transcript of the text in figure 7. Degrassi 1947, 51.

in play on this document: one unit depends for its meaning on the date of foundation, the other on the principle of eponymity.

The most telling innovation introduced by the foundation-era notation is that it generates a clash between two concepts of civil time. One has it that the real time of Rome begins with the foundation of the city; the other has it that the real time of Rome begins with the foundation of the Republic.[46] The traditional consular lists chart the time of the city from the foundation of the Republic, implying that the time before the consular lists is somehow out of the reckoning, just as traditional annalistic history has no era system for the time of the kings, and begins real, properly structured temporal history with the beginning of the Republic.[47] By putting a foundation-era count beside the consuls' names, Augustus subverts this understanding; in being aligned with the counting from the foundation of the city, the list of names loses a large part of its significance as a chart of Republican time.[48] "There was," as Purcell has recently reminded us, "a structural association between the Capitoline cult [instituted at the foundation of the Republic] and the institution of eponymity."[49] This "structural association" is now severely weakened, in a way that makes the modern name of Augustus's list—the *Capitoline fasti*—look profoundly ironic.

A related derogation from the prerogatives of the Capitoline cult comes with the dedication of Mars Ultor in 2 B.C.E., and the invention of a new rite linked to the new temple, calqued upon the tradition of the annual nail driven into the door of Jupiter's temple on the Capitoline by the consul.[50] Augustus laid down that the censors should hammer a nail into the temple of Mars Ultor at the conclusion of each five-year *lustrum;* since one of these censors would always be the emperor, the new rite is in direct competition with the traditional Republican and Capitoline association "of the driving of the nail, the dedication of a temple to the chief state deity, and the beginning of a new form of government characterized by annual magistrates."[51] Instead of the temple of Jupiter, there is now the temple of Augustus's Mars; instead of a tradition of annually successive eponymity, there is a new tradition of five-yearly cyclical repetitions of the same name, "Augustus."[52]

The censors have a role to play also in the Augustan consular *fasti,* and once again an apparently minor annotation has far-reaching consequences for the time frames being evoked, with the symbolically laden watershed of the expulsion of the kings once again being transgressed.[53] The Republican Fasti Antiates already record the censors, whose names occur at five-year intervals, although the patterning is not perfect, for in the years covered by the Fasti Antiates there were occasionally six or seven years between censors.[54] As may be seen in figure 9, which reproduces the Fasti Antiates for the years 164–137 B.C.E., the censors punctuate the regular run of consuls' paired names, which are painted in black and lined up in paired columns separated by a slight gap. The names of the two censors, painted in bright red, start one or two letter spaces to the left of the normal consular margin; their names run across the gap that separates the two consuls' names, and underneath the censors' names, indented and likewise running across the gap, is the phrase *lustrum fecerunt* ("performed the lustration"). The norm is the paired black consular names, with the censors' lustration in red providing a cyclical punctuation, ideally on a five-year rhythm. Augustus's inscribed *fasti* do not have the color distinction of the painted Fasti Antiates, but they have a related way of offsetting the censors' names from the consuls', slightly indenting their names from the normal left margin. The difference from the earlier *fasti* is that after the formulaic abbreviated phrase *l(ustrum) f(ecerunt)* now comes a number, marking that the censors "performed the lustration for the nth time": the last lines of figures 7 and 8 show the numeral LV at the very end, noting that the censors for the year had performed the census for the fifty-fifth time. Since the census and lustration were inaugurated according to tradition by the sixth king, Servius Tullius, this significant rhythmical pattern of the city's life is now being marked as one that goes back before the time of the Republic, its Capitoline cult, and its consuls.[55]

These changes, however slight in appearance, have the cumulative effect of reconfiguring the status of the eponymous consular list as the distinctive way of charting the city's time under the Republic. Of course, the nature of the office of the consulship itself is being reconceived under the Principate, as the power of the supreme magistracy is drained away into the hands of the emperor. The iconography of Augustus's consular *fasti* represents this particular transformation in two principal ways, reflecting a revolution in what the magistracy and its *fasti* were for and about.[56]

The first innovation here concerns the conventions for recording the names of the suffect consuls, those who came into office for any reason after the first two consuls of the year, the *ordinarii*.[57] Under the Republic, suffect consuls were rare, coming into office on the unusual occasions when one of the *ordinarii* died or was deposed. In the Republican Fasti Antiates, the suffects' names, like those of the censors, represent a supplement to the fundamentally eponymous parade of consular names, and the suffects' names are accordingly marked in red in the same way as the censors'.[58] In the year 154 B.C.E., for example, as may be seen in figure 9, the name of the first consul is preceded by the red Greek letter theta, standing for the first letter of θάνατος, *thanatos,* the Greek word for "death"; under his name, indented by three letter spaces to the right, and painted in red, are the words *suffectus M.' [Acili(us) G]labrio.*[59] With the exception of the color distinction and the use of theta, this is very much what one sees in the first four tablets of Augustus's Fasti Capitolini, which extend to the year 12 B.C.E. in the current state of tablet IV. A suffect's name is underneath that of his predecessor in office, indented by about three letter spaces, introduced by the phrase *in eius locum factus est* ("in his place was elected"). If the suffect replaces the leading *ordinarius* of the year, his indented name is underneath his predecessor's on the left-hand side of the column; if he replaces the other consul, then his indented name is underneath his predecessor's on the right-hand side. The overall effect, as in the Republican Fasti Antiates, is "to mark the eponymous magistrates of each year and to indicate by a hierarchical sequence of indentation the subordinate status of any substitute officials serving during the same year."[60]

Tablet V, however, beginning as we now have it in the year 1 C.E., and added at

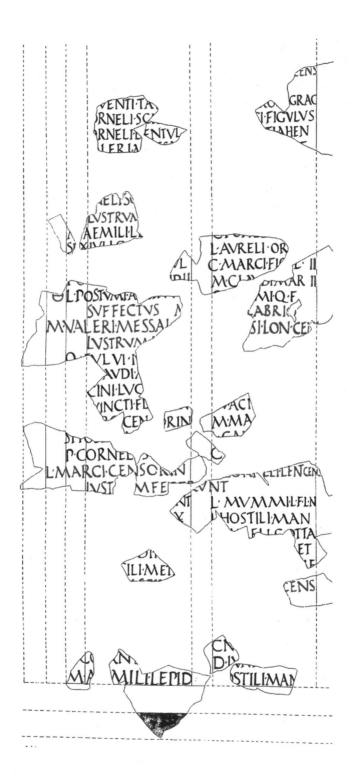

ENS

VENTI·TA   GRAC
RNELI·SC   T·FIGVLVS
RNELI LENTVL   LAHEN
LER LA

RELI·S
LVSTRVA
AEMILI L   L·AVRELI·OR
S XVII   C·MARCI·F   L·II
                  M CL   MAR II
L·POSTVMA   MI·Q·F
SVFFECTVS   ABRI
M·VALERI·MESSAL   SI·LON·CE
LVSTRVM
VLVI·I
AVDI
INI·LVC
INCTI·F   ACI
CEN   RIN   M·MA

P·CORNEL   C
L·MARCI·CENSORIN   ELI LEN CEN
IVST MFE ERVNT
             NT   L·MVMMI L·FI N
             X   P·HOSTILI·MAN
                  F L COTTA
                  ET
ILI·MEI
                  ENS

N   CN·
MA   MMI L LEPID   D I   STILI MAN

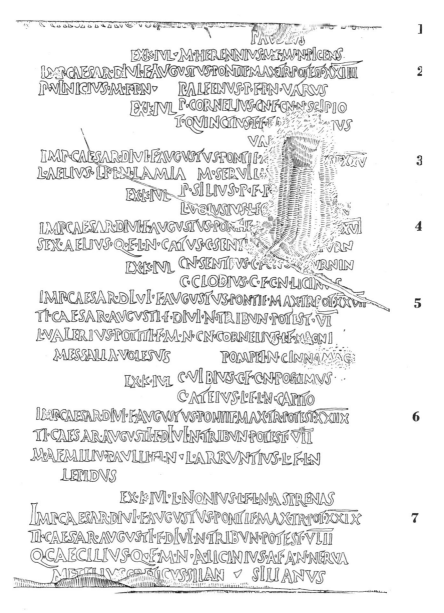

FIGURE 9. *(left)*
The Republican Fasti Antiates Maiores for the years 164–137 B.C.E. Degrassi 1947, 160.

FIGURE 10. *(above)*
The Capitoline Fasti for the years 1–7 C.E., showing the repetition of Augustus's name in each year. Degrassi 1947, 60.

a later date, is quite different, "marking the *suffecti* of each year as a group by list-ing them in a single column beneath the names of one of the *ordinarii*," and for the first time marking the day of the year on which they entered office.[61] This is a great change in emphasis, one that goes hand in hand with the new imperial practice of having supplementary consuls every year as a matter of course. The Republican convention of representing the suffects adheres to the principle that the consulship is an office, and what counts is to show who replaced whom in that office, rather than when; the new Augustan convention does not indicate who replaced whom, but rather gives explicitly the day on which the suffect began his term. The Repub-lican convention depends on the principle of succession, but the Augustan con-vention reduces the importance of the office as an office and makes the governing principle that of the date.[62] The consuls are now there primarily to chart a chronol-ogy: it is this change in convention that highlights more effectively than anything else the limitations of seeing the original eponymous lists as dates.[63]

The second innovation is far more striking, immediately obvious to anyone who looks at the Augustan years of the *fasti* on their wall in the Capitoline Museum or in Degrassi's edition. In the year 23 B.C.E. the name of Augustus, as consul for the eleventh time, heads the list. Then we are told that he abdicated and that L. Sestius became consul in his place; immediately thereafter, we read that Augustus, after abdicating from the consulate, accepted *tribunicia potestas*. In the entry for the next year, 22 B.C.E., after the consuls' names comes Augustus's name, followed by "with tribunician power" (*tribunicia potestate*). At this point, unfortunately, there is a gap of ten years, until the year 12 B.C.E., where we find the names of the two consuls and three suffects followed by "Augustus with tribunician power for the eleventh time," now with a partner in this novel office, whose name comes under, not beside, his own—M. Agrippa, "for the sixth time." When the new, fifth, tablet begins afresh in the year 1 C.E., the revolutionary implications of Augustus's new office have been fully worked out: [64] figure 10 shows Degrassi's drawing of the first section of the fifth tablet, covering the years 1–7 C.E., with his transcription in figure 11. Now Augustus's name leads off each year, before the names of the con-suls, with the new imperial dating era of the emperor's tenure of *tribunicia potestas* "for the twenty-third time." From now on, to the end of the tablet in 13 C.E., the last full year of Augustus's life, each year opens with the full width of each column being covered by Augustus's name and titles, beginning with *Imp. Caesar* and end-ing with the remorselessly increasing numerals of his tenure.[65] In the year 5 C.E. his name is once again joined by that of a colleague in *tribunicia potestas*, his desig-nated heir Tiberius; from then on the pair of them introduce each year, with

Augustus on top and Tiberius underneath, to be followed by the consuls and their suffects.

The effect is bizarre, following on from the consuls of the Republic. Every year there appears the same name, with a power that is not consular, nor Republican; this name is accompanied by a sequentially numbered office that has a dating power independent of the consuls' eponymy, so that the *fasti* of the Roman people start to look like a king list. The addition first of Agrippa and then of Tiberius creates the impression of a new collegial magistracy with a novel hierarchy built into it, a magistracy to rival and supplant the consulship, for this is "a quasi-magistracy reserved for the emperor and his chosen successor."[66]

The so-called Fasti Triumphales, right next to the consular lists in the original site in the Forum, reinforce the impression that a new cycle has begun, with the time of the city now regulated by different mechanisms from the eponymous parade of consuls.[67] If the consular *fasti* have a numerical date from the foundation of the city at regular ten-year intervals, then the list of *triumphatores* emphatically begins in that very moment of origins: the first two lines of the inscription read *Romulus Martis f. rex ann. [I]/de Caeninensibus k. Mar[t.]*, "Romulus, son of Mars, King, in Year One, over the Caeninenses, on the Kalends of March."[68] In an unbeatably primal moment, Romulus is celebrating the first Roman triumph on Day One, Year One, of Rome, and from then on every one of the triumphs has the year from the foundation of the city recorded, as well as the day of the year.[69] After Romulus, there is not another son of a god on the list until the year 40 B.C.E., when the name appears of *Imperator Caesar Diui filius*.[70] The Fasti Consulares by definition cannot list kings, so the list of *triumphatores* was the only one that made it possible for Augustus to create for himself this loop back to the time of divine origins. Having served its purpose of generating a time frame that begins with the city's foundation by the first king and provides a connection to the living son of a god, the list of the *triumphatores* may now be closed, for "the rest was imperial ceremonial."[71] The last name on the list, that of Cornelius Balbus in 19 B.C.E., comes at the very bottom of the slab: "there was no room for future triumphs, and the arch closed a chapter in Roman triumphal history."[72]

Yet another system of charting time is in place in this extraordinary complex, for following on from the names of the magistrates of the year 13 C.E. there is a notice of the performance of the Ludi Saeculares in the year "17 B.C.E.," marked as the fifth performance of the games; the earlier performances were likewise commemorated in the inscription.[73] Augustus's name stands prominently at the top of the entry for the fifth games, so that he has sealed his authority as the teleological

1   *[Imp. Caesar Divi f. Augustus, pont(ifex) max(imus), tr(ibunicia) potest(ate) XXIII]*
        C. Caesar August[i f. Divi n.]   *[L. Aemilius Paulli f. L. n.]*
                                                    Paullus
                ex k(alendis) Iul(iis) M. Herennius M. f. M.' n. Picens

2   *Imp. Caesar Divi f. Augustus, pontif(ex) max(imus), tr(ibunicia) potest(ate) XXIIII*
        P. Vinicius M. f. P. n.   *P. Alfenus P. f. P. n. Várus*
                                   P. Cornelius Cn. f. Cn. n. Scipio
                ex k(alendis) Iul(iis) *T. Quinctius T. f. T. n. [Crispi]nus*
                                        Val[erianus]

3   *Imp. Caesar Divi f. Augustus, pontif(ex) m[ax(imus), tr(ibunicia) pot]est(ate) XXV*
        L. Aelius L. f. L. n. Lamia   *M. Serviliu[s M. f. – n.]*
                                   P. Silius P. f. P. [n.]
                ex k(alendis) Iul(iis) *L. Volusius L. f. Q. [n. Saturni]n(us)*

4   *Imp. Caesar Divi f. Augustus, pontif(ex) [max(imus), tr(ibunicia) potest(ate) X]XVI*
        Sex. Aelius Q. f. L. n. Catus   *C. Senti[us C. f. C. n. Sa]turn(inus)*
                                   Cn. Sentius C. f. C. n. S[a]turnin(us)
                ex k(alendis) Iul(iis) *C. Clodius C. f. C. n. Licinus*

5   *Imp. Caesar Divi f. Augustus, pontif(ex) max(imus), tr(ibunicia) pot(estate) XXVII*
        Ti. Caesar Augusti f. Divi n. tribun(icia) potest(ate) VI
        L. Valerius Potiti f. M. n.   *Cn. Cornelius L. f. Magni*
         Messalla Volesus   *Pompei n. Cinna Mag(nus)*
                                 C. Vibius C. f. C. n. Postimus
                ex k(alendis) Iul(iis) *C. Ateius L. f. L. n. Capito*

6   *Imp. Caesar Divi f. Augustus, pontif(ex) max(imus), tr(ibunicia) potest(ate) XXIIX*
        Ti. Caesar Augusti f. Divi n. tribun(icia) potest(ate) VII
        M. Aemiliu⟨s⟩ Paulli f. L. n.   *L. Arruntius L. f. L. n.*
         Lepidus
                        ex k(alendis) Iul(iis) L. Nonius L. f. L. n. Asprenas

7   *Imp. Caesar Divi f. Augustus, pontif(ex) max(imus), tr(ibunicia) pot(estate) XXIX*
        Ti. Caesar Augusti f. Divi n. tribun(icia) potest(ate) VIII
        Q. Caecilius Q. f. M. n.   *A. Licinius A. f. A. n. Nerva*
         Metellus Creticus Silan(us)   *Silianus*
                  [ex k(alendis) Iul(iis) – Lucilius – f. – n. Longus]

FIGURE 11. *(above)*

The Capitoline Fasti for the years 1–7 C.E., a transcript of the text in figure 10. Degrassi 1947, 61.

FIGURE 12. *(right)*

The Republican Fasti Antiates Maiores for 1–16 January. Degrassi 1963, 2.

goal of this rhythm of the city's time as well. With his redefinition and appropriation of the Romans' eponymous lists, past triumphs, and past Ludi Saeculares, Augustus over the years created a profound reconfiguration of the systems of representing the past time of the city. This reconfiguration centered on his own person and that of his heir, in the process forging links with Rome's divine origins and creating a new imperial dating era. The Republican time systems appear to be still in place, but by the end of Augustus's reign their symbolic power, iconography, and resonance have been compromised and redrawn.

A K·IAN F
B F ⌐AESCVLA·CO·O
       VEDIOVE
C
D
E
F NON F
G ⌐VICAE·POTAE
H
A
B
C CAR·N⌐
D ⌐CIVTVRNAE
E EIDVS
F EN
G CAR·N⌐
H ⌐C·CARMENT

AUGUSTUS'S CALENDRICAL YEAR

If the phenomenal pressure of the Principate's new power warped the distinctive patterning of time's arrow at Rome, then time's cycle, in the form of the calendrical *fasti*, was even more systematically and overtly redrawn.[74] Here the impact of Augustus and his family is at its most obvious and pervasive: the changes took place swiftly and within two generations fixed themselves as normative and became foundational for the future empire. Simply looking at the Republican Fasti Antiates and then at an Augustan or Tiberian calendar such as the Fasti Praenestini or Amiternini brings home what different documents they are, and it soon emerges what different ideological ends they are serving.

The Republican *fasti* are a beautifully clean and austere document, one that embodies the idealized corporatism of the Republic.[75] Each month has a column to itself, with the total of the month's days at the bottom; the first sixteen days of January from the Fasti Antiates may be seen in figure 12. In each column's left-hand margin are the nundinal days, the market-day cycle marked by the recurring letters *A–H* (an eight-day cycle to our eyes, but a nine-day one by the Romans' inclusive counting).[76] Kalends, Nones, and Ides are marked on the first, fifth, and thirteenth days, while notations give the legal and religious status of each day: the letter *C (comitialis)* means that assemblies could meet and vote on that day, *F (fastus)* denotes a working day without legal restrictions, and so on.[77] Large letters mark the major state festivals such as the Carmentalia (11 and 15 January) and Lupercalia (15 February); in smaller letters are marked other festive days, overwhelmingly the names of a particular temple cult in the dative ("to Vica Pota," 5 January; "to Juno Sospita Mater Regina," 1 February; "to Concordia," 5 February). It is very striking that the calendar shows no names of human beings.[78] Indeed, only two historical events are recorded, the foundation and the near destruction of the city: 21 April, *Roma condita* ("Rome founded"), and 18 July, *Alliensis dies* ("the day of [the battle at] the Allia").[79] Jörg Rüpke has recently argued that the notices of gods in the dative do have a historical force; according to his argument, these are dedication days *(dies natales)* of temples, introduced by Fulvius Nobilior into his *fasti* in the temple of Hercules Musarum, intended to commemorate the victories and dedications of great *nobiles* and to provide an abbreviated symbolic image of the history of the Roman people.[80] In a very general sense these notices may have a historical power in evoking the institution of various cults, and there is no doubt that the *dies natalis* is an important part of any cult.[81] But is hard to see a distinctively political and historical power in such a vague form of notation, in which the traces of a foundational act by an individual (if that is in fact what the dative denotes) are always liable to be swallowed up by the cyclical and corporate momentum of the document. As Rüpke himself acknowledges, a genuinely historical notice should look something like "On this day in the consulship of A and B, this temple was dedicated to god C by personage D."[82] This, however, is not at all what we see. What the Republican calendar shows is "First day of January: to Aesculapius, on the island": this is an enduring day, the same every year, that repeats at the same place every year, a day that belongs to the god and the people, not to any individual.

With the coming of the Principate, which has its own new *fasti* in the form of Julius Caesar's reformed calendar, including a month that now bears his name, a revolution in the style as well as the calendrical content of the *fasti* takes place: "every few days, another imperial anniversary, another commemoration of the *princeps* and his family, a positive invasion, a planned and systematic act of intrusion which has the cumulative effect of recasting what it means to be Roman."[83] After centuries in which no human being was named on the calendar, the imperial family is now everywhere, with specific year dates often attached to their various doings. Births, deaths, apotheoses, assumptions of power, accessions to priesthoods, comings of age, dedications of temples, victories in battle—the *fasti* of the Roman people take on an increasingly crowded and fussily annotative look.[84] Figures 13 and 14, showing Degrassi's drawing and transcript of the Fasti Praenestini for 6–15 January, convey a vivid impression of the way in which the imperial family have transformed the old calendar with the new battery of commemorative material. Contemporaries immediately saw the point. In 13 B.C.E. Horace addresses Augustus with an ode in which he asks how the Senate and People will make his virtues live forever into the future "through inscriptions/titles and the memory-preserving/memory-endowed *fasti*" (*tuas, Auguste, uirtutes in aeuum/per titulos memoresque fastus, Carm.* 4.14.3–4). The word *tituli* refers both to the "inscriptions," including *fasti*, on which he will appear, and to the "titles," including especially the name "Augustus," which will denote him there;[85] the *fasti* will remember Augustus and preserve his memory with their welter of citations of his name and deeds. Horace is perhaps alluding in particular to the Augustalia of 12 October, instituted six years earlier in 19 B.C.E., the first Roman festival ever to be named after a historical human being and, so far as we know, the first new large-letter festival to be incorporated into the calendar since its original publication.[86] Horace's phrasing looks distinctly prophetic of the most conspicuous way in which the *fasti* would preserve the name of Augustus, through the renaming of the month Sextilis five years after this poem was published.

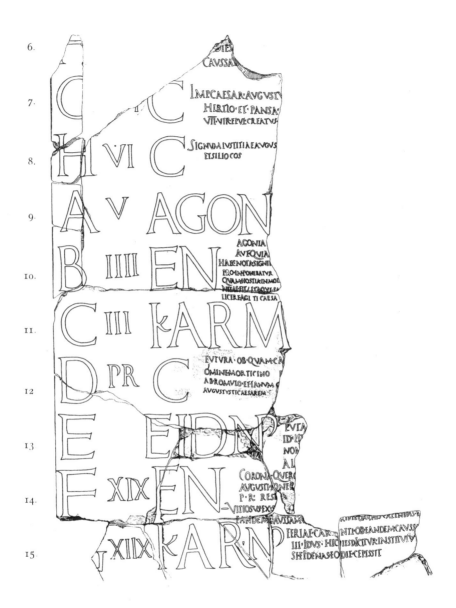

FIGURE 13.
The Fasti Praenestini for 6–15 January. Degrassi 1963, 112.

6. F [VIII f(astus). Hic] dies [religiosus est, ut sunt dies postridie omnis nonas ob eandem]
caussam [quod postridie omnis calendas]

7. G [VI]I c(omitialis). Imp. Caesar Augustu[s – – – primum fasces sumpsit]
Hirtio et Pansa [co(n)s(ulibus). Ti. Caesar – – – – – – – – – – – – – –]
VIIvir epul(onum) creatus [est]

8. H VI c(omitialis). Signum Iustitiae Augus[tae – – – Ti. Caesar dedicavit Planco]
et Silio co(n)s(ulibus)

9. A V Agon(alia), [np. –]
Agonia [– –]
aut quia [– –]

10. B IIII en(dotercisus). Haec nota signif[icat diem intercisum; nam endo antiquissima aetate]
pro in ponebatur. [Die interciso nefas est mane – – – – – – – – – – – – – – – – – – ante]
quam hostia inmol[etur et post exta porrecta – – – – – – – – – – – – – – – – – rursus]
nefas fit. Itaque sa[epe responsum est – – – – – – – – – – – – – – – – – medio tempore]
licere agi. Ti. Caesa[r – – – – – – – – – – – – – – – – – –]

11. C III Karm(entalia), [np. –]
[– – – – – – – – – – – – – – – – – – Carmentis partus curat omniaque]
[f]utura, ob quam ca[ussam in aede eius cavetur ab scorteis omnique]
ómine morticino. D[ebellavit hostes Imp. Caesar Augustus tertium]
ab Romulo et Ianum c[lausit se V et L. Appuleio co(n)s(ulibus). Imp. Caesar]
Augustus Ti. Caesarem [– – – – – – – – – – – – – – – – – –]

12. D pr(idie) c(omitialis) [– –]

13. E eid(us), np. [–]
puta [–]
id est [–]
non [–]
al[–]
Corona querc[ea, uti super ianuam domus Imp. Caesaris]
Augusti poner[etur, senatus decrevit, quod rem publicam]
p(opulo) R(omano) rest[it]u[it].

14. F XIX en(dotercisus). Vitiosus ex s(enatus) [c(onsulto), qu]o[d Antoni natalis. Idem religiosus ob]
eandem caussam q[uod post]ridie omnis calendas n[onasque]

15. G XIIX Kar(mentalia), np. Feriae Car[me]nti ob eandem caussa[m quod]
III idus. Hic [d]ies dicitur institutu[s a Romulo],
si Fidenas eo die cepiss[e]t

FIGURE 14.

The Fasti Praenestini for 6–15 January, a transcript of the text in figure 13. Degrassi
1963, 113.

Some twenty years after Horace's fourth book of *Odes,* at the beginning of his
calendar poem, Ovid shows how aware he is of the differences between the old and
new calendars, and also of the way that this annotation of the *fasti* is something
that will continue on into the future, with each succeeding generation. Here he is
addressing Germanicus Caesar, the heir apparent, the nephew and adopted son of
the emperor Tiberius (*Fast.* 1.7–12):

sacra recognosces annalibus eruta priscis
et quo sit merito quaeque notata dies.
inuenies illic et festa domestica uobis;

saepe tibi pater est, saepe legendus auus,
quaeque ferunt illi, pictos signantia fastos,
    tu quoque cum Druso praemia fratre feres.

You will recognize sacred rites dug out from old annals, and what each day
is entitled to be marked by. There you will find in addition the festivals of
your house; often your father and grandfather are to be read there, and the
rewards that they bear, picked out in the painted calendar, you too will bear
with Drusus your brother.

The first of the quoted lines (7) refers to Ovid's sources, including older commentaries on the *fasti;* the second line (8) refers to the calendar itself, with the
strong implication that the days marked are the ones marked in the old calendar,
since the following lines are signaled by the new material of the new imperial *fasti*,
introduced by "there you will find *in addition* . . ." At the beginning of book 2,
when he addresses Augustus, Ovid describes the *fasti* as "your names, your titles"
(*tua . . . nomina, . . . titulos . . . tuos*, 15–16).

By writing themselves into the *fasti* in this way, the imperial family are behaving
like the first king, according to Ovid, who represents Romulus as a proto-Augustus,
putting his family into the calendar. Romulus named March (the first month
according to him) after his father, Mars, and the "second" month, April, after
Venus, the mother of the race through Aeneas (1.39–40).[87] The second king,
Numa, does not follow this precedent but puts Janus and the month of the ancestral
shades, February, in first and second place (1.43–44). The power of the use of the
fasti as a venue for honorific work was, then, clear from the start. It attracted much
adverse comment from critics such as Tacitus, who delivers himself of a number of
mordant comments about "the befouling of the *fasti* by flattery" (*fastos adulatione
foedatos, Hist.* 4.40.2).[88] The emperor Tiberius himself turned down a proposal that
September should be given his name, and October that of his mother, Livia;[89] typically, he asked the Senate what they would do if there were thirteen Caesars.[90]

The process had begun with the honors voted to Julius Caesar by the Senate for
his various victories in the civil wars, and his new calendar provides a new venue
for innovation within an increasingly structured system of honors: the late Republic had seen experiments with statues, funerals, crowns, and so on, but only with
Caesar and his new calendar do the *fasti* themselves become part of the honorific
"language of power."[91] Various imperial *fasti* record the addition of *feriae publicae*,
marked with *NP*, on the anniversaries of the victories at Munda (17 March), Alex-

andria (27 March), Thapsus (6 April), Ilerda and Zela (2 August), Pharsalus (9 August)—not to mention Caesar's birthday (12 July, first performed as a festival in 42 B.C.E.).[92] For the first time the name of a human being is on the *fasti*, even if the actual creation of a named festival in honor of a living human had to wait, as we have seen, for the Augustalia of 19 B.C.E.[93] Other ideas were mooted in Caesar's lifetime that did not get carried through, but that anticipated the kind of honorific acts that later *fasti* would commemorate. Cicero tells us, for example, that Antonius proposed that an entry should be made in the *fasti* for the Lupercalia, saying that on this day the kingship was offered to Julius Caesar by M. Antonius the consul, but that he had refused it.[94] Cicero himself, a great adept in the invention of honors, proposed in April 43 B.C.E. that the name of D. Brutus should be written in the *fasti* beside his birthday, since by chance this was the day that his victory at Mutina on 21 April was announced at Rome: although Cicero does not mention Caesar's name in this passage, Caesar was clearly the prototype for the idea that D. Brutus too should have "a perpetual mark in the *fasti* of his most welcome victory" (*notam . . . in fastis gratissimae uictoriae sempiternam*).[95] The wish to avoid Caesar's example means that Cicero has to resort to the desperate expedient of pointing to the legendary Acca Larentia as a precedent for honoring a living human being in the *fasti* in this way: in making his proposal, he tells M. Brutus, "I followed the precedent of our ancestors, who gave this honor to the woman Larentia, to whom you *pontifices* make your regular sacrifice at the altar in the Velabrum" (*sum maiorum exemplum secutus, qui hunc honorem mulieri Larentiae tribuerunt, cui uos pontifices ad aram in Velabro sacrificium facere soletis*).[96] Cicero is perfectly well aware that Caesar and D. Brutus have in fact no precedents for their presence on the *fasti*.

The revolutionary Julian calendar, with its new use in constructing the Principate's part in Roman practice, played a profoundly important role in the integration of the regime into the changing religious and ideological patterns of post-Republican life. In adding all these meanings to the dense semiotic displays of the Roman year, the new *fasti* progressively redefined the meaning of what living as a Roman now meant.[97] The period of Augustus's rule was when the greatest part of this work on the *fasti* was done; Rüpke well points out that much of the impetus for addition and elaboration died away as the regime consolidated itself and the reign of Augustus became itself a foundational period in its own right.[98] By the time of Claudius the revolutionary momentum was more or less played out, even though the calendars clearly continued in use. All of our surviving monumental inscribed imperial *fasti* come from the reigns of Augustus and Tiberius, although additions are occasionally registered on them up to Claudius's reign.[99]

THE YEARS OF HISTORIOGRAPHY

The emperors' encroaching presence also warps the distinctive Roman form of historiography, that of annalistic history *(annales)*, inaugurated by the first Roman to write history, Fabius Pictor.[100] The narratological correlative to the monumental *fasti* with their paired consuls, *annales* are organized around the Republican format of the successive pairs of annually elected consuls and give a year-by-year account of the life of the city and its empire.[101] Ideally, the subject matter and the format are mutually determining "due to the structure of the state," which is based precisely on "annually elected magistrates who actually ran the state."[102] The consuls not only provide a backbone for the city's dating system together with an organizing principle for the events of a given year; they also generate the action that is the material for the historian.

The richest and best-studied departures from this tradition are to be found in Tacitus, and a fine study exists on the subject in Ginsburg (1981). Already in Livy, however, whom Ginsburg and others take as the norm from which Tacitus departs, there are numerous examples of self-conscious variation to show how pressure on Republican patterns is mirrored in the narrative. Rich (1997) has well demonstrated the way that Livy departs from his year-by-year format "probably for the first time" when he comes to the tangled and constitutionally hideous years from the Social War to the revolt of Lepidus in 78 B.C.E. (books 71–90); here he narrates "in a single section events taking place in one region over two or more years," using flashbacks as he covers widely disparate events. As Rich says, "Republican institutions were in disarray in those years, and it would have been wholly inappropriate, and indeed impossible, to retain the old regular pattern for the annual narratives."[103] When he came to the final collapse of the Republic, Livy may well have forsaken the annalistic patterning and returned to the personality-dominated format of his first book, where the narrative of the kings is not structured around the annual rhythm.[104] Even within the securely Republican period of the early fourth century, a constitutional crisis can produce a narratological one. When the tribunes Licinius and Sextius veto the election of the curule magistrates for the years 375–371 B.C.E. (Livy 6.35.10), then dating and proper narrative both become impossible: "by eliminating the authorities by whom time is measured the tribunes effectively take control of narrative authority as well, while the state and its record simply stop."[105]

In the light of these highly self-referential Livian moments, Rich is certainly right to say that the Livian norm that Ginsburg posits as the foil for Tacitus's aberrations is too rigid. Nonetheless, Ginsburg's fundamental insights into Tacitus's procedures remain valid, as Rich likewise stresses. This is especially clear in the way Tacitus systematically reduces the consuls' role in the narrative from that of actors to ciphers. Instead of leading off the year in the nominative and being projected into actually doing something, as regularly in Livy, Tacitus's consuls are cited in the ablative absolute construction as a mere date: this narratological move is the historiographical correlative of the consulship's demotion from office to date in the Fasti Capitolini.[106] Further, even in terms of the comparison with Livy, this is a case where the later author is himself performing an act of reductionism on his predecessor in order to highlight his own departures. It is Tacitus, after all, not just Ginsburg, who keeps speaking of annalistic technique as a confining norm and affecting to chafe at its restrictions.[107] As Rich says, it is only at *Annales* 6.31–37 that Tacitus for the first time explicitly comments on his including material from more than one year in one section, so carefully does he go through the motions of adhering to the format whose meaninglessness he illustrates.[108] Tacitus, in other words, needs to posit a hyper-Republican and hyper-annalistic Livy in order to heighten his own ironic contrasts between Republican sham and imperial reality in the period he is treating.[109] The very first sentence of annalistic history in Tacitus's oeuvre is already driving wedges into the fault line between Livian form and Tacitean content: *Initium mihi operis Seruius Galba iterum Titius Vinius consules erunt* ("The beginning of my work will be Servius Galba (for the second time) and Titius Vinius as consuls," *Hist.* 1.1.1).[110] Tacitus is "forced" to begin on 1 January with the entry into office of the new consuls. This is a formally correct date for beginning, but it is at odds with the fact that the narrative should "really" have begun with the real transfer of power six months earlier, when Nero died. The first of these consuls, after all, has actually been emperor since June of the previous year, and the sentence at first looks as if it will shape up into something like "The beginning of my work will be Servius Galba *as emperor*." It is the word *iterum* that derails this "other" opening; you can be consul for the second time, but not emperor.

One can observe this technique in operation in a rich passage from early in the reign of Nero (13.10–11). Here Tacitus lays hold of all three of his interrelated inherited time charts (both kinds of *fasti* together with the annalistic historiographical format) and shows them all buckling and cracking under the new dispensation, so as to reveal the radical incommensurability between the imperial monarchy and the fundamental rhythms of Roman time. Immediately before the passage in question, Tacitus carefully reminds his readers of the Republican annalistic norm by creatively transgressing it.[111] Tacitus has just been narrating foreign affairs, in Armenia. Ostensibly in order to preserve the coherence of the mininarrative about that piece of business he has continued the story until the next consuls, narrating the events of 54 and 55 in sequence as one unit, when he should strictly have split them up into one year: *quae in alios consules egressa coniunxi* ("Events extending into other consulships I have here linked together," 13.9.3).[112] Once the annalistic norm has been reinforced by this mild violation, Tacitus then shows us the Senate proposing to jettison altogether the fundamental basis of annalistic history and of civil life: they vote to change the beginning of the year from 1 January to Nero's birthday on 15 December, even though Nero, still in his "good" phase under the tutelage of Seneca and Burrus, declines this honor: *quamquam censuissent patres ut principium anni inciperet mense Decembri, quo ortus erat Nero, ueterem religionem Kalendarum Ianuariarum inchoando anno retinuit* ("Although the fathers had voted that the start of the year should begin in the month of December, in which Nero had been born, he retained the old reverence for the Kalends of January to initiate the year," 10.1).[113] The closeness of the escape is straightaway brought out at the beginning of the next section, when Nero and Antistius, in the ablative absolute, mark the new year as the consuls of 55 (11.1). Of course, one of these consuls is only a consul, and the other one is the emperor. Unlike the beginning of a new year in Livy or in the Republic, with this new year no power is transferred, no change in the underlying realities takes place; the names are in fact reduced to being a date.[114]

The pressure exerted by the new regime on both kinds of *fasti* is brought out in a devastating pun in *Annales* 4.70, finely elucidated by Morgan (1998). Here, on the first day of the new year 28, the emperor Tiberius appropriates the consuls' prerogative of inaugurating the new year by taking over their prayers for the state in a letter to the Senate (*sollemnia incipientis anni Kalendis Ianuariis epistula precatus*, 4.70.1). The letter turns to denounce one Sabinus, who is forthwith condemned and led off to execution; as he is led away, Sabinus cries out "that such was the year's inauguration, these were Sejanus's victims that were being felled in sacrifice" (*sic inchoari annum, has Seiano uictimas cadere*, 70.1). As Morgan shows, the name of Tiberius's henchman here hides the name of the god who should be receiving proper attention as custodian of ordered Roman time and procedure, namely Janus, the custodian of the calendrical *fasti* and the god who receives first sacrifice from the new consuls: "It was a token of the smooth and proper running of the Roman state that sacrificial victims fell in honour of *Ianus* on 1 January, but in the corrupt circumstances of A.D. 28 the sacrifice, of Sabinus, is to *Se-ianus*."[115]

The consuls in this passage are no longer the ones who "open up" *(recludant)* shrines and altars, but prisons instead (4.70.3). Exactly as in the Nero passage we have just discussed, this derangement of the traditional *fasti* is closely associated with a self-referential comment on the confines of annalistic historiography, for immediately after the death of Sabinus comes another letter from Tiberius, at which point Tacitus makes one of his most famous remarks about the restrictions imposed by his conventions: *ni mihi destinatum foret suum quaeque in annum referre, auebat animus antire statimque memorare exitu* ("If it had not been my design to refer events each to their proper year, by inclination I would be anxious to anticipate and immediately to recall the outcomes," 4.71.1). Once again, all of the fundamental categories of Roman time are being subjected to destructive pressure.

A CALENDAR THAT MEASURES TIME

We turn now to the impact of Julius Caesar's reformed calendar. So far we have focused on the ideological power of the revolution in representations of the calendar, with all the additional exegesis and imperial commemoration that adhered to the new *fasti*. Yet the mechanism of the 365¼-day calendar was itself a revolution, one that had wide-ranging repercussions for the Romans' apprehension of time in many guises. Caesar's new calendar, perfected by Augustus, represents a huge watershed in the organization of time not just in ancient Rome, but in post-Roman Europe, and eventually the whole modern world. In the late sixteenth century, Joseph Scaliger was still extraordinarily impressed by the improvement Caesar's reform represented over the ramshackle Republican calendar it superseded: "The Julian calendar . . . marked a victory in the realm of culture more lasting than any Roman victory on land or sea."[116]

The mesh between civil and natural time that the reformed calendar provided was one that had never before been seen in the Mediterranean, and never before aimed at. No civil calendar in the Mediterranean world before 1 January 45 B.C.E. had pretended to approximate a harmony with the high degree of astronomical accuracy that scholars had achieved in their construction of observation-based calendars. The pre-Julian Republican calendar was certainly no better off than any other in this regard—indeed, according to Scaliger, it was considerably worse: "No nation in human memory has used a worse calendar than theirs."[117] Astronomical observations show how adrift the Republican dates often were from the natural year. The solar eclipse of 190 B.C.E. that can be given the Julian date of 14 March was observed in Rome on the fifth day before the Ides of Quintilis, that is,

"11 July," while the eclipse of 21 June 168 B.C.E. was observed at Pydna in north-eastern Greece on the third day before the Nones of September, that is, "3 September."[118] State festivals that were notionally keyed in to seasonal events had no link with the relevant time of year: before Caesar's reform, says Suetonius, the calendar was so disturbed "that the harvest festivals did not coincide with the summer nor the vintage festivals with the autumn" (*ut neque messium feriae aestate neque uindemiarum autumno competerent, Jul.* 40.1).

We are all disposed to side with Scaliger and see the supersession of the Republican by the Julian calendar as a self-evident triumph for science and common sense. We do so because as inhabitants of Caesar's grid we take it for granted that a calendar is there precisely to *measure time,* to create an ideal synthesis of natural and socially or humanly organized time and in the process to capture a "time" that is out there, waiting to be measured. In virtually all societies throughout most of human history, however, this is not what calendars have been for, since time is not something waiting to be measured, but the product of the operation of measurement. Stern's important study of time and calendar in ancient Judaism makes the issues clear:

> The calendar should not be perceived, necessarily, as a time-measuring scheme. Its primary purpose, in any society, is to facilitate the co-ordination of events and activities, and to measure the duration of activities and processes . . . for instance, to determine the dates of festivals, establish the length of contracts and agreements, etc. The calendar is fully purposeful without any underlying notion of the time-dimension.[119]

The fact that all calendars operate in conjunction with either the sun or the moon or both likewise predisposes us to feel that they are attempting to measure time, on the post-Caesarian assumption that the relationship between the movements of earth and sun somehow *is* what time is.[120] Yet this is not the case, as Stern again makes clear: "The reason why the moon and sun are employed in the construction of calendars is that their courses are universally knowable, and reasonably regular and predictable. . . . The courses of the moon and sun do not have, however, intrinsic time-measuring properties."[121]

When observing ancient societies it is natural for a modern person to feel frustration that they did not have more "accurate" or "useful" calendars, yet it is the result ultimately of a post-Caesarian frame of mind to assume that what counts in a calendar is accuracy and that what calendars are for is to be "useful" in a sense that corresponds to a modern sense of utility. The calendars of Athens are a valuable caution against such assumptions.[122] Athens simultaneously ran two calendars without reconciling them. The first was the archon's calendar, which regulated the festivals and divided the year into twelve lunar months, with an extra month being intercalated usually every other year. This calendar had a notional relationship to the true phases of the moon, so that "the beginning of the month approximated the appearance of the new lunar crescent."[123] Second-century B.C.E. inscriptions, indeed, regularly give two dates, one "according to the archon" (κατ᾽ ἄρχοντα), and one "according to the god" (κατὰ θεόν): here the date "according to the archon" is that of the festival calendar, while the date "according to the god" is a designation according to the actually observed phase of the moon.[124] Adjustments were sometimes made to the archon's calendar to bring it into closer relation to the actual lunar phases, usually by adding one or more days.[125] In addition to this festival lunar calendar, with its reasonably close but varying relationship to lunar phases, democratic Athens maintained a calendar based on the organization of its council, the βουλή. This council was composed of representatives of the ten tribes, each of which took turns serving as "presidents," πρυτάνεις, of the council; their period of officiating was called a "presidency/prytany" (πρυτανεία), and the prytany calendar was therefore divided into ten units, not twelve months.[126] Until the fourth century B.C.E. the festival calendar and the prytany calendar began and ended on different days, and inscriptions can give dates from both of them.

From the fifth century B.C.E. onwards Athens certainly had at its disposal all the astronomical knowledge necessary for creating a calendar that would be in harmony with the natural seasons, and that could harmonize these differing systems into a united solar and civil calendar. Yet the sophisticated astronomical models of the time were not even used as a control for the different civil calendars, let alone as a template for a new calendar altogether.[127] It has even been argued that the prytany calendar was in fact run as a 365/366-day solar calendar for an extended period in the late fifth century.[128] It is all the more striking, then, that the city did not take what might strike a modern observer as the natural step of perpetuating a reformed single civil calendar on this "accurate" model; instead, the prytany's solar calendar was abolished toward the end of the fifth century. There are various possible explanations as to why this happened, but all the explanations concern internal and external political ideology, not astronomical considerations.[129] What appear to moderns to be criteria of accuracy and utility are very considerably less important than relationships between council and archon, or between metropolis and allies.

The Athenian calendars are not in place to measure time, but to regulate mean-ingful civil, religious, and interstate activity in ways that best serve the city's inter-ests as understood in the light of changing circumstances. The fact that their cal-endrical systems did not do a very good job of tracking natural phenomena is of marginal significance. It is clear that highly complex and sophisticated societies, including international empires such as those of Athens or Republican Rome, could operate perfectly successfully under these apparently ramshackle systems. Before Caesar's reform, the very idea that the calendar ought to track celestial movements accurately could strike a Roman as almost quaint. Twenty-five years before the reform, Cicero tells the audience of the *Verrines* about the way that Greeks add a day or two every now and then to recalibrate their calendars, in the way we have just observed the Athenians doing. This is, he says, a "habit of the Sicilians and other Greeks" (*consuetudo Siculorum ceterorumque Graecorum, Verr.* 2.2.129); he is struck by the fact that they bother to "make their days and months fit with the ordered pattern of the sun and moon" *(quod suos dies mensesque con-gruere uolunt cum solis lunaeque ratione)*. It is very revealing that a Roman in 70 B.C.E. could see the Greek calendars (to our eyes, so defective) as striving for con-gruence with *ratio*, "ordered pattern"; Cicero's language also incidentally reveals how far it is from the Roman attitude to see such a goal as part of what the Roman calendar should be about.

THE HARMONIES OF CAESAR'S YEAR

This whole situation changed, literally overnight, as the final, 445th, day of the final year of the Republican calendar terminated at midnight of the final day of December 46 B.C.E., the last time that December would not have 31 days.[130] Only after 1 January 45 B.C.E. was it for the first time feasible in the Mediterranean world to have the civil and natural years in harmony under the same standard of repre-sentation. This revolution was one whose implications were immediately appre-hended by contemporaries, for no educated Roman could fail to be impressed by the phenomenal improvement in consistency that Caesar's calendar represented in comparison with the Republican calendar. Not only the novel accuracy of the reform became apparent, but also the power that accrued to Caesar's authority by it.[131] Plutarch preserves a splendid joke by Cicero that brings out the realization of the power of both the calendar and its author. When someone remarked that the constellation of the Lyre would be rising the next day, Cicero said, "Yes, by decree."[132] Here the power of Caesar is seen as controlling the celestial movements themselves, and since the Lyre rises on the fifth day of January according to Caesar, Cicero was making his epochal observation when the new calendar was not yet four days old.[133]

Cicero's joke captures very well the intuition that Caesar's revolutionary reform is part of a larger revolution of systematizing and personal control in many departments of Roman life, by which Caesar's name and presence were made indispensably central.[134] The reform of the calendar is the first item mentioned by Suetonius in his catalogue of the ways in which Caesar undertook "to put the condition of the state into order" (*ad ordinandum rei publicae statum, Jul.* 40.1). It is very attractive to see the same Caesarian regularizing and ordering urge at work in the reform of the calendar as in his grammatical work *On Analogy,* which argued for the same kind of systematizing approach to the Latin language: Caesar was seeking a kindred harmony between nature and grammar and between nature and the calendar.[135] Julius Caesar was Pontifex Maximus, and it was in this capacity that he instituted the calendrical reform of what remained fundamentally a festival calendar. The matrix of Rome's religious life was now being harmonized by Egyptian and Greek science, personified by the astronomer Sosigenes who accompanied Caesar from Alexandria and oversaw the details of the reform: the figure of the calendar's author was stamped on it for all time with the renaming of the month Quintilis as Julius.[136] The full commemoration of this nexus of knowledge and power had to wait almost another forty years, until 9 B.C.E., when Augustus set up his remarkable *horologium* complex on the Campus Martius.[137] This extraordinary monument was designed to be in place for the next year, 8 B.C.E., to celebrate his definitive recalibration of the Julian year, whose intercalation had gone awry in the intervening years: 8 B.C.E. was also the year in which the name of Augustus took over from the month of Sextilis.[138] Although many of the details remain controversial, there is no doubt that this complex displays the power of the *princeps* to control time through his mastery of foreign knowledge.[139] The *gnomon* of the massive sundial was provided by the first Egyptian obelisk imported to Rome; dedicated to the Sun by Augustus in his capacity as Pontifex Maximus, the obelisk cast its shadow at noon on a meridian line whose zodiacal demarcations were annotated in Greek.[140]

The new calendar, for all its accuracy in correlating the civil cycle with astronomical phenomena, was still only one of a number of mechanisms available for charting time, since the rhythms of the Roman festival calendar were not the only ones pulsing through the life of the city and empire. The people of Rome and Italy responded to the new calendar's success in tracking the solar year by adapting the old format of the parapegma to take account of various other cycles not covered by Caesar's calendar.[141] By Caesar's time there were plenty of parapegmata in book form, but the parapegma was still very popular in the original form from which it took its name, as an inscription with holes into which a peg was stuck, to be moved each day so as to keep tracking whichever cycle the inscription was concerned with. In Greece, where the civil calendars were lunar and made no attempt to follow the sun, the parapegmata concentrated on supplementing the civil calendars with information keyed in to the annual motion of the sun, especially stellar phases and the astrometeorological phenomena that were associated with them. In post-Caesarian Rome and Italy, once a calendar was in place that could very successfully capture the solar year, parapegmata concentrated on other rhythms—local nundinal cycles, the 29- or 30-day lunar cycle, and eventually the cycle of the seven-day week. The parapegmata, as Lehoux puts it, are "*extra-calendrical* devices used for keeping track of non-calendrical cycles," and the cycles that interest them will be precisely the ones not covered by the local calendar.[142] The new calendar's remarkable success in aligning the civil and solar years did not, then, preempt the need for any other mechanisms for tracking cycles of time but provided a basis for a symbiotic relationship with the parapegmata, which very probably impinged more directly on most people's daily experience. The reach of the new calendar was restricted in other respects as well. Our conceptions of utility might lead us to imagine that the new calendar should transform itself into an empire-wide web, but, as we shall see at the end of this chapter, such was not the case: the diffusion of the calendar was limited and culture-specific, and many other civil calendars remained quite happily in place for as long as the Empire lasted.

Despite these qualifications, the new Julian calendar undoubtedly had a profound impact in the wide areas that it did reach. In our attempt to see what difference the reform made to the Romans' apprehension of time we are very fortunate to have a control in the form of two works by the polymath Varro. Varro wrote two surviving works that included substantial sections on the rhythms of the year, and it is very good luck for us that one of these sections was written immediately before Caesar's reform, and the other nine years after it.

First, Varro has a long passage on the calendar in book 6 of his work "On the Latin Language" *(De Lingua Latina);* even though this work was finally published sometime shortly after the reform, the section on the calendar is clearly written with the Republican calendar in mind.[143] At the beginning of this portion of his work he describes the natural divisions of the year—the year itself, months, days, seasons (6.1–11). He then turns from "the division made by nature" *(naturale dis-*

crimen) to "the names of the days as given by the city" *(ciuilia uocabula dierum,* 6.12).[114] He will first speak of the days "that have been instituted for the sake of the gods, then those instituted for the sake of men" (*prius qui deorum causa, tum qui hominum sunt instituti*); by this he means first the festivals (6.12–26), to be followed by the calendrical terminology of Kalends, Nones, Ides, *dies comitiales, nefasti,* and so on (6.27–32). As he begins his discussion of the festivals, it becomes immediately apparent that Varro shows virtually no interest whatever in the relationship between the natural cycle that he has just been expounding in the first eleven sections and the civil and religious calendar. The Roman festivals are either fixed in the calendar or else movable *(conceptiuae),* and in his entire discussion of the fixed festivals Varro mentions only two as being related to the natural year in any way. One is the Robigalia, on 25 April, when sacrifice is made to personified Blight to protect the standing corn (6.16).[145] I give the date of the Robigalia, although Varro very seldom refers to the festivals by date: he goes through the year sequentially from January to December but mentions the date of only three festivals, with specific reasons for doing so in each case.[146] The other festival that Varro keys in to the natural year is the Vinalia (Wine Festival). There are in fact two Vinalia, each of them mentioned by Varro. On its first mention he means the Vinalia of 23 April, and here he gives an elaborate description of how the *flamen Dialis* inaugurates the vintage, orders the picking of the grapes, sacrifices a lamb to Jupiter, and in the middle of the sacrifice himself first picks a bunch of grapes (6.16). This is very odd, because April is not the time of harvesting grapes, but a time to celebrate the fact that the young grapes are now secure from the threat of frost.[147] The vintage festival falls much later in the year, on 19 August; when Varro mentions this later Vinalia, however, he makes no reference to the vintage or to any natural cycle but rather mentions a cult of Venus and a holiday for kitchen gardeners (6.20). It is very striking that Varro inserts his battery of information about the harvesting of grapes when he mentions the earlier festival, in April, and not at the "right" moment, in August. Grapes are not harvested in April, but a quick read of Varro would give you the impression they are: he is simply putting his dossier on the Vinalia into the text when the first Vinalia occurs, even if it is the "wrong" one.

It is not that Varro is unaware that some festivals notionally have a relationship with the natural cycle.[148] When he has finished with fixed festivals and gets to the section on movable feasts, which do not have a fixed day marked in the calendar but are announced by the priests each year (6.25–26), two of the five he mentions are agricultural festivals, the Feriae Sementivae (Seed-Sowing Festival) and the Paganicae (Country-District Holiday). Why some festivals keyed into natural processes are fixed and others movable is not something that engages his interest; certainly, it is not an instinctive reflex to conceive of the civil operations and the natural operations as a duet. Varro is still in precisely the same situation as Cato a century before, for in the *De Agricultura* Cato "uses the civil calendar only for the dates of business affairs, such as contracts. For other purposes he reckons mainly by the stars."[149] For Varro, as the case of the Vinalia shows, the opportunity to make a meaningful connection between the state's calendar and the operations of the natural cycle of the year is not taken up. From this perspective, Suetonius's famous comment on the disarray in the Republican calendar, quoted above, reveals itself as coming from a post-Julian point of view: it is hard to believe that the man who saw no difficulty in discussing a vintage festival in April was very concerned "that the harvest festivals did not coincide with the summer nor the vintage festivals with the autumn" (Suet. *Jul.* 40.1).[150]

We turn now to Varro's *De Re Rustica*, which was published after the Julian reform, in 37 B.C.E.[151] When Varro talks in the first book of this later work about the divisions of the year and their relationship with agriculture and nature we are, all of a sudden, in a completely different world (1.28.1). First he gives the natural divisions of the year, linking the beginning of the various seasons to the time when the sun is in various constellations: *dies primus est ueris in aquario, aestatis in tauro, autumni in leone, hiemis in scorpione* ("The first day of spring is [when the sun is] in Aquarius, that of summer in Taurus, of autumn in Leo, of winter in Scorpio," 1.28.1). He then gives the lengths of these natural seasons (spring contains ninety-one days, summer ninety-four, and so on). Now he does something he could not possibly have conceived of ten years earlier, and he marks the novelty of what he is about to do with a telling phrase, referring to "these figures, correlated to our civil days, *the ones that are now in existence*," *quae redacta ad dies ciuiles nostros, qui nunc sunt*[152]—at which point he proceeds to the extraordinary step of giving Roman calendrical dates for these seasonal phenomena, in a way that would have been simply and literally impossible before 1 January 45 B.C.E.: spring now begins on 7 February, summer on 9 May, autumn on 11 August, and winter on 10 November.[153] Not ten years have gone by since the calendar's reform, and the reorientation that Varro has performed is profound. In the first of these two works, the festivals are in chronological order but for the most part undated and not related to natural processes that they might be thought to track; in the second, the Roman calendar is capable of capturing the cyclical predictability of nature itself. This is the first documented step in a process that will eventually lead to the calendrical dates ousting stellar phases from Latin parapegmata as the index to meteorological phenomena: when the calendar has such an unprecedentedly tight bond with the movement of the sun, then there is no longer any need to make the rising and setting of constellations the organizing principle of time.[154]

Varro's adaptation to the reform and its implications is still not complete. When he continues from the section we have just investigated to give information on when to perform various agricultural activities, he is still working from the data of a parapegma, and not giving calendrical dates.[155] It is fascinating to observe the elder Pliny, some hundred years after Varro, plotting the natural rhythms of the agricultural year systematically against the Roman calendar itself. Here we see the fully developed mentality of someone utterly at home in the Julian grid, able to comment shrewdly on the implications of the exercise of harmonizing the calendar and the natural world. Pliny devotes a long piece of book 18 of his *Natural History* to a discussion of the rhythms of the seasonal—especially agricultural—year (18.201–320). He pays regular attention to the issue of how these rhythms relate to the calendar, going much farther than Varro in systematically giving calendrical dates for the risings and settings of the various constellations and for many other associated meteorological phenomena.[156] The entire section begins as an inquiry into the right time to sow crops (18. 201), and for many pages we are instructed on all kinds of natural phenomena in their rhythmically occurring, and datable, patterns. Pliny remains perfectly well aware, however, that this is not a watertight grid, and he repeatedly comments on the fact that meteorological and calendrical patterns have a complex interrelationship. In an important section at the beginning of his treatment he discusses the different dates for sowing different crops and opens up a crucial question in the process. Some people, he remarks, say you should use seasonal signs such as the arrival of the west wind or the spring equinox to determine times for sowing (201–4). Some, however, pay no attention to the fine points of meteorology and lay down guidelines by means of calendrical time (*quidam omissa caelesti subtilitate temporibus definiunt*, 205): they will bluntly give calendrical prescriptions for the times appropriate for sowing different crops. These people, according to Pliny, pay no attention to nature, while the first group pay too much (*ita his nulla naturae cura est, illis nimia*, 205). In other words, it is as much an error to pay no attention to natural phenomena in such matters as it is to pay no attention to the calendar. In the end, however, the world of nature will not submit to the calendrical constraints. Pliny uses a deft legal metaphor to drive this point home, introducing a reference to a realm where the calendar really did have a prescriptive force: "We cannot expect changes of weather to answer to bail on dates fixed in advance" (*non ad dies utique praefinitos expectari tempestatum uadimonia*, 231).

THE CIVIL AND THE NATURAL

The kind of distinction Pliny is working with is one that matters profoundly to many Romans who write on the calendar. It would have made instant sense to Varro, for it fits into his favorite polarized pair, the "civil" and the "natural," which we have already observed in his antithesis in *De Lingua Latina* between "the division made by nature" (*naturale discrimen*) and "the names of the days as given by the city" (*ciuilia uocabula dierum*, 6.12). This pairing likewise figures heavily in the work of Censorinus, who is greatly indebted to Varro's work. Much of the organizational backbone of Censorinus's *De Die Natali* is provided by the interplay between the civil and the natural, especially in terms of *saecula* (17.1), years (19.4), months (21.1), and days (23.1). The working method is to establish that in each case there is a measurable unit of time "out there" in nature, which different societies approximate or represent in different ways.[157] Whether the issues are framed in precisely this Varronian manner or not, the fascination of the interplay between the natural and the constructed underpins much of the Romans' engagement with the Caesarian calendar, which invited appraisal as the most successful attempt by any society to capture the natural world's rhythms in a human construction. The calendar thus becomes indispensable to Roman thinking on the problem of culture. The calendar can seem like the quintessential cultural product in its profound constructedness *and* its inextricability from realms of nature that are ultimately independent of human control; its shaping of natural experience can seem so successful that its shaping power is naturalized. The debate the Romans conducted about the naturalness or conventionality of their representations of time is, as we saw in the introduction, one that continues to be conducted today, even if in rather different terms.

It is not surprising that Ovid is the author who responds with greatest zest to the challenge of exploring these problems, in his calendar poem, *Fasti*. In his treatment, to which we now turn, the Julian calendar feels at once profoundly natural, for it tracks the seasons and cycles of the natural year with unprecedented success, and profoundly conventional, since it is up to society's interpretation to impose meaning upon these cycles and to mark them out in language and symbolic representation.[158]

Ovid represents the development of Roman time as the cumulative construction of an ever tighter mesh between civil and natural time, culminating in Caesar's reform. At first "the stars ran free and unobserved through the years" (*libera currebant et inobservata per annos/sidera*, 3.111–12); astronomy assisted the early Roman calendar, he continues (3.151–54), "but the times were still wandering around, until

Caesar took charge of this along with many other things" (*sed tamen errabant etiam tunc tempora, donec/Caesaris in multis haec quoque cura fuit*, 3.155–56). The Roman calendar is a microcosm or even an allegory of the Roman world, moving from a ramshackle freedom to increasing regulation under the Caesars. Here again we see the force of the "fall from grace" template we investigated in chapter 4, as humans move from a supposed time before time into the increasingly tight control of the conditions of modernity. Ovid sees very clearly the ideological motivation behind Caesar's reform, as is revealed by the way he describes Caesar "taking charge of the times along with many other things": shortly thereafter, the point is reinforced when Ovid says that Caesar "wanted to know in advance the heaven that had been promised to him; nor as a god did he want to enter, a guest, into homes he didn't know" (*promissumque sibi uoluit praenoscere caelum/nec deus ignotas hospes inire domos*, 159–60).

For all the success of Caesar's harmonizing procedures, Ovid knows, just as Pliny does, that the controlling power of the grid falls short of controlling nature, or of ultimate success in tracking its day-to-day unpredictability. The inherent arbitrariness of the human plotting of time is an important theme in Ovid's poem, highlighting the way in which the Romans could appreciate that even the web that Caesar had thrown over the flow of time was fundamentally a convention, a human grid for human convenience, ultimately incommensurable with the phenomena it purported to capture.[159] The first line of Ovid's poem announces his subject matter as *Tempora cum causis Latium digesta per annum* ("Times arranged/ organized/classified through the Latin year, along with their causes/origins"), and in line 27 he mentions the first Roman to start this arranging process, Romulus (*tempora digereret cum conditor Urbis*, "when the founder of the city was arranging/ organizing the times"). The *tempora*, "times," announced as his subject in the first line are humanly determined time units, as is clear from the fact that they have *causae*, human "causes" or "origins." *Natural* time, however, is not arranged by human agency through the year but is indivisibly continuous: *ter sine perpetuo caelum uersetur in axe* ("Let the heaven revolve three times on its perpetual/ unbroken axis," 4.179).[160] The flow of time and the human grid can never finally be one and the same. Ovid reminds us early on that there are gaps between the times of the year and the days of the calendar, when he is searching for the "Day of Sowing" *(dies Sementiua)* in his book of *fasti* (1.657–58). The Muse intervenes to tell him that this is a movable feast, to be announced by the priests; as she says, *tempora* and *dies*, season and day, are sometimes disjointed (*utque dies incerta sacri, sic tempora certa*, 661).

The acculturated impact of the calendar is so deep that it can make us feel that its demarcations are part of nature, but Ovid follows normal ancient learning in reminding us that, for example, even such a powerful marker as 1 January is a contingent one. Numerous ancient sources discuss the fact that there are many possible places to begin the circle of the year. Plutarch dedicates one of his "Roman Questions" to "why the Romans begin the year in January"; using the same binary pair of nature and convention, he remarks, "In general, by nature (φύσει) there is neither a first nor a last point for things that are revolving in a circle, and it is by custom (νόμῳ) that different people adopt different beginnings of the year" (*Mor.* 268C).[161] Many states began the year in high summer, or in autumn, and one can see why Samuel's authoritative work on ancient calendars should describe the Romans' choice as an "arbitrary beginning point" as opposed to the "natural beginning points" of many Greek states, keyed in to natural astronomical phenomena such as solstices.[162] Plutarch, indeed, in the passage just quoted, ends by saying that the best beginning of the year is the winter solstice, for it is somehow "natural" (κατὰ φύσιν) for human beings, as the point at which the amount of light shed by the sun begins to increase (*Mor.* 268D).

Why, then, did the Romans begin the year in the dead of winter? The Romans themselves were not sure why their civil year began in January, and the names of the months after June (going from Sextilis to December) made it easy for them to imagine that originally their calendar and civil year must have begun at the more "natural" beginning time of the spring, with March as the first month.[163] Ovid asks the god Janus a pointed question in the first book of the *Fasti: dic age frigoribus quare nouus incipit annus, /qui melius per uer incipiendus erat?* ("Tell me, how come the new year begins in the cold season, when it would have been better for it to start in spring?" 1.149–50).[164] Ovid highlights his point by marking the discrepancy between the natural newness of spring and the newness of the civil appurtenances that are on display on the state's artificial beginning point of 1 January. In his description of the year's opening ceremonials, the *fasces*, purple, and rumps of the consuls are all new (*iamque noui praeeunt fasces, noua purpura fulget, /et noua conspicuum pondera sentit ebur,* 1.81–82); when he describes to Janus the newness of spring, which would have been an ideal beginning for the year and for his poem, all the newness of nature is wistfully signposted with repeated "then": *omnia tunc florent, tunc est noua temporis aetas, /et noua de grauido palmite gemma tumet, . . . tum blandi soles . . . tum patitur cultus ager* (151–59). "This," he says, "should by rights have been called the newness of the year" (*haec anni nouitas iure uocanda fuit,* 1.160).[165]

Mars himself is able to indulge complacently in a description of spring at the "right" moment, when he speaks to the poet at the beginning of his own month of March (3.235–42); since spring is now beginning, all of Mars's description is dotted with "now," instead of "then": *nunc fecundus ager, pecoris nunc hora creandi, / nunc auis in ramo tecta laremque parat* (3.241–42). The month of Mars is also presented as an ideal place for the Roman year to start for reasons other than those of natural congruence with the seasons. At the beginning of the book, when Ovid begins telling the story of how the Vestal Silvia became pregnant with Mars's sons Romulus and Remus, he asks a loaded question: *quid enim uetat inde moueri?* ("What prevents me from starting from here?" 3.11). As Barchiesi has pointed out, if we think of our Ennius, where the rape of Silvia is the beginning of the Roman foundation story in epic, then "Why don't I take this as my starting point?" becomes a very powerful question.[166] Under one interpretation of what being a Roman is all about, for the Roman year to start with the month of Mars is appropriate ideologically and historically as well as from the point of view of the seasons. Mars's month used to come first, put there by his son Romulus, but it has since been displaced, by Greek science, which taught the Romans that there were actually twelve months in the year, not ten (3.97–102).[167] In the first two books Ovid has already given us snippets of the Romulus and Remus story, but the beginning of book 3 gives the proper beginning of their narrative at last, with their conception and birth—except that this foundational narrative of origins is no longer at the beginning of the year, or the poem. Ovid creates the idea that calendar time and seasonal time and narrative time ought to be in harmony, and he insinuates that at Rome they used to be more in harmony, in the beginning. Caesar's calendar, for all its success in creating a harmony between the city's time and nature's time, is continuing to preserve disharmonies of other kinds at the same time. Overall, the main effect of reading the poem continuously is one of contingency, not of harmony, as the reader experiences the utter unpredictability of moving through something that is grounded in nature but that is continually having unmotivated juxtapositions flung upon it, as one day of the *fasti*, with all its possible connotations and associations, follows without natural rhyme or reason after another.[168]

Ovid presses harder yet on the categories of civil and natural as they relate to the representation of time in the calendar. As we have already seen, the *tempora* that Ovid announces as his subject in the first line of the *Fasti* are for the most part not natural, since they have human causes. In the second line of the poem, he says he will in addition treat of celestial phenomena, "constellations/signs, their settings beneath the earth and their risings" (*lapsaque sub terras ortaque signa*). These "signs" look at first like a natural system in contrast to the human ordering of the first line, and so, in an important sense, they are;[169] yet Ovid works at breaking down this distinction too. The *signa* are themselves in fact the product of human ordering and distinction, part of a signifying system, as Ovid implies when he points out that the early Romans of Romulus's time did not recognize the patterns in the sky that were picked out by Greek astronomers (3.105–12). The early Romans, according to this highly tendentious representation, are as ignorant as men in the Golden Age, who just look up at the sky and see pretty dots, not semiotic patterns.[170] Both as celestial patterns and as indices of such foreign myths as Andromeda or Arion, the *signa* are Greek. Here we catch a glimpse of the inveterately schizophrenic Roman attitude toward Greece, as the land of culture and learning and as the land of a natural, especially mythic, existence.[171] Both these ways of thinking underpin Ovid's *signa,* which are marked out by Greek astronomical science and are simultaneously the repository of Greek natural myth as opposed to the arranged human time units, *tempora digesta,* of the Roman *fasti* grid. This Roman double perspective on the Greeks likewise finds expression in the Greek zodiacal and seasonal annotations to the meridian line of Augustus's *horologium* on the Campus Martius. In the excavated portions, the names of the zodiacal constellations are in Greek, together with the phrases ΕΤΗΣΙΑΙ ΠΑΥΟΝΤΑΙ ("the Etesian winds stop"), or ΘΕΡΟΥΣ ΑΡΧΗ ("the beginning of summer").[172] Greek is the language of science for the Romans, and the *horologium* complex recognizes and celebrates the way that Rome now controls the Greek knowledge systems that made the new calendar possible; yet Greek is also the "natural" language for marking the passage of the natural year.[173]

THE COUNTRY'S TIME
AND THE CITY'S TIME

The binary opposition between natural and civil, then, is the default mode for exploring this conundrum of culture, however much someone like Ovid may deconstruct it. With the Romans, a discussion of the interplay between natural and civil will almost inevitably be filtered through the lens of the rural and the urban. It is interesting to observe how carefully Roman authors could keep the prerogatives of the city's *fasti* from encroaching upon the world of the country; here we may see the limits of the reach of the city's *fasti,* and these limits throw into relief the power of other forms of time representation, which are not inscribed in the *fasti.*

Virgil's *Georgics* were published some fifteen years after the Julian reform, more than enough time, if we remember the precedent of Varro's *De Re Rustica*, for the poet to have fully assimilated the new technology. The poem, however, rigorously keeps within a pre-reform Hesiodic tradition, based on meteorological patterns and lunar parapegmata. There is not a single date in the *Georgics*. The poem's time markers are all "natural": time is organized and signaled in the georgic world by the constellations, the seasons, the forces of wind and rain, the sun and the moon. Like Hesiod in the *Works and Days* (765–828), Virgil has a section on "days" (1.276–86), but the days here are not Roman calendar days; in particular, they are not Caesar's solar days, but Greek lunar days, as in the parapegmata.[174] The first line tells us that the moon is in control of these days: *ipsa dies alios alio dedit ordine Luna/felicis operum* ("The Moon herself has appointed different days in different order as favorable for work," 1.276). In the last line of his section on days Virgil has a *dies nona*, a "ninth day" (1.286), but this is emphatically not the Roman Nones: the Nones in the Roman calendar do not denote the "ninth" day into the month, as must be the meaning here. Roman calendrical dates are not the only element of the *fasti* missing from the *Georgics*. Virgil names no months in the poem, even though he gives an etymological pun on Aprilis.[175] Nor does he name any festivals. He tells the farmer to "perform annual sacrifice to great Ceres" (1.338–39), but his references are generalized and cannot denote a specific festival, such as the Cerealia or the Ambarvalia.[176] Virgil captures the relentless pressure of the farmer's opportunity-cost time, but he does so without dating it or plotting it into the grid of the city's calendar.[177] His country world is somehow exempt from the *fasti*, in such a way as to reinforce his general picture of detachment between the rural and urban worlds.

Horace picks up the point in his second *Epode*, where we read a long praise of the country life only to discover at the end that all of this has been coming out of the hypocritical mouth of the usurer Alfius (67–70):

haec ubi locutus faenerator Alfius,
    iam iam futurus rusticus,
omnem redegit Idibus pecuniam,
    quaerit Kalendis ponere.

When the usurer Alfius had said this, just on the point of becoming a rustic, he called all his money in on the Ides, and seeks to lend it out again on the Kalends.

Heyworth has well observed the way that the named dates in the last two lines of the poem, the Ides and the Kalends, drive home the disjunction between the richly described round of cyclical life in the country and the hard-nosed, unvarying urban environment of the usurer Alfius.[178] Until the surprise ending, the poem follows a natural rustic calendar straight out of the *Georgics*, a seasonal progression in an annual round: "there is . . . a progression in lines 9–16 from spring to early summer activities which balances the more clearly articulated movement in lines 17–36 from autumn to winter."[179] Horace has surely noticed that the world of the *Georgics* goes on in a noncalendrical environment, for his *Epode* shows only one date or festival of any kind, the Terminalia, when a lamb is killed (*agna festis caesa Terminalibus*, 59).[180] The life of the country follows its natural round without supervision by the *fasti*, just as in the *Georgics*, whereas the last two lines of the poem introduce the two dates that regulate the flow of cash in the city, two dates of exclusively financial significance—the Ides for calling in debts and the Kalends for making new loans—days that are the same every month, rain or shine, summer or winter.[181]

The point about the *Georgics* that Horace had noticed is also picked up on by Ovid when he writes his own didactic poem—not the *Fasti*, of course, which is entirely full of calendrical dates and festival days, but his other didactic poem, the *Ars Amatoria*, which follows Virgil and Hesiod in having its own section on "days."[182] Ovid knows very well what didactic—especially *rustic* didactic—ought to look like, but no one before him had written a didactic poem on sex and the city. In Ovid's case, the days to avoid are ones where the lover might be expected to buy his *puella* a present (so "bad" days are *good*, because the shops will be closed). He introduces his "days" section with the key word *tempora*, the first word of the *Fasti;* and he makes the point that it is not just the denizens of the georgic world who need to know the "times" (1.399–400):

> Tempora qui solis operosa colentibus arua,
> fallitur, et nautis aspicienda putat.

> He is mistaken who thinks that only those who cultivate the plow lands with their work, or sailors, need to look out for times.[183]

Ovid's "times," however, are radically different from Virgil's, for he is situating his work at the heart of cosmopolitan urban life. The days he proceeds to itemize, then, are not Hesiodic or georgic lunar days, but a cluster of all kinds of time markers, including especially the days of the *fasti* that Virgil (and Horace) had so carefully avoided: Roman calendar and festival days (405–6), birthdays (405, 417–18), astronomical markers (409–10), the black day of the Allia (413–14), and even the Jewish Sabbath (416). This is an international panoply of civilized time division, all to be found in the metropolis, the heart of ordered and conventional time.

THE CITY'S TIME
AND THE EMPIRE'S TIME

As Beard (1987) has shown, the distinctive power of the Roman calendar derives overwhelmingly from its specificity to the culture, since it is a religious and political instrument for shaping Roman cultural memory before it is an instrument for measuring time.[184] We can gauge this specificity by reflecting on the question of why the Romans did not make an imperial machine out of the calendar. Once the Romans had organized this extraordinarily successful instrument of time control, it might seem natural to us that they would impose it on their subjects as a means of facilitating worldwide communication and administration. One might expect them to do this not solely on grounds of "utility," which is so often a snare for the modern observer of ancient instruments of time. After all, the organization of time is one dimension of the organization of power, as we have seen very clearly with the case of the Caesarian reform, and the calendar is a necessary medium for regulating and controlling human activity in any empire.[185] Alfred Gell relates an intriguingly revealing fact concerning the Muria, a people of central India among whom he did fieldwork. According to him, only three words from English have entered the normal Muria vocabulary: one is "time," and "the others are 'power' and 'officer.'"[186] In other empires, the calendar has served as a universalizing grid for the whole of the imperial dominions. The ancient Chinese term for incorporating some new region into the empire was to say that its inhabitants had "received the calendar."[187]

In the light of this comparative evidence, it is very striking that the Romans did not attempt to make all the inhabitants of the Empire "receive the calendar." Dating by the consuls was the imperial norm, used together with the regnal year of the emperor, but there was no systematic effort made to impose the calendar itself as a standard throughout the Empire, and many cities that already had their own calendars continued to use them.[188] In the originally less urbanized Latin West the Roman calendar rapidly became normative, but especially in the long-established civil culture of the East local calendars in all their discrepant variety continued in use.[189] Numerous Eastern calendars did adapt themselves to the Julian calendar, sometimes doing no more than taking over the Roman names for months, and sometimes harmonizing more systematically;[190] yet many remained unaltered. The Romans' Greek or Egyptian or Syrian or Jewish subjects had to work with the Roman calendar at the level of interface with the imperial authority, yet they tended not to abandon their own calendars but to synchronize them with the Roman one as needed.[191] Complex negotiations went on as the presence of the imperial system settled, and many local initiatives have left their traces in recast local calendars, but the imposition of a centralized empire-wide system was not at issue. Partly this is a reflection of the Romans' general administrative preference for laissez-faire and subsidiarity, and the lack of interest in imposing the calendar is related to a wide range of similar policies in other spheres.[192] Partly, however, this hands-off tendency reflected the way that the Roman calendar itself continued to be a distinctive marker of Romanness. Its reach was not universal: it was not meant to be a unifying grid for all the peoples of the Empire, but it retained its specific power for Roman citizens as a context for apprehending and exploring Roman identity.[193]

This irreducibly Romanocentric dimension of the calendar potentially enabled any Roman anywhere in the Empire to feel part of a shared community of citizens. In this way the calendar comes close to enabling the "homogeneous" time that Anderson picks out as so crucial to the formation of the consciousness of modern nationalism: Anderson's "homogeneous" time fosters the feeling that disparate individuals are part of a community that is connected laterally, sharing a jointly mapped-out grid of connected time.[194] This sense of shared time is vividly present in the numerous coordinated sets of *fasti* that were erected throughout Italy in the early years of the Principate; Italy had a particularly close relationship with the metropolis, reflected in the display of shared religious cult and synchronized time that was embodied in the *fasti*.[195] These links stretched throughout the diaspora of Roman citizens across the Mediterranean, above all in the case of the colonies, whose cults and calendars linked them back to the center of the Empire, in Rome.[196] Especially within the army, the calendar discharged an important acculturating function as it massaged the diverse recruits into an empire-wide unit through shared anniversaries and festivals. Where the army went, the calendar went too.[197]

Despite all these tendencies toward homogeneity among a widely dispersed citizenry, the Roman calendar, like all other ancient calendars, continued to derive a great deal of its symbolic power from its local grounding, as we saw in the case of Virgil's presentation of time and place in *Aeneid* 8.[198] Even Roman imperial time had a localized dimension. The festivals that mark each month were in many cases cloned and reproduced in other places, but it is not certain that all of them could be, especially if they were related intimately to particular places and buildings in the metropolis.[199] The degree of synchronized homogeneity, then, must have been qualified to some extent by the apprehension that not all of the Roman times could elicit the prescribed responses outside the city itself. Rome's greatest authority on time, Ovid, draws out the full consequences of the localized aspect of the city's time when he writes his exile poetry.[200] For Ovid in exile, the usual contours even of natural time are blurred and become increasingly meaningless;[201] especially, Ovid's banishment to the very fringe of the Roman world has made his participation in Roman time tenuous.[202] In *Tristia* 3.13, when his birthday comes around, Ovid rejects it, in a kind of "inverse *genethliakon.*"[203] As Williams well puts it, "the Roman birthday as a marker of time and progress in life is . . . redundant in exile, where [Ovid's] existence lacks all positive development and the years merge into each other without meaningful distinction."[204] Ovid's identity as a Roman is intimately bound up with the calendar—and not only because he is a poet of the Roman calendar. His estrangement from the city threatens to put him outside Roman time as well as Roman place.

The special importance of the calendar in the Romans' work on their identity is nowhere more clearly visible than in the outsider's view provided by Plutarch in his so-called "Roman Questions." Plutarch composed two sets of *Aetia* (Origins or Causes), one Greek, one Roman, commonly called the "Greek and Roman Questions" after their Latin title *Quaestiones Graecae et Romanae.* A dozen of Plutarch's 113 Roman *aetia* concern calendrical questions, beginning with the one we discussed above: "Why do they adopt the month of January as the beginning of the new year?" (*Mor.* 267F).[205] Plutarch has 59 Greek questions, and only one of them refers to a calendar.[206]

The disparity is partly due to the fact that the Greeks did not have a single calendar for all Greeks, in the way that the Roman calendar can embrace all Roman citizens. Plutarch could, one imagines, have posed more than one question about individual Greek calendars, but the Roman calendar provides more of a unifying focus for inquiry.[207] Still, the disparity goes much farther. The exercise in comparison brings out how deeply Roman culture is implicated in the temporal and calendrical. For Plutarch, it is not possible to talk about Roman culture without engaging with the Romans' representations of time. What was true for Plutarch remains true for us.

Epilogue

The reach of the Romans' time schemes was very great. They extended to heaven to chart the constellations, in the knowledge that the constellations are the result of human work. They extended back to the fall of Troy when the Roman story could be said to begin, and sideways to take in the developments of the empires of Greece and the Near East. Working in history, or operating synchronistic comparisons with other contemporary time schemes, required genuine sophistication of a kind from which our universalizing and homogeneous schemes shield us. Simply living at anything beyond subsistence level required operating with a calendar of genuine complexity and dense semiotic power. The Romans created time machines that we still inhabit, and they were working creatively on time from the beginning of our historical understanding of their culture, in formats that I have not been able to touch on. A chronologically organized study of Roman time would perhaps begin with the layout of the *comitium* area in the Forum, with its lines of sight used for determining and announcing sunrise, noon, and sunset; it might then continue to investigate the use of buildings and of sundials to organize the timely routines of law, politics, and commerce.[1]

As I said in the introduction, I have on the whole excluded from the survey the ways in which the individual person experienced and constructed the passage of time. A powerfully condensed sequence of lines from Horace will have to atone for this omission, since they itemize all of the principal time schemes that enfolded an individual's progress through time. The frames of time alluded to by Horace here capture the recurrent cyclical rhythms of hourly, daily, monthly, seasonal, and annual time, all of them squeezing on the individual's forward movement toward death (*Carm.* 4.7.7–16):

> immortalia ne speres, monet annus et almum
>   quae rapit hora diem:
> frigora mitescunt Zephyris, uer proterit aestas
>   interitura simul
> pomifer Autumnus fruges effuderit, et mox
>   bruma recurrit iners.
> damna tamen celeres reparant caelestia lunae:
>   nos ubi decidimus
> quo pater Aeneas, quo Tullus diues et Ancus
>   puluis et umbra sumus.

The year warns you not to hope for immortality, and the hour that snatches the life-giving day. The cold grows mild with the Zephyrs, summer treads down spring, itself due to perish once apple-bearing autumn has poured out its fruits, and soon inert winter runs back. The swift moons nonetheless restore their heavenly losses; we, once we have fallen down where father Aeneas, rich Tullus, and Ancus fell, are dust and shade.

The sequence is introduced by the large unit of the year (7), followed by the hour and day (8). There follow the four seasons, from the cold of winter in line 9 to the very middle of winter again at the end of the round, with *bruma* in line 12: not just another word for "winter," *bruma* is precisely "the shortest day," a contraction (fittingly) of *breuissima*.[2] Next come the moons, standing for the months, which are able to "*re*store" their losses (*reparant*, 13). The recurrent prefix *re-* organizes the whole structure of the poem, from the "*re*turn" of the grass in line 1 (*redeunt*) to the "*re*currence" of winter in line 12 (*recurrit*) to the triply negated "*re*storation" of the individual human being in lines 23–24 (*non, Torquate, genus, non te facundia, non te/restituet pietas*).[3] Our fate is to be "dust and shade"—exactly what the moon would become if it suffered the fate it looks as if it suffers every month. Virtually every unit of time that affects the individual is here.[4] Since they had no seconds or minutes in use, the hour is the smallest unit Horace deploys.[5] He does not mention the *saeculum*, which might seem an odd omission from the poet of the *Carmen Saeculare*, until we reflect that the *saeculum* is not a unit of time an individual can *experience*, by definition.

Horace's generation, and the ones immediately before and after it, are the ones to which I have returned repeatedly in this book. This was a period when things were changing fast, and many people were actively engaged in creative work with Roman time. Caesar's calendrical reform was only part of a revolution in the representation of time under the evolving new order, with all the inherited forms undergoing profound change. All of this work went hand in hand with revolutions in the organized and encyclopedic representation of knowledge systems of many kinds, especially those to do with space.[6] Ovid, as usual, puts his finger on the point when he tells us that Roman space and natural space are merging in the same way as Roman time and natural time (*Fast.* 1.85–86, 2.683–84).

To quote a scholar whose work on chronology has been indispensable to me over the last few years, Anthony Grafton: "The Romans of the late Republic and early Empire were as obsessed with time, in their own way, as the Europeans of the sixteenth and seventeenth centuries."[7] The Romans' obsession in that period derived above all from their attempts to digest their conquest of most of the known world and their transformation from a republic to a monarchy. Most of the impetus for the later European obsession with time came from their stunned discovery of new parts of the world, ones that had their own ancient time systems, and ones that imposed new time systems on navigators if they were going to sail to and return from them without dying.[8] But part of the impetus for the Renaissance obsession with time came from their own new reengagement with the Romans. In the Romans who were emerging from the new work of contemporary chronographers and historians, they could see a society that looked uncannily modern in the work it devoted to the control and representation of time in all its aspects.

The Romans' chronographic perspectives were in many respects superseded by their successors in the Renaissance, but not before they had contributed fundamentally to the creation of a new set of instruments for the charting of time. If we use the sixteenth and seventeenth centuries as a perspective for comparison, we may see that the Romans' special obsession with time had itself also been the product of encounters with new parts of the world and with new technologies. The work they performed to assimilate these novelties transformed their world in the process and turned them into something close to the first modern society.

NOTES

INTRODUCTION

1. Macey 1991, xviii. Not to mention the roughly 180,000 articles that Macey figures on for the same period (xvi).

2. Adam 1994, 508.

3. Respectively, Lynch 1972; Carlstein, Parkes, and Thrift 1978.

4. On the impact of the Industrial Revolution on the experience of time, see Whitrow 1989, 157–69; cf. Elias 1992, 135–41; Adam 1994, 515.

5. Laurence and Smith 1995–96, 133; cf. Graf 1997, 11–12. My thanks to Joseph Farrell for stimulating discussion of Rome's status as a modern society.

6. Bettini 1991, 113–93, on Roman temporal metaphors; Putnam 1986 on Horace's (im)mortality-obsessed fourth book of *Odes*. James Ker is currently at work on Roman representations of time in a more "private" sphere; our concerns overlap to some degree, but I hope that they will in the end complement each other.

7. As in my last book (Feeney 1998), where comparison between Greece and Rome was the main theme in a discussion of the issues facing both us and them in understanding the interaction between literature and religion at Rome.

8. For an account, and critique, see Gell 1992; Adam 1994.

9. Worsley 1997 is an important study of the multiplicity of knowledge systems in any society. Note, for example, his summary after discussing Australian Aboriginal knowledge systems for classification of the natural world: "There is . . . no such thing as Aboriginal thought with a capital T, all of a piece and based on a central unifying principle: in Durkheim's case, the elements of the social structure; in Lévi-Strauss', the

categories built into the human mind. Thinking, rather, is a plural, not a unitary phenomenon; there are different modes of thought within any one culture" (119).

10. Gell 1992, 326: "Ritual representations of time do not provide a 'world-view' but a series of special-purpose commentaries on a world. . . . Because ritual collective representations of time only cohere in the light of their implicit relation with the practical, they cannot be singled out as constituting the unique, culturally valid representations of time operated by members of a particular society." Cf. Bloch 1989, esp. chap. 1, and Hassig 2001, 61–63, against the common view that the cyclical constructions of Aztec priestly ritual and calendars are somehow *the* Aztec view of time, instead of being one mode of representing time in certain circumstances.

11. Mazzarino 1966, 2.2:412–20; Momigliano 1977b, 179–85; Vidal-Naquet 1986, 39–60; Stern 2003, 8–9; Brettler 2004.

12. Möller and Luraghi 1995, 7.

13. Adam 1994, 508.

14. Appadurai 1981, 201, cautioning against the view that "concepts of time (and indeed the perception of duration itself) are fundamental cultural variables"; Bloch 1989, 7–12; Gell 1992; Adam 1994. Cf. Worsley 1997, 14–15, on how very close Aboriginal classifications of the natural world are, in certain contexts and for certain purposes, to those of "Western biologists, zoologists and botanists."

15. Gell 1992, 315. Stern (2003, 16–17) strongly criticizes Gell, but I am not sure he is right to see Gell depending on the kind of view Stern objects to, namely, that "time is an objective component of the physical world" (17). Gell is not defending a Western objective notion of "pure" time so much as using concepts of shared cognitive capacities to question those who think that some cultures are timeless even within the terms of Stern's own processual understanding of time.

16. Aveni 1989, 18–29.

17. Adam 1990, 89; cf. Gosden 1994, 9: "Biological rhythms are to human time what sex is to gender: a biological structure which is always worked on culturally."

18. As indeed do Bloch (1989), Gell (1992), and Adam (1990, 1994), who all have as their ultimate goal the understanding of discrete cultural forms.

19. Gell 1992, 84–92.

20. An important part of the argument of Adam 1994.

CHAPTER 1. SYNCHRONIZING TIMES I:
GREECE AND ROME

1. Wilcox 1987, 7–8 (a highly important book, that deserves to be better known amongst classicists); Cobet 2000, 9–10.

2. Daffinà 1987, 31–45; Greenway 1999, 132–34; Holford-Strevens 2005, 124–25.

3. Wilcox 1987, 142–43.

4. Grafton 1993, 312–15 (date of incarnation); 278, for the absence of the incarna-

tion ⟨xa⟩ in *Emendatio Temporum;* and 676–77, for its appearance as an era in *Isagogici Chronologiae Canones,* which formed the armature of the later *Thesaurus Temporum* (1606). Grafton regularly and defensibly inserts B.C./A.D. dates in parentheses when quoting Scaliger's text.

5. Grafton 1993, 133.

6. Wilcox 1987, 207; cf. Zerubavel 2003, 52, 92.

7. E.g., Gomme 1945, 7: "Numbering years was a device half adopted by the Romans (A.U.C. together with the consular names), but, by one of the curiosities of history, it long eluded the Greeks." As we shall see in chapter 5, counting years A.U.C. was never an official or even historiographically canonical practice in Rome; similarly, as we shall see throughout the first three chapters, while the Olympiad dating system was an important one for the Greeks and Romans, it never came close to being a universal and self-sufficient era like our C.E. system, even among historians, who always used it as only one of a number of ways of fixing events in a temporal network.

8. A question addressed principally by Hunter (1982) and Wilcox (1987).

9. Wilcox 1987, 9 (on centuries); Zerubavel 2003, 96. The *saeculum,* as Nicholas Horsfall reminds me, is an important unit for the Romans, especially in prophetic or religious contexts, as the longest life span of a human being, regularly rounded to one hundred years (see Censorinus *DN* 17 for a long discussion of various possible lengths for the *saeculum*); as such, the *saeculum* could be used for "interval-counting" to give a sense of depth in time (e.g., Cic. *De Orat.* 2.154, *duobus prope saeculis ante*). Vance Smith points out to me that Dante similarly counts back "venticinque secoli" from his own time to the sailing of the Argo in the final canto of the *Divina Commedia* (*Paradiso* 33.95). But the distinctive power of the modern "century" comes from the fact that it is not a mobile unit, to be used as an interval marker from any ad hoc point of departure, but locked in to a preexisting grid.

10. From "The Sydney Highrise Variations" (L. Murray 1991, 177); quoted with kind permission of Carcanet Press.

11. Note, for example, the "short twentieth century, 1914–1991" of Hobsbawm (1994); the "long nineteenth century, 1780–1920" of http://www.kennesaw.edu/hss/wwork/overview.htm; the "American century" of Slater and Taylor (1999); the "German century" of Fukuyama (1999).

12. Shaw 2003, 29; cf. M. L. West 1978, 376: "Our system . . . appears to us to have an almost objective validity, to be etched into the design of the universe."

13. Such considerations go a long way to explaining why ancient societies did not take up as a universal time chart the system of the astrologers, which, as Tony Grafton points out to me, really did provide a supranational and agreed-upon scheme of time. If (*per impossibile*) someone had wanted or managed to impose a universal time scheme on the Empire, this would have been the best candidate.

14. Whitrow 1989, 159. Until the rapid transport of the last two centuries, far more

was local than we now remember. Music, for example, had localized standards. Any European town might have a different pitch for A from the next town, keyed to the organ in the local church (my thanks to Magen Solomon for this parallel).

15. Note how he continues: "We should not wonder at the inconsistency of the days, since even now, when astronomical matters have been made more exact, different people mark a different beginning and end of the month." Cf. *Rom.* 12.2, where he says that "even now the Roman months have no agreement with the Greek ones."

16. As noted at the end of the preface, the quotation marks enclosing "384 B.C.E." mean that this date corresponds to what we call 384 B.C.E.

17. My thanks to my colleague Tom Hare, who supplied me with this example, and to Stephen Young, for alerting me to the Asian parallel; cf. Greenway 1999, 129, for an example from Anglo-Saxon England.

18. It is a pleasure to acknowledge and recommend the indispensable work of my colleague Tony Grafton on Joseph Scaliger, who is usually hailed as the father of modern synchronistic studies, and, in consequence, as the father of modern historical scholarship (not that this is quite the picture that emerges from Grafton [1993]). Contested synchronisms are only just beneath the surface of our apparently uniform picture of preclassical ancient history. Synchronism with Egpyt underpins the entire dating systems of the Near Eastern and Greek world down to the end of the Dark Age: if the Egyptian dates are out, then so are all the others, and there was no "Dark age" after all: see James et al. 1991. On synchronism in general, Momigliano 1977a, 51; 1977b, 192–93; Asheri 1991–92.

19. A point eloquently argued by Shaw (2003); cf. Wilcox 1987.

20. Asheri 1991–92, 52 (a fundamentally important study of synchronism, to which I am much indebted); cf. Gell 1992, 28, making the crucial related point that objects do not have dates, only events.

21. Stern 2003, 21; my thanks to David Levene for referring me to this important study. Leibniz is the first modern to propound this approach, according to Whitrow 1989, 129; as Whitrow points out, Epicureanism anticipates him (58–59, citing Lucr. 1.459–63).

22. Damasio 2002, 71; cf. Gell 1992, 159, making the identical claim, but moving from the philosophy of time toward an anthropological perspective; cf. also Zerubavel 2003, 40, for the manufacturing of contiguity between isolated moments of time.

23. Aveni 1989, 121; Greenway 1999, esp. 138–39.

24. Twain 1968 (1883), 389, quoted by Zerubavel (2003, 90), who remarks: "In marking significant historical breaks, 'watersheds' often serve as extremely effective *chronological anchors*" (original emphasis).

25. Wodehouse 1987 (1947), 70.

26. πόσα τοι ἔτε᾽ ἐστί, φέριστε;/πηλίκος ἦσθ᾽, ὅθ᾽ ὁ Μῆδος ἀφίκετο; DK 21 B 22.5. Cf. Shaw 2003, 23, on the way that Thucydides follows "the practice, current before

his time, of identifying significant moments by reference to the well known figures involved."

27. Mazzarino 1966 is an excellent introduction to this interval-spacing mentality, in the section on time in ancient historiography, which is incomprehensibly tucked away at the back of his masterpiece as the forty-nine-page-long footnote 555 in vol. 2.2: note especially pp. 439, 446–47, and 448, with his favorite reference to Hor. *Carm.* 3.19.1–2, *Quantum distet ab Inacho/Codrus* (where see also the enlightening note of Williams 1969). See too the lucid discussion of Möller 2004, 170–71, and Möller and Luraghi 1995, 8–10, touching also on the related issue of the ancient historians' practice of linking up the beginning of their narrative to the end of a predecessor's (for which see the charts in Marincola 1997, 289–92).

28. *FGrH* 241 F 1a. Compare the use of the war against Perseus of Macedon (171 B.C.E.) as an interval marker in Cato's *Origines* (F. 49 Peter) and in Sallust (*Hist.* fr. 8). Especially for Cato, who could not date by consular names thanks to his refusal to use personal names in his narrative, it was important to have a hook that was recent and memorable.

29. We return to this issue below, in chapter 5.

30. A famous embassy, this, memorable for the confrontation between Roman imperial power and Greek theoreticians of power: see Purcell 1995, 146–47; Zetzel 1996.

31. Note how the character of Atticus in Cicero's *Brutus* describes his *Liber Annalis*, a book that we would call a chronography, implying a collection of dates: Atticus calls it a "memorial of achievements and officeholders" (*rerum et magistratuum memoriam*, 19).

32. This is the general theme of Wilcox's important book: particularly concise formulations in Wilcox 1987, 9, 13, 74.

33. The phrase "absolute time" is that of Wilcox (1987).

34. Other clear-headed accounts include Cornell 1995, 399–402 and Möller and Luraghi 1995. Stern (2003) offers an excellent approach to these issues via ancient Judaism, finding there the same commitment to "process" rather than "absolute time" that Hunter (1982) finds in Greek historiography.

35. Hunter (1982) made great progress on an original path, so it is not patronizing to observe that she remains still, half-consciously, invested in the idea that Herodotus or Thucydides really knew about dates in our sense but are more interested in their place within the "process," while Wilcox and Shaw see that the relativizing process is what there is: "Classical authors possessed no cognitive awareness of absolute chronology, nor had they a means of identifying each day by a universally acknowledged date. What is more important, they did not expect to do so, or to be able to do so, nor did they think it necessary" (Shaw 2003, 25). Accordingly, Hunter (1982, 254) cites Herodotus's mention of Calliades as the archon at Athens when Xerxes invaded Attica

(8.51.1) as "the one 'absolute date'" in Herodotus, but that is not the function of the mention of Calliades' archonship in the text: Herodotus is not helpfully providing a key to archon lists so that everyone will be able to fix the moment in time, but rather signaling the moment of overlap into Athenian time. Calliades' archonship is only an "absolute date" to us as a result of two millennia of synchronistic work. See rather Wilcox 1987, 57–59, and Shaw 2003, 21, 32.

36. Daffinà (1987, 28–29) comments on how hard it was for a Roman to use the consular lists intuitively as a means of orientating himself in temporal space. Still, for those who were practiced at it, the exercise was clearly not the impossibility it may appear to be to us: note the language of Velleius Paterculus, criticizing those who get the date of Pompey's birth wrong, "even though the ordering of the years from the consulate of C. Atilius and Q. Servilius is so easy" (*cum a C. Atilio et Q. Seruilio consulibus tam facilis esset annorum digestio*, 2.53.4). Many readers of this book will recall scholars of an earlier generation who moved around lists of consuls and archons with this same facility.

37. *Ad Att.* 13.30, 32, 33, 6, 4, 5 = Shackleton Bailey 1965–70, 303, 305, 309, 310, 311, 312. The last in the series, 316, is not keyed in to this legation but forms part of the same pattern of inquiries for a planned dialogue setting. I am heartened by the beginning of the second of these letters, where Cicero says, "You don't quite understand what I wrote to you about the Ten Commissioners"; even Atticus, it appears, found it hard to follow. See Badian 1969 for discussion of the prosopography, with praise for the accuracy of Cicero and Atticus; esp. Sumner 1973, 166–70, on these letters, and 161–76, in general on "Cicero at work" in *Ad Atticum*.

38. Bettini 1991, 143, 167–68.

39. Sumner 1973 on *Brutus*, and Douglas 1966b, esp. 293: "The Leges Annales ensured that Roman politicians were as conscious of such dates as any graduate of his 'year' or 'class'"; cf. Aveni 1989, 178–83, on analogous apprehensions of age groups among the Nuer and the Mursi.

40. We could compare the way in which Cicero speaks of Solon in *Brutus* as being an old man in a Roman time frame but a youth in a Greek one (39).

41. Samuel 1972, 57–138; Hannah 2005, 48–56.

42. Gomme 1945, 2–8, remains the first place to go for a discussion of the problems facing Thucydides in chronology.

43. Jacoby 1954, 1:15; cf. Möller 2001, 248.

44. Jacoby 1954, 2:279—not to mention the Theban equivalents, the Boeotarchs, Pythangelus and Diemporus, who are part of his narrative of the incursion into Plataea.

45. Note the argument of Smart (1986) that Thucydides was intent on making the beginning of the war part of a "natural" process, not dependent on the artificial and discontinuous eponymous dating; cf. Dunn 1998b, 40–41. Timaeus appears to have

marked this lesson: see Meister 1989–90, 63, for the way Timaeus uses natural (i.e., Panhellenically comprehensible) calendrical markers such as harvest time or the decline of the Pleiades.

46. Gomme 1945, 5.

47. An insistent theme in Jacoby's writings: see Jacoby 1949, 200–25; cf. Purcell 2003, 20. Davidson (2005, 13) acutely observes that Thucydides uses unlocalized time frames as part of the general strategy, already set in train by Herodotus, of creating a form that "had no local structure . . . , no local occasion . . . and no local space"; as he puts it, in Greece history "is structurally supra-local, belonging to the pan-Greek 'middle.'"

48. As argued by, for example, Asheri (1991–92, 54); see, rather, Dunn 1998a, esp. 224, on the common modern error of assuming that the ancients have utility in mind in their time arrangements. On the use of natural markers, not synchronization of calendars, to fix the Panhellenic Olympic festival (at the second full moon after the summer solstice), see the decisive arguments of Miller (1975); Statius appears to refer to this kind of arrangement with his fine phrase about the celebration of the Nemean Games in honor of Archemorus: *maestaque perpetuis sollemnia iungimus astris* ("We join the sad solemnities to the perpetual stars," *Theb.* 7.99).

49. Walbank 1957–79, 2:348.

50. Polyb. 12.11.1 = *FGrH* 566 T 10.

51. On Timaeus's chronological work, see, conveniently, Walbank 1957–79, 2:347–48; for his pivotal importance in the Greek historiographical tradition, Jacoby 1954, 1: 382.

52. On Eratosthenes' *Chronographiae*, see Pfeiffer 1968, 163–64; Fraser 1970, 198–200; 1972, 1:456–57; on Apollodorus's *Chronica*, see Jacoby 1902; Pfeiffer 1968, 255–57; in general, Jacoby, *FGrH* 239–61 (Zeittafeln), Komm., 661–65; Mosshammer 1979, esp. 97–100.

53. Indeed, according to Grafton and Swerdlow (1986), Eratosthenes even gave a calendrical date for the sack of Troy, the seventh or eighth day before the end of the month Thargelion, a date that Virgil, according to them, alludes to in *Aen.* 2.255, *tacitae per amica silentia lunae*.

54. As we have seen, Timaeus synchronized Argive priestesses, Spartan ephors, and Athenian archons with Olympic victors, and he certainly gave dates counted back from a "first Olympiad" (Dion. Hal. *Ant. Rom.* 1.74.1 = Timaeus *FGrH* 566 F 60): the vexed question then arises of whether he had already fixed on the "776/5" date before Eratosthenes. Jacoby is convinced that Timaeus devised the "776/5" benchmark for the first Olympic Games and was followed in this by Eratosthenes: Timaeus *FGrH* 566, Komm., 538, Noten, 321; Eratosthenes *FGrH* 241, Komm., 662–63. We return to this problem in chapter 3: see p. 84 below.

55. Geus (2002) is highly skeptical about whether the work was designed to estab-

lish a chronology per se, and Grafton (1995) reacts strongly against traditional scholarship's reverence for the supposedly modern and scientific nature of the work. But Möller (2003) rightly qualifies Geus's extreme skepticism, and Grafton's justified reaction against anachronistic interpretations still leaves plenty of room for Eratosthenes to be demarcating and dividing for his own reasons, as we shall see in chapter 3.

56. Wilcox 1987, 87. One cannot put much weight on the language used by Clement of Alexandria to report how Eratosthenes divided time from the fall of Troy to the death of Alexander, since Clement need not be using Eratosthenes' actual diction (*Strom.* 1.138.1–3 = Eratosthenes *FGrH* 241 F 1a). But, for what it is worth, when Clement says that Eratosthenes "draws up the epochs in the following way" (τοὺς χρόνους ὧδε ἀναγράφει), the verb he uses is a metaphor from mathematics or geography, where it describes using lines as bases, or establishing visual demarcations (*LSJ* II.3).

57. For Apollodorus's choice of iambic verse, designed to aid memorization and to make his learning more accessible to a larger audience, see Pfeiffer 1968, 255.

58. Jacoby 1902, 25, 29; cf. Jacoby, *FGrH* 239, Komm., 667, on the same phenomenon in the Marmor Parium.

59. This is an idea that will cheer up half the readers of this book and depress the other half.

60. Jacoby 1902, 57–58.

61. See Jacoby 1904 for the Marmor Parium, an anonymous work inscribed in Paros sometime after 264/3 B.C.E., the year that provides the anchor for the interval counting throughout (e.g., "so many years from the fall of Troy to the archon of '264/3'"). See Higbie 2003 for the (misleadingly named) "Lindian Chronicle," an inscription from 99 B.C.E. that catalogues offerings to the goddess Athena in Lindos, from heroic times to the present; the "Chronicle" owes much to the chronographic tradition.

62. On the importance of this initiative, see below, pp. 63–64.

63. Pais 1905, 176–78, on Cremera; 178–84, 221, in general; important discussions since include Ogilvie 1965, 315, 359–60; Wiseman 1979, 23–24; esp. Griffiths 1998. For interesting conjectures about the role of synchronism in constructing Roman tradition about the expulsion of the Tarquins and the tyranny of Aristodemus in Cumae, see Gallia forthcoming.

64. So Griffiths (1998), arguing that the Thermopylae parallels behind the Cocles and Scaevola stories show the original author presenting "his compatriots as being in some sense western counterparts of and successors to the Spartans."

65. Wiseman 2000; contrast Wiseman 1979, 23–24.

66. Pliny *HN* 34.17.

67. As would Purcell (2003, 24–26). I vote rather with the skeptical Griffiths (1998). This is not to deny the deep impact of Greek culture at every level in early

Rome, including law (Horsfall 1994, 62, with reference to Delz 1966). The question is rather to find what preliterary mechanism would faithfully preserve verifiably accurate details of particular cross-cultural transmission for three hundred years: see Finley 1985, 16–17.

68. The conclusions of chapter 2 will make this late appearance of Roman chronographical scholarship less surprising.

69. On Catullus and Nepos, see, most recently, Rauk 1996–97 and B. J. Gibson 1995. On Nepos's *Chronica*, see Wiseman 1979, 157–58; Geiger 1985, 68–72; Horsfall 1989b, 117–18.

70. Aul. Gell. *NA*. 17.21.8 = Peter, *HRRel.* F 4.

71. Horsfall (1989a), xx n. 30, summarizing the important argument of Geiger (1985), 70.

72. Aul. Gell. *NA* 17.21.3 = Peter, *HRRel.* F 2 (Homer); Solin. 40.4 = Peter, *HRRel.* F 6 (Alexander).

73. My thanks to Tony Woodman for alerting me to the significance of Velleius as a key text for chronological inquiry; Woodman (1975, 286) makes a connection between Nepos and Velleius. There is an important discussion of Velleius's construction of past time in Gowing 2005, 41–43.

74. In general, Jacoby, *FGrH* 239–61 (Zeittafeln), Komm., 664–65; Bickerman 1980, 70, 76–78.

75. Livy *Per.* 47.

76. Bickerman 1980, 70.

77. A clear account of the issues in Bickerman 1980, 67–77. In *De Die Natali* 21.6 Censorinus provides a good example of how counting from the foundation of Rome to "now" will produce different results depending on whether you are counting Olympiad years or from the Parilia or from 1 January: cf. Grafton and Swerdlow 1985, 454. Burgess (2002, 22–23) explains the makeshifts of Eusebius and Jerome in their chronicles. Eusebius simply imposed the civic Macedonian calendar of his home city of Caesarea, which began on 3 October, on all of the differing year counts, so that all the regnal years and years of Abraham begin in 3 October; but Jerome made the start of the Roman consular year, 1 January, the start of his year, "and for him all years of Abraham, regnal years, and Olympiads began on 1 January"; cf. Burgess 1999, 28–29. This may seem like a quaint foible from an alien world, but identical issues pertained in Europe until 250 years ago. A recent British naval history of the period 1649–1815 notes the range of beginning dates for the year across Europe for much of the period, together with the issues of the discrepancy between Julian and Gregorian years, and declares: "All dates up to 1752 are Old Style unless otherwise indicated, but the year is taken to begin on 1 January throughout" (Rodger 2004, xix).

78. For acts of Parliament, the date in the United Kingdom was expressed in regnal years down till 1962: Holford-Strevens 2005, 114. If the C.E. dating system had not

been in use, the United States might well have continued using the era count that documents from the early Republic employ. Robert Knapp kindly supplies me with this information: "Some official documents from those early years make reference to the number of years of U.S. independence, with 1776 being regarded as the first year of independence. This is in addition to the Common Era date affixed to these documents. The official texts of U.S. treaties with Algiers (1816), Spain (1821), and Mexico (1826) are a few examples of this practice."

79. Cic. *Brut.* 13–15; *RE* Suppl. 8.520–21; Münzer 1905.

80. Münzer 1905, esp. 84–85.

81. We should remember, after all, that Gellius's book is called *Noctes Atticae*, "Attic Nights"; he represents himself as writing up the notes that he started taking when he was in Athens.

82. *RE* Suppl. 6.1237–42; Rawson 1985, 244–46; Grafton and Swerdlow 1985.

83. Rawson 1985, 245.

84. Varro's *Imagines* were much shorter, accompanying portraits: see Horsfall 1982a, 291; 1989b, 11; Rawson 1985, 198–99. On Nepos, see also Geiger 1985. Dionisotti 1988, 38, has interesting speculation on the newly topical relevance for Nepos of the comparison between the strife of fifth-century Greek history and the impending chaos of his own times.

85. Cf. Rawson 1985, 231: "What is perhaps most important about both Varro's and Nepos's works is that for the first time Greek and Roman subjects are placed together on a level"; cf. Horsfall 1989b, 102: "What the two works have in common is comparison of famous Greeks and Romans by category on a huge scale." Geiger 1985, 72, well situates Nepos's work in general within a period including Catullus and Cicero, one that saw "a concentrated attempt to bring Latin literature up to par with Greek."

86. As Nicholas Horsfall put it to me, via e-mail.

87. On this two-edged nature of simile, see Lyne 1989, 135–48; Feeney 1992a. J. Z. Smith (1990), chap. 2, "On Comparison," is fundamental to the whole topic. Purcell (2003, 20) compellingly makes the case that the comparison making of synchronism is fundamental to history: "When two ancient communities tried to work out what they had in common, and from what point they had shared this, history was invented. Thus, synchronism was a far more vital instrument of historiography than differentiation— or the delineation of the alien." I would only stress that "differentiation" and "the delineation of the alien" are integral to comparison, and hence to synchronism.

88. Jacoby 1902, 26–28; Leuze 1909, 166–67; Fraser 1972, 1:457 with 2:660–61; cf. Gabba 1991, 198.

89. Fabian 1983; my thanks to James Ker for discussion of this point.

90. Modern histories of the ancient Mediterranean regularly further such focalization, producing grand narratives in which "marginal" areas such as Sicily or central

and southern Italy only feature when they are involved in the affairs of the main actors such as Rome or Athens: Dench 2003, 295.

91. Irad Malkin, oral remark reported by Griffiths 1998, n. 12.

92. Rawson 1985, 231.

93. Rambaud 1953, esp. 58–106; Fantham 1981, 13–17; Rawson 1991, chap. 4, esp. 62–66 on *De Re Publica*.

94. Rambaud 1953, 57–58; Rawson 1991, 74. Note that Cicero has Atticus say that he was fired to write the *Liber Annalis* after reading his friend's *De Re Publica* (*Brut.* 19), with the implication that it was Cicero's historical vision that inspired him.

95. Douglas 1966b, 291: "When he wrote *Brutus,* Cicero was as excited by Atticus' *Liber Annalis* and the chronological researches of Varro and possibly Nepos as any modern scholar by *Adelsparteien* or *Magistrates of the Roman Republic* or by Badian's own contributions in this field. His interest in chronology is almost obsessive." I doubt that Nepos's *Chronica* was part of this excitement for Cicero in 46. He had been living with the book for some years, having used it in *De Re Publica* (Zetzel 1995, 175); something new had happened to quicken his interest. See Horsfall 1989b, xvi, for discussion of the possibility that Cicero's attitude to Nepos may well not have been warm or admiring. As for Varro, his main chronological work, *De Gente Populi Romani,* is too late for Cicero to use, dating to late 43 B.C.E. at the earliest: Horsfall 1972, 124–25.

96. Münzer 1905, then, still seems to me to have been on the right track: see esp. 51–55, 78–80; cf. Douglas 1966a, lii–iii; Habinek 1998, 95–96.

97. Cf. Fantham 1981, 15–16, for Cicero's attempts in *De Oratore* 3.27–28 and 56 "to create cultural parallels"; 2.51–53 is a similar passage. My thanks to Stephen Hinds for getting me to rethink my first thoughts on Cicero's approach in the earlier dialogues.

98. Zetzel 1995, 174. Cf. Cornell 2001, 55, on Cicero's representation of early Rome as already developed to a level "comparable to that of Sparta": his stress on the specificity of Cicero's targets and tactics in this work is salutary.

99. *Brut.* 39; cf. *Tusc.* 1.3, 4.1. Contrast *De Or.* 1.6–16, where Cicero talks at length of the paucity of the names in Roman oratorical history, without deploying any of the language of "late" or "recent" that we might expect to see with the hindsight of the passages from *Brutus* and *Tusculans.* In *De Oratore* his apprehension of temporal "unlikeness" is not at all as developed.

100. Note in particular *Brut.* 26–51, where his survey of Greek oratory is basically taken over from his earlier survey in *De Or.* 2.93–95 but has been "amended, elaborated, and in places . . . confused" (Douglas 1966a, xlv). A principal source of the difficulty is that Cicero is gripped by his new understanding of the chronological issues of earliness and lateness, so that he keeps deliberately backtracking in order to set up the comparative points he will need when he comes to the Roman section.

101. This paragraph is taken from Feeney 2002, 15–16, with kind permission of Michael Paschalis; see there for fuller discussion of Cicero's (and Horace's) attitudes to cross-cultural comparison.

102. Habinek 1998, 95.

103. *OLD* s.v. §4, "(mil.) to extend in line of battle, deploy." The use of *ordines* is crucial to the metaphor, for *explicare* seems to have "an almost technical sense" in Roman chronographic writing of this period: *explicare* is used by Catullus in his reference to Nepos's *Chronica* (1.6), and the verb "is a favourite word of Nepos in his extant work and . . . is used by Cicero to describe the (evidently very similar) *Liber Annalis* of Atticus": Woodman 2003, 193, for both quotations, with references to earlier scholarship.

104. Jacoby regularly asserted that Timaeus pioneered the use of columns: e.g., Jacoby 1954, 1: 382; cf. Asheri 1991–92, 54. But this is highly unlikely in the light of Eusebius's proclamations of his novel layout, and so far as I can see Atticus is the only possible predecessor of Eusebius in this regard: on Eusebius's innovation in design, see Mosshammer 1979, 37 and 62; Grafton and Williams (2006), chap. 3.

105. Burgess 2002, 8.

106. Mosshammer 1979, Burgess 1999, and Grafton and Williams (2006) are fundamental; see Burgess 2002 for an invaluable introduction to Jerome, and to the exemplary edition of Jerome's *Chronicle* by Helm (1956). Donalson 1996 provides a translation and commentary of Jerome's continuation from 327–378 C.E.

107. Adler 1989 is an excellent introduction to the whole subject, stressing how disparate and unmonolithic the Christian chronographic tradition is; cf. Adler and Tuffin 2002, a translation of one of the most important post-Eusebian chronicles, that of George Syncellus.

108. Zerubavel 2003, 105–9; on the Christians' agenda, see Adler 1989, 18–20.

109. Herodotus 2.143, on which see Brown 1962; R. Thomas 2001, 208–10; Moyer 2002. The most memorable expression of the Greek apprehension of their being "out-past-ed" by the Egyptians is in Plato's *Timaeus* (22a–23a). The Christians are also taking over polemic of the kind one sees in Josephus's *Contra Apionem*, in which the Jewish author asserts that Hebrew and Eastern history is incomparably older than Greek. Cf. Sacks 1990, 64, on the "particularist strife among Egyptians, Jews, and Greeks" in first-century B.C.E. Alexandria, with the various groups arguing "for the chronological primacy of their own founding legends and hence of their respective races." On such polemic between Christians and pagans in fourth-century C.E. Rome, see Ando 2001, 392–93.

110. Cobet 2000, 20. Augustine is a fascinating figure in the longer history of synchronism, although he would take me too far from my competence and my pagans. In *The City of God* (esp. 18.1–2), he shows a profound understanding of the mechanisms and implications of synchronism. In these chapters he lays bare the comparative nature of the whole enterprise, declaring that his purpose is to allow the city of God and the

city of men to be compared by his readers (*ut ambae inter se possint consideratione legentium comparari*, 18.1); he also reveals an understanding of the *translatio imperii* theme that, as we shall see in the next chapter, underpins the developed form of the pan-Mediterranean synchronistic project. He takes Assyria and Rome as the two great representative Eastern and Western empires of mundane human history (18.2); here, too, it is very striking that he understands how the Roman time line has been accommodated to the Greek time line, showing that Rome's status as the inheritor of Hellenism is a contingent fact of human history.

111. One thinks of how Velleius Paterculus inserts notices of literary efflorescence into his history: 1.17; 2.36.

112. Ted Champlin makes the attractive suggestion to me that Lucilius comes last as the Roman who invents a genre that is regarded as distinctively native and non-Greek: cf. Quint. 10.1.93, *satura . . . tota nostra est*.

113. See above, pp. 25–28; cf. Hor. *Epist.* 2.1.161–63 for the same Ciceronian insight.

114. Zerubavel 2003, 87–88. Naturally, the arrival of Greek culture in Rome is by no means straightforwardly a Good Thing: the mention of the first literature in Rome is followed five years later (44) by the citation of the first divorce in Rome.

115. On Accius's scholarship, especially the *Didascalia*, see E. Stärk in Suerbaum 2002, 163–65; and, for Gellius's knowledge of Accius, Holford-Strevens 2003, s.v. index, esp. 158 for *NA* 3.3.

116. This famous embassy led by Carneades, the same one referred to in Cicero's correspondence with Atticus (above, pp. 14–15), forms a piece of ring composition, with the figure of Carneades featuring at the beginning of Gellius's essay (1). For the later development of the configurations of Greek "culture" and Roman "power," remembered in this tradition as beginning with this embassy, see Whitmarsh 2001, esp. chap. 4.

117. To allude to the title of the important paper of Wallace-Hadrill (1988).

118. On *translatio imperii*, see, briefly, Momigliano 1987, 31–59; Cobet 2000, 15–18; further below, p. 55. It is a theme that J. M. Alonso-Núñez made distinctively his own: see Clarke 1999b, 274, for a full bibliography.

119. Leuze (1911) saw this essential point in his still fundamental paper; see esp. 237 n. 2.

120. Similarly with Pompeius Trogus, who only introduces Rome into his universal history with Pyrrhus (book 23); cf. Wilcox 1987, 110. Modern histories mark this moment accordingly; note Errington 1989, 83: "One side-effect of the defeat of Pyrrhus was that it put Rome on the map for the Greek world. Ptolemy II Philadelphus was sufficiently impressed to choose this time to send presents to the Senate and to form an informal friendship; the Romans returned the diplomatic gesture." Cf. Pearson 1987, 143, on the way that Western Greece does not become part of Hellenic history until the Peloponnesian War, especially with the Athenian expedition to Sicily.

121. My word "invasion" is itself, of course, anachronistically Romanocentric in its focalization.

122. Their obliteration, at least, might have registered: Cornell 1989, 302: "The Sack . . . was the first event of Roman history to impress itself on the consciousness of the Greeks."

123. In general, Morello 2002, esp. 71–72, on Livy's linking of the two Alexanders. Tony Woodman refers me to Walsh 1961, 201–3, for Livy's fondness for small-scale counterfactuals ("TheRomans would have been defeated if not for the arrival of another group"), and to Moles 1984, 242, for a list of places where Velleius toys "with the 'ifs of history' (46.3, 47.5, 48.2, 72.2, 86.1)."

124. Above, p. 21

125. Leuze 1911, 247–48. See Pearson 1987, 157, for speculation that this year was an important synchronism between Athenian and Sicilian constitutional history in Timaeus. Velleius is careful to mark the various changes in Athens' constitution, with the end of the monarchy (1.2.1), and the end of the life archonship (1.8.3); the lost portion of book 1 would no doubt have registered the annual archonship and the thirty tyrants.

126. From Xerxes' invasion, for example, he mentions Salamis and not Plataea (12); cf. below, p. 41.

127. Another extremely valuable way into this comparison mentality is via Horsfall 1993, which shows how the Roman writers of Augustus's time were insistently comparing themselves to their Greek predecessors and counterparts, and noting how far they still had to go to catch up.

128. Lamberton 1997, 155, 158; cf. RE 2R 21.936–37; Desideri 1992, esp. 4475–78; Duff 1999, 287–309; Pelling 2002, 349–63, esp. 359–61.

129. I realize that this is perhaps not a good metaphor to use in a land where the automatic transmission reigns supreme, but my father taught me to drive on the beach in New Zealand in a 1955 Austin Gypsy, a variety of jeep, in which you had to double-declutch between each gear change as you went up or down the gears.

CHAPTER 2. SYNCHRONIZING TIMES II:
WEST AND EAST, SICILY AND THE ORIENT

1. Translation by M. Hubbard in Russell and Winterbottom 1972.

2. It is worth pausing to remind ourselves of how much more difficult it was for the Greeks and Romans to establish that events in different parts of the world, with their different calendars, happened on "the same day": Brown 1958, 74; Pearson 1987, 157. How did one set about claiming that a day on the calendar of Syracuse was the same as a day on the calendar of Athens? To correlate particular events, counting back was standard: see Hdt. 9.101.2, linking Mycale and Plataea; Caes. BCiv. 3.105.3–6, linking the battle of Pharsalus in Thessaly with an omen in Ephesus. See Miller 1975 for the

Greeks' reliance on natural, astronomical, phenomena, rather than calendars, for synchronizing the Panhellenic games.

3. Asheri 1991–92, 58.

4. Asheri 1991–92, 87.

5. "One of those coincidences that in ancient history would be dismissed as obvious fictions," Blackburn and Holford-Strevens 1999, 282. Let me recommend this splendid book in the warmest terms: every household should have a copy. For a diverting collection of ancient coincidences, see Plut. *Quaest. Conv.* 717C–D.

6. For the ancients' fondness for deaths of famous men in the same year, see Diod. Sic. 15.60.3–5 on the deaths in the same year of Amyntas of Macedon, Agesipolis of Sparta, and Jason of Pherae; esp. Polyb. 23.12.1–14.12, Diod. Sic. 29.18–21, and Livy 39.50.10 on the deaths in the same year of Hannibal, Scipio, and Philopoemon; cf. Walbank 1957–79, 1:229, 3:235–39; Clarke 1999b, 268. In British history the most striking coincidence of dates is a linear, not a parallel, one—3 September, the day on which Oliver Cromwell won the victories of Dunbar (1650) and Worcester (1651), and the day on which he died (1658).

7. How many people do you need together in a room to guarantee a 50-percent chance of two of them having the same birthday? The answer is twenty-three; Belkin 2002, 35 (my thanks to Michael Flower for the reference). See Charpak and Broch 2004, chap. 2, "Amazing Coincidences," for a demonstration of how knowledge of elementary statistics dispels the sense of amazement.

8. Hdt. 8.15.1 for Artemisium and Thermopylae; 9.101.2, with explicit mention of counting up the days to establish the coincidence of Plataea and Mycale: Asheri 1991–92, 60; Flower and Marincola 2002, 276–77. The tradition continued: see App. *BCiv.* 4.116 for the amazing synchronism of a naval battle in the Adriatic and the land battle at Philippi. Salamis also figured in a meaningful chain of coincidence supposedly linking the three great Attic tragedians—Aeschylus fought in the victory, Sophocles danced in the chorus celebrating it, and Euripides was born on the very day itself: Mosshammer 1979, 309–10.

9. *FGrH* 70 F 186; see Pearson 1987, 134; Vattuone 1991, 82; Asheri 1991–92, 57.

10. Dench 1995, 51, on Himera and Salamis; cf. Dench 2003, 299, on the Tarentines' attempt to get in on this act by claiming that their victories over "various south Italian *barbaroi*" are part of "the struggle against the now generic barbarian."

11. T. Harrison 2000b, 96. On the ideological resonances of the Himera-Salamis synchronism, and the links between the wars against the Carthaginians and Persians, especially in Pindar and Herodotus, see Gauthier 1966; Bichler 1985; Asheri 1991–92, 56–60; S. P. Morris 1992, 238, 374. There will be an important reassessment of these topics in the forthcoming book by Sarah Harrell, based on her 1998 Princeton PhD dissertation.

12. Asheri 1991–92, 56–57.

13. 7.159, alluding to *Il.* 7.125.

14. 7.161.3, alluding to *Il.* 2.552–54.

15. Clarke 1999a, 121, on Diod. Sic. 13.114.3 (an artful passage, where Diodorus reinforces his sense of closure by announcing the end of the book).

16. Diod. Sic. 16.88.3: Asheri 1991–92, 86; Purcell 1994, 391 ("a sign of how eagerly parallels between East and West were observed"); Clarke 1999a, 121.

17. Note the "reverse simile" character of the significance of the synchronism between the peace of Antalcidas and sack of Rome drawn by Justin 6.6.5 (quoted by Walbank 1957–79, 1:47): *hic annus non eo tantum insignis fuit quod repente pax tota Graecia facta est, sed etiam eo quod eodem tempore urbs Romana a Gallis capta est.*

18. Purcell 1995, 139.

19. On this theme, see above all Momigliano 1977a, esp. 53–58; cf. Vattuone 1991, chap. 9, "Timeo, Pirro e la 'scoperta' di Roma." Vattuone 2002 provides a condensed introduction, together with an invaluable bibliographical discussion (226–32).

20. For his synchronistic chronological work, see *FGrH* 566 T 10–11.

21. Mendelssohn 1876; Brown 1958; Momigliano 1977a; Pearson 1987; Walbank 1989–90; Meister 1989–90; Vattuone 1991; Asheri 1991–92.

22. Mendelssohn 1876, esp. 185–89; Brown 1958, 13–14, 43–44; Pearson 1987, 57–59; Walbank 1989–90, 47, 53; Asheri 1991–92, 88. Synchronism was not his only tool: he claims a "direct" physical link between West Greece and Hellas "proper" by elaborating on Pindar's claim that the river Alpheius runs under the sea from the Peloponnese to reemerge in Syracusan Ortygia (Pind. *Nem.* 1.1–2; Polyb. 12.4d = *FGrH* 566 F 41b): see Dench 1995, 51.

23. Plut. *Mor.* 717C = *FGrH* 566 F 105, alluding to, without necessarily quoting, Timaeus's words. Plutarch actually says this was the year of Dionysius's birth, but all agree this is a slip on his part.

24. Asheri 1991–92, 79; cf. above, p. 40; other speculation in Pearson 1987, 157.

25. Hanell 1956, 151, 166; Walbank 1957–79, 1:48; Mazzarino 1966, 2.2:447.

26. Walbank 1957–79, 1:48.

27. See Asheri 1991–92, 56, for some trenchant remarks on the fashion for "discovering, or rather inventing, an 'Axial Age' in a roughly synchronous line of great names that presumably represents a period of spiritual breakthrough." A fair hit (directed, without naming names, against Karl Jaspers 1953), but the question of simultaneous parallel developments in cultures without necessarily close ties continues to engage the attention of serious historians: see C. Kidd 2004, 14, for discussion of the claim in Bayly 2004 that "the mid 19th-century witnessed a second age of revolutions. The Europe of 1848 was part of a wider bout of global dislocation which included the Indian Mutiny, the Taiping rebellion in China and the American Civil War." My thanks to Tony Woodman for drawing my attention to this issue. For an overview of

the history of the concept of the "Axial Age," see Arnason 2005, part of a collection of essays devoted to the paradigm (my thanks to Peter Brown for this reference, and for discussion of the issue).

28. *FGrH* 566 F 150; see Asheri 1983, 87, for a charitable interpretation of this moment as an attempt to register the "nuova èra che stava per inaugurasi nella storia universale."

29. Diod. Sic. 13.108.4–5 = *FGrH* 566 F 106.

30. Vattuone 1991, 299.

31. On the Athenian context, see esp. Momigliano 1977a; Vattuone 1991, 72–73.

32. Momigliano 1977a, 39–41.

33. *Quam ait Timaeus Graecarum maxumam, omnium autem esse pulcherrimam,* Cic. *Rep.* 3.43 = *FGrH* 566 F 40.

34. *FGrH* 115 F 153; trans. Connor 1968, 78 (my thanks to Michael Flower for this reference). On the Athenocentric representation of the Persian Wars both in antiquity and the modern world, inflating Salamis and downplaying the predominantly Spartan victory at Plataea, see Flower and Marincola 2002, 28–31.

35. Cf. Lowenthal 1985, 53: "*Remoteness* is another quality that commends antiquity, the 'so *old*' of the American tourist for whose countrymen, a British observer comments, 'it must be an embarrassment to possess a national history less than five centuries old.'" In the case of the Sicilians, the conventional colonial response, that the new society is more vigorous, is perhaps already present in Gelon's jibe at the Greek ambassadors before Himera, that they have lost the spring of the year (7.162.1): "Gelo might . . . compare the youthful vigour of the colony, Sicily, to the spring, and the effete mother-country to the later duller months of the year" (How and Wells 1912, ad loc.).

36. Pearson 1987, 143.

37. Irad Malkin, oral remark reported by Griffiths 1998, n. 12, alluded to also in the case of Rome and Greece, above, p. 25.

38. Pearson 1987, 57–59, on *FGrH* 566 F 164.

39. Cicero makes gentle fun of this tendency in *Brut.* 63, reporting Timaeus's strained attempts to represent Lysias as really Syracusan, not Athenian (*FGrH* 566 F 138; see Jacoby, Komm., 590, for Timaeus's mission). Cicero exemplifies the pattern Timaeus objected to, representing Greek oratory as essentially coextensive with Athenian oratory (*Brut.* 26), and only mentioning the Sicilian aetiology with Corax and Tisias in the "technical" part of his account (46).

40. *FGrH* 566 F 119a; see Vattuone 1991, 92, 98.

41. Another place where Timaeus tried to tie Western affairs into the Persian Wars was with his synchronism between the capture of Camarina in Sicily and what he calls "the crossing of Darius," presumably the Marathon expedition of 490: Asheri 1991–92, 73–75.

42. *FGrH* 566 F 94.

43. First argued by Mancuso (1909); good discussions, especially on the urge to raise Sicily at the expense of Athens, in Pearson 1987, 132–40; Walbank 1989–90, 43; Asheri 1991–92, 58.

44. Connors 2002, 16; her fine discussion of Chariton shows how long into the Roman imperial period Syracuse's imperial associations resonated. See Jaeger 2003 for a discussion of Livy's presentation of Syracuse as "a failed Rome" (233).

45. Cf. Arnold-Biucchi 2002: "Most handbooks of Hellenistic history . . . seem to think of the West as too insignificant to be part of the Hellenistic kingdoms. Even numismatic treatises . . . ignore Sicily." The Roman tradition could overlook Syracuse as well: when Cicero says that Rome had only three rivals as aspirants to world empire, he mentions Carthage, Corinth, and . . . Capua (*Leg. Agr.* 2.87). Apart from the fact that it begins with *C*, it is initially hard to see why Capua is in that list instead of Syracuse, which was described by Timaeus, in words twice quoted by Cicero, as the largest of the Greek cities and the most beautiful of all cities (*Verr.* 2.4.117; *Rep.* 3.43). For the role of Capua as a potential second Rome in Silius Italicus, see Cowan 2002, 52–53.

46. On this theme in Thucydides, see Hunter 1982, 46–47, 263 n. 58; Connors 2002, 16. In general, on the theme of the contention for imperial status in the Mediterranean, see the outstanding study of Purcell (1995), to which I am indebted throughout.

47. Sparta was not a maritime city (despite its depiction in the film *Troy*), and for the imperial theme in which Athens and Carthage are involved, this is crucial: Purcell 1995.

48. *Alc.* 17.2; *Nic.* 12.1–2.

49. Livy 25.24.11–13; Plut. *Marc.* 19. The scene has been the subject of some fine recent discussions: Rossi 2000; H. I. Flower 2003; Jaeger 2003; Marincola 2005.

50. Marincola 2005, 228–29, well brings out the metahistorical function of Livy's description of Marcellus's tears; Marcellus's memory of the key points commemorated in Sicilian history is Livy's way of pinpointing the fact that Western Greek history is now ending, to be subsumed in Roman history, just as the work of the Western Greek historians is now being subsumed in his own *Ab Urbe Condita*.

51. Hanell 1956, esp. 149, 152, 166, 169; cf. Brown 1958, 15; Momigliano 1977a, 57–58.

52. Cornell 1975, 24; cf. Jacoby, *FGrH* 566, Komm., 536–37; Momigliano 1977a.

53. Dion. Hal. *Ant. Rom.* 1.74.1 = *FGrH* 566 F 60. I agree with Meister 1989–90, 58–59, that this date was given in the *Histories*, not the supplementary *Pyrrhica*.

54. Jacoby, *FGrH* 566, Komm., 536.

55. See the discussion between Momigliano and Hanell in Hanell 1956, 183–84.

56. Momigliano 1977a, 55.

57. Aubet 2001, 227.

58. Plut. *Cam.* 22.2.

59. Strabo 2.1.40 (meridian), 1.4.9 (constitutions); cf. Fraser 1972, 1:483, 769; Asheri 1991–92, 73.

60. Serv. ap. *Aen.* 4.682 = F 80 Peter; cf. Cic. *Rep.* 2.41.2, with Zetzel 1995, ad loc.

61. Horsfall 1973–74.

62. A fundamental contribution on this function of Thebes in the Athenian imaginary is Zeitlin 1986; P. Hardie (1990) demonstrated how profitably this model could be transferred to Rome. I am indebted to Cowan's outstanding analysis of the role of Capua in Silius Italicus, where he shows the multiple mirroring role of Capua as *altera Carthago* and *altera Roma*, arguing that Silius's Capua resembles "Rome so closely that important but dangerous issues can be safely explored within its bounds without openly admitting their presence at Rome" (Cowan 2002, 52–53).

63. For other weeping conquerors, see Labate 1991, 169; Rossi 2000. In general on the *urbs capta* motif, see Paul 1982.

64. Rossi 2000, 61–63; H. I. Flower 2003, esp. 47; Marincola 2005, 226. The first such moment in Livy's history is the capture of Veii in book 5, where the themes of corrupting wealth are already present, even if the threatening victim is Etruscan, not Greek: Miles 1995, 79–88.

65. Sall. *Cat.* 10.1; *Jug.* 41.2–3; cf. Purcell 1995, 143.

66. The reference to Troy is telling, coming from a Roman. The theme that the fates of Carthage and Troy are linked is likewise sounded in the *Aeneid*, where the suicide of Dido evokes Homer's reference to the fall of Troy. When Dido collapses on the pyre, the lamentation of the women is marked by a simile that refers to the destruction of Carthage or Tyre, "just as if the enemy had been let in and all Carthage or ancient Tyre were plunging" (*non aliter quam si immissis ruat hostibus omnis/Karthago aut antiqua Tyros, Aen.* 4.669–70). The simile alludes to Homer's simile of the lamentation at the death of Hector (*Il.* 22. 410–11). The death of Hector makes the fall of Troy inevitable a few weeks later: the death of Dido makes the fall of Carthage inevitable hundreds of years later—a characteristically different epic-historical span of time for Virgil.

67. Scipio likewise refers to the changeability of fortune as he receives the supplication of the Carthaginian commander, Hasdrubal (Diod. Sic. 32.23); in both passages he seems to be quoting the words of his natural father, Aemilius Paullus, who animadverted on the mutability of fortune after the battle of Pydna in 168 B.C.E., to an audience including his young son (Plut. *Aem.* 27). A related use of the topos is in the mouth of Hannibal, speaking to the elder Scipio Africanus before Zama (Polyb. 15.6.4–7.9; Livy 30.30–31).

68. Appian's version of Polybius's account of Scipio's words at Carthage does explicitly have Scipio reflecting on the succession of empires, going over Troy, then Assyria, Media, Persia, and Macedonia (App. *Pun.* 132). It is keenly debated whether this developed version of the "four plus one" imperial succession theme can have been

in Scipio's or Polybius's mind in 146 B.C.E.: Mendels 1981; Alonso-Núñez 1983; Momigliano 1987, 40–42; Suerbaum 2002, 428. The question is sharpened by debate over whether the topos in classical historiography goes back to a pre-Greek Eastern template, introduced via Hebrew apocalyptic or anti-Roman propaganda: Flusser 1972; Collins 1998, 92–98 (a reference I owe to Dan Sobaer); Cobet 2000, 15–16; otherwise, it is argued that the imperial succession theme we see in Daniel is one that is taken in the reverse direction, from the Greek world: Momigliano 1987, 48–52; Millar 1997, 103–4. Given that Polybius had, as we have seen, a vision of Rome following on from Macedonia and Persia as a world power, and since he could have read in his Herodotus that Persia was the inheritor of imperial power from the Medes, who had taken over from Assyria (1.95, 130), then he does at least have a potential framework of Assyria-Media-Persia-Macedonia-Rome, and the possibility remains that Appian preserves a good trace of Polybius's vision, even if he has codified it systematically in a way that Polybius perhaps did not do. Such is basically the position of Trompf 1979, 79–81; Momigliano 1987, 40–42; cf. Dench 2005, 58–59, 88–89.

69. Hanell 1956, 155; Momigliano 1977a, 54, 58; Vattuone 1991, 301; cf. Asheri 1991–92, 72–73: "The discovery of Rome as the new political and military counterpart of Carthage, replacing the declining Graeculi of post-Agathoclean Sicily and of the semi-barbarized Magna Graecia, and inheriting their traditional position in the network of political and commercial relations in the western Mediterranean, was the great contribution of Timaeus to early Hellenistic historiography."

70. Dench 1995, 69–70. On the late development of any consciousness of "Hellenicity" among the Greeks in Sicily in particular, see J. Hall 2004. See now Dench 2005 for a reexamination of the whole issue of self-definition against barbarism on the part of both Greeks and Romans.

71. See Walbank 1957–79, 1:42, on the Greek historians of the Hannibalic War, "who wrote mainly from the Punic point of view."

72. See Roussel 1970 for an argument that the Sicilian Greeks at the time of the First Punic War were if anything more inclined to be pro-Carthaginian than pro-Roman.

73. Harrell (1998) provides an excellent account of Herodotus's nuanced representation of the Greek/non-Greek situation in Sicily. She shows how the Deinomenid rulers of Syracuse could play up their "Eastern" origins, and it would be worthwhile to follow in her footsteps and see how much the "Trojan" Romans learned from Pindar, Bacchylides, and their Sicilian patrons about how to project themselves "as colonists of eastern heritage whose families achieve rule in the colonial land where they have settled" (221).

74. See Dench 2003, 300, for Daunian Arpi casting the Romans as Greeks and the Samnites as barbarians; and 302–3, for Romans and Samnites competing over the role of Greeks (cf. Dench 1995, 54).

75. Feeney 1991, 119.

76. Naevius fr. 8 Büchner; see Feeney 1991, 118, for discussion and earlier bibliography.

77. Purcell 1995, 139.

78. Rawson 1989.

79. Rawson 1989, 428, 430, 434, 438, 446.

80. Purcell 1994, 403.

81. Rawson 1989, 446.

82. Polyb. 15.35.6; cf. Rawson 1989, 434, 438.

83. Wiseman 2000, esp. 299, well brings out the Roman interest in Athens from around 300 B.C.E. at least; cf. Purcell 2003, 22, on Hellenistic antiquarian interest in "elucidating the complexities of the vast and singular Athenian state"—an interest Romans will have shared as they contemplated their own vast and singular state. On the power of Athens as a potential counterweight to Rome in Ovid's *Metamorphoses*, see Gildenhard and Zissos 2004, esp. 71. Lamberton (1997, 153–54) rather exaggerates the lack of interest in the Athenian political paradigm during the Hellenistic period, but he well captures the enduring power of Athens as a cultural magnet over the long term.

84. Jacoby, *FGrH* 239 §52 (Plataea), with Komm., 666–67. Compare Gellius's description of Chaeronea as an Athenian defeat (*NA* 17.21.30), above, p. 41.

85. Above, p. 20.

86. Grafton and Swerdlow 1988, 24. Cf. Champion 2000, esp. 429–30, for how Polybius could treat Romans as "honorary Greeks." Plutarch's *Lives* are the most dramatic instantiation of this Athenocentrism: see Lamberton 1997, esp. 156. There are ten Athenians; four Spartans; two Macedonians; two Thebans (one, Epaminondas, now lost); then five more, scattered. Tellingly, there is no Sicilian apart from Dion, son-in-law of Dionysius I and friend of Plato, who is there as a pair for Brutus as a "philosopher in politics." Another major figure from Sicilian history, Timoleon, finds his way in, but he is by origin a Corinthian, whose mission in life is to overthrow Sicilian tyrants.

87. For a lucid account of his operating principles, see Walbank 1972, 97–114; cf. Walbank 1975.

88. Esp. 2.37.4; 5.31.6; see Wilcox 1987, 83–84, and Clarke 1999a, 114–28, on the universal ambitions of Polybius's history.

89. Walbank (1975, 201) points to the treaty of Naupactus in 217 B.C.E. as the moment when the weaving together (συμπλοκή) really became operative in linking all the regions (4.28.3–4; 5.105.4–9).

90. The quoted phrase is from Purcell 1995, 139.

91. Wilcox 1987, 85.

92. Cf. Clarke 1999a, 118.

93. In general, Clarke (1999a, 307–28; 1999b) sets the scene very well.

94. Wilcox 1987, 113: "The Hellenistic Oecumene changed the face of time. To describe and explain the new integration of world affairs, historians created a time of vastly greater chronological scope than that of their Hellenic predecessors."

95. As Tony Woodman points out to me, the later Romans did not make this mistake: see Tac. *Ann.* 15.25.3 for acknowledgment of the sweep of Pompey's pirate command.

96. Millar 2002, 223–24. As he goes on to say, "for a brief moment in 87–86 B.C., indeed, at the height of Mithridates' westward expansion, Rome controlled nothing east of the Adriatic except parts of Greece and Macedonia" (225).

97. Gruen 1984, esp. 609–10, 670.

98. In so doing he raised himself to the rank of Agamemnon, King of Kings: see Champlin 2003a. His neglected predecessor Lucullus, meanwhile, who had done so much to pave the way for him, has become a Thersites.

99. Kuttner 1999.

100. See above all Kallet-Marx 1995, 331–34.

101. *Mith.* 94–95, 119. Pompey was "like a king of kings" (94), and his defeat of Mithridates made the Roman Empire extend "from the setting of the sun to the river Euphrates" (114).

102. Pliny *HN.* 7.95: *aequato non modo Alexandri Magni rerum fulgore, sed etiam Herculis prope ac Liberi patris;* Purcell 1995, 139, for this description of Hercules and Dionysus.

103. Clarke 1999a, 308. Lucan refers to Pompey's triumphs over the three parts of the world, and to the irony that he and his two sons each died in one of them: *Europam, miseri, Libyamque Asiamque timete:/distribuit tumulos uestris fortuna triumphis* (6.817–18).

104. Gruen 1984, 285; cf. Nicolet 1991, 31–38; Mattern 1999, 166. Nicholas Horsfall points out to me that the impact of Pompey on the contemporary Hellenistic literary world and on the later imperial discourse of panegyric is strangely understudied. As he says, much of the raw material for such a study could be accessed via the entry "Pompeius" in the index of Susemihl (1891–92).

105. Clarke 1999a, 311. Woodman 1983, 214–15, collects references to the rich material of "Alexander-imitation" at Rome. Gruen 1998—a reference I owe to Ted Champlin—redresses the balance with a caution against overreading the evidence, but Gruen's skepticism about interest in Alexander among the protagonists of the 60s and 50s goes too far.

106. Wiseman (1992, 34–35) deftly inserts Catullus's poem into the contemporary atmosphere of world conquest.

107. I print the *horribiles uitro ultimosque* of McKie (1984) in lines 11–12, and the *quacumque* of Nisbet (1978a, 94–95) in line 13. My thanks to Tony Woodman for stimulating discussion of the problems of text and translation of this extraordinary poem.

108. For play on this epithet, see Feeney 1986. In the Pliny passage just quoted, he makes a similar joke, noting that Caesar was *maior* than *Magnus*, "bigger" than "Mr. Big" (*HN* 7.99). There are traces of provincial attempts to transfer the name from the old Roman Alexander, Pompey, to the new one, Caesar: see Reynolds 1982, 159–60, for a triumviral-period inscription from Aphrodisias that refers to Julius Caesar as ὁ μέγας (my thanks to Tony Woodman for the reference).

109. On the numinous aura of the Britons and of the boundary of Ocean, see Braund 1996, chap. 1, "The Conquest of Ocean": he refers, tellingly, to Nicolaus of Damascus's *Life of Augustus* 95 for the claim "that Caesar was preparing a Parthian campaign at the time of his death in 44 B.C. in order to reach the Ocean in the east as he had reached it in the west" (20).

110. Gruen 1984, 285; Clarke 1999a, 307–8.

111. Above, p. 29.

112. *FGrH* 250 F 14 for Moses.

113. Cf. Bickerman 1952, 73, on how late it was for the Greeks to accept the antiquity of the Eastern figures: "At last, in Caesar's time, Castor harmonized the Greek and Oriental chronologies." Castor's was the breakthrough, despite the fact that there had long been available the histories of Egypt and Babylon written in Greek by Manetho and Berossus: on the scant attention paid by Greeks to these histories, written by "local savants," see Kuhrt 1987, 33; Dillery (forthcoming), in an interesting discussion of the audiences for Manetho and Berossus, makes the lack of attention from mainstream Greeks less surprising.

114. Adler 1989, 17.

115. *FGrH* 250 T 1 (Suidas).

116. Mosshammer 1979, 135; cf. Vell. Pat. 1.6.1, linking the epochs of the foundation of Rome and the end of life-archonships at Athens.

117. *FGrH* 250 F 5. Pompey celebrated his triumph on his birthday (Pliny *HN* 37.13); we return to the significance of this in chapter 5.

118. Jacoby, *FGrH* 250, Komm., 815. Kallet-Marx's important modern history of Rome's integration of the Eastern Mediterranean chooses the same terminus (Kallet-Marx 1995, 7).

119. Gruen 1984, 356.

120. See Jacoby, *FGrH* 250, Komm., 815, for his impact on Varro's *De Gente Populi Romani* (43 B.C.E.); invaluable discussion of Castor's impact on Varro and thence on Ovid's *Metamorphoses* in Cole 2004; in general, Mazzarino 1966, 2.2:448–49: "L'età pompeiano-cesariana, cioè l'età di Castore, ha avuto così un'enorme importanza nella storia della cronografia classica." The most telling influence of Castor came later, with the Christians, who took over his schemes for their new teleological visions: Mazzarino 1966, 2.2:450.

121. On this general point, see Millar 2002, 194, 196, 199.

122. Numerous good recent accounts exist of the universal history boom in the late Republic and early Principate: Burde 1974; Woodman 1975; Momigliano 1987; Alonso-Núñez 1987; Sacks 1981, 96–121; Sacks 1990; Clarke 1999a and b; Wheeler 2002.

123. Clarke 1999b, 251–52, against Livy's universal status.

124. Cf. Momigliano 1987, 44, for how the world conquest of Pompey and Caesar is a "congenial atmosphere" for universal history; Clarke 1999b.

125. My label of the "Walter Raleigh" periodization trap is owed to Sellar and Yeatman (1930, 69–70), who point out that James I had "a very logical and tidy mind, and one of the first things he did was to have Sir Walter Raleigh executed for being left over from the previous reign."

126. Note that Appian carefully and explicitly registers that Pompey did not enter into Egypt itself: *Mith.* 114.

127. Spain (44.5.8, the very end of the work); Parthia (42.5.10–12).

128. 41.1.1; cf. Alonso-Núñez 1987, 64–65, on how Trogus "intended to show the Parthians as the moral heirs of the Persians and to emphasize the duality between East and West." For material on the Parthian empire as the equivalent of the Roman, see Woodman 1977, 126; Mattern 1999, 66, 107.

129. Here I can do no more than gesture at a vast bibliography, beginning with the classic work of Kermode (1967). We return to these issues in a discussion of Virgilian time in chapter 5.

130. And, I argue below (pp. 143–44), with the resulting dedication of Hercules Musarum in 184.

131. Tempting as it has been to some to hypothesize that Ennius's three-book extension culminated with the triumph of Aemilius Paullus over Macedonia in 167 B.C.E., the evidence of Cicero that Ennius died before that year is insurmountable: see Skutsch 1980, 103–4, on Cic. *Brut.* 78 and *Sen.* 14.

132. 3.3.8–9; cf. Alonso-Núñez 1983, 424.

133. 39.8.6.

134. See Kraus in Kraus and Woodman 1997, 54, for the controversy over whether Livy had a planned end point that he extended, like Polybius, or whether "the endpoint of the *Ab Urbe Condita* was incessantly deferred, as Roman history moved on, and the history of Rome moved with it."

135. Clarke 1999a, 312.

136. Clarke (1999a, 254–55 and 287) well brings out the way that Strabo's post-Actium world is no longer divided.

137. On the map of Agrippa, and its implications, see esp. Nicolet 1991, 98–111; Wiseman 1992, advancing the attractive argument that Julius Caesar had already laid the path.

138. B. Anderson 1991, 188.

1. E.g., T. Harrison 2000a, 197–207.

2. On modern distinctions between myth and history, see H. White 1978, 56–61, 83, 89, 103–4.

3. Ford 1992, 46: "What defines this 'heroic' poetry is time: these mortals are closer and earlier to the powerful origins of the world order"; cf. 47 on the sense of stratification within the "continuous sacred history"; also 148–49, 155; cf. Cobet 2002, 389. See also the important discussion of this Homeric feature, and Virgil's departures from it, in Rossi 2003, 145–49.

4. Bellerophon, too, from an earlier generation, fought Amazons and the Chimaera (6.179–86). On Homer's exclusion of such material from the time frame of his narrative, see Griffin 1977, 40–41; in general, on these stratifications in Homer, see Most 1997, 121–22.

5. Ford 1992, 46–47; Boardman 2002, 12–13.

6. See the important discussion in Haubold 2002; note especially the parallel Greek and Akkadian chart on p. 10 of that article.

7. R. L. Fowler 2000, xxviii: "The subject-matter of tragedy, almost without exception from the mythical period, implies incontrovertibly that the large body of tales we call the Greek myths was indeed recognized as a distinct category of stories." Cf. E. Hall 1989, 66: "Greek visual arts, like the epics from which most tragic plots were to be drawn, had previously confined themselves almost exclusively to the deeds of gods and legendary heroes, which is proof in itself that the Greek could distinguish myth from immediate recent history."

8. E. Hall 1989, esp. 62–69; in general, on this dialectic, see S. P. Morris 1992, 271–361.

9. Frr. 10–18 West²; on this Simonidean theme, see Boedeker 2001 and S. Hornblower 2001.

10. My thanks to David Lupher for drawing this point to my attention.

11. Cf. Boedeker 2001, 159–60; S. Hornblower 2001, 137–40. Translating μεμυθολόγηται as "mythologized" begs the question, no doubt; the Loeb translator offers "found their way into poetry." Yet the crucial insight remains, that what normally translates the dead into this special honorific status is time. Cf. Parker 1996, 226–27, on the way that "myth has become 'ancient'" by this period, citing Aeschines' distinction between the "ancient myths" about Amphipolis from the time of the sons of Theseus and "events that have occurred in our own time" (Aeschin. 2.31).

12. Osborne 1998, 176–84.

13. See Erskine 2001, 72, for details.

14. Boardman 1977.

15. A crucial intervention was that of Shimron (1973). Bibliography in Hunter 1982, 19, 44 n. 47; T. Harrison 2000a, 198. Besides Hunter and Harrison, important recent discussions include Darbo-Peschanski 1987, 25–38; Asheri 1988, xxxvii–xliii; Canfora 1991; Cartledge 1993, 18–35; Moles 1993b; Howie 1998, esp. 80–81; S. Hornblower 2001; Cobet 2002, 405–11; B. Williams 2002, 149–71; Moyer 2002, esp. 86, on Herodotus's creation of "a double past: one to which human chronology relates, and another which is the time of divine origins and exists far away in the distant past"; Vannicelli 2003. The phrase *spatium historicum* is taken over from Jerome, who has a "historical space" for recording events between his columns.

16. Translation and ellipses as in Moles 1993b, 97.

17. Shimron (1973)—though his overall argument is more nuanced than it is often represented as being.

18. Pelling 1999, 333; T. Harrison 2000a, 201. Shimron (1973) knows these passages and has his own account of them.

19. Raaflaub 1987, 241–45, well demonstrates the justification for Herodotus's choice of Croesus as "first" within the economy of the causal narrative as a whole; cf. the illuminating discussion of Węcowski (2004, 149–55).

20. So, rightly, H. I. Flower 1991, 60; Vannicelli 1993, esp. 15–16. Flower's general argument for Croesus's special significance to Herodotus is very compelling: Herodotus thought he had information about Croesus of a kind he had about no one before Croesus as a result of the rich oral tradition at Delphi that had grown up around the magnificent monuments dedicated there by the king.

21. Pelling (1999, 334) calls attention to the "demythologizing and rationalizing" in Herodotus's accounts of Io and the others, but I take Herodotus to be poking fun at Hecataeus's rationalizing technique *en passant*, showing that rationalizing the myths does not redeem them from the point of view of knowledge. Moles 1993b, 96, well brings out how "Herodotus has it all possible ways" in his accounts of the women from myth and Croesus, while still making "a distinction between myth and solid, verifiable history."

22. Knowledge and space are also linked. One of Herodotus's two uses of the word μῦθος is in connection with Ocean, which is "not seen and not verifiable. I at any rate know of no river Ocean" (2.23; cf. Wardman 1960, 404).

23. On Herodotus's debts to Homer, see Huber 1965; Krischer 1965; Woodman 1988, 1–4; Moles 1993b, 91–98.

24. Clearly argued by Huber (1965, esp. 46); his insight has not passed into *communis opinio* as it should have.

25. Clay 1983, 12–20; Ford 1992, 60–61. On the crucial importance of this distinction in the historiographical tradition from Herodotus on, see Marincola 1997, 63–86.

26. The other half of the Homeric antithesis has already appeared in the first sentence of the work, when he announces his subject. There he says that he is writing so

that the κλέος of the great deeds of the Greeks and barbarians will be not be lost, and the agent that will destroy the things he will narrate if he does not narrate them is, precisely, time (ὡς μήτε ... τῷ χρόνῳ ἐξίτηλα γένηται, μήτε ... ἀκλεᾶ γένηται).

27. As Moles 1993b, 97, paraphrases 7.20.2–21.1; good discussions in Momigliano 1977b, 105; J. Gould 1989, 125.

28. T. Harrison 2002a, 203, 205, on 7.170–71. The deeper context for this report is the same as the one we observed in chapter 2 (p. 46 above): Herodotus is reporting why the Cretans did not join the alliance, after reporting on the failure of the Sicilians and the Argives. I do not mean to associate myself with the view that reported speech is an automatic sign of personal skepticism, a view well countered by Mikalson 2003, 145; the issue here is the way in which Herodotus is setting out the terms for the technology of his new form of rhetoric.

29. Pelling 1999, 334.

30. For a compelling and lucid account of Herodotus's perception of divine forces at work in his historical account, see Munson 2001, 183–206; cf. Cartledge and Greenwood 2002, 357–58: "Thus Herodotus claims to be able to infer divine involvement in human events, but he achieves these inferences through a process of independent inquiry based on the realm of human knowledge." Mikalson 2003, a comprehensive study of Herodotus's representation of religion, is very much in accord with such positions: note esp. 146.

31. See Luraghi 2001, 146, for the variance in Herodotus's view of how far back knowledge of the past can be taken, depending on locality: "Not all communities are thought able to perform this transmission of memory to the same degree."

32. Shimron 1973, 49; Cobet 2002, 406; van Wees 2002, 334. Cf 2.44, where he makes declarations about the antiquity of Heracles on the basis of information he supposedly got from priests of Heracles in Tyre. Moyer 2002 is an interesting reexamination of the whole issue; Moyer shows how Herodotus rethinks the time of the Greek past in the light of what he learns about Egypt.

33. Thucydides, as a careful student of Herodotus, is very clear about this issue of time and knowledge. In 1.21.1 he says that what makes things "approximate untrustworthily to the status of the mythical (τὸ μυθῶδες)" is, precisely, time. Events in the deep past are qualitatively harder to know about; it is not possible to find out anything clear about events before roughly what we call 500 B.C.E., but it is possible to use τεκμήρια, "inferences drawn from evidence," to get some trustworthy results: Gomme 1945, 135–36, for the periodization and the translation of τεκμήρια; cf. Nicolai 2001, esp. 245–47. On the vexed question of τὸ μυθῶδες, see Moles 2001, 201–2.

34. B. Williams 2002, 155 (my thanks to Harriet and Michael Flower for drawing this book to my attention). A parallel passage in Thucydides proves the point: when Thucydides, in the course of his introduction to Sicily, first mentions the Laestrygonians and Cyclopes, he says that he is not in a position to say what their *genos* was (6.2.1). This

Thucydidean usage is actually a counter to Williams's argument that Thucydides introduces a distinctively new concept of an objective historical past, for Thucydides' stance here is in fact very close to Herodotus's. In general, it seems to me that Williams does not appreciate what Herodotus achieved, and claims too much for Thucydides. For a good account of how much Thucydides owes to Herodotus in "his method of enquiry and in the temporal scope of his work," see Węcowski 2004 (quotation from 158).

35. The uncertainty here is very similar to the kind of indeterminacy that Lloyd 1979 suggests for Herodotus's attitudes to *physis* and illness: see 29–32, esp. 32 n. 108: "What must remain in some doubt is the extent to which Herodotus saw nature as a *universal* principle, and *all* natural phenomena as law-like" (emphasis in the original).

36. Von Leyden 1949–50, 93; Hunter 1982, 103.

37. I quote from a communication from Bob Kaster, whom I thank for discussion of this issue.

38. As argued by O. Murray (2001 [1987]); cf. Finley 1975, 18; R. Thomas 2001, 202.

39. Esp. Lloyd 1987; cf. the confessedly undeveloped but highly suggestive comments on the connection between historiography and science in Hunter 1982, 283–84. R. Thomas 2000 makes many important connections between the intellectual and performance environments of Herodotus and his peers in medicine and science.

40. Lloyd 1979, 235; 1987, 27–28.

41. Lloyd 1979, 250; cf. 1987, 99; R. Thomas 2000, chaps. 6–9.

42. Lloyd 1987, 258.

43. Lloyd 1987, 266.

44. Lloyd 1987, 70. For "prominence of authorial ego" in Herodotus as a marker of difference from Homer, see Huber 1965, 46.

45. Cf. H. White 1978, 103, on the Lévi-Straussian view that "*all* sciences . . . are constituted by *arbitrary* delineations of the domains that they will occupy. . . . This is especially true of a field such as historiography."

46. Von Leyden 1949–50, 94–96; Poucet 1987, 73.

47. I misunderstood this point about the mobility of the demarcation line in Feeney 1991, 256–57, and as a result very much underplayed the importance of chronology in the demarcation of history.

48. *FGrH* 70 T 8 = Diod. Sic. 4.1.3.

49. *FGrH* 70 F 9 = Harp. s.v. ἀρχαίως.

50. *Thes.* 1, following the translation of Pelling 2002, 171.

51. On such histories, see, conveniently, Pearson 1975. Without the actual texts, it is impossible to know how they represented this material; after all, as we have seen, even Herodotus's very careful and intelligent procedures continue to be regularly misunderstood, when his text survives intact. On the important fragment of Theopompus about his strategy concerning myth (*FGrH* 115 F 381), see the decisive arguments of

M. A. Flower (1994, 34–35), showing that Theopompus claims to be signaling explicitly when he incorporates myth, unlike his predecessors.

52. Marincola 1997, 118, part of a very valuable discussion; cf. Wardman 1960, 411–12.

53. On the generic interface between history and myth/epic, see Woodman 1988, index s.v. "historiography, ancient, and poetry"; Moles 1993a and b. As S. Hornblower (2001, 146) remarks, in advancing a strong claim for Pan's role in Herodotus 6.105.1–2: "Generic crossover can be a very arresting device." For the analogous procedures in epic and elegiac poets, see, conveniently, Hinds 1987, esp. 115–17.

54. A classic example of a process referred to by H. White (1987, 95): "The implication is that historians *constitute* their subjects as possible objects of narrative representation by the very language they use to *describe* them" (original emphasis). Feldherr 1998, 64–78, is an important discussion of Livy's approach to these problems. In a forthcoming volume edited by Toni Bierl I treat in more detail the vexed issue (recently revisited by Wiseman 2002) of how to interpret the mythic or fantastic material mentioned in historical texts.

55. To allude to the title of H. White 1987, *The Content of the Form*.

56. Feeney 1991, 44, 255.

57. Finley 1975, 15–18.

58. Veyne 1988, 74.

59. Sacks 1990, 65–66; Marincola 1997, 119–20. παράπηγμα, which I translate as "chronological system," is a device like a cribbage board for tracking regular meteorological phenomena, and Diodorus's use here of this time device from another sphere is metaphorical, graphically conveying the lack of an ordered system for these mythic times; he uses the same word in the same context at 40.8.1.

60. Finley 1975, 18.

61. Sellar and Yeatman 1930, 5. Cf. Munz 1977, chap. 5, esp. 121–22; Atkinson 1978, 22 ("It is the essence of history . . . that it should locate events in space and time"); B. Williams 2002, chap. 7, esp. 162–63: "There is an intimate relation between historical time and the idea of historical truth. To say that a statement about an event is historically true is to imply that it is determinately located in the temporal structure; if it is not, historical time leaves it nowhere to go, except out of history altogether, into myth, or into mere error."

62. Cf. Asheri 1988, xxxviii, on how Herodotus already distinguishes himself in this regard from the genealogists and local historians of his day.

63. Von Leyden 1949–50, 91; R. L. Fowler 2000, xxviii; Möller 2001, 251: "[Hellanicus] dealt primarily with mythical genealogies, which are autonomous in being unconnected to measured time. Measuring the past was in no way their purpose." In this sense, then, it is not the case that "from the very beginning the mythic past was firmly situated in historical time" (Green 1997, 38).

64. Veyne 1988, 76–78; Alcock 1997, 33–34; S. Hornblower 2001, 136–37.

65. *FGrH* 239 §§ 1, 3, 12, 21; cf. Dowden 1992, 51–52.

66. It is telling that when geographers reach their limit of knowledge at the edges they resort to language very similar to that of historians at the limit of their time charts: see Romm 1992, 172–73, for Herodotus's refusal to commit himself about matters on the edge of known space, just as he will not commit himself to matters on the edges of known time. In the *Germania*, Tacitus uses very similar language of noncommittal agnosticism when he is talking about the remote past of the heroic epoch (3.3) and of the remote edges of the nations he describes (46.4).

67. Alcock 1997 and Greene 1997; Higbie 2003, 163, 207–8, well evokes the first-century B.C.E. mentality, visible in the "Lindian Chronicle," of a seamless web of time going back to Lindos, Cadmus, Minos, and Heracles; cf. Chaniotis 1988, 178, on the way that the local histories show "Anachronismen, Fehlen einer Unterscheidung zwischen Mythos und Geschichte, Vergegenwärtigung uralter Ereignisse."

68. Adler 1989, 18–19.

69. Adler and Tuffin 2002, xxxiii–iv.

70. E.g., Green 1997, 38.

71. Jacoby 1954, 382–83; Momigliano 1977b, 192; Asheri 1988, xxxviii.

72. Sacks 1990, 65.

73. On the issues involved in this kind of periodization, see the stimulating discussion of I. Morris 1997.

74. On the likelihood that Varro's divisions here ultimately go back to Eratosthenes, see Jacoby, *FGrH* 241, Komm., 709; cf. Adler 1989, 15–16. For Castor of Rhodes as the proximate source, see Ax 2001, 301–2; Cole 2004.

75. In general, Porter 2004, 320.

76. Just before §§1 and 25. Jacoby does not signal these *spatia* in his text in Jacoby 1904 or *FGrH* 239; he discusses their significance in Jacoby 1904, V–VI, 88.

77. Fraser 1972, 1: 456–57.

78. *FGrH* 241 F 1a (= Clem. Alex. *Strom.* 1.138.1–3) gives the time intervals from the fall of Troy to the death of Alexander.

79. Horsfall 2000, 175.

80. Jacoby 1902, 10.

81. Feeney 1999, 19. The details are obscure thanks to textual corruption in Censorinus *DN* 21.2; see Cole 2004, 419–20.

82. Helm 1956, 6.8–7.3; Burgess 2002, 26.

83. One may compare the way that Cato in his *Origines* did not date the foundation of Rome by Olympiads, but from the fall of Troy (Feeney 1999, 16, on Dion. Hal. *Ant. Rom.* 1.74.2). De Cazanove 1992, 95 n. 139, well points out that when Solinus (1.27) refers to *nostra tempora* he is counting from the fall of Troy, while *Graeca tempora* means "Olympiads."

84. Feeney 1991, 130–31, on Virg. *Aen.* 1.12–28.

85. On Aeneas as the last of the demigods, a theme glimpsed in the Homeric Hymn to Aphrodite, see Clay 1986, 166–70. A. Barchiesi (1999, 117) is right to call this an "(unprovable I think) theory," but it coheres closely with Virgil's vision.

86. This helps the interpretation of the vexed lines 469–70, *namque aliud terris, aliud regionibus ipsis/euentum dici poterit quodcumque erit actum.* Here *terris* must be "the world *qua* body," with *regionibus* "places *qua* space," as suggested by Long and Sedley 1987, 2:26: two lines later *terris* is picked up by *materies,* and *regionibus* is picked up by *locus ac spatium* (471–72).

87. In general, Jacoby, *FGrH* 239–61 (Zeittafeln), Komm., 663; Samuel 1972, 189–90; Bickerman 1980, 75–76.

88. *FGrH* 566, Komm., 538; a judicious discussion in Möller 2004.

89. *FGrH* 566 T 10 = Polyb. 12.11.1; on this point, see Vattuone 2002, 223–24.

90. Möller 2004, 176–77, on the Timaean evidence, and on the "so-called Olympiad chronicle from Athens."

91. *FGrH* 241, Komm., 707: "E die eigentliche beglaubigte geschichte erst mit Ol. 1 begann." Jerome's *Chronicle* has a revealing note on the first Olympiad: *Ab hoc tempore Graeca de temporibus historia uera creditur. Nam ante hoc, ut cuique uisum est, diuersas sententias protulerunt* ("From this time Greek chronological history is held to be true; for before this they gave different opinions as each one saw fit," Helm (1956, 86 [d]).

92. Censorinus's report of Varro's divisions, which very probably are ultimately Eratosthenic, has a fascinating remark on the tantalizing status of the last years of the "mythical" period, before the first Olympiad: these years, "although they are the last of the mythical time, some have wanted to define more precisely, because they are adjacent to what is transmitted by historians" (*quamuis mythici temporis postremos, tamen quia a memoria scriptorum proximos quidam certius definire uoluerunt, DN* 21.2). Grafton 1995, 25, well catches the (potentially fruitful) ambivalence of the whole passage: "It divides the age of myth into periods and both reflects and criticizes efforts to define the last of these very precisely. The original passage could thus have served as a warrant for, as well as a critique of, chronological argument about the mythical time that preceded the first Olympiad." Cf. van Groningen 1953, 105–4, on the "genealogical no man's land, which has no other function than to establish a connection, to join the historical and the mythical."

93. See the references to Mazzarino 1966 in chapter 1, n. 27.

94. Grafton 1995 skewers this fat target with relish; cf. Möller 2004.

95. Even the highly judicious Mosshammer (1979, 96). See, rather, Hedrick 2002 for skepticism on the use of records, and for an interesting discussion of the kind of monumental sources the first list compilers could have used.

96. See Shaw 2003, 50, on this crucial point; cf. Möller 2004, 180. The other Pan-

hellenic games were much more recent: the Pythian and Isthmian games were dated back to "582 B.C.E.," and the Nemean to "573 B.C.E." See Purcell 2003, 28–29, on the significance of the Panhellenic festival world for constructing time schemes that linked the Greek world.

97. My thanks to Tony Woodman for tutorials on the soccer offside rule.

98. The bibliography on the foundation of the city is, needless to say, large. I have found the following particularly helpful: Bickerman 1952; Classen 1963; Strasburger 1968; Schröder 1971, 57–94; Cornell 1975; 1983; 1995, chap. 3; Poucet 1985; Bremmer and Horsfall 1987, chaps. 2 and 3; Gruen 1992, chap. 1; Wiseman 1995; Erskine 2001.

99. Against the view that Hellanicus, a contemporary of Thucydides, wrote of Aeneas and Odysseus jointly founding the city, see Horsfall in Bremmer and Horsfall 1987, 15–16, with references; Gruen 1992, 17–18.

100. Purcell 1997 makes this point very clearly; cf. Bickerman 1952, 66–68; Cornell 1975, 27; Horsfall in Bremmer and Horsfall 1987, 16, 18; Gruen 1992, 19–20.

101. See Bickerman 1952 for the motivation; a still very helpful collection of evidence in Sanders 1908.

102. A catalogue in Sanders 1908, 317–19; discussion in Wiseman 1995, 50–54. Schröder 1971, 57–94, is extremely valuable for an overview of the evidence for the various foundation stories; cf. Horsfall in Bremmer and Horsfall 1987, chap. 2, for the Aeneas legend in particular.

103. Della Corte 1976, 133; Piérart 1983, 51; Poucet 1987, 81; Wiseman 2002, 332.

104. Jacoby, *FGrH* 97, Komm., 301.

105. As might have been expected from his name, "Four-Square." And "Jackass" to boot.

106. Poucet (1987, 81, 82, 85) well remarks that there are no hard and fast periodization criteria in the Roman tradition, though the foundation was a nodal point of discussion.

107. On Cicero's tactics in *De Re Publica* 2, see Feldherr 2003, 209.

108. My thanks to Tony Woodman for discussion of Livy's agenda. Moles (1993a, 149), in the course of an otherwise excellent discussion, misinterprets *Pref.* 7 to mean that "it remains a plus if historical work can include the mingling of divine and human." For the role of the Romulus and Remus story in relations with the Greek East, see the remarkable inscription from Chios (*SEG* XVI 486, from the late third or early second century B.C.E.) that speaks in language close to Livy's of how the story of the twins' parentage might be rightly considered true because of the courage of the Romans (following the interpretation of Derow and Forrest 1982, 86).

109. Pelling 2002, 189 n. 1.

110. Good remarks in Fox 1996, 43.

111. Veyne 1988, 50.

112. Overview in Horsfall in Bremmer and Horsfall 1987, chap. 2.

113. I call this an "extraordinary shift," but it attracts oddly little attention, apart from Asheri 1991–92, 69.

114. Cornell 1995, 125, comes close to spelling this assumption out: "Problems arose, however, when Roman historians and antiquarians in the second [*sic*] century B.C. began to examine the chronological implications of these pleasing anecdotes. The work of Hellenistic chronographers had made this possible, and the discrepancies that emerged were problematic, not to say embarrassing. The *discovery* that several centuries separated Romulus from Aeneas made it necessary to fabricate the dynasty of Alban kings" (emphasis added).

115. Gruen (1992, 20) frames the issue very well.

116. The phrasing of Momigliano (1989, 83) is typical: "We simply do not know why Roman tradition chose to fix the date of the birth of Rome in the eighth century." But this way of putting it begs the question of whether it was Romans who chose this date.

117. On this Capitoline/Republican era, see Mommsen 1859, 197–200. We return to this era at the beginning of chapter 5.

118. Purcell 2003, 29.

119. Skutsch 1985, 316: "The only dating possible before a foundation date for the city was more or less fixed by the antiquarians was *post primos consules* or *ab aede in Capitolio dedicata*." Purcell 2003, 29, confusingly adduces Timaeus's foundation date as confirmation that it was "possible for such ways of thinking to ante-date formal history." But Timaeus *was* writing "formal history," even if from outside the city. And even if it was possible for Timaeus to come up with a time frame for a Roman foundation date, it is not proved that it was possible or desirable for Romans at the time, before their own "formal history," to do so.

120. Cf. Cornell 1995, 218–21. We return in chapter 5 to the importance of such constitutional changes as interval markers in chronologies at Rome (pp. 140–41).

121. On this point I recommend the fine argument of De Cazanove (1992, esp. 91). As he shows (92–93), the evidence of Dion. Hal. *Ant. Rom.* 1.74 strongly implies that the first people to give historical foundation dates were not working back from the fall of the monarchy at all.

122. De Cazanove 1992, 85–86. The dates vary from Timaeus's "814 B.C.E." to Cincius's "728 B.C.E."

123. De Cazanove 1992, 98: "La durée de la période royale a donc été déduite de la date assignée à la fondation, et non l'inverse."

124. Walbank 1957–79, 1:668–69.

125. On this debate, see the conclusive arguments of Cornell (1975).

126. For the Roman stage hypothesis, and for an account of modern discussion of the dramatic form of the story, see Wiseman 1998, chap. 1; for the theory of Diocles modeling the story on Sophocles' *Tyro*, see von Holzinger 1912; Frier 1999, 261–62.

Timpe (1988, 275–81) mounts a very powerful case for Fabius's use of Diocles for the structure of the foundation story, arguing that the literary forms of historiography are crucial, and that Fabius is not simply writing down what was somehow already "there" in an oral tradition; cf. Gabba 2000, 31, 66–67; Beck and Walter 2001, 1:59; Dillery 2002, 18–21; Hillen 2003, 113. Gabba 2001, 591, memorably evokes the context for the new historiography: "La <creazione storiografica> a Roma alla fine del III secolo rispondeva ad esigenze politiche di fronte al mondo magnogreco e greco, che prima non esistevano. Questo non è un preconcetto, è un dato di fatto."

127. Finley 1975, 28–29, is devastating on the subject of the capacity of "tradition" to preserve a chronology, or to be interested in one in the first place; cf. the important discussions of von Ungern-Sternberg (1988, esp. 255–58) and Timpe (1988, 280).

128. So, rightly, Gabba 2001, 591, summing up much previous work.

129. Schröder (1971, 170) well demonstrates how this "coincidence" is meaningless; cf. De Cazanove 1992, 72–73. And it may well not be a coincidence at all, if Ridgway (2004, 19–22) is right to suggest that dendrochronology is going to force a reassessment of accepted Iron Age dates for Italy and "turn the 8th century B.C. south of the Alps into a kind of chronological black hole" (22). As he says, "it will be interesting to see what happens when historians of early Rome realise this" (20). As Forsythe (2005, 85) points out, modern focus on the Palatine, the result of following ancient tradition, has meant that the other hills have received comparatively little archaeological attention.

130. Burkert 1995; cf. Daffinà 1987, 17.

131. A century later, the opinion of Sanders (1908, 316) still holds: "The time of the founding of Rome was, both to Greeks and Romans, a matter of pure guesswork."

132. Cornell 1995, 72, for the 1000 date, and for skepticism about attempts to link the eighth-century archaeological remains with the literary tradition.

133. So far as I discover, Jacoby first made this point explicitly: *FGrH* 566, Komm., 564, and it is stressed in Asheri 1991–92, 66–67, and visible between the lines in Cornell 1975, 23–24; Vattuone 2002, 221, is characteristically acute: "Timeo è il primo a distinguere nettamente tra la Roma <troiana> e quella <storica>, a fissare una data precisa per la più recente." But in general it is very surprising that so many discussions of the various foundation stories do not seem to regard it as significant to ask who first made this highly important shift.

134. Erich Gruen suggests to me Hieronymus of Cardia as a possible competitor for the distinction of first giving Rome a nonmythical foundation date, since he is mentioned by Dionysius of Halicarnassus as "the first who touched on the early history (ἀρχαιολογίαν) of the Romans" (*Ant. Rom.* 1.5.4). Certainly the possibility remains open, although Dionysius does not mention Hieronymus in his later discussion of the various foundation dates of Rome (1.74). Jacoby takes Hieronymus's coverage to be an ethnographic excursus in the context of the Pyrrhic wars: *FGrH* 154, Komm., 547 (on

Γ 13), as does J. Hornblower (1981, 248). If Hieronymus did discuss the origins of Rome, it is likely that he gave a Trojan origin: J. Hornblower 1981, 250. A Trojan origin is of course not incompatible with a historical date of foundation, as Timaeus's case shows, but it seems more likely that Hieronymus was giving the more or less standard pre-Timaean version of a foundation in the time of the *nostoi*.

135. *Ant. Rom.* 1.74.1. It is still sometimes claimed, following Jacoby, that Timaeus had two epochs for the foundation of Rome: a "heroic" one in his *Histories* and a "historical" one in his *Pyrrhica* ("Affairs of Pyrrhus," a supplement, it appears, to the *Histories*, covering the wars of Pyrrhus in Italy and Sicily): see Jacoby, *FGrH* 566, Komm., 564–65. There is in fact no testimony to a Timaean heroic foundation era, and Jacoby bases his argument solely on the conviction that the Rome/Carthage synchronism only makes sense on the brink of the First Punic War and must therefore have been included in the *Pyrrhica*, so that the earlier *Histories* will have given the conventional heroic epoch for Rome's foundation. The *Histories*, however, very likely already contained substantial treatments of Rome (Meister 1989–90, 58–59), and there are many other contexts than 264 B.C.E. to explain the significance of the synchronism (Momigliano 1977a, 54–55; Asheri 1991–92, 72–73). Further, if Timaeus had given a heroic date in his *Histories* and then the "814" date in a later book, surely Polybius would have commented, as well as Dionysius of Halicarnassus: Dionysius knew Timaeus well, went into this question in a lot of detail, and was very puzzled by the "814" date (Momigliano 1977a, 54).

136. Asheri 1991–92, 70 n. 31, firmly establishes that Timaeus fixed the fall of Troy in "1334 B.C.E.," the same year as that of Duris of Samos. On the significance of the date, see pp. 142–43 below.

137. Asheri 1991–92, 66. Philistus of Syracuse, for example, dated Carthage's foundation to "1215 B.C.E." (*FGrH* 556 F 47). Once the mid-eighth-century date for Rome's foundation had become canonical, it was still possible to achieve the synchronism by moving Carthage's date: Apion (first century C.E.) put the foundation of Carthage in "752 B.C.E."—the same year as the Exodus from Egypt (Joseph. *Ap.* 2.17 = *FGrH* 616 F 4a).

138. My thanks to Josephine Quinn for the suggestion that Timaeus could have obtained his information about a Carthaginian foundation date from Carthaginians, and for discussion of this whole question. Asheri (1991–92, 62–67) argues for Timaeus finding the Carthaginian date in translations of Tyrian annals, but the very existence of these annals is disputed, let alone their accessibility to a Greek around 300 B.C.E.: for a skeptical view, see Garbini 1980, and for a view closer to Asheri's, Aubet 2001, 27–29, 215–19.

139. For Dionysius's genuine expertise in chronology, see Schultze 1995 and Cornell 1995, 401.

140. As reported by Cornell 1975, 26–27; Gabba 1991, 197–98, for a development;

see above, pp. 24–25. Even Servius could remark that it was not possible to find a consensus about the true origin of the city (*Aen.* 7.678): Ando 2001, 392. The topicality of the general problem is clearly seen in the discussion in Aubet 2001 of the value of the traditional classical foundation dates for Phoenician settlement in the Western Mediterranean: "In this sense, to consider the western establishments as the end result of a more or less long-term process of trial and error and barter, like the one described by Herodotus on the Altantic coasts of Africa (Herod. 4:96), is not the same as to interpret the Phoenician expansion as a socio-economic phenomenon, arising from needs that are of an equally economic nature, but are concrete and set within a defined time space" (195; cf. 201). See Lomas 2004, 5–6, for a discussion of what is at stake in the language of "pre-colonisation" in debates over Western Greek settlement.

141. Ridgway 1992, 110–11.

142. For differing speculation on Timaeus's interest in the Romans' Trojan connections, see Vattuone 1991, 275–86; Gruen 1992, 27–28, 37–38; Erskine 2001, 152; Hillen 2003, 83–86.

143. Dion. Hal. *Ant. Rom.* 1.67.4 = *FGrH* 566 F 59.

144. Polyb. 12.4b–c1 = *FGrH* 566 F 36.

145. On the "invention of tradition," see the influential collection of essays in Hobsbawm and Ranger 1983.

146. Brown 1958, 59; Pearson 1987, chap. IV; Walbank 1989–90, 47–48, 53; Vattuone 1991, 286, 308, 310, 318. Modern students of Greek and Phoenician colonization regularly wish to preserve both the classical literary tradition and the evidence of archaeology by positing a very similar Timaean pattern of traces in the precolonizing period proper being picked up by the actual colonization itself: for discussion, see Aubet 2001, 200–201, on Phoenician scholarship; Ridgway 2004, 17–18, on Greek.

147. Jacoby, *FGrH* 555, Komm., 489; seconded by Prinz 1979, 162–63. Heracles, on the other hand, had already made his impact felt: Pearson 1987, 59–62. On Pindar's techniques, most clearly embodied in the stories of Cyrene, see Calame 2003; in general, on "double foundations" in mythic and in historical time, see Malkin 1998, 4.

148. Jacoby, *FGrH* 555, Komm., 489.

149. Testimonia alone can very seldom help on this kind of point. If Livy's account of Hercules and the Ara Maxima, for example, had not survived except in paraphrase, we would have a totally misleading impression of how Livy reported a "mythological" event in a history with distanced reporting techniques of analepsis (1.7.3–14).

150. Cf. Dougherty 1991 for the way that colonization is figured by Greeks as a return, not an intrusion.

151. Quite how this retracing or refoundation might have worked is an extremely vexed topic: Vattuone 1991, 274–86; Gruen 1992, 37–38.

152. Vattuone (1991, 289 n. 70) claims that Timaeus very probably had the same pattern for Carthage as for Rome. Certainty is not possible, but in the absence of any evi-

dence for a Carthaginian connection to mythic time, I find it more attractive to hypothesize that Timacus made a distinction between Rome and Carthage, maintaining the by now traditional Greek view of the Trojan dimension to Rome's past, with nothing comparable for Carthage. Rome, then, would be more "like us," with a purchase in "our" mythical maps, while by comparison Carthage's otherness would be stressed.

153. Dion. Hal. *Ant. Rom.* 1.74.1. If he had not used an Olympiad date then Dionysius would certainly have told us, because in the next section he remarks on the fact that Cato does not.

154. So much is clear from Plutarch, our source on this point both for Fabius and for *his* source, Diocles of Peparethus (*Rom.* 3.1–2). The whole problem of Alba Longa as a bridge between the epochs of myth and history is a very important one, but not one I can treat here. I find much to agree with in Poucet 1985 and 1986. Schröder 1971, 87–88, 170–71, remains a valuable resource; cf. Schultze 1995, 197–99. Schröder 1971, 87, rightly stresses that Alba is important in the tradition from early on and was not foisted onto the founding myths just to allow the chronological gap to be plugged: cf. Cornell 1975, 15; Gruen 1992, 25. Indeed, in Ennius's version Alba is already in existence when Aeneas arrives: Skutsch 1985, 190. The beauty of Alba was that the main thing it was known for was its destruction by Tullus Hostilius: it was no longer there (if it ever had been), and provided malleable material as a result.

155. For Diocles as Fabius's source here, see von Holzinger 1912; Timpe 1972, 942–44; Frier 1999, 260–62, 265–68; Momigliano 1990, 101–2; Dillery 2002, 18–21. On the Alban list in particular as Diocles' contribution, see Gruen 1992, 20; Hillen 2003, 12, 114. As Nicholas Horsfall points out to me, Schwegler 1867, 345, already showed that the Alban list must have been the work of a Greek, not a Roman.

156. We do not know the date of the publication of the *Chronographiae* of Eratosthenes, but since he was born around 285–280 (Fraser 1972, 2:490), it is entirely possible that the book was available to Diocles as a precursor of Fabius, who was writing at the end of the century.

157. Brown 1958, 31.

158. Beck and Walter 2001, 92; cf. 59; Dillery 2002, 8.

159. How important such generational number-crunching may have been for these writers, and for others who followed them in coming up with variations on eighth-century foundation dates, I do not know. Cornell (1995, 73) is no doubt right to suggest that "some kind of mechanical calculation" was employed in fixing the foundation dates. Asheri (1991–92, 69–70) suggests that Timaeus's date is thirteen 40-year generations from his Troy date of "1334/3"; and he points out that thirteen generations of 33.3 years (= 433 years) cover the span between Eratosthenes' Troy date of "1184/3" and a foundation date of "751/0." If such generational counting was so important, it is curious that so little explicit discussion of it survives, after the initial exposition of Herodotus (2.142.2).

160. The year 748 is two 33-year generations down from 814. Curti (2002) offers a fascinating argument about the coincidence between the eighth-century foundation dates for Rome and for the Greek colonies in Italy, although we differ over whether we are dealing with a genuine memory or a third-century reconstruction, and over whether the agency in defining this tradition is Greek or Roman.

161. Velleius Paterculus does the same, claiming that Cumae was founded at the same epoch as the Ionian colonies (1.4.1–3). On the general ancient lack of distinction between what we call the "Ionic migrations" and the later colonizing period, see Mazzarino 1966, 1:110.

162. Eusebius has Cumae founded in "1050," 867 years after Abraham (Helm (1956, 69b [b]); this is three years after his date for Magnesia in Asia, and eleven years before Carthage. Aubet 2001, 195–97, has very similar conclusions regarding the worthlessness of the traditional classical historical foundation dates for Cadiz and other western Phoenician settlements, which are grounded in *a priori* Trojan War time frames and have no independent historical value.

163. Gomme, Andrewes, and Dover 1970, 206.

164. Jacoby 1902, 161–62. The dates of Antiochus look sacrosanct to modern observers because they are in Thucydides book 6, and we have all read Thucydides book 6, but in fact there were many variant dates even for the Sicilian colonies (Gomme, Andrewes, and Dover 1970, 206–7), and it may be no more than coincidence that these dates of Antiochus turn out to approximate to the dates modern archaeologists give; in addition, we face the circularity problem that the archaeologists have all read Thucydides book 6 as well.

165. Strabo 6.1.12 = *FGrH* 555 F 10.

166. Strabo 5.4.4; see the very helpful discussion and collection of evidence in Oakley 1997–98, 2:631–32.

167. A. Barchiesi 2005a, 282; cf. Horsfall 1989a, an eye-opening discussion of the importance of Greek colonization to Virgil's framing of the *Aeneid*.

168. In an important forthcoming paper, John Dillery independently argues that Cincius Alimentus's eccentric-looking foundation date of "728 B.C.E." should be put in the context of colonization in Sicily, where he had served as praetor: this is the date of the foundation of Megara Hyblaea.

169. Beck and Walter 2001, 92; cf. Rawson 1989, 425, on Fabius's attempts to represent Rome as Hellenic.

170. On Rome's persistent barbarianization and rusticization of its non-Greek Italian neighbors, see Dench 1995; the Romans are reacting against the tendency of the Greeks to label them as Opici, "assimilating them to rough Italic tribes of southern Italy against which the Greek colonial cities had long struggled" (Rawson 1989, 423). On the concept of "allochrony," see Fabian 1983.

171. Aubet 2001, 198–99, sheds fascinating light on the persistence of such tactics,

as she demonstrates how the scholarly debates in the early twentieth century replayed these ancient chauvinist maneuvers, arguing for or against Phoenician or Greek priority as colonizers. The debate continues, even if not conducted in these chauvinist terms: J. Hall 2004, 35 with n. 1.

172. J. Z. Smith 1990, 51.

173. Suggestive remarks in Curti 2002.

174. On such motifs in colony-foundation myths, see Mazzarino 1966, 1:212–17; Dougherty 1993; on the importance of seeing the foundation of Rome as such a colony-foundation, see Piérart 1983, 57; Cornell 1983, 1110–11; 1995, 70–72; Poucet 1985, 133–34, 189; Vattuone 1991, 291; Purcell 1997.

175. Sanders 1908, 319.

176. Bickerman 1952, 67, developed by Cornell 1975, 25–27, and Gruen 1992, 38–40.

177. In both poets Romulus is the son of Aeneas's daughter, Ilia (Serv. Auct. *Aen.* 1.273); Eratosthenes had said that Romulus was the son of Aeneas's son, Ascanius (ibid. = *FGrH* 241 F 45).

178. Following M. Barchiesi (1962, 524) in the opinion that Naevius had read Fabius.

179. Dion. Hal. *Ant. Rom.* 1.74.1 = Peter, *HRRel.* F 4 = *FGrH* 810 F 1.

180. Jocelyn (1972, 1012–13) very oddly says that Ennius was following "a local tradition" in giving the conventional Hellenistic epoch of just after the Trojan War.

181. Gruen 1992, 36–37: "The origins of the Roman people in Troy were the paramount point, long since entrenched and firm"; cf. M. Barchiesi 1962, 527. Naevius strenuously kept open the gap between myth and history, even though there was an aetiological power to the mythical portion, since he had no continuous narrative joining his mythical and historical sections. Even the style differs between the mythic and historical sections; M. Barchiesi 1962, 225, 328–29.

182. *Semigraeci* (Suet. *Gram.* 1). Erskine (2001) inadvertently reveals the importance of the Greekness of Naevius and Ennius. He stresses, even to excess, how small a role the Troy legend played in Roman life and literature before Julius Caesar and Augustus on occasions when "Romans were addressing other Romans" (37). His rather strained arguments about Naevius and Ennius, trying to show that the importance of the Troy legend in their poems is not an exception to his case, are unnecessary. Naevius and Ennius, mediating between Greece and Rome and participating in Roman culture from the outside, as *semigraeci,* in fact corroborate the power of his general insight in the book, that it is precisely such interstitial spaces that are the prime venue for the mobilization of the Trojan myth. He is able to do more justice to Fabius Pictor's treatment of the Trojan myth of descent, as a result of seeing him as someone who writes in Greek in order to mediate between the worlds of Rome and Greece (38–41).

183. Horsfall (1974), however, crucially stresses how remarkably independent Virgil could still be in manipulating the by now canonical dates of Troy and Rome. On the

vital interplay between "myth" and "history" in the Roman epic tradition, especially in Naevius and Virgil, see A. Barchiesi 1989, 133–38.

184. Frier 1999, 263.

185. The first history of Rome to be written in Latin was of course Ennius's *Annales*.

186. Dion. Hal. *Ant. Rom.* 1.74.2 = Peter, *HRRel.* F 17.

187. Feeney 1999, 16.

188. I have been especially influenced by the fundamental work of Miles (1986 = (1995, chap. 2), Kraus (1994b), and Edwards (1996, 45–52); cf. Kraus (1998) on "good" and "bad" repetition in Livy, building on the Virgilian work of Quint (1993, chap. 2). There is a major discussion of the link between city-destruction and -foundation in Serres 1991, and of the general significance of the sack of Rome by the Gauls in J. H. C. Williams 2001, chap. 4.

189. This is the date as fixed by the Polybian synchronisms with the peace of Antalcidas and Dionysius's siege of Rhegium (1.6.2); the later conventional "Varronian" chronology put the sack in a year corresponding to 390 B.C.E.: see Cornell 1995, 399–400. How Ennius conceived of the year of the sack in a time grid is very uncertain.

190. Ennius somehow had to massage a long chronology, with only seven kings to fill the gap between a foundation three generations after the fall of Troy and the beginning of the Republic a hundred years or so before the sack of Rome by the Gauls around 390: for an introduction to the problem, see Cornell 1986, 247. But we can be quite sure that Ennius is not making a mistake, or failing to keep up on the latest research; he is making conscious decisions for serious reasons.

191. Dreizehnter 1978. If someone wrote a novel in which a scholar called Mr. Thirteenth wrote a book called *The Rhetorical Number,* they would be accused of overdoing it. After all, "thirteen" is not just a number; it is a *rhetorical* number.

192. Dreizehnter 1978, 90–92; cf. Syme 1958, 772; Asheri 1991–92, 67. Orosius (7.2.9), in saying that Carthage lasted a little more *(paulo amplius)* than seven hundred years, and Macedonia a little less *(paulo minus)*, interestingly replays the language of Ennius's Camillus, avoiding an overly fussy precision.

193. On the coverage of book 4, see Skutsch 1985, 306.

194. My translation of the first clause attempts to capture the way in which "the *res* is in the first instance the historian's subject-matter but it then 'slides' into being the Roman state itself" (Moles 1993a, 146). On the prominence of allusion to Ennius in Livy's preface, see Moles 1993a, 142, 155, 157.

195. Chaplin 2000, 200–201, with her reference to Fornara 1983, 73; cf. Miles 1995, 77–79.

196. In accordance with the crucial themes of repetition and refoundation, this is actually Camillus's second speech on this theme: his first (much shorter, and in *oratio obliqua*) occurs earlier in book 5, just after the capture of Veii (5.30. 1–3).

197. On the significance of the number, Hubaux 1958, 38, 60–88; Mazzarino 1966, 2 2:44 with n. 196; Pinsent 1988, 3. At 5.40.1 Livy speaks in rounder numbers, of 360 years since the foundation. Cassius Hemina, writing in the second quarter of the second century B.C.E., mentioned that the sack occurred in the 363rd year after the foundation of the city (Macr. *Sat.* 1.16.22 = Peter, *HRRel.* F 20 = Chassignet 1999, F 23); it looks as if Livy is using the Julian calendar to tidy up and improve upon what was presumably a fortuitous and unsymbolic numeral in his predecessor.

198. The crucial point about Camillus's halfway position between Romulus and Augustus was seen by Miles (1995, 95), even if his arithmetic does not quite work as he claims, to locate the year 27 B.C.E. as the other end of the calculation. See, rather, Pinsent 1988, 3–4.

199. Dilke 1967, 323–24; P. Hardie 1986, 351 n. 51. For Virgil's detailed exploitation of Livy's first pentad in this section of his poem, see Woodman 1989.

200. In addition to the already cited works of Miles (1986), Serres (1991), Kraus (1994b), and Edwards (1998), note Rossi 2003, chaps. 1 and 8, on the fall of Troy and Alba Longa and the new identity of Rome; and, in general, Woodman 1988, 138–39, on the importance of cyclical views of history to Livy.

201. Kraus 1994a, 25–26; cf. Kraus 1994b, esp. 269 and 283–84. Livy's language to describe the span of 1–5 looks very like a description of a self-contained work about a city's entire history from beginning to end: *ab condita urbe Roma ad captam eandem* (6.1.1); but searching in *FGrH* yields no traces of any such works, nor does examining the interesting section "The City Necrology" in Pomeroy 1991, 255–57 (my thanks to Tony Woodman for this reference). Corinth, Thebes, and Carthage are the obvious candidates.

202. Kraus 1994a, 26; cf. Henderson 1998, 318: "Was I–V a mythical preface to the history 'proper' of VI–CXX?"; J. H. C. Williams 2001, 140–41.

203. The talk of lost written records and a new clarity in the refounded history is, naturally, specious—fifth-century Rome did not have archives, and later writers did not use such material for the early period. Cf. Oakley 1997–98, 1:382: "Books ii–x become increasingly more full of useful material, but there is no clear point at which authentic records begin."

204. Frier 1999, 121–23; Kraus 1994a, 25, pointing out how Livy improves on Claudius by beginning his new book with the recovery, not the sack; cf. Oakley 1997–98, 1:381 with n. 1, 718; J. H. C. Williams 2001, 182, on "the date of the sack of Rome as 'Year 0' in later Roman chronologies." Note that Livy's Camillus, when recapitulating the events that led to the sack, marks the war with Veii using the same demarcating language of "firstness" with which Livy opened the *History. Iam primum omnium satis constat Troia capta*, says Livy in the *History*'s first sentence; *Iam omnium primum Veiens bellum*, says Camillus (5.51.6).

205. See above, p. 48 It is clear from Dion. Hal. *Ant. Rom.* 1.74.4 that the Gallic sack

is the keystone of his entire chronological edifice. The sack's epochal nature in the early Roman historical tradition is evident from the fact that Fabius Pictor dates the election of the first plebeian consul as taking place twenty-two years after the Gauls captured Rome (Gell. *NA* 5.4.3 = Chassignet 1996, F 23). As Chris Kraus points out to me, Livy even manages to place a quasi-fabulous story just before the demarcation of the refounding so that he can pass the same sort of noncommittal judgment that he had given on the status of fabulous stories before the "first" founding: compare *Pref.* 6 and 5.21.8–9.

206. Livy puns on the close association between destruction and refounding in 5.49.7. As Camillus celebrates his triumph he is hailed as another founder *(conditor)* of the city, while his soldiers are shouting out *iocos . . . inconditos.* These are "unpolished or rough jokes," but *inconditus* means literally "unfounded." Coming as it does only six words before *conditor,* the adjective activates the sense that the fate of the city is on a knife-edge, able to tip toward "unfounded" or "founder": Camillus's great speech persuading the Romans not to leave for Veii is still to come.

207. On the proleptic resonances of the geese here, see Gildenhard and Zissos 2004, 52–53.

208. *Fast.* 6.351–94, alluding to Enn. *Ann.* 51–55 Skutsch, a passage he also alludes to in *Fast.* 2.481–90 and *Met.* 14.805–17, where he describes the apotheosis of Romulus. For the foundation of the city as the likely occasion for the Ennian council, see Feeney 1984, 190. A related case is Propertius 4.4, where the day of Tarpeia's attempted betrayal of the city is given as the Parilia, the day of the city's foundation (4.4.73): once again, foundation and barely averted catastrophe are linked. On ancient attempts to construct possible links between the stories of Tarpeia and the Gallic sack, see Horsfall in Bremmer and Horsfall 1987, 68–70.

209. Michels 1967, 25; Rüpke 1995b, 359, 415 (with 560–70 on the *dies Alliensis*).

210. Since the Fasti Antiates are a Republican calendar, I should really give the date of the Allia as 18 Quintilis, or as fifteen days before the Kalends of Sextilis.

211. Here again one sees how much recent discussion of these topics owes to the insights of Quint (1993, chap. 2) and Kraus (1994b).

212. *De Reditu Suo* 121–28; my thanks to Peter Brown for this reference.

213. B. Anderson 1991, esp. 192–99.

214. On the link between the Republic and the temple of Jupiter, see above, p. 89. My thanks to W. S. Anderson for pointing out to me the importance of this watershed.

215. Livy's use of the verb *numero* here is very striking (reinforced, as Chris Kraus points out to me, by the other "number words" in the sentence, *magis* and *deminutum*). *Numero* really means "to count," but here it must mean "to consider/estimate." The Loeb translation's "reckon," which I have borrowed, very well catches the syllepsis: "considering/estimating" the origin of liberty is the same as "counting" the consuls. We return to the conflation of liberty with counting consuls in chapter 6.

216. Kraus 1994a, 25.

217. In the earlier historiographic tradition (Fabius Pictor and Cato), the establishment of the Decemvirate in 458 B.C.E. will have been another crucial staging post: Chassignet 1986, xi n. 5.

218. Tacitus makes a great deal of the refoundation of the destroyed temple of Jupiter, begun in a ceremony on 21 June 70 C.E. (*Hist.* 4.53). Kathleen Coleman compellingly suggests to me that Tacitus is using the refoundation of the temple to respond to the way the Flavians used Republican imagery to stress their return to pre-Neronian norms, as he capitalizes on the identification of the initial foundation of the temple and the Republic after the expulsion of the Tarquins. A key piece of evidence for the Flavian recycling of Republican nomenclature is the use of the anachronistically Republican phrase *ex manubiis* to describe the construction of the Colosseum, reclaiming land from the autocrat's pleasure palace for public use: Coleman 2000, 229–30, referring to the reconstruction of the original dedication by Alföldy (1995).

219. In general, on the fabulous dimension to Nero's portrayal in Tacitus, see Woodman 1998, 187–89; O'Gorman 2000, 162–70.

220. Good discussions in Kraus 1994b, 285–87; O'Gorman 2000, 172–75; Champlin 2003b, 194–200.

221. Note that Tacitus uses the Republican name of the month in this anniversary context, Sextilis, not Augustus.

222. First worked out by Grotefend (1845)—actually, as he says, 454 years minus 8 days.

223. J. H. C. Williams 2001, 177.

224. On the distinction between the two periods implied in Tacitus's sentence here, see Rouveret 1991, 3067–68.

225. I have learned much from discussions with Tony Woodman, who is working on this topic.

226. Zeitlin 1986 continues to be richly thought-provoking for students of Rome to work with: Nero's Rome is locked into the eternal regress that the paradigm of reenactment always threatens, just as Thebes is in Attic tragedy.

CHAPTER 4. TRANSITIONS FROM MYTH INTO HISTORY II: AGES OF GOLD AND IRON

1. In describing this template I do not mean to endorse it. The fantasy of a natural human life in harmony with nature is precisely that—a fantasy. On the inextricable mutual implication of the "natural" and the "human," see Cronon 1995a.

2. Mazzoli 2001, 136: "Dalla preistoria alla storia, al tempo relativo, il passaggio è traumatico."

3. In general, Lowenthal 1985, 371–72; Heinberg 1989; Slater 1995, on "Edenic narratives"; Herman 1997, a study of the concept of decline concentrating on the last two centuries; Zerubavel 2003, 16–18.

4. Excellent account in Munz 1977, 139–41, beginning with "the conception of Ferdinand Tönnies that the development of human groups in history goes from community (*Gemeinschaft*) to society (*Gesellschaft*), with the clear indication that a community is something valuable and meaningful in which there is a common life and a sense of belonging and that a society is a mere conglomerate of individuals in which there is not only a division of labour but also a division of value, opinions, and of leisure time activities" (140). Munz gives a wide range of examples, curiously not mentioning Marxism explicitly. For the power of such Marxist-informed views in British cultural materialism, see Felperin 1990, 167–69; for an eloquent expression of the fantasy that "there was a time when things were both more beautiful and less fragmented," and for a protest against succumbing to it, see B. Williams 1993, 166–67.

5. Dupont 1999 is extreme, but representative.

6. Lévi-Strauss's various contributions are lucidly discussed and criticized by Gell (1992, chap. 3); he remarks that Lévi-Strauss's "interest in the sociology of time is focused primarily, and perhaps with a degree of envious nostalgia, on the ways in which societies can annul time and its effects" (24). N. Thomas observes, more broadly, that anthropology's distinctive object of study "was and is essentially a social or cultural system or structure out of time" (1996, 120).

7. Fabian 1983. This was a very common conception in the ancient world: R. F. Thomas 1982b, 55; Cobet 2002, 405; Campbell 2003, 189; Nisbet and Rudd 2004, 271. One brief example: when Lucretius speaks of contemporary people without Iron Age technology, he uses the same language of rumor and report (*ut fama est*, 5.17) that he just before uses of mythical events in deep time (*fertur*, 5.14). For a compelling presentation of the geographically remote also embodying the future, see Murphy 2004, 183–88, on Seneca's picture of the Chauci in his evocation of cataclysm (*QNat.* 3.27–28).

8. Horace's sixteenth *Epode*, with its fantasy of an escape to the Blessed Isles, is the finest example: see Watson 2003 for copious comparative material, and, in general, Bichler 1995; Evans 2003, for Roman utopias.

9. *The Economist*, 16 April 2005, 71.

10. Mann 2005, 289, 304. Mann's book synthesizes recent research that dispels the view of a "natural" Edenic existence in the Americas before 1492, and that asserts that the inhabitants of America were then, and have continued to be, fully part of history. Cf. Worsley 1997, 41–50, on the Aborigines of northern Australia.

11. "The switch from hunting and gathering to farming may have been . . . even more gradual than was previously thought" (*The Economist*, 7 August 2004, 65–66). For a severe questioning of the "revolution" model, see Gamble 1986.

12. Diamond 1997, 86, 113.

13. Hughes 1994, 29–30.

14. N. Davis 1996, 71; cf. Heinberg 1989, 166–70.

15. M. L. West 1997, 312–19. Most (1997) attempts to contest the Near Eastern

contribution, together with the conventional interpretation of the myth as charting a progressive decline. He makes some important points about how the conventional view has not done justice to Hesiod's particular vision, and he well stresses the fundamental tension between the state of the Golden Race and the current Iron Race (114); but it is very strained to argue that the imagery of metal is not inherently degenerative.

16. The topic has "generated an enormous amount of scholarly discussion," as Woodman and Martin (1996, 240) remark in the course of their valuable account. Key references to general discussions concerning the ancient world include Lovejoy and Boas 1935; Edelstein 1967; Gatz 1967; Cole 1967; Wallace-Hadrill 1982; Blundell 1986; Kubusch 1986; Versnel 1994, 89–227; Campbell 2003, 336–53 and index s.v. "golden age"; S. J. Harrison 2005. The bracing common sense of Horsfall (2003) is salutary, as he reminds us that "what we think of as traditional Roman prejudice ('new is worse', 'development is degeneration', etc.), has no bearing on the content and attitudes of popular culture" (32).

17. As Froma Zeitlin points out to me, the main emphasis in archaic and classical Greek versions of the myth of the age of Cronus is not so much on a succession of ages or races as on the use of the rule of Cronus as a counterfactual world: see, above all, Vernant 1981 and Vidal-Naquet 1981, and, on the importance of this theme in Old Comedy, Dunbar 1995, 5–6. On Cronus and the festival of Cronia, see the important discussion of Versnel 1994, 89–135.

18. Gatz 1967, 204–5; cf. Momigliano 1987, 33–35, on the limited afterlife of Hesiod's myth.

19. Cole 1967, 1.

20. Wallace-Hadrill 1982, 25. As we shall see, the Augustan poets were certainly also interested in the use of the Fall myth "to explain the present state of humanity." At the end of the chapter we return to the Augustan Golden Age.

21. *Ann.* 3.26, with Woodman and Martin 1996, 239–40, on Tacitus's "description of primitive man and his 'golden age.'" Note that Tacitus begins by talking of the "oldest of mortals" (*uetustissimi mortalium*) and does not explicitly use a phrase such as *aureum saeculum*, in the way that he had in his other "Golden Age" passage, in the *Dialogus De Oratoribus* (12.1–4). In the *Dialogus* Maternus praises poetry, in self-consciously poetic fashion, as the mode of *felix illud et, ut more nostro loquar, aureum saeculum* (3), before the corruption of crime and oratory: see Heilman 1989; Mayer 2001, 123–26. Heilmann well stresses that the view expressed in both passages is part of a coherent and sophisticated historical vision.

22. Excellent discussion in Della Corte 1976; cf. Baier 1997, 176–79. The Varronian passage is Dicaearchus fr. 54 in the new edition of Mirhady (2001).

23. Kubusch 1986, 47–51; Boys-Stones 2001, 14–17. This Dicaearchan view of the Golden Age may be glimpsed behind Cicero's modifications of Aratus's visions of plenty: see A. Barchiesi 1981, 184–87 on Cic. *Arat.* fr. 17 Traglia, suggesting Dicae-

archus as an influence, although Cicero has taken the austere line even farther. On the high opinion of Dicaearchus among Cicero and his contemporaries (Varro and Atticus), see Rawson 1991, 60–61. It is not easy to discriminate Dicaearchus's own positions from the reports of Varro and of Porphyry (*Abst.* 4.2.1–9 = fr. 56A Mirhady 2001). Saunders (2001) argues strongly that Dicaearchus was not a "primitivist," but rather an "*ironic* progressivist" (254); cf. Schütrumpf 2001, 257–58, on the question of whether the "falling-off" model is Varronian or already present in Dicaearchus.

24. For conflicting claims over the status of oldest city (the top candidates are usually Athens, Argos, Sicyon), see Pliny *HN* 7.194: the Egyptians win, with Diospolis.

25. In Latin the point is reinforced by the fact that *antiquus* in the comparative can anyway mean "better, preferable, more desirable" (*OLD* s.v. §10): see Bettini 1991, 117–19, for the fundamental sense of "coming before," "out in front."

26. Schütrumpf 2001, 258–59.

27. North 1995 on the Roman version of this perspective.

28. R. Williams 1973; note the reassessments offered in MacLean, Landry, and Ward 1999.

29. Della Corte 1976.

30. Versnel 1994, 190. See Della Corte 1976, 130, for the coexistence in Varro's *Res Rusticae* of the two ideas of progress and decadence. For an interesting discussion of Greek theories of language within this framework, see Gera 2003, which focuses on language as either a trace of a lost form of communication between humans and animals and gods or else one of civilization's appurtenances.

31. Herman 1997, 13; I am much indebted to his discussion.

32. Farrell 1995. Lucretius thus anticipates the insight of Horden and Purcell 2000, 303: "Things have always got worse as well as better."

33. On the Lucretian dimension, see Gale 2000, 38–43, 63–66. The bibliography on the Golden and Iron ages in Virgil is colossal: a recent overview in Perkell 2002 provides very helpful orientation.

34. Kubusch 1986, 94–98; R. F. Thomas 1988, 1:16–17, 87.

35. On the close links here to Varro's reworking of Dicaearchus's third stage, see Kubusch 1986, 100–103. Varro likewise speaks of farmers being regarded by the Romans as "the only ones left from the stock of King Saturn" (*solos reliquos esse ex stirpe Saturni regis, Rust.* 3.1.5).

36. So Zetzel 1994, 21; cf. 1997, 190–95; Horsfall 1981, 146–48; O'Hara 1994; O'Hara (forthcoming), chap. 4; R. F. Thomas 2004.

37. My translation is based on the commentary of Woodman and Martin (1996), ad loc.

38. On this crucial shift, see Baldry 1952; Gatz 1967, 205–6; Blundell 1986, 136, 156–57. As Gatz acutely observes, and as we shall see further below, the shift from

"race" to "age" represents a Roman politicizing and historicizing of an originally more anthropological framework; cf. Momigliano 1987, 33–34.

39. Gatz 1967, 229.

40. See Campbell 2003, 345–49, for a fuller conspectus. Aratus is an interesting exception to the universal ban on plowing in the Golden Age: see *Phaen.* 112–13, with D. Kidd 1997, ad loc.; cf. Kubusch 1986, 89–90.

41. Blundell 1986, 104–5, 135–36; Versnel 1994, 106–7; Most 1997, 114.

42. The omission of any word for "before" is idiomatic, but here the omission of the time word reinforces the complete absence of time divisions before Prometheus's intervention. Greek sources usually attribute to Palamedes the credit for inventing nocturnal astronomy, and the sundial as well: Gratwick 1979, 311.

43. See Murgia 2000 for a defense of the transmitted *propter odores* in 5.1445, and for a clear statement of Lucretius's antipathy to sailing (a topic to which we return shortly): my thanks to Charles Murgia for discussion of this passage.

44. Quoted by Gell. *NA* 3.3.5; my thanks to Stephen Hinds for pointing out to me the relevance of this fragment. Gratwick (1979) identifies Menander as Plautus's model, writing at a time when the sundial was indeed a recent introduction to the city of Athens.

45. On Dicaearchus fr. 56A Mirhady (2001) (= Porph. *Abst.* 4.2.1–9), see Della Corte 1976, 128; on the Stoics, Boys-Stones 2001, 18–43.

46. Important discussion in Clay 1986, 166–68, identifying Aeneas as the last demigod; cf. Scodel 1982, 35–36, and Burkert 1995, 143, on the crucial significance of Troy as the cut-off point; cf. Clauss 2000, 24, on this theme in Apollonius's *Argonautica*. In general, on the theme of the gods hiding themselves after the Golden Age, "ever since the world became real," see Veyne 1988, 72.

47. I am indebted to the thought-provoking remarks of Janan 1994, 109, discussing Catullus 64, to which we turn in the next section.

48. Canonical version of the myth in Pind. *Isthm.* 8.26–48; see Slatkin 1991, 70–77.

49. Cf. van Groningen 1953, 97–100, on the static quality of the gods' narrative time.

50. Suggestive observations on these strategies of accommodation in Ando 2001, 391. Veyne 1999 is an interesting discussion of these issues in Plutarch; I thank Peter Brown for the reference, and for discussion of the topic.

51. Well stressed by Mazzoli 2001, 138.

52. Jackson 1997, 249–51. As Jackson well shows (253–55), the "firstness" of the Argo in pre-Apollonian versions consists in its being the first Greek ship to penetrate the Black Sea; Eratosthenes, in *Catast.* 35, written probably after Apollonius, "is the first Greek writer, so far as we know, to have referred to Argo as the first ship" (255). Ovid wittily combines the Greek version of the Argo as the first to enter the Black Sea with the developed Roman version of the Argo as harbinger of the Iron Age, when he

represents Tomis as an Iron Age locale, on a sea first entered by Jason (*Pont.* 3.1.1): for Ovid's Tomis as an Iron Age locale, see G. Williams 2002, 346. For collections of material relating to the motif of the "first ship," see K. F. Smith 1913, 246–47 (on Tib. 1.3.37–40); Pease 1955–58, 770 (on Cic. *Nat. D.* 2.89); McKeown 1998, 224–26 (on Ov. *Am.* 2.11.1–6).

53. See the material collected by Jacoby (1904, 41–42); cf. Jackson 1997, 251–52; Pliny also reports the Danaus version (*HN* 7.206).

54. See Jocelyn 1967, 353, on "the pleonastic gerund *inchoandi*," and also for the reading *cepisset*, rather than the usually quoted *coepisset*, which would be even more deliciously pleonastic (signaled as such in *OLD*, s.v. *coepi* §4a ["*pleon.*"]; but I cannot construe *coepisset* in the sentence). On Ennius's stress on the "initiatory moment," and on his exploitation of "associations with the end of the Golden Age," see Theodorakopoulos 2000, 124.

55. O'Hara (forthcoming), chap. 3, emphasizes the importance of Catullus's stress on the Argo as "first"; I have benefited very much from his discussion of this difficult poem. As he says, commenting on line 11, "even the most recent proponent of removing *prima* (in favor of *proram*) thinks we are still dealing with the first ship" (referring to Heyworth in Harrison and Heyworth 1998, 105–6). The point is well made by Bramble (1970, 35–37).

56. For such gradualist views, see Most 1997, 105–6; cf. Watson 2003, 529, on the model according to which "one age shades in to the next without a sharp break." The Stoic view of the corruption of natural rationality by civilized arts is another gradualist model of this kind: Boys-Stones 2001, 42–43.

57. Maltby 2002, 194 (on Tib. 1.3.35–48).

58. Bramble 1970, 36: "Two elements which were previously distinct have now been mixed together." On Catullus's Argo as harbinger of culture, see Konstan 1977, 23–30.

59. *OLD* s.v. *proscindo* §1; see Fordyce 1961, ad loc., citing Varro *Rust.* 1.29.2, *terram cum primum arant, proscindere appellant;* cf. R. F. Thomas 1988, 200 (on Virg. *G.* 2.237). On the metaphor of "plowing" the sea, see McKeown 1998, 218 (on Ov. *Am.* 2.10.33–34); as he remarks, "Sailing the sea, like ploughing the land, signalled the end of the Golden Age." As Chris Kraus reminds me, in Virg. *Ecl.* 4.32–33 agriculture and sailing are intertwined.

60. Following the supplement and correction of Bergk: see Fordyce 1961, ad loc., for the text. As we shall see shortly, the stress on "*that* day" is a "correction" of the version of Apollonius, now being superseded, which marked the departure of the Argo with the phrase "on that day" (ἤματι κείνῳ, 1.547).

61. Fitzgerald 1995, 150; cf. Munich 2003, 48.

62. *The Corrupting Sea* is the title of Horden and Purcell 2000, a book to which I am much indebted in this section.

63. D. Kidd 1997, 222, commenting on Aratus *Phaen.* 110, one of the few Greek texts to speak explicitly of sailing as an evil that did not exist in the Golden Age, well speaks of "the Latin poets' theme of seafaring as a crime." My thanks to Peter Brown and to Robert Knapp and the Berkeley classics majors for stimulating discussion of why the ship was such a dangerous subject for the Romans.

64. A passage alluded to by Aratus (*Phaen.* 110–13).

65. The second simile is another technological simile, comparing the sizzling of the eye to the noise from water into which a smith has dipped iron to temper it (391–94). For shipbuilding and navigation as the supreme emblem of human intelligence, and for Odysseus as their supreme exponent, see Detienne 1981.

66. Griffith 1999, 181, well elucidates the ode's interest in "the ambiguous moral character of 'technology' . . . and of human ingenuity in general."

67. Solon fr. 13.43–46; Eur. *IT* 408–21: my thanks to Donald Mastronarde for pointing out the significance of these passages to me.

68. Horden and Purcell 2000, 278; cf. 300, 342. For extensive material on views of seafaring in the ancient world, see Heydenreich 1970, 13–62.

69. Pl. *Phd.* 109b.

70. Polyb. 1.20.12; cf. Casson 1971, 121; Finley 1973, 129–30. Note the qualifications of the Roman view in Cornell 1995, 388, documenting Roman naval and maritime interests before 264 B.C.E.

71. Casson 1971, 173.

72. Horden and Purcell 2000, 134–35, on Cic. *Prov. cons.* 31; see Aelius Aristides' *Encomium of Rome* (200–201) for an evocation of Rome as the center of trade from all over the world, together with the satiric countervision of the Romans as "consuming the world" with their shipborne trade in Petronius's civil war fragment (*Sat.* 119: see Connors 1998, 104–14). More than trade is involved. Scheidel (2004, 26) remarks on the distinctively Roman character of large-scale population movements: "Short lives were common to all pre-modern populations. By contrast, physical mobility far beyond one's native environment was a much more specific and culturally contingent determination of what it meant to be 'Roman'." On this Roman "diaspora," see Purcell 2005.

73. Finley 1973, 42–61, on Cic. *Off.* 1.150–51. For the *plebiscitum Claudianum* of 218 B.C.E., which banned senators from owning ships that were bigger than needed to transport produce from their own agricultural estates, see Livy 21.63.2, with the discussion of D'Arms (1981, 31–39), on its causes and impact: my thanks to Harriet Flower and Brent Shaw for these references. For ancient (and modern) double-think about the supposed gulf between Mediterranean trade and agriculture, see Horden and Purcell 2000, 342 ("The gulf is as unhistorical as the Golden Fleece"); D'Arms 1981 is a general study of the whole "relationship between upper-class attitudes towards commerce and the realities of behavior" (17). The Athenians of the 440s already embody this double-

think, torn between their status as a great naval power and their inability to escape from dominant Greek aristocratic ideologies of landed wealth: Griffith 1999, 185.

74. As Chris Kraus points out to me, such a mentality leads to the attempt to locate the city of Rome in an ideal situation, neither too close to nor too far from the sea (Cic. *Rep.* 2.5–10, with Zetzel 1995, 162–63).

75. He is thus widening his focus from the previous poem (*Carm.* 1.2), which had used the end of *Georgics* 1 as a way of concentrating on the more circumscribed topic of Roman national guilt for the civil wars: Nisbet and Hubbard 1970, 16–17.

76. Mynors 1990, 28.

77. Horace's primary lyric model, Alcaeus, is regularly cast by him as the sailor (*Carm.* 1.32.7–8; 2.13.27).

78. Rosen 1990, 104, on Hesiod's metaphorical activation of farming and sailing; I thank Stephen Hinds for this reference, and for alerting me to the issue. On this programmatic dimension to Horace's poem, see Basto 1982 and Sharrock 1994, 112–14.

79. I quote the translation of D. West (1995).

80. As Sharrock (1994, 113) puts it, in the course of an enlightening discussion. She well brings out how the poem combines an understanding at once of "progress, the attempt to push back the boundaries of human civilization," and "transgression, which attempts to burst the boundaries of human nature and the condition of man" (115).

81. On Valerius Flaccus's exploitation of the similarity of flying and sailing in his treatment of the Argo's ending of the Golden Age, see Feeney 1991, 330–32.

82. Nisbet and Hubbard 1970, 57: "The long final vowel is an archaism."

83. W. S. Anderson *per litteras* kindly points out to me another striking departure in this portion of the poem, "the daring enjambement between 32 and 33, which acts out the Latin *corripuit gradum*. It is the only case where the fourth line [of the stanza] does not come to a full stop in the poem."

84. It is interesting to see what the great commentary of Nisbet and Hubbard said about this poem in 1970: "Horace turns to an attack on human inventiveness in general. The ancients by no means lacked appreciation of such enterprise"; they give examples: "Yet poets and moralists regularly stressed the other point of view, not necessarily with any overwhelming conviction. Prometheus was too often the symbol not for man's conquest of nature, but for impious defiance of the gods" (Nisbet and Hubbard 1970, 44). "Man's conquest of nature" was a phrase that could still be used in straightforward approbation in 1970. Their further comment (45) sounds genuinely ironic early in the next, steadily warming, millennium: "The diatribe against enterprise has none of the universal validity which we expect from Horatian commonplaces, and though no more foolish than the conventional praises of poverty, it sounds particularly unconvincing to modern ears." Syndikus 1972, 62–63, offers a more sympathetic view.

85. Note, however, that Catullus "refrained from mentioning the Argo by name":

R. F. Thomas 1982a, 148. It is of course by no means at all straightforwardly the case that the sailing of Catullus's Argo takes us simply from the Golden to the Iron Age: as we shall see, the confusion of the various eras is vital to Catullus's project, and the "heroic race" of Hesiod is as much at issue as the "Golden Age" (Syndikus 1990, 105–6, 188). Still, he is undoubtedly capitalizing on the crucial concept of a turn from a blessed to a fallen state, however much the apparent transparency of this concept is put under pressure as he proceeds. Marincic (2001, 484, 488–89) provides a convincing framework for this problem, arguing for Catullus's blending of Hesiodic and Aratean paradigms of degeneration. For the possible influence of Dicaearchus on Catullus's conception of a falling-off from proximity to the divine, see Della Corte 1976, 128 n. 29.

86. Cf. Fitzgerald 1995, 151. In Apollonius, when the nymphs look on in wonder at the first sailing of the Argo, they do so from mountaintops, not from the sea (1.549–52): Clare 1996, 63.

87. This is very different from Apollonius's *Argonautica*, as is well pointed out by Clauss (2000, 25 n. 55), who remarks that Apollonius "does not appear to envisage seafaring per se as a symptom of a fall from grace." On the hidden presence of Jason and Medea in the poem's opening, see Zetzel 1983, 258–61.

88. Cf. Bramble 1970, 36–37; Munich 2003, 48: "While the ship brings about the occasion for Peleus's and Thetis's meeting and is responsible for their union, it is also an agent of separation—pine trees are uprooted, man is separated from land, and the sea nymphs abandon their usual home."

89. On the rich literary tradition concerning the wedding, see Syndikus 1990, 113; for the iconographic tradition, see *LIMC* VII.1, s.v. "Peleus," 265–67. In book 4 of Apollonius's *Argonautica* we see an encounter between Peleus and Thetis that is the only depiction of a conversation between a divorced couple that I can think of in ancient literature, given that in the plays of Euripides and Seneca Jason and Medea are still in the stage of custody dispute, and that in *Odyssey* 4 Menelaus and Helen are reconciled and "remarried." It is not much of a conversation, since Peleus sits and listens in silent shock while Thetis tells him what is going to happen to the ship (4.851–68). She even begins by addressing him in the plural, as if addressing the ship's company (856–61), before switching to the singular (862–64).

90. Prisc. *Gramm.* 2.79.8, *ab humo humanus;* Maltby 1991, s.vv. *humanus* and *humus;* see Ahl 1985, 108, on Varro *Ling.* 5.23–24.

91. Best captured in the analysis of Gaisser (1995). The powerful arguments of Versnel (1994, 90–227) on crises of inversion and reversal associated with Cronus and Saturnus do not provide a model with which to *solve* the problems of poem 64, but his analysis of the total ambivalence generated in these moments of transition and caesura is very good to think with for students of the poem, not least for those interested in its ambiguities of moral judgment: note his evocation of the coexistence in transitional

Saturnian contexts of "sadness, anxiety, despair" with "elation, joy and hope" (121). For chronological distortions in particular see Versnel 1994, 130, 177, 188.

92. Fundamental discussion in Weber 1983; Gaisser (1995) and O'Hara (forthcoming) add much to the debate over chronological inconsistency. As Tony Woodman reminds me, this is not to deny the careful overall structure of the poem, which is meticulously divided into different time zones: Traina 1975, 148–51.

93. In the *Argonautica*, for example, Apollonius shows us the wife of the Centaur Chiron holding up the baby Achilles to wave good-bye to his father as the Argonauts head out to sea for the first time (1.557–58); and on the return voyage there is a meeting between Peleus and Thetis, who have clearly been divorced for some time (4.851–68: see n. 89 above).

94. Weber 1983, 264–65, gives details. Theseus's father refers to him as "returned to me in the extreme limit of my old age" (217), an allusion to Call. *Hec.* fr. 234, where Aegeus says to Theseus, "You have come against expectation."

95. Reading Baehrens's supplement of *ex*.

96. *Utinam ne in nemore Pelio . . .* , Enn. *Medea Exul*, fr. 1.1. W. S. Anderson reminds me that Ovid likewise refers to the Argo as the first ship (*prima carina*) in the last line of *Metamorphoses* 6, even though he has already told of another journey by ship (*carina*) earlier in the book (444, 511): Anderson 1972, on *Met.* 6.721. Likewise, Wheeler (1999, 138) shows how Ovid reactivates the chronological problems of the marriage of Peleus and Thetis in *Metamorphoses* 11.

97. For Minos as the first thalassocrat, Thuc. 1.4.1; Call. *Aet.* fr. 4, καὶ νήσων ἐπέτεινε βαρὺν ζυγὸν αὐχένι Μίνως ("and Minos stretched a heavy yoke on the neck of the islands"). This is a doubly primary moment in Callimachus, for it is part of the first aetion in the *Aetia*, explaining why the Parians sacrifice to the Graces without flutes and garlands. Phaedrus plays on the issue in 4.7: he produces a parody of the opening of the *Medea*, with the sailing of the Argo, the first ship (6–16), only to provoke a retort from the reader that this is "dumb and falsely spoken" (*insulsum . . . falsoque dictum*, 17–18), since Minos had long before tamed the Aegean with the first empire (18–20).

98. The apparently unemphatic *quondam*, the second word of the poem, now looks much more powerful. "Once upon a time" in the first line is a generic marker for this kind of poem already in Callimachus (*Hec.* fr. 230), but now *quondam* really does mean "at some indefinite time in the past."

99. Well discussed by Theodorakopoulos (2000, 139–40), who also has excellent remarks on the metapoetic implications for Catullus's own project of originality (126–27). Cf. Malamud and McGuire 1993, 196–97, on the cognate issues in Valerius Flaccus's *Argonautica:* "In both Catullus and Valerius, as the *Argo* sails, it comes upon traces of earlier voyages—even for the first ship, it turns out that there is nothing new under

the sun. By the time Valerius inherits it, the myth of the *Argo* has become a trope for the impossibility of discovering an origin; for Valerius it seems also to be a metaphor for the impossibility of creating a truly original text. . . . The *Argo* myth which seems at *first* glance to be about origins, exploration, and innovation, becomes in Valerius' hands a vehicle for exploring the endless repetitions and variations of a profoundly derivative literary world" (emphasis added).

100. So Godwin 1995, ad loc.

101. *OLD* s.v. §5a; see Kroll 1922, ad loc., for the *simplex pro composito* construction.

102. On the importance of Prometheus in the cultural history of the poem, see Gaisser 1995, 609–10.

103. Cf. Bramble 1970, 24: "The demarcation between heroic past and sinful present is deliberately blurred"; Gaisser 1995, 613: "All ages may be the same."

104. Above, p. 118.

105. Fine discussions in Fitzgerald 1995, 140–68, and Munich 2003. Syndikus (1990, 104) well remarks on how unlike "bourgeois" Theocritean or Callimachean epyllia Catullus's poem is in its fascination with the glamorous and grand heroic (however qualified).

106. Especially Catullus 68, and 8, 58, 72, 76: see Putnam 1961; Traina 1975, 150–51; Mazzoli 2001, 136–37; Marincic 2001, 485, 488.

107. Good treatments are available in Fyfe 1983, on *Medea;* P. J. Davis 1983 and Boyle 1987, esp. 18–24, on *Phaedra;* and Segal 1983, in general.

108. On this article of the Stoic creed, see Long and Sedley 1987, 1:400–401.

109. In the *Natural Questions,* likewise, his discussion of the winds turns into a long denunciation of the abuse of winds to enable sailing (5.18.4–16), ending with the observation that "different people have different motives for launching a ship, but none has a good one" (*non eadem est his et illis causa soluendi, sed iusta nulli,* 16).

110. Fyfe 1983, 87.

111. Tony Woodman attractively suggests that *pingitur aether* may be a reference to a model of the night sky.

112. In *Epistle* 90, to which we turn shortly, Seneca offers a wonderful counterpart to this moment, contrasting the fake ceilings above modern heads with the "remarkable spectacle of the nights," which were there for early man to gaze upon (*insigne spectaculum noctium,* 42).

113. It is worth remarking that this kind of perspective is no part of Seneca's counterpart in Greek, Euripides' *Hippolytus.*

114. P. J. Davis 1983, 114–15; Boyle 1987, 18–19, on Hippolytus's assertion of violent control here.

115. Note how Theseus, the "normal" man *par excellence,* marks time through agri-

cultural demarcations in his first words on stage, informing us that he has been in the underworld for four years by saying, "This is the fourth time that Eleusis has cut the gifts of Triptolemus" (*iam quarta Eleusin dona Triptolemi secat*, 838).

116. In using the Phaedra myth, with its central theme of aberrant sex, Seneca follows Ovid's use of this sexual theme to explore these same issues of human nature (Feeney 1991, 195–96); it is distinctive that Seneca incorporates the larger natural dimension of the *Georgics* so seamlessly into the sexual one. Uncontainable sexual impulse and madness had of course already been part of Virgil's universe in the *Georgics*, as Chris Kraus reminds me (*amor omnibus idem*, 3.244).

117. Gellner 1983, 51.

118. N.b. *Rust.* 3.1.4, where Varro makes a distinction between the fields as the gift of divine nature and the cities as the product of human art, with land cultivation going back into time immemorial. Blundell (1986, 145) well points out that Aratus's location of an agricultural life in the Golden Age (*Phaen.* 112–14) is "almost certainly a reflection of the sophisticated urban society out of which Golden Age beliefs are now issuing: Hesiod could never have made an idyll out of the farming life, because he was a farmer himself and knew too much about it; but Aratus could."

119. Pfligersdorffer 1982; Kubusch 1986, 75–86; Boys-Stones 2001, 18–24, 45–49.

120. §9 (*G.* 1.144); §11 (*G.* 1.139–40); §37 (*G.* 1.125–28).

121. How fair any of this may be to Posidonius is another matter: as I. G. Kidd (1988, 969) points out, Seneca's polemic is so hyperbolical that it is impossible to recover Posidonius's real position in detail. Still, at the very least, it is clear that Seneca "wishes to draw a sharp and excluding line between philosophy and the arts and sciences; Posidonius, while distinguishing them, wanted to emphasise their natural and necessary relationship" (968–69).

122. Boys-Stones 2001, 38.

123. Seneca demonstrates a characteristic unwilling fascination with the details of technology as he goes on to itemize the intricacies of sailing and steering, adding a gratuitous sentence on the modeling of the rudder on the tail of a fish. Similarly, in the *Medea*, when he is describing the sails of a ship, he shows a keen zest for the ingenuity of human technology even as he is denouncing its folly (323–28); cf. *Epist.* 77.1–2 for yet more intrigued description of sailing technology.

124. Pfligersdorffer 1982, 306–7; Kubusch 1986, 77, 84–85. I. G. Kidd (1988, 962–63), in his commentary on Posidonius F 284, derived from Seneca's *Epistle*, leaves open the question of how committed Posidonius himself was to the concept of a Golden Age, allowing room for Seneca's innovation with reference to the strong appeal of the concept "in the Roman world of the 1st centuries B.C. and A.D."

125. Pfligersdorffer 1982, 321; Kubusch 1986, 81–82.

126. Cf. Blundell 1986, 218–19.

127. A lead into the copious material is provided by DuQuesnay 1977, 43. I can

only repeat the observation of Versnel (1994, 192) on the "awe-inspiring quantity of studies" on the subject of the return of the Golden Age. Beside Versnel's own study (192–205), note in particular Gatz 1967, 135–43; Wallace-Hadrill 1982; Kubusch 1986, 91–147; Zanker 1988, 167–83; Galinsky 1996, 90–100.

128. On the imperial drive to repeat these fundamental patterns in successive generations, see Henderson 1998, 258–59.

129. Above, n. 38.

130. Momigliano 1987, 34. On the difference between the Greek use of the time of Cronus as a point of comparison and the Roman idea of a return, see Gatz 1967, 90, 134–35; cf. Wallace-Hadrill 1982, 20–21.

131. Gatz 1967, 90, 134–35, with reference to, for example, Arist. *Ath. Pol.* 16.7, on the rule of Pisistratus as the life under Cronus. Among the overpowering bulk of studies of *Eclogue* 4, orientation is provided by Gatz 1967, 87–103; DuQuesnay 1977; Nisbet 1978b; Marincic 2001; Perkell 2002, 12–18.

132. DuQuesnay 1977, 72; Galinsky 1996, 92; Marincic 2001, 490.

133. Gatz 1967, 92–93; Perkell 2002, 14–15.

134. Munich 2003, 44.

135. So Versnel (1994, 119), referring to the work of Weidkuhn (1977, 174–75), on a legitimacy that refers "to a mythical reality outside ours, . . . lying beyond the borders of history and space, an eternal truth that existed before time but still exists behind it and behind our reality, and occasionally mingles with ours in 'periods of exception'."

136. Macleod 1979; my thanks to Stephen Hinds for this reference.

137. Watson 2003, ad loc. For this reading of the "Prioritätsfrage," see Cavarzere 1975/6, esp. 39; Horsfall 1991, 357.

138. Especially helpful for orientation are Zanker 1988, 167–83; Galinsky 1996, 90–100.

139. Galinsky 1996, 90–91; cf. Barker 1996, 434: "a complex myth at the centre of a complex discourse."

140. Barker 1996, an important discussion, to which I am indebted throughout this section.

141. Weinstock 1971, 196; Horsfall 1976, 86–87, with references to a possible earlier date for the Ludi, in 23 B.C.E.—though Virgil's allusions are compatible with longer-range planning.

142. *Romane, memento* (*Aen.* 6.851) translates μεμνῆσθαι, Ῥωμαῖε of the third line of the oracle (Zosimus 2.1.6). I wish Norden (1927, ad loc.) had elaborated on his remark that this is "eine Konkordanz, aus der sich interessante Schlüsse ziehen liessen." In his note on 6.70 he detects a Virgilian anticipation of Ludi Saeculares, in honor of Apollo and Diana.

143. Barker 1996, 438–42.

144. Barker 1996, 443–46.

145. As Stephen Hinds points out to me, Ovid is alert to these paradoxes in his account of the ages: the Ovidian iron race start mining, and they dig up "harmful iron, and—more harmful than iron—gold" (*nocens ferrum ferroque nocentius aurum, Met.* 1.140–41); cf. *Ars Am.* 3.123–24, with R. K. Gibson 2003, ad loc.

146. Virgil may again be picking up on a theme from Catullus 64, where the Golden Age metaphor is also complicated and "literalized" in the splendid gold of Peleus's palace (64.44), as shown by Bramble (1970, 39); cf. Fitzgerald 1995, 149.

147. Cf. Galinsky 1996, 98, on this "dilemma" as "one of the many creative tensions of the Augustan culture"; cf. P. White 1993, 189. We return at the end of the next chapter to the importance of the site of Rome in *Aeneid* 8 for the theme of chronological disjunction.

148. Wallace-Hadrill 1982, 27; Galinsky 1996, 99–100; R. K. Gibson 2003, 135–36; especially A. Barchiesi 1997, 232–37.

149. Cf. P. Hardie 1991, 62–63.

150. This devastating puncturing of the Golden Age balloon is repeated shortly thereafter when Janus says that Saturn, the presiding deity of the pre-Iron Age, came to Latium on—of all things—a ship (233–34).

151. Cf. A. Barchiesi 1997, 235–36: "'Gold' has changed its place in the sequence of the Ages, but it has not brought a moral renaissance with it. . . . Rome is now a city of gold, but only for the splendor of her monuments and the political and social power of finance."

152. Syme 1978, 47: "A delightful passage. The god corroborates the poet's modernity and dismisses, by implication, the archaic fancies and fraudulence on high show in Augustan Rome."

153. A. Barchiesi 1997, 236.

154. *Met.* 15.857–60: cf. Feeney 1991, 221; on Tacitus's analogous undoing of the Golden Age ideology of Augustus at *Ann.* 3.28.3, see Woodman and Martin 1996, ad loc.

155. Champlin 2003b, 127–28.

156. *Ep.* 115.12–13, quoting Ov. *Met.* 2.1–2, 107–8.

157. Champlin 2003b, 128.

158. *Aen.* 1.353–59. At the end of the episode (16.3.2), Tacitus describes Bassus's Dido-like end, as he regains his senses and commits suicide to escape shame and fear (Tacitus prefers this version to a less sensational one, of arrest, confiscation, and release).

159. In general, on Tacitus's hostility to Virgilian concepts of a return to an Age of Gold, see Heilman 1989, 389–90, 394–97.

160. See especially Courtney 1987; Baldwin 1995; Horsfall 1997; Champlin 2003c.

161. Champlin 2003b, 9–21 ("an afterlife that was unique in antiquity," 9); cf.

Horsfall 1997, 193–94, for this context, and others, as possible explanations for the interest of a later poet in the figure of Nero.

CHAPTER 5. YEARS, MONTHS, AND DAYS I:
ERAS AND ANNIVERSARIES

1. Speakers of German, Italian, and French presumably find it less possible to evade the origins of the era, since they do not pronounce an abbreviation in the way English does with "B.C.," but incorporate the name of the Messiah in normal speech when referring to dates "vor/nach Christus/Christi Geburt," "avanti/dopo Cristo," "avant/après Jésus-Christ" (though French will also refer to dates "avant notre ère").

2. Ginzel 1906, 2:358; Leschhorn 1993, 11.

3. In general, on ancient eras, see *RE* 1.606–52, Suppl. 3.24–30 (Kubitschek); Samuel 1972, 245–48; Bickerman 1980, 70–78; Leschhorn 1993; Hannah 2005, 92–94, 146–57.

4. *RE* 1.632–34 (Kubitschek); Samuel 1972, 245–46; Bickerman 1980, 71–72; Leschhorn 1993, 22–43; Hannah 2005, 92–94.

5. Daffinà 1987, 19–20; cf. Sherwin-White 1987, 27: "Royal time now had continuity and was *Seleucid*, not an individual king's."

6. Ma 1999, 148: "The imposition of a Seleukid conceptual geography and a Seleukid time are acts of symbolical violence."

7. Ginzel 1906, 1:263.

8. Stressed by Samuel 1972, 247 n. 1.

9. *Att.* 5.13.1 = Shackleton Bailey 1965–70, 106.1; cf. *Mil.* 98. On this era of Bovillae, see Weinstock 1971, 189. Chris Kraus points out to me that Caesar opens book 7 of the *De Bello Gallico* with a reference to the murder of Clodius, as if marking an era in the same way.

10. Kallet-Marx 1995, 14, against the conventional view that the era marks the annexation of the province of Macedonia.

11. Samuel 1972, 247; Leschhorn 1993, 221–25 (era of Pharsalus), 225–28 (Actium).

12. Samuel 1972, 246–47: cf. Kallet-Marx 1995, 48, on the Achaean era of 145/4 marking not the annexation of the province but "the 'freedom' granted by the Romans in the Mummian settlement."

13. Leschhorn 1993, 419, 434.

14. Knapp 1986, 120.

15. Knapp 1986, esp. 132–35; the period of the inscriptions would be from 391 to 557 C.E., on Knapp's hypothesis.

16. Bickerman 1980, 77–78; Blackburn and Holford-Strevens 1999, 676. Compare the case of the era of the Incarnation, which took so long to take hold in historiogra-

phy for the analogous reason that scholars could not agree on the date of Christ's birth (above, p. 8).

17. *BM Coins, Rom.Emp.* III.cxxxii; Schmidt 1908, 81 n. 1.

18. Grant 1950, xv n. 2.

19. Oakley (1997–98, 2:191–92) collects examples; Pinsent (1988, 4) well brings out the symbolic significance of Livy's examples, focusing on constitutional change and on the subdividing of his material in groups of books.

20. Cf. Frier (1975, 86 n. 28), who collects cases.

21. Macr. *Sat.* 1.16.22 = Peter, *HRRel.* F 20 = Chassignet 1999, F 23; similarly Gellius, also cited by Macrobius ad loc. = Peter, *HRRel.* F 25 = Chassignet 1999, F 24.

22. Pliny *HN* 29.12 = Peter, *HRRel.* F 26 = Chassignet 1999, F 29. Hemina also notes that the fourth Ludi Saeculares took place in the 608th year: Censorinus *DN* 17.11 = Peter, *HRRel* F 39 = Chassignet 1999, F 42.

23. Censorinus *DN* 17.13 = Peter, *HRRel.* F 36 = Chassignet 1999, F 39.

24. Wilcox 1987, 94.

25. Above, pp. 13–14.

26. Mommsen 1859, 197–200, citing, *inter alia*, Varro *Rust.* 1.2.9, Cic. *Rep.* 2.60, *Brut.* 62; cf. Pinsent 1988, 5–6. Whether the Republic was as a matter of fact founded in the same year as the temple—or indeed what it means to speak of the Republic being "founded" in a certain year—is another question altogether, once that does not concern us in investigating beliefs from the later Republic: on the question, Cornell 1995, chap. 9, esp. 218–23.

27. Oakley 1997–98, 2:75, on this tradition; of course, the story of the annual nail is not the only piece of evidence that links the foundation of both the temple and the Republic.

28. Purcell 2003, 27–30; cf. above, pp. 89–90.

29. Cornell 1995, 219–21.

30. Magdelain 1969, 266–68; Richard 1978, 442–44.

31. Purcell 2003, 26–33; cf. on the temporal power of the Capitoline complex, Hölkeskamp 2004, 139–42, 144–46. On Juno "Remembrancer" (the translation is that of Linderski 1985), see also the important paper of Meadows and Williams (2001).

32. Dion. Hal. *Ant. Rom.* 1.74.2 = Peter, *HRRel.* F 17 = Chassignet 1986, F 17; above, p. 99.

33. Clem. Alex. *Strom.* 1.39.2 is the testimonium for Duris (*FGrH* 76 F 41); Mendelssohn (1876, 185–86) made the case that this was Timaeus's date as well. Jacoby repeatedly argued that Timaeus cannot have used the date of "1335/4," but rather the date of "1194/3" transmitted by Censorinus (*DN* 21.3): Jacoby 1902, 147; *FGrH* 566 F 125–26, Komm., 587. He argues partly on the basis that Timaeus can have had no interest in Alexander panegyric; but note F 106 (linking the profanation of Apollo of Gela with the capture of Tyre by Alexander) and F 150 (linking the birth of Alexander with

the burning of the temple of Artemis at Ephesus), but a Timaean date of "1335/4," see the arguments of Asheri (1983, 55–60; 1991–92, 69–70).

34. The first two of the four books of Apollodorus's *Chronica* are organized to bring out this pattern in history, since book 1 went from the fall of Troy to the Persian Wars, and book 2 from the Persian Wars to Alexander: Jacoby 1902, 10.

35. Lane Fox 1973, 111–15, 124; Asheri 1983, 65–67; Higbie 2003, 238–39.

36. Gratwick 1982, 65.

37. Cic. *Brut.* 79, with Livy 39.44.10 for the year of the colony's establishment.

38. Cornell 1986, 250, seeing a link back to the opening of book 1, with the first treaty between Aeneas and Latinus (frr. 31–32). The second pentad may well have ended with a restatement of the Romans' Trojan descent, in the appeal of the people of Lampsacus in 197 or 196 B.C.E. (frr. 344–45).

39. Gratwick 1982, 65: "It can hardly have escaped the attention of contemporaries that Cato became censor 1,000 years after the fall of Troy."

40. On the crucial significance of the poem's culmination with the importation of the Muses into Fulvius's temple, see Skutsch 1985, 144–46, 553, 649–50; on the nexus of Muses and temple, see further Goldberg 1995, 130–31; Hinds 1998, 62–63; A. Hardie 2002, 195–200; Gildenhard 2003, 95–97. H. I. Flower (1995, 184–86) provides an up-to-date account of the evidence for the triumph and temple.

41. Livy 38.9.13; cf. Pliny *HN* 37.5 for Pyrrhus's famous agate ring depicting Apollo and the Muses, each Muse with her appropriate emblems.

42. Skutsch (1985, 143–44) does not convince me that *Musae* was not the first word of the poem, even though the fragment is not explicitly attested as the first line.

43. Jocelyn 1972, 1005.

44. Pythagoreanism may provide another dimension, if Pythagorean numerological schemes of incarnation underpinned the Trojan date calculations of Heraclides Ponticus and Eratosthenes (Asheri 1983, 95); on the importance of Ennius's Pythagorean interests for his own account of reincarnation and for the programme of Fulvius's Hercules Musarum, see Skutsch 1985, 144–46, 164–65; A. Hardie 2002, 199–200.

45. Jacoby, *FGrH* 97, Komm., 301; cf. above, p. 87.

46. Nilsson 1920, 1719. The arithmetic may look incorrect, since 753 + 248 = 1001, not 1000, but in calculating anniversaries across the B.C.E./C.E. watershed it is important to remember that there is no year 0, and we pass directly from 1 B.C.E. to 1 C.E.—except for astronomers, for whom, tidily, 1 B.C.E. is year 0, and "2 B.C. is -1, 3 B.C. is -2, and so on" (Blackburn and Holford-Strevens 1999, 782). The C.E. figure is therefore always one more than it would be in simple mathematics: the bimillenary of Horace's death in 8 B.C.E. was 1993, not 1992, and the bimillenary of Virgil's death in 19 B.C.E. was 1982, not 1981: Horsfall 1982b. Needless to say, this is a problem only for moderns, not for the Romans: Philip was using a totally different calculus.

47. On the various Christian millenary calculations, see Blackburn and Holford-Strevens 1999, 787–88. Prophecies of Rome's doom, constructed around significant numbers, abound in the Sibylline literature (Potter 1990, 236–40), and are reported by historians as well: Dio, for example, reports a prophecy with 900 years as Rome's fated span (57.18.3–5).

48. Nilsson 1920, 1717–18.

49. Syme 1958, 772–73: even if this particular case is very strained, his discussion of the anniversary mentality is indispensable (771–74).

50. Grant (1950, 3–4) collects many examples of temple and colony foundations timed to the century and its multiples or subdivisions.

51. "It cannot have escaped notice that his death took place a hundred years after the fall of Carthage": Nisbet and Hubbard 1978, 25.

52. For the possibilities, see the index of Grant 1950 under "anniversary years." For speeches in honor of later emperors' five- and ten-year anniversaries of accession to power, see Nixon and Rodgers 1994, 82 n. 5; compare the special care Augustus put into festivities in the year 13 B.C.E., "the thirtieth anniversary of his *dies imperii* (7 January 43 B.C. . . .), of his first *acclamatio* as *imperator* (16 April 43 B.C.), and of his first consulship (19 August 43 B.C.)": DuQuesnay 1995, 141.

53. The meaning of "100 years" must, however, have been a possible one from the start: see Watkins 1995, 351, for the "ideal human lifespan of 100 years" as "Indo-European patrimony."

54. So, emphatically, Weinstock 1971, 191, whose whole account of the concept is most valuable (191–97); see further Nilsson 1920; *Neue Pauly* 10.1207–8.

55. For Varro's use of this distinction, see, for example, *Ling.* 6.12 on the natural division of time and the civil names of days, with the closing comments of Hinds (2005b). On Varro's *Antiquitates* as Censorinus's prime source, see Grafton and Swerdlow 1985.

56. There are clear links with two Greek schemes, Hesiod's succession of generations and the transmission of empire: Weinstock 1971, 192; Valvo 1988, 64–73. What the Etruscan connection may be to these structures, and/or to the oriental patterns that ultimately lie behind them, remains irrecoverable.

57. See Horsfall 1974, 114–15, for fascinating speculation on the possible impact of this event on Virgil's numerology in *Aen.* 1.257–72, where Jupiter prophesies 333 years from the last year of Aeneas's wandering to the foundation of Rome. As Horsfall points out, the portentous year 88 B.C.E. is 666 A.U.C., with a foundation date of 754/3, and it is possible that Virgil has halved this significant number into the significant 333 and added them together in order to go back to the time of Aeneas.

58. Text in Lachmann 1848, 350–51; full discussion of the many textual problems in Valvo 1988, 1–18.

59. The translation of Harris 1971, 34 n. 4, for the difficult phrase *ob auariiam prope novissimi octavi saeculi*.

60. Adams 2003, 182.

61. Serv. Auct. *Ecl.* 9.46.

62. So Weinstock 1971, 195, correcting the version given in Serv. Auct. on Virg. *Ecl.* 9.46, that the man said he would die because he had revealed divine secrets. It is very telling that, as Serv. Auct. informs us, Augustus related this incident in book 2 of his autobiography, associating his own advent in Rome with the dawn of the new *saeculum*.

63. Harris 1971, 36–37.

64. Hubaux 1945, 5–6; Grafton and Swerdlow 1985, 461. Vettius's calculation puts the terminus of Roman power in the middle of the fifth century C.E., which makes him a better prognosticator than most of his ilk (at least as far as the Western Empire is concerned).

65. Nilsson 1920; Pighi 1965; Beard, North, and Price 1998, 71–72, 111, 201–6; Watkins 1995, 353: "a ritual to assure the long life and orderly succession of the generations . . . a reaffirmation of the crossing of the *saecula* of a hundred years." Augustus for his own purposes fixed on 110 years as the span, capitalizing on the flexibility of the unit: his commemorative inscription refers to the span of 110 years (line 25 of the edition of Pighi [1965]) but also divertingly records that the games were due to be held "after a certain number of years," *post complures annos* (line 52).

66. "No one," says Augustus's commemorative inscription, "will ever again be present at a spectacle of this kind" (*tali spectaculo [nemo iterum intererit]*, line 54); "it is not allowed to any mortal to see them more than once" (*neque ultra quam semel ulli mo[rtalium eos spectare licet]*, line 56).

67. Beard, North, and Price 1998, 372.

68. Tony Woodman refers me to a letter written by Martin West to the *Times* (3 February 1998), chastising the pedants who insisted that the millennium only really ended at the end of 2000, not the beginning. As West says, the crucial point is that "*all the numbers will change.* It is like seeing 99,999 turn into 100,000 on the car mileometer. That's what it's all about" (original emphasis; my thanks to Dr. West for kindly sending me a copy of his letter).

69. Grant 1950, 1.

70. Johnston 1991; Zerubavel 2003, index s.v. "anniversaries."

71. Grafton and Swerdlow 1998.

72. Grant 1950, xii–xiii, 171. The ideal places to start in studying anniversaries in the Roman calendar are Beard 1987 and Hopkins 1991.

73. Argetsinger 1992. On the importance of anniversaries in the poetry of Horace, in particular, see Feeney 1993, 59–60; esp. Griffin 1997. It would be highly interesting

to follow up Griffin's acute pinpointing of differences between poets and genres in this regard: no calendar dates of any kind in the first three books of Propertius, for example (55–56, 59).

74. A. Barchiesi 2005b, 28–29. Horsfall (2006), on Virg. *Aen.* 3.301, collects much valuable material on such ceremonies, with Andromache's sacrifice to Hector as the point of departure: Servius ad loc. takes *sollemnis* to mean *anniuersarias*.

75. Wissowa 1912, 56–57.

76. Schmidt 1908, 12–14; Burkhard 1991, 13–14; Mikalson 1996 for the unusual cases of annual birthday celebrations (often posthumous) for outstanding individuals such as Plato, Epicurus, Aratus of Sicyon, or the Hellenistic monarchs, all of whom regularly had monthly celebrations anyhow: on the revealing case of Epicurus, see Sider 1997, 156. Argetsinger (1992, 192) well remarks on the significance of the fact that "in the West, the emperor's birthday was always celebrated annually rather than monthly, as those of the Eastern monarchs had been."

77. Collection of evidence in *RE* 13.1142–44; cf. Balsdon 1969, 121–22. For the highly organized empire-wide celebrations of the imperial family's birthdays, see Weinstock 1971, 209–10.

78. Cic. *Att.* 4.1.4 = Shackleton Bailey 1965–70, 73.4; *Sest.* 131; cf. Argetsinger 1992, 176 n. 1; Hinds 2005a, 206 n. 5.

79. Weinstock 1971, 38; for the date, Pliny *HN* 37.13. Caligula later certainly celebrated an *ouatio* on his birthday in 40 C.E. (Suet. *Cal.* 49.2), and Messalla may have celebrated his triumph on his birthday in 27 B.C.E. (Tib. 1.7): Weinstock 1971, 209.

80. Vell. Pat. 2.53.3 (the day before); Plut. *Pomp.* 79.4 (the day after); Plut. *Quaest. Conv.* 717c (either the day itself, as at *Cam.* 19.7, or the day before).

81. Cic. *Ad Brut.* 1.15.8 = Shackleton Bailey 1980, 23.8; cf. *Fam.* 11.14.3 = Shackleton Bailey 1977, 413.3.

82. App. *BCiv.* 4.113.

83. Plut. *Brut.* 24.4 (in the year 44 B.C.E.); App. *BCiv.* 4.134 (by whose dating it is, symbolically, Brutus's last birthday, celebrated on Samos); cf. Val. Max. 1.5.7.

84. Full discussion of the anecdotes in Moles 1983; my own "birthday" connection with Apollo and Octavian by no means contradicts the meanings Moles suggests for Brutus's choice of quotation.

85. Cf. Hopkins 1991, on the changing meanings of the Lupercalia in the transition to Christianity.

86. A. Barchiesi 1997, 130. We follow up this Ovidian clash between "traditional" and contemporary imperial resonances in the next chapter.

87. Blackburn and Holford-Strevens 1999, 682. Once the initial correction of dropping ten days had been made, the reform allowed much more precise accuracy by ordaining that centennial years would only be leap years if they were divisible by 400: "Thus 1600 (reassuringly) remained a leap year, and likewise 2000, but 1700, 1800, and

1900 became common" (682); the new system, then, "saves" three days every 400 years, which is enough to keep us on track until the year 4000 C.E. (M. L. West 1978, 376 n. 1).

88. As remarked above, "days that are significant for one thing can fortuitously become significant for something else altogether" (p. 149).

89. As of 1999, at any rate: Blackburn and Holford-Strevens (1999, 883) report that the year "is decreasing by about 0.53 seconds in a century."

90. Blackburn and Holford-Strevens 1999, 670; cf. Suerbaum 1980, 336–37.

91. The date 2 September was immediately followed by the fourteenth, leading to the famous cry "Give us back the eleven days we were robbed of": Blackburn and Holford-Strevens 1999, 373. One more day needed to be dropped than in 1582 (eleven instead of ten) because of the extra accumulated error in the meanwhile.

92. A rich and diverting account in Blackburn and Holford-Strevens 1999, 87–88 (although one of the book's extremely few misprints gives "1752" as the year Washington came of age, not 1753). The issue confronted Russians after the Revolution; indeed, as Nicholas Horsfall points out to me, Rostovtzeff, as a practicing Orthodox, preferred the old Julian calendar in general, especially for celebrating his birthday: J. Andreau makes the point in his introduction to Rostovtzeff (1988, xxvi).

93. On the positioning of festivals in Caesar's reform, see Michels 1967, 180–81; Suerbaum 1980, esp. 330–31; Rüpke 1995b, 376–77; Hannah 2005, 122–24.

94. Bickerman 1980, 47.

95. Valuable introductions in Michels 1967, 18–22; Blackburn and Holford-Strevens 1999, 672.

96. So—to simplify drastically—did the Greeks, at least for the first two-thirds of their month, at which point they generally started counting down backwards to the beginning of the next month. For a lucid account of the many diverse Greek practices, see M. L. West 1978, 349–50; and Hannah 2005, 43–44, for Athens.

97. Macr. *Sat.* 1.15.17; cf. Horace's pun on this etymology in *Carm.* 4.11.14–16, addressed to the Etruscan Maecenas: *Idus . . . /qui dies mensem Veneris marinae/*findit *Aprilem.*

98. This is *not* the ninth day *into* the month.

99. Named, so the Romans believed (probably correctly), from a verb *kalare* meaning "to call" or "to announce," relating to the fact that the priests used to "announce" on this first day when the Nones would fall in the coming month: Varro *Ling.* 6.27.

100. As Joshua Katz reminds me, by this way of counting the Romans called "the day before yesterday" *nudius tertius.*

101. I give them in that order according to the old mnemonic: "In March, July, October, May, the Ides fall on the fifteenth day." In the Republic, it goes without saying, July was not July, but Quintilis, "Month Number Five": it was renamed after Julius Caesar in 44 B.C.E.

102. Hence the necessity for constant intercalation, and the inevitability of chaos if intercalation was omitted. Laurence and Smith (1995–96, 137–38) well stress that the system fell down badly during two particular periods of crisis, the Hannibalic War and the last years of the Republic.

103. And he had to add another day every fourth ("leap") year to get a more precise average of 365¼.

104. So that the mnemonic of "March, July, October, May" works for the position of the Ides in the Julian as well as the Republican calendar. The extra day in February that needed to be added every fourth year for the "leap" year was not added at the end of the month, as now; rather, the sixth day before the Kalends of March ("24 February") was counted twice (hence *bissextus*, giving our "bissextile"). Caesar chose this point in the month because it was here that the intercalary month was inserted under the old calendar.

105. See Macr. *Sat.* 1.14.8–9 for Caesar's care on this point. The only major festival held between the Kalends and Nones anyway was the Poplifugia on 5 July: Wissowa 1912, 436.

106. It is very clear from Macr. *Sat.* 1.14.11 that what counted was the position relative to the preceding Ides, not to the following Kalends: cf. Suerbaum 1980, 330–31; Hannah 2005, 123–24. The net effect was to preserve a curious feature of the old calendar, whereby the main *feriae* fall on odd days, reckoned by our normal method of forward counting, with the exception only of the Regifugium on 24 February and the "second" Equirria on 14 March: Wissowa 1912, 436–37; cf. Dumézil 1970, 562, for discussion of these anomalous festivals. This apparent bizarre departure from the "backward-counting" structure of the calendrical system is to be explained by the fact that this distribution avoids having two *feriae* back to back: Wissowa 1912, 437. Caesar's solution is interestingly different from what had happened to the two festivals that fell after the Ides in February when there was intercalation in the Republican calendar. In this case, the Regifugium and "first" Equirria kept exactly the same notation and hence the same distance from the following Kalends and did not maintain the same position relative to the preceding Ides: "It is clear . . . that . . . the intercalary month was inserted after the Terminalia, *a.d. VII Kal. Mart.* (February 23) and that the Regifugium and Equirria, which in ordinary years were celebrated on *a.d. VI* and *a.d. III Kal. Mart.* (February 24 and 27), were celebrated on *a.d. VI* and *a.d. III Kal. Mart. mense intercalario*" (Michels 1967, 160). It is no doubt significant that the Regifugium and the "second" Equirria are anomalous in their placement in the calendar, since the Regifugium and "first" Equirria in February are closely connected with the "second" Equirria in March: Michels 1967, 17–18.

107. On Augustus's birthday, see Michels 1967, 180–81; Suerbaum 1980, 334–35; Hannah 2005, 124–25; Pasco-Pranger 2006, chap. 4.

108. Suerbaum 1980, 334–35.

109. Michels 1967, 180–81; Franchetti 1990, 39 n. 59.

110. Suerbaum 1980, 327–29, 332–34; my presentation here is merely a précis of his impressive argumentation.

111. The date is fixed by the Fasti Verulani for 14 January: Degrassi 1963, 158.

112. Suerbaum 1980, 329.

113. Again, Suerbaum 1980, 335–37.

114. Her birthday is marked in the Acta of the Fratres Arvales: Degrassi 1963, 405.

115. E.g., Radke 1990, 81–82. On the extra ninety days Caesar had to add to the year 46, *ultimus annus confusionis*, in order to bring it into line with the seasons before his reformed calendar began, see Macr. *Sat.* 1.14.7 (the source for the often-quoted tag); Censorinus *DN* 20.8.

116. Briscoe 1991.

117. My thanks to Bob Kaster for helpful conversation on this point.

118. Indeed, the British Parliament knew this in its bones as well: "The Act of Parliament that introduced the New Style from 14 September 1752 prescribed that a 21st year of age current at the time of the change should be assigned the same number of days as if the reform had not been made" (Blackburn and Holford-Strevens 1999, 87).

119. The details of Republican intercalation are still contested: I follow Michels (1967, 161) and Hannah (2005, 107–8) in thinking that an intercalary month of twenty-seven days was added to a shortened February, beginning on either 24 February or 25 February, thus adding either twenty-two or twenty-three days to the year's total. Hence one of the meanings of the Terminalia ("23 February"), which would terminate the month of February in a year when the intercalary month began on 24 February.

120. Hinds 2005a, 221–22, with n. 38 (original emphasis); my thanks to him for dialogue on the anniversary. This is only one example of the fundamental transformations of the apprehension of time enforced upon the Romans by Caesar's reform: this transformation will be the main subject of the next chapter.

121. Sider 1997, 153, commenting on poem 27 (= *Anth. Pal.* 11.44).

122. Coleman 1988, 197; Burkhard 1991, 37–141; Argetsinger 1992; for Ovid's exploitation of the form, see Hinds 2005a. As Nisbet (2002, 83) points out, citing Tib. 1.7, 2.2, 3.11, 12, 14, 15, an interest in such poems "is particularly noticeable in the circle of Messalla." Note the interesting letter Augustus wrote on his own birthday to his grandson Gaius, congratulating himself on having lived through the climacteric year, the sixty-third (Gell. *NA* 15.7.3).

123. Russell 1996, 629.

124. *Anth. Pal.* 6.227 (to "Proklos" = Proculus, a Roman); 6.261 (to a Greek, "son of Simon"); 6.345 (roses speak as they are sent to an anonymous woman, who could be either Greek or Roman).

125. Burkhard 1991, 142–45.

126. My thanks, then, to the Merton College students by whose suffering I learned.

127. Syme 1939, 524; the dates are 19 August 43 B.C.E. and 19 August 14 C.E.

128. 1 Sextilis: the month later called Augustus. See Lowrie 1997, 342, on the time games here.

129. And the same place, too—on the Island: see Miller 2002, 174, for fine observations on the "temporal and spatial coincidence" here.

130. Zerubavel 1981, 114 (original emphasis); cf. Zerubavel 2003, 46–48, on "'Same' Time"; and Kraus 1994a, 250, on the day of the Allia, 18 July, as a test case of historical repetition.

131. On the various World Calendar proposals, see Zerubavel 1985, 75–77, 80, 82; Blackburn and Holford-Strevens 1999, 689–92.

132. Döpp 1968, chap. 6; Newlands 1995, 80 ("Ovid emphasizes rupture and contradiction rather than continuity"), 231; Graf 1996; A. Barchiesi 1997, passim, esp. 106–19, 214–37. As a poet of the aetiological *Fasti* Ovid makes the problem of continuity of identity an autobiographical one at the beginning of book 2. He used to write facile love poetry, but he is now writing grander and purer stuff: "I, *the same person*, am writing of religious rites and times marked in the *fasti;* is there anyone who would think there was a route from there to here?" (*idem sacra cano signataque tempora fastis:/ecquis ad haec illinc crederet esse uiam?* 2.7–8).

133. See Fraschetti 1990, 36–38; A. Barchiesi 1997, 106–10.

134. A. Barchiesi 1997, 109. On Augustus's institution of the Lares Augusti, see Lott 2004, 101–6. Lott well brings out the distinctive nature of Augustus's associating his own Lares Augusti with the older Lares Praestites on 1 May (116–17).

135. On this problem, see Feeney 1991, 93–94; Goldhill 1991, 321–33. Pasco-Pranger (2000) well illustrates that the whole question of continuity between past and present was at the heart of the antiquarian project even before Ovid got to work on it.

136. The crucial words enter as soon as the future site of Rome comes into sight, setting the scene for the whole scene: *nunc/tum* (99–100); cf. *nunc, olim* (348). On this "Einst-Jetzt" motif here and its influence on Ovid, see Döpp 1968, 77–94.

137. P. Hardie 1994, 17–18.

138. Dio 55.6.6; Censorinus *DN* 22.16.

139. Drew (1927, esp. 16–17) began this whole line of inquiry; cf. Grimal 1951, 51–54; Binder 1971, 42–43; Mueller 2002. Horsfall (1995, 162–63) is skeptical about large-scale historical allegory, but even he remarks that "the case Drew makes for a precise reference to the events of 12–13 Aug., 29 B.C. . . . is remarkably neat" (163).

140. On the triple triumph itself, Gurval 1995, 19–85.

141. Grimal 1951, 54–55; for Antonius's cultivation of Hercules, see Ritter 1995, 70–81. Further evidence of Octavian's planning is to be found in the name of the suffect consul who welcomed him when he arrived outside the city on 12 August (Drew 1927, 17–18): Valerius Potitus was the man chosen, and his *cognomen* recalls the *nomen* of the now-extinct family of the Potitii who shared the care of the cult of Hercules until

312 B.C.E., when the state took it over (Mueller 2002 gives details). Virgil carefully highlights the name Potitius in his description of the ritual (269, 281).

142. Gransden 1976, 14–20.

143. On wormholes, space-time tunnels connecting two disparate regions of space-time, see Gott 2001, 118–24; I happily acknowledge my borrowing of the metaphor from a Princeton seminar paper by Rob Sobak on the layering of time in Pindar. The analogy with Virgil's collapsing of timescales is not exact, because, crucially, in Virgil's universe the calendrical time traveler is always in the *same place*. This wormhole effect is fundamental to Ovid's technique in the *Fasti*, as A. Barchiesi (1997) has shown.

144. The year "1177" is plucked out of the air, as being seven years after the Eratosthenic date for the fall of Troy.

145. As Philip Hardie points out to me, referring to Wills 1996, 147 n. 54, for the uniqueness of this "line-final repetition" in Virgil.

146. R. F. Thomas 2004 for Aeneas terminating the Saturnian Age; above, p. 83, for Aeneas as the last demigod.

147. For the Arcadian acorn diet and their birth before the moon, see Ap. Rhod. *Argon.* 4.264–65, with Livrea 1973, ad loc. The conventional location for the beginning of the calendar at Rome is in the reign of Numa: note how Serv. Auct., in referring to the reign of Romulus, can say *adhuc fasti non erant* (*Aen.* 8.564).

148. My thanks to a Princeton undergraduate, Dan-el Padilla Peralta, for permission to quote these words from his essay, "Virgil's Hercules and the Foundation of the Ara Maxima." As Philip Hardie points out to me *per litteras*, the other candidate for a day marked in Evander's calendar is the Carmentalia: Carmentis certainly has an altar (337–38), and she may well have a day also.

149. Clarke 1999a, esp. 17–21.

150. Edwards 1996, 46: "Places in the city are, in religious terms, parallel to days in the calendar. The place and time prescribed for a particular rite are an essential part of that ceremony's meaning and power." On *"loca sancta,"* see MacCormack 1990; Horden and Purcell 2000, chap. X.

151. Stephen Hinds suggests to me a very attractive double play on *lucus* here: *lucus* suggests *locus* (Hinds 1987, 38 with n. 44), while by the antonymical etymology of *lucus a non lucendo*, the grove of Hercules provides both a *lucus* and a *lux* (= *dies*). The same effects will be felt later in the book, when Virgil says that the Pelasgians set up a cult of Silvanus at Caere, inaugurating *lucumque diemque* (601).

152. The phrase *ante urbem in luco* refers back to the identical phrasing in the same *sedes* in 3.302, where it refers by contrast to the futile and backward-looking sacrifices of Andromache: Binder 1971, 43 n. 13.

153. Zerubavel 2003, 46 (original emphasis); cf. Gell 1992, 28, on the "illusion of time-travel engendered by the contemplation of ancient objects."

154. Above, p. 134.

155. For a recent account of Aeneas's tour with Evander, with bibliography, see Klodt 2001, 11–17.

156. Edwards 1996, 12–14, 31–32, a discussion to which I owe much; cf. Gransden 1976, 34–35, quoting at length from the unforgettable words at the beginning of the seventy-first, and final, chapter of Gibbon's *Decline and Fall* ("The wheel of fortune has accomplished her revolution.... The forum of the Roman people, where they assembled to enact their laws and elect their magistrates, is now enclosed for the cultivation of pot-herbs, or thrown open for the reception of swine and buffaloes.")

157. See Strabo 2.5.17 for this fashion. Small (1997, 234–35) and Klodt (2001, 17–18) engagingly suggest that Evander's walk acts out the mnemonic technique of having the memory prompted by monuments in an ordered sequence: *Aeneid* 8 would, then, not only be about memory and be itself a repository of memory but comment on an alternative mnemonic technique that allows memory to be stored and recalled.

158. On the location of the Porta Mugonia, and its status as the entrance to the Palatine from the Sacra Via, see Coarelli 1992, 26–33. In his parody of this Virgilian passage, Ovid has his mock-Evander figure take the book of *Tristia* 3 along the same route, up the Sacra Via, past Vesta and the Regia, and then turning to the right through the gate of the Palatine to the house of Augustus (*Tr.* 3.1.28–34).

159. *Anth. Pal.* 9.101–4; cf. 9.28, on the devastation of Mycenae, without mentioning animals. The epigrams are undatable, though Gow and Page (1968, 2:429) comment on 9.104 that it could have been written "at any time in the late Republican and early Imperial periods." See P. Hardie 1992, 59, on the relevance of these epigrams to the themes of Virgil. Much comparative material in Horsfall 2000, 283 (on Virg. *Aen.* 7.413), for "the familiar tradition of lamenting the past glory of cities famed in myth or history but now reduced to insignificance."

160. 9.104.6 has the adjective "mooing" (εὐμύκων), though it describes the cattle who are now stalled in Argos, not Mycenae.

161. Cf. Martindale 1993, 49–53. Propertius responds to Virgil's collocations of gold and cows by using Veii as Rome's twin. In Prop. 4.1 Rome was once the home of Evander's cows and is now golden (1–5); in 4.10 Veii was once golden and is now the home of cows (27–30). See Labate 1991, 176–78. Besides Propertius and Virgil, other key passages juxtaposing the bucolic past and the luxuriously civilized present include Tib. 2.5.25; Ov. *Ars am.* 3.119–20. Fantham 1997 is a valuable survey of the whole issue, focusing especially on Propertius; cf. on Propertius, La Penna 1977, 187–91; on Tibullus, Buchheit 1965.

162. Ambrose 1996, chaps. 14–15.

163. Zetzel 1994, 21; cf. Zetzel 1997, 200.

164. Above, p. 55.

165. Labate 1991; P. Hardie 1992, 59–60; D. Fowler 2000, 125; Rossi 2004, 30–40.

166. For the contemporary context of speculation on the length of Rome's tenure

of the inheritance, see Trompf 1979, 186–87. Virgil and his readers will have been as aware of this template as Kipling and his readers: "The British . . . knew too much ancient history to be complacent about their hegemonic position. Even at the zenith of their power they thought, or were reminded by Kipling, of the fate of Nineveh and Tyre. Already, there were many who looked forward uneasily to the decline and fall of their own empire, like all the empires before it" (Ferguson 1993, 247–48). In general, I am indebted to Zetzel 1996, an important discussion of Virgil's debt to Cicero's *De Re Publica* in his reflections on Rome's limits "in both space and time" (317).

167. P. Hardie 1992, 69–72; in general, P. Hardie 1993, esp. 1–3, 76; Rossi 2004, 36–37, on the poem's "two competing historical visions," with Jupiter's teleological plan competing with "a tragic dialectic, in which the constant antithesis between rise and fall produces numberless beginnings and numberless ends."

168. On this great scene, P. Hardie 1992, 59–60; Martindale 1993, 49–51; Edwards 1996, 11–12.

169. Barkan 1986, 87–88; P. Hardie 1992, 60–61; Tissol 1997, 186–88; Habinek 2002, 54.

CHAPTER 6. YEARS, MONTHS, AND DAYS II: THE GRIDS OF THE *FASTI*

1. Exiguous remains survive of two other such lists: Fasti Triumphales Urbisalvienses (no. 35 in Degrassi 1947, 338–40); Fasti Triumphales Barberiniani (no. 36 in Degrassi, 342–45). There certainly had been triumphal lists before Augustus's, for the "Barberiniani" predate his, but it is uncertain, and unlikely, that such triumphal and consular lists had been exhibited together before: Degrassi 1947, xiv. An arch to the south of the temple of Divus Julius remains the location favored by many scholars as the original site of Augustus's consular and triumphal lists, but the whole question is extremely controversial: Rich 1998, 103–6. It can be confusing that these Augustan *fasti* from the Forum are regularly described as the Fasti Capitolini, after their location in the Capitoline Museum, where they have been kept since their discovery in the sixteenth century.

2. *Fasti consulares* occurs twice in one passage, in the late (c. 400 C.E.?) *Historia Augusta* (*Ael.* 5.13–14), and has been in modern use since at least the early seventeenth century, with Carlo Sigonio's *Fasti Consulares* of 1609. Degrassi's term "Fasti Anni [Numani et Iuliani]" comes from Mommsen's editions in *CIL* 1²; neither this phrase nor "Fasti Triumphales" ever occurs in ancient texts, as Degrassi himself stresses in the case of the Fasti Triumphales (Degrassi 1947, xiv). What we refer to as Augustus's Fasti Triumphales are labeled *Acta Triumphorum* in the edition of Mommsen, Henzen, and Huelsen in *CIL* 1².

3. *TLL* 6.327.31–32: *nonnullis locis diiudicari uix potest, utrum de unius anni fastis an de perpetuis annis cogitetur.* For an instructive example from Horace, see p. 185 below.

4. Mommsen 1859, 200–201: see Hanell 1946, 69, for acknowledgment of Mommsen's crucial insight. As we shall see, it was no part of the original purpose of the lists of consuls to assist historical chronology, but they can certainly work in tandem with the calendar to make it possible to mark points in time.

5. There is no doubt that the term *fasti* was applied first to the calendar and then later, by extension, to the closely linked list of chief magistrates. The word is an adjective from *fas* (divine right); *fas* itself derives from *for/fari*, "to utter," and the term *dies fasti* refers to days on which proper utterance is allowed. A digest of days when proper utterance was allowed came to be called *fasti: Neue Pauly* (Rüpke), s.v.

6. Hanell 1946, 69: 'Im Grunde ist nämlich die Eponymenliste ein Verzeichnis der nach Eponymen benannten Jahre, ist also kalendarischer Natur, ein Teil des Kalenders." Hanell's achievement is rightly stressed by Ridley (1980, 283–85); cf. Rüpke 1995a, 185–86; for criticisms of Hanell's views, especially the idea that originally there was only one name per year, see Michels 1967, 215–17; Cornell 1995, 221–22.

7. Bickerman 1980, 69.

8. Once again, Mommsen (1859, 208 n. 394) first made the point, stressing that *fasti tribunicii, aedilicii,* and so on are misnomers, for these officials did not give their names to the year: cf. Hanell 1946, 69.

9. On these close links, see Degrassi 1947, xiii; 1963, xxi; Taylor and Holland 1952, 140: "The two types of *Fasti,* consular list and calendar, enumerations of years and days, belonged together, and at least six of the thirty-five consular lists which have come to light were accompanied by calendars." Further, the forum at Praeneste that displayed the famous "calendrical" Fasti Praenestini also had "consular" *fasti,* which were almost certainly put up at the same time: Degrassi 1947, 260. On the many other kinds of time charts in addition to these two, which adorned the so-called Codex-Calendar of 354, each evoking its own dimension of the past, see the important study of Salzman 1990, esp. 24: there are birthdays of the emperors, signs of the zodiac, urban prefects, and bishops of Rome.

10. Taylor and Holland 1952, esp. 138; for Janus as the first god to receive sacrifice, see Cic. *Nat. D.* 2.67, with the copious documentation ad loc. of Pease (1955–58); Wissowa 1912, 103. On the reform of 153 B.C.E., see p. 171 below.

11. Degrassi 1947, xiii; Rüpke 1995a, esp. 199–200.

12. Taylor and Holland 1952, 140; doubted by Rüpke 1995a, 194.

13. See Salzman 1990, 35–36, for the Codex-Calendar as the culmination of a tradition of paired consular and calendrical *fasti;* cf. Rüpke 1997, 81–84.

14. Popularized by S. J. Gould (1987).

15. A. Barchiesi 1991, 6–7.

16. Laurence and Smith 1995–96, 145, on the imperial *fasti:* "In effect, linear events of history were inscribed into circular time."

17. Fantham 1985.

18. Degrassi 1947, xiii; for the date, above, p. 143.

19. Degrassi 1963, xx; Rüpke 1995b, 341–45.

20. Degrassi 1963, xx, citing Macr. *Sat.* 1.12.16 (March and June); Varro *Ling.* 6.33 (a translingual etymology from Greek to explain April); Censorinus *DN* 22.9 (Romulus's names for the months).

21. Skutsch 1985, 313; Rüpke (1995b, 362) is more guarded.

22. For Ennius's use of consuls as part of his intermittent cultivation of an annalistic format, see Rüpke 1995a, 200–201, citing fr. 290 Skutsch (*Quintus pater quartum fit consul* = 214 B.C.E.) and fr. 304–6 (*additur orator Cornelius suauiloquenti/ore Cethegus Marcus Tuditano collega/Marci filius* = 204 B.C.E.).

23. It is not necessarily surprising that later sources should not cite the consular *fasti* of Fulvius in the way they cite the calendrical *fasti*. Antiquarians who work on the calendar are working in a tradition that encourages citation from earlier antiquarians, and once Fulvius's calendar is in the tradition it is going to get cited. Antiquarians, however, do not write on the consular *fasti;* it is historians who use the consular *fasti*, but it is not part of their tradition to cite their sources and haggle over them in the antiquarian manner.

24. Gildenhard 2003, 95–96. Whether the names of censors as well as consuls were on this early list is not certain.

25. Gildenhard 2003, 97. Gildenhard's view is explicitly indebted to the important research of Jörg Rüpke. It is, however, at odds with Rüpke's own idiosyncratic conviction that the Fulvian consular list did not extend back in time from the temple's dedication but rather began in 179 B.C.E. and will therefore at first have contained only a few lines (Rüpke 1995b, esp. 365; 1995a); Rüpke himself sees the main burden of the complex's historical meaning residing in Fulvius's calendrical *fasti*, especially with the new addition of temple-dedication notices (Rüpke 1995b, 354–55, 359–60; 1995a, 199). I do not have space here to argue the case in detail, but I see an extensive consular list reaching some way back into the past as having far more symbolic and historical power than the anonymous, year-less, and sparse dedication notices of the calendar, which overlook the great majority of past military successes. It seems perverse to locate more historical denotation in the calendrical than the consular *fasti*. Rüpke's main ground for believing that the Fulvian consular list began around 179 is that this is where the Fasti Antiates' consular list may have begun. It is in fact uncertain at what date the Fasti Antiates began, since there may well have been more slabs before (i.e., to the left of) our first surviving piece (Degrassi 1947, 164: the consular list is only 1.36 m wide compared to the 2.5 m of the calendar); anyway, if there is a connection between the two consular lists, it is more economical to suppose that the Fasti Antiates began where the Fulvian *fasti* left off. Rüpke sees the Fasti Antiates as intimately dependent on the Fulvian *fasti*, so that, for example, no more temple-dedications have been added to the Fulvian ones; yet it is not certain that the Fasti Antiates contained no temple-

dedications after Rüpke's *terminus post quem* date of 173 B.C.E. (Sehlmeyer 1996), and it is very striking that the Fasti Antiates do not follow the Fulvian *fasti* in having their distinctive learned exegetical comment, of which there is not a trace in the surviving fragments from Anzio (Degrassi 1963, 28). I thank Jörg Rüpke for generous correspondence on these issues; at the time of writing, we each remain unpersuaded by the other.

26. Wallace-Hadrill 1987, 223.

27. Compare the observations of Williamson (1987) on the functions of legal documents inscribed on bronze tablets, concentrating on their "symbolic functions which are distinguishable from the efficient functions usually given priority by scholars" (161): my thanks to Nicholas Horsfall for this reference.

28. Shaw 2003, 29—an important discussion.

29. Related points in connection with Greek eponymous lists in Hedrick 2002, 27–28; Shaw 2003, 29–34: n.b. 32: "In ancient Greek societies the original function of eponyms, calendars, and systems of reckoning was not chronological *per se* although . . . they could be put to such use." Cf. Stern 2003, 59, on the difference between calendars and chronologies.

30. Cornell 1995, 401, quoted also by Shaw 2003, 29.

31. Laurence and Smith 1995–96, 142. My selection of this sentence is not meant to question the great value of this excellent paper, from which I have learned much.

32. See Woodman and Martin 1996 on Tac. *Ann.* 3.52.1, *C. Sulpicius, D. Haterius consules sequuntur, inturbidus externis rebus annus.*

33. Lucidly expounded by Michels (1967, 98): "The consular year defines the period during which a particular pair of consuls was in office. It can begin on any day of the calendar year and it may be shorter than a calendar year if the consuls leave office before their full term has expired. . . . The calendar year, on the other hand, contains no variable elements, but is valid for any year. Its function is to provide dates within any one year, or dates which recur in a regular cycle. The dates of religious observances are determined by the calendar year, as are those of business transactions. In treaties between Rome and other states periods of time were defined in terms of the calendar year."

34. Livy *Per.* 47.

35. Bickerman 1980, 70. On the varying dates of entry to the office, see Mommsen 1859, 86–104; for the early Republic, Oakley 1997–98, 2:612–14.

36. Richardson 1986, 128–32.

37. I have found the following studies of particular value for the large subject of the Principate's reconfiguring of time and consequent impact on the *fasti* of both kinds: Beard 1987; Wallace-Hadrill 1987; Fraschetti 1990, 5–120 ("*Parte prima:* Il tempo"); Hinds 1992; Newlands 1995; Rüpke 1995b, 396–416; A. Barchiesi 1997, esp. 47–78; Pasco-Pranger 2006. Much of this work relates to Ovid's calendar poem, *Fasti*, which has been central to the rethinking of the ideological power of Augustus's work on time.

38. See above, n. 1.

39. Degrassi 1947, no. 1; 1–63, 88–142.

40. Degrassi 1947, 42–51, contains the transcript of the columns in this section, Frag. XXI.

41. This system is true of the first four of the five tablets, down to 12 B.C.E.: we return shortly to the significance of the change in the fifth and final tablet.

42. Similarly, the censors of 131 B.C.E. are annotated as being "the first both to come from the plebs."

43. Wallace-Hadrill 1987, 223; I am particularly indebted to the arguments of Rüpke (1995a), highlighting the nature of Augustus's innovations in the consular *fasti*.

44. Well pointed out by Rüpke (1995a, 193): 'Mit der Beifügung der *a.u.c.*-Daten verliert die eigentliche Namensliste ihren ohnehin fraglich gewordenen Charakter als Zeitrechnungsinstrument."

45. Bickerman 1980, 78.

46. I thank W. S. Anderson for discussion of this point.

47. Frier 1999, 204–5; Kraus 1994a, 10 n. 44.

48. Compare the way that writers other than historians abandon reference to an era *post reges exactos* in favor of *ab urbe condita* in the early Principate: Pinsent 1988, 5 ("perhaps for ideological reasons").

49. Purcell 2003, 30, building on the insights of Hanell (1946).

50. Here I merely paraphrase the incisive arguments of Bodel (1995, 290–92).

51. Bodel 1995, 291.

52. For related Augustan strategies of diminishing Jupiter in favor of Mars Ultor (and also Apollo Palatinus), see Feeney 1991, 216–17.

53. Here I follow the clear analysis of Rüpke (1995a, 191–92).

54. Degrassi 1947, no. 3; 159–66.

55. Livy 1.44.1–2 for Servius Tullius's institution of the census and lustration. In the early part of the *fasti*, the censors are by no means regularly in office every five years, and the first recorded lustration, for 474 B.C.E., is already the eighth. It is this haphazard patterning of *lustra* in so much of the period covered by the *fasti* that makes me cautious to accept Rüpke's interesting suggestion that an alternative, quasi-Olympiad dating system is being set up in Augustus's lists (Rüpke 1995a, 192–93): only in the second half of the third century B.C.E. does something like a regular pattern of five-year *lustra* begin to take hold, and even then it is by no means fixed.

56. The two crucial changes I am about to discuss were picked out with lapidary concision by Degrassi (1947, 20), writing of the changes in the last portion of the Fasti Capitolini: "Qui fasti et diebus quibus consules suffecti inierunt indicatis et tribuniciis potestatibus Augusti et Tiberii ante consulum nomina positis et scriptura et ratione uersuum a ceteris longe differunt." On the subversion of the consular office under the Principate, see Kraus and Woodman 1997, 94, on Tac. *Ann.* 1.1.1 and 1.81.1–2.

57. Throughout this section I am deeply indebted to the important papers of Bodel (1993 and 1995), and to his generous correspondence with me on this question.

58. Rüpke 1995a, 191.

59. This is to be seen in the middle of the illustration of the Fasti Antiates in fig. 9. The year 130 B.C.E. is very fragmentary, but it is clear that the same convention is followed there as well.

60. Bodel 1993, 262.

61. Bodel 1993, 264. The Fasti Tauromenitani similarly "purport to indicate the day on which each suffect entered office, with the natural consequence that the *suffecti* of the year, like the *ordinarii* of the various years, appear in chronological order" (265).

62. As Lucan points out with his mordant comment that the consular office lost its power with Julius Caesar, but that "just so the time does not lack a name, monthly consuls mark the epochs onto the *fasti*" (*tantum careat ne nomine tempus,/menstruus in fastos distinguit saecula consul,* 5.398–99).

63. We are still left with the issue of locating the change in convention as indeed an Augustan one, given that the Fasti Venusini have the same convention of dating suffects as Tablet V of Augustus's *fasti* yet originally went back to the Social War (Degrassi 1947, no. 8; 249–56). The extant remains of Fasti Venusini cover only the years 35–28 B.C.E., so that it is unfortunately impossible to know how they recorded suffects in the early years of the list. It is certainly possible that they recorded suffects in the "new" way for the early years, in which case they may well have had a pre-Augustan source. These *fasti*, however, were inscribed some time after 16 B.C.E. (Degrassi 1947, 250), and it is far more compelling to see them responding to an Augustan transformation of the office and of the *fasti;* as Bodel points out, the Fasti Venusini "may or may not have recorded suffects by date from their inception *a bello Marsico*" (Bodel 1995, 281 n. 9). Augustus's own *fasti*, after all, change their convention at a certain stage, and it is possible that the Fasti Venusini did as well. If the Fasti Venusini did record suffects by date from the start, then it is still possible that they retrojected the Augustan convention, approximating or inventing dates in the process. I thank John Bodel for enlightening discussion of this vexed question.

64. Bodel 1993, 263: "The whole system changes." Lacey (1979) well brings out the way in which the use and significance of *tribunicia potestas* evolved as Augustus felt his way forward in the unparalleled circumstances of his new institutions.

65. Since each year now has its suffects, introduced by the date "from the Kalends of July" and moved over to the far right, the words *Imp. Caesar* at the beginning of each year are strikingly "paragraphed" each time, with a blank space above them. The year 13 C.E. is the end of the document as we have it, for there is no room for additions at this point: whether it was continued elsewhere is unknown (Degrassi 1947, 20).

66. Lacey 1979, 33. Bodel (1995, 292–93) makes a persuasive case for 2 B.C.E. as the crucial year in which many of these threads were pulled together by Augustus, as he

dedicated his temple of Mars Ultor—tellingly enough, in the last year in which he held the consulship.

67. Degrassi 1947, no. 1; 1–4, 8–23, 64–87.

68. Degrassi 1947, 64–65.

69. For the idea that March was the beginning of Romulus's civil year, see below, p. 205. As Rüpke (1995a, 193) points out, it is significant that the year of each triumph is dated AUC, not by the names of the consuls. Other "triumphal" *fasti* vary: the Fasti Triumphales Urbisalvienses (Degrassi 1947, no. 35; 338–40) give the day of the year plus the *triumphator*'s magistracy, which is a kind of date; the Fasti Triumphales Barberiniani (Degrassi, no. 36; 342–45) give the day of the year, but no magistracy, and no other kind of date.

70. Note that he is not called *Diui filius* when he appears for the years 40, 36, and 29 B.C.E. on the Fasti Triumphales Barberiniani (Degrassi 1947, 342–45).

71. Wallace-Hadrill 1987, 224.

72. Wallace-Hadrill 1987, 224.

73. Degrassi 1947, 20, for the details.

74. For initial bibliography, see n. 37 above.

75. The classic work of Michels (1967) remains standard for the notations of the Republican calendar. Graf 1997 is a highly stimulating essay on the possible semiotic power of the calendar, concentrating on the sequence of festivals from December to March.

76. Michels 1967, 84–89.

77. Michels 1967, 22–83; cf. Scullard 1981, 44–45; Rüpke 1995b, 245–88; Linderski 1997–98; Scheid 2003, 46–54.

78. Fraschetti 1990, 13 (although his use of Varro's terminology of "days instituted for the sake of men" misrepresents what Varro means: see below, p. 199, for the meaning of Varro's language); cf. Michels 1967, 142.

79. Michels 1967, 25; Rüpke 1995b, 359, 415; above, p. 103.

80. Rüpke 1995b, 345–60; 1995a, 199. This proposal looks as if it may be becoming *communis opinio:* Gildenhard 2003, 95–97; Scheid 2003, 56, 181–82 ("a discreet way of writing the history of Rome and above all that of the victorious generals").

81. There are other possible explanations of the dative form besides that of the temple-dedication notice, canvassed by Rüpke (1995b, 355–58).

82. Rüpke 1995b, 355. It is highly strained to argue, as he does there, that this form was not used because it would have made the cost of the inscription higher and obscured the underlying format of the *fasti* as Fulvius had inherited it from Cn. Flavius. Of course, if there were consular *fasti* present as well as calendrical, then the historical power of the consular format will have made itself felt.

83. Feeney 1992b, 5; again, my debt to Wallace-Hadrill (1987) in particular is great.

84. Herz 1978, 1148–51, gives lists of the principal additions honoring Augustus

and Tiberius. A sample from the first few days of the Fasti Praenestini (cf. Wallace-Hadrill 1987, 229–30): Augustus's first assumption of *imperium* in the consulship of Hirtius and Pansa, and Tiberius's election as a *VIIuir epulonum* (7 January); Tiberius's dedication of an image of *Iustitia Augusta* in the consulship of Plancus and Silius (8 January); Augustus's closing of the gates of Janus in his (fifth) and Appuleius's consulship (11 January); award of an oaken wreath to Augustus by the Senate for restoring the Republic to the Roman people (13 January); the birthday of M. Antonius, *uitiosus* (14 January); name of "Augustus" conferred in his (seventh) and Agrippa's (third) consulship, and dedication of temple of Concordia Augusta by Tiberius in the consulship of Dolabella and Silanus (16 January). By contrast, for the same days in the Fasti Antiates, we find only the Carmentalia on the eleventh and fifteenth, and "to Juturna" on the eleventh.

85. In the first sense, *OLD* s.v. §§1 and 2; in the second, §4b (including a reference to Flor. *Epit.* 2.34, *sanctius . . . uisum est nomen Augusti, ut . . . ipso nomine et titulo consecraretur*). Cf. Ov. *Fast.* 2.16, referred to below, p. 188.

86. Institution of Augustalia: *Res Gestae* 11; Tac. *Ann.* 1.15.2; on its revolutionary import, Taylor and Holland 1952, 140, expressed in a more qualified way in Michels 1967, 141. Interestingly, *OLD* s.v. *fasti* §3 lists this Horatian passage under the "wrong," i.e., consular, *fasti; TLL* 6.327.12–13 correctly has it under the calendrical *fasti* (cf. Rüpke 1997, 76 n. 61).

87. Ovid explains the translingual etymology whereby Venus = Aphrodite = April at *Fast.* 4.61–62.

88. Cf. *Ann.* 15.74.1 for the renaming of April as Neroneus, and 16.12.3 for the renaming of May and June as Claudius and Germanicus.

89. Suet. *Tib.* 26.2.

90. Dio 57.18.2.

91. On the development of the honorific "system" in the transition from Republic to Principate, see Wallace-Hadrill 1990.

92. Wissowa 1912, 445; Michels 1967, 142; Weinstock 1971, 157, 206 (for Caesar's birthday); Fraschetti 1990, 15–16; Rüpke 1995b, 393. *NP* denotes "days on which *feriae* were celebrated at public expense for the benefit of the whole people, by the state" (Michels 1967, 74), and the ligature itself probably means *(dies) nefasti publici* (76).

93. An important prototype is clearly given by the so-called Ludi Victoriae Sullanae, instituted in 81 B.C.E. and running from 26 October to 1 November, but it is significant that these were originally called simply Ludi Victoriae, and Sulla's name was added later to distinguish his victory games from Caesar's (20–30 July): Degrassi 1963, 526.

94. *Phil.* 2.87; cf. Rüpke 1995b, 391–92.

95. *Ad Brut.* 1.15.8 = Shackleton Bailey 1980, 23.8. On Cicero's facility with "the language of power," see Wallace-Hadrill 1990, esp. 166–67.

96. *Ad Brut.* 1.15.8 = Shackleton Bailey 1980, 23.8.

97. Again, Beard 1987 is fundamental.

98. Rüpke 1995b, 416: "Nun dienst die Augusteische Zeit selbst als die begründende Vergangenheit."

99. Michels 1967, 142; Rüpke 1995b, 417–25.

100. For Fabius as the originator, see Frier 1999, 201, 271, 283–84.

101. Kraus (1994a, 10–12) and Rich (1997) offer qualifications of a sometimes reductive version of the practice of Livy and his predecessors. Verbrugghe (1989) gives an important analysis of the ancient meanings of *annales* and well qualifies overly rigid assumptions about a set form of history writing descended from the supposed *Annales Maximi.* It is essential to remember that Thucydides and Polybius likewise organized their narratives on an annual basis; the crucial point is that in Rome this annual unit is identified with the chief executive officers and commanding generals of the state.

102. Verbrugghe 1989, 222.

103. Rich 1997, text to nn. 36–38.

104. Kraus 1994a, 10 n. 44.

105. Kraus 1994a, 281.

106. Tacitus's consuls begin the year in this ablative absolute construction 70 percent of the time, as opposed to 25 percent in Livy, according to the selection of Ginsburg (1981, 11); cf. Woodman and Martin 1996 on *Ann.* 3.2.3.

107. Ginsburg (1981, 2–3) collects the main passages: note esp. *Ann.* 4.71.1 (with Martin and Woodman 1989, ad loc.); 6.38.1.

108. Rich 1997, n. 36. This becomes more common in the later books (12.40.5; 13.9.5): as we shall see, this is because the presence of the maniacal Nero exerts even more pressure on the norms than does Tiberius.

109. Ginsburg 1981, 100; Martin and Woodman 1989, 32; Rich 1997, text to n. 3. Compare the way that Virgil creates a misleading impression of a monolithically corporatist Ennius for his own ends, or that Lucan retrospectively rewrites Virgil as nothing but a committed mouthpiece of Augustus.

110. Damon 2003, 77.

111. To use the very helpful model of Hinds (1987 and 1992), to describe the way that Roman poets mark their generic boundaries by transgressing them.

112. Cf. Polyb. 14.12, with Walbank 1957–79, ad loc. Here as elsewhere in this chapter I give the translation of Woodman (2004).

113. Similarly, in 12.40.5, the scrupulous notice that he has put together the material of a number of years in one section is immediately followed by the bland ablative absolute construction for the consuls of the next year, and by the sinister news that time was speeded up for Nero, so that he could assume the toga of manhood early and enter public life (*uirilis toga Neroni maturata,* 41.1). Nero can wreck even Greek time: see

Champlin 2003b, 53–54, for the way that Nero forced a unique postponement of the Olympic Games (from 65 to 66) to coincide with his tour of Greece.

114. Even the consuls' value as a date is called into question at *Ann.* 4.1.1, as Martin and Woodman (1989) point out ad loc.; here the consuls' names are followed by the emperor's regnal year (*nonus Tiberio annus erat*); cf. Morgan 1998, 587.

115. Morgan 1998, 586; as he remarks, "with the privative *se* 'Sejanus' is almost literally 'lacking in Janus'" (587 n. 8).

116. Grafton 1993, 233, referring to Scaliger 1583, 157.

117. *Post hominum memoriam nulla gens in terris ineptiore anni forma usa sit,* Scaliger 1583, 126 (trans. Grafton 1993, 233).

118. Respectively, Livy 37.4.4, 44.37.8; Michels 1967, 102–3.

119. Stern 2003, 59–60.

120. Modern science's measurements of years and days and minutes and seconds has recast even this conception of the relationship between the thing being measured and the units being used to measure it (Burnett 2003, 9–10; Holford-Strevens 2005, 15). For most of modern scientific history, the movement of the earth through space in relation to other bodies has been both the phenomenon we *want* to measure and the phenomenon we *use* to measure. Scientists eventually reached such accuracy in the measurement of other time-lapse intervals that their calibrations have outstripped and become independent of the astronomical relationships that the process of measuring was originally designed to capture. See Holford-Strevens 2005, 15, and Benson 2005 for the hard case of the "leap second," the unit that is periodically inserted into international time measurement in order to calibrate between time measured as a function of the earth's rotation ("Universal Time 1," U.T.1) and time measured as vibrations of the cesium atom ("International Atomic Time," T.A.I.). As Benson shows, to use only T.A.I. as the standard, and omit the leap second as a way of calibrating the two measures, would be "to uncouple our time-keeping from the rotation of the earth"—to him, a perilous step. In November 2005, after considerable debate by the responsible body in Geneva, it was decided to insert a leap second after all, so that our measurement of time continues to be linked notionally to the movement of the earth through space.

121. Stern 2003, 60.

122. Cf. Dunn 1998a, 224: "We tend to think, with our modern prejudices, that a calendar should somehow be regular or precise, and that an irregular calendar must be diverging from a more regular or more accurate counterpart. But there is no reason to imagine that Greek festival calendars were ever designed to be, or were ever expected to be, precise. Their purpose was to schedule monthly and annual festivals, and to allow these to be performed at a regular or convenient time." Cf. Michels 196, 16 n. 19, on the Roman Republican calendar as a "purely civil calendar, designed to guide the religious, political, legal, and business activities of Roman citizens."

123. Dunn 1998a, 224.

124. I follow the interpretation of Dunn (1998a, 444) on this very vexed question, he suggests that the date "according to the god" was meant to facilitate coordination from city to city.

125. Dunn 1998a, 221–22.

126. Samuel 1972, 61–64.

127. On the failure to use, for example, the Metonic cycle as a control for the calendar, see Bickerman 1980, 35; Samuel 1972, 52–55; Dunn 1998b, 42; Lehoux (forthcoming), chap. 4.

128. Dunn 1998b, 43–46.

129. Dunn 1998b, 47; Hannah 2005, 69–70.

130. Again, on the extra ninety days Caesar had to add to the year 46 B.C.E., see above, p. 281 n. 115.

131. Cf. Schiesaro 2003, 219, on how Caesar's new calendar emblematizes his overall creation of a new order.

132. Ναί, ἐκ διατάγματος, Plut. Caes. 59.3—a translation of something like immo, ex decreto. Similar jokes had their day after the introduction of the Gregorian reform in England, where "it was observed that the Glastonbury thorn flowered on Old Christmas Day, and not according to Act of Parliament" (Blackburn and Holford-Strevens 1989, 687).

133. For the Lyre's date of rising, Ov. Fast. 1.315–16; Pliny HN 18.234. Plutarch himself misses the point of the joke, saying that "men were compelled to accept even this dispensation." Rather, human power is seen as controlling the celestial movements; Ovid catches at this also when he speaks of how we "shall fix to the wandering stars their own days" (ponemusque suos ad uaga signa dies, Fast. 1.310).

134. Rawson 1994, 454, on Caesar's building works: "Thus Caesar imposed his presence on the very heart of Rome, and in every public act of his life the Roman citizen was to be reminded of him"; cf. 444–48 for his colonization plans, and 455–56 for his overhauling of corn supply and transport. Suet. Jul. 40–44 lists many such schemes; cf. Momigliano 1990, 69: "There was never again a situation in which the discovery of new facts was pursued so relentlessly and effectively as in the time of Caesar."

135. My thanks to Neil Coffee for this intriguing suggestion, and to John Dugan for a reference to Sinclair 1994, which brings out the systematizing and rationalizing approach of the De Analogia to language (esp. 92–96).

136. Pliny HN 18.211.

137. Buchner 1982, 10.

138. On Augustus's correction of the errors introduced after Caesar's death, see Bennett 2003, esp. 232–33, for the convincing hypothesis that it was the travails of the new Pontifex Maximus, Lepidus, that caused the problems.

139. Many of the detailed claims of Buchner (1982) have been impugned by Schütz (1990).

140. Revealed by the excavations of Buchner (1982); we return to this complex below, p. 206. Wallace-Hadrill (1997, 16–18) well brings out how the calendrical work of Caesar and Augustus depends on specialized knowledge to produce a rationalization that massively reinforces their "social and political authority."

141. On parapegmata, see Taub 2003, 15–69; Hannah 2005, 59–65; especially Lehoux (forthcoming), a systematic reexamination from which I have learned much. My account here merely gives a précis of the valuable overview in Lehoux's chapter 4.

142. I quote from the end of the first section of Lehoux's chapter 4 (forthcoming); emphasis is in the original. On the gulf between the calendar and parapegma tradition in Latin, see also Rüpke 1995c, 299–300. This separation between the two traditions helps to explain the near-total absence of astronomical information in calendrical *fasti* (on which see Gee 2000, 10–11). In the Republican calendar it would of course have been impossible to plot this information anyway, since the calendar made no pretense to track the natural year; but even after the Julian reform, when it would have been possible, the tradition of demarcation remained.

143. Varro's discussion of the Terminalia explicitly mentions the Republican intercalation (6.13), and the fifth month is still Quintilis, not Iulius (6.34): cf. Fraschetti 1990, 11. Yet in July 45 Cicero was still expecting the book (*Att.* 13.12.3 = Shackleton Bailey 1965–70, 320.3).

144. See Hinds 2005b for the links in structure between this "Book of Time" and the preceding "Book of Place," *De Lingua Latina* 5; Hinds well brings out the crucial shared underpinnings of the "civil" and the "natural."

145. For a New Zealander who is fond of Italy and of anniversaries, the Robigalia has a special place: as New Zealand's most popular festival, Anzac Day, it commemorates the day the Australian and New Zealand Army Corps landed at Gallipoli in 1915, and as la Festa della Liberazione it commemorates the popular revolt against the Nazis and Fascists in Italy in 1945 (witnessed by the Second New Zealand Division, campaigning in northern Italy).

146. He gives the date of the Quinquatrus (in March) because he explains it as falling *five* days after the Ides (6.14); he likewise dates the "lesser" Quinquatrus, to the Ides of June (6.17); the Vinalia are dated to 19 Sextilis (*a.d. XII Kal. Sept.*, 6.20), to differentiate them from the earlier Vinalia (23 April); the Larentalia are said to be celebrated "on the sixth day after the Saturnalia" (6.23).

147. My thanks to Steve Miller for enlightenment on these agricultural matters.

148. Similarly, in the *De Legibus*, written in the late 50s B.C.E. (Rawson 1991, 125–29), Cicero can provide some idealized legislation to ensure that intercalation is properly performed, so as to allow offerings of first fruits and flocks to be made at the right time (2.29).

149. Michels 1967, 16.

150. North (1989, 602–3) well argues that it is a misunderstanding of the Republi-

can calendar to assume that it posited a primitive one-to-one correspondence between the performance of a particular festival and the desired effect in the natural world.

151. The author's eightieth year (*Rust.* 1.1.1).

152. Rüpke (1995c, 298) remarks on the significance of these words but misinterprets them as a result of placing the date of the *De Re Rustica* before, rather than after, the Julian reform.

153. Cf. Brind'Amour 1983, 15–21, on this section, and on how the hard work of synchronization between the seasons and the civil year must have been done by Sosigenes and Caesar.

154. So Lehoux (forthcoming), chap. 3. Gee (2001, 520–21) attractively suggests that Cicero's *Aratea* may be similarly used as a control for attitudes to natural time before and after the reform. When Cicero translated Aratus in his early youth, the *ratio* of the heavens was inspiringly ordered, but it was, as it were, self-contained, for the regularity of celestial processes was its own clock; when the character Balbus quotes from the *Aratea* in *De Natura Deorum*, after the reform, his comments show a new apprehension of a new kind of harmony, for the *ratio* of the heavens is now measurable by a calendar for the first time: as she says, Pease (1955–58, ad loc.) drew out the implications of Balbus's comments on how "day, month, year have been given boundaries by humans" (*ab hominum genere finitus est dies, mensis, annus*, 2.153).

155. E.g., *Rust.* 1.29.1, on the things to do "between the onset of the west wind and the vernal equinox"; 1.30, on the things to do "between the vernal equinox and the rising of the Pleiades."

156. Note especially 18.234–37 for the dates of various constellations' and stars' risings and settings.

157. The framework is still useful: cf. Whitrow 1989, a valuable study of concepts of time through history, which begins with a discussion of "conventional" and "civil" time in relation to perceived "absolute" time (3–4).

158. I am indebted here to Marie Louise von Glinski and Martin Sirois, students in a Princeton seminar on Ovid's *Fasti*, who wrote fine papers exploring these questions in the context of Romulus's construction of the calendar (Ov. *Fast.* 1.27–42).

159. Cf. Hinds 1992, 148–49, on Ovid's questioning of the degree to which Augustus's "version of the calendar" is "natural and 'given.'" After all, as Gosden 1994, 122, points out, "there are no natural patterns of time" for humans.

160. On these different concepts of time in Ovid, and their interaction, see the important discussion of Newlands 1995, esp. 27–50.

161. Cf. Censorinus *DN* 21.12–13; Blackburn and Holford-Strevens 1999, 784–85.

162. Samuel 1972, 16–17.

163. Ov. *Fast.* 1.39, *Martis erat primus mensis*, with Bömer 1957–58, 1:39–44.

164. In Britain and the Empire until 1752, the year *did* begin in the spring, on 25 March—a "natural" beginning date for another reason also, in that this day, the Feast

of the Annunciation, comes exactly nine months before Christmas. Only with the adoption of the Gregorian reform and the dropping of eleven days from the year 1752 did Britain and the colonies move the beginning of the year to 1 January. To avoid the bookkeeping chaos, however, that would have followed having a financial year of only 354 days in 1752, Parliament decided to keep the beginning of the financial year 365 days from 25 March 1752; in 1753, allowing for the eleven days dropped between 2 September and 14 September 1752, the 365th day from 25 March 1752 fell on 6 April. Hence the reason why the British tax year still runs from 6 April to 5 April.

165. Ovid affects to convey a little envy of Lucretius, who had been able to begin his didactic poem with a splendid evocation of spring: cf. P. Hardie 1991, 50 n. 6.

166. A. Barchiesi 1997, 63.

167. Hinds 1992, 121–24.

168. Such are the "paratactic" effects analyzed by A. Barchiesi (1997, esp. 70–78).

169. Newlands 1995, 50: "In the opening couplet of the poem Ovid introduces two different temporal codes: the artificial and the natural." As emerges from her discussion, the "artificial" is fundamentally Roman, and the "natural" is fundamentally Greek.

170. Cf. pp. 127–28 above.

171. See Farrell 2001, 24–25, for the Romans' persistent representation of "the Greek" as a natural ground.

172. Buchner 1982, 63–66 (with plates), 96–103, 107–12.

173. So much so that the Greek annotation of the end of the Etesian winds is copied over, despite the fact that "it is irrelevant to the western Mediterranean" (Hannah 2005, 129).

174. "We are probably to imagine the husbandman marking off the age of the moon by moving a peg every day in a *parapegma*" (Mynors 1990, 62). Lehoux (forthcoming), chap. 2, describes Virgil as following a Greek lunar calendar here. Compare the observation of D. West (2002, 193) on Phidyle's prayer to the new moon in Hor. *Carm.* 3.23.1–2: "The farmer does not bother with the Roman Kalends, which tend to be out of kilter with the moons. He or she goes by the farmer's calendar."

175. See R. F. Thomas 1988 and Mynors 1990 on 1.217–18, *candidus auratis aperit cum cornibus annum/Taurus.*

176. Mynors 1990, 76.

177. See Gell 1992, 89, for the continued popularity of farming almanacs (the modern parapegmata) among modern peasants: "These documents, whose stipulations are more honoured in the breach than the observance . . . none the less epitomize the essential—temporal—form of the farmer's predicament, offering a magical surrogate for control over time and chance which the peasant, always on the horns of some planning dilemma, never has."

178. Heyworth 1988, 80.

179. Watson 2003, 76, summarizing the conclusions of Plüss (1913, 84–85) and Heyworth (1988, 74–77) (though Watson does not follow Heyworth in transposing lines 23–28 to follow line 16). No one denies that there are powerful responsions between Horace's poem and Virgil's *Georgics*, but there is much debate over which way the influence goes. Although all the evidence points to the *Epodes* being actually published before the *Georgics*, I agree strongly with Watson (2003, 76–77) that Horace is responding to Virgil rather than the other way around.

180. I am not sure why Horace mentions this one festival: see Mankin 1995, ad loc., for some possibilities. In light of the crucial Ides and Kalends coming up ten lines later, it is possible that Horace has chosen a date that used to have calendrical significance (as the site for intercalation in the Republican calendar), but that no longer does.

181. Well put by Heyworth (1988, 80). Horace's meticulous demarcation of the calendrical world of Alfius and of the farmer corroborates again the arguments of Griffin (1997) concerning the highly discriminating use made of the calendar by the Augustan poets.

182. Hollis 1977, 104.

183. My translation of *operosa* as "with their work" is a little labored; it is meant to bring out the way that Ovid, at the beginning of his "days" section, puns on Hesiod's title of Works *and Days*, just as Virgil had at the beginning of *his* "days" section: see R. F. Thomas (1988) on *G.* 1.276–77 for the way that Virgil's *dies . . . operum* alludes to Hesiod's title ("the first attested reference"). On the pun on Hesiod's title to be found in the *Fasti* (*uates operose dierum*, 1.101), see P. Hardie 1991, 59.

184. Cf. Rüpke 1995b, 17–36, 593–628.

185. Hassig 2001, 71.

186. Gell 1992, 89.

187. Gell 1992, 313.

188. Bickerman 1980, 49–50; Laurence and Smith 1995–96, 143, 148. The Aztecs provide an interesting comparison: see Hassig 2001, 83, 123, for the way the Aztecs' own calendar spread through their empire and was used to coordinate payment of tribute but was not systematically imposed on the subject peoples and did not necessarily supplant the local calendars.

189. Compare the way that cities in the East continued to mint their own coins while those in the West did not: Millar 2000, 17–18.

190. Samuel 1972, 171–78, 186–88; Hannah 2005, 131–38.

191. Samuel 1972, 186.

192. Cf. Beard, North, and Price 1998, 316–17, for the "relatively diffuse and unintegrated" nature of Roman religion's spread throughout the Empire, likewise with comparative evidence from other empires that imposed their own religions much more

systematically on their subjects; Adams 2003, esp. 634–37, for the Romans' lack of interest in imposing their language in Egypt and in the Greek East in general, with their "view of Greek as a suitable lingua franca in the east" (635).

193. Laurence and Smith 1995–96, 148.

194. B. Anderson 1991, 24–26; cf. Zerubavel 2003, 4, for the related phenomenon of "mnemonic synchronization."

195. Beard, North, and Price 1998, 322–23; cf. Crawford 1996, 426, especially on how local Italian calendars were dying away even before the massive diffusion of the Julian calendar; Dench 2005, 214.

196. A. Barchiesi (2005b) on this Roman connectivity as a major theme of the *Aeneid* (esp. 29 on the role of the calendar).

197. For the important evidence of the calendar found at the army base in Dura Europus on the Euphrates (the "*feriale Duranum,*" edited by Fink, Hoey, and Snyder [1940]), see Webster 1969, 267–68; Beard, North, and Price 1998, 324–26.

198. Above, p. 163.

199. Beard, North, and Price 1998, 323.

200. Here I am indebted to the fine discussions of Hinds (1999 and 2005a); G. Williams (2002).

201. Hinds 1999, 65–67; 2005a, 213–18 (§3 "The *Tristia:* Time at a Standstill"); G. Williams 2002, 354–56. Note esp. *Tr.* 5.10.1–14.

202. G. Williams 2002, 356. Note esp. *Tr.* 3.12.17–26.

203. So named by Cairns (1972, 137).

204. G. Williams 2002, 356.

205. Nos. 19, 24, 25, 32, 34, 55, 68, 77, 84, 86, 100, 105. This list does not include the numerous "Questions" relating to festivals, such as no. 45, on the Veneralia (275E).

206. The second part of a double question about Delphi: "Who is the Consecrator among the people of Delphi, and why do they have a month called *Bysios?*" (292D).

207. Compare the title of a lost prose work of Callimachus, "Names of Months by tribes and cities" (Pfeiffer 1949, 1:339); also the "Months," written in the early third century B.C.E. by the poet Simmias of Rhodes.

EPILOGUE

1. Laurence and Smith 1995–96, 140–41.

2. So understood by Varro (*Ling.* 6.8) and other authorities: Maltby 1991, 85. See Putnam 1986, 137 n. 10, for the significance of the word here.

3. Commager 1962, 279; Putnam 1986, 141.

4. Horace does not incorporate the nundinal cycle: he mentions it nowhere else either.

5. Barnett 1998, 150: "By 1500, public clocks were beginning to strike on the quar-

ter-hour, but the minute could not be accurately counted until the pendulum clock [1657], and the second had to await the invention of the 39.1-inch pendulum in 1670." On divisions below the level of the hour, see Holford-Strevens 2005, 7–10.

    6. Nicolet 1991; Wallace-Hadrill 1997.

    7. Grafton 2003, 82.

    8. Wilcox 1987, 189–90; B. Anderson 1991, 69–70.

BIBLIOGRAPHY

Adam, B. 1990. *Time and social theory.* Oxford.

————. 1994. Perceptions of time. In *Companion encyclopedia of anthropology*, ed. T. Ingold, 503–25. London and New York.

Adams, J. N. 2003. *Bilingualism and the Latin language.* Cambridge.

Adler, W. 1989. *Time immemorial: Archaic history and its sources in Christian chronography from Julius Africanus to George Syncellus.* Washington, D.C.

Adler, W., and P. Tuffin. 2002. *The chronography of George Synkellos: A Byzantine chronicle of universal history from the creation.* Oxford.

Ahl, F. 1985. *Metaformations: Soundplay and wordplay in Ovid and other classical poets.* Ithaca and London.

Alcock, S. E. 1997. The heroic past in a Hellenistic present. In Cartledge, Garnsey, and Gruen 1997, 20–34.

Alföldy, G. 1995. Eine Bauinschrift aus dem Colosseum. *ZPE* 109: 195–226.

Alonso-Núñez, J. M. 1983. Die Abfolge der Weltreiche bei Polybios und Dionysios von Halikarnassos. *Historia* 32: 411–26.

————. 1987. An Augustan world history: The *Historiae Philippicae* of Pompeius Trogus. *G&R* 34: 56–72.

Ambrose, S. 1996. *Undaunted courage: Meriwether Lewis, Thomas Jefferson, and the opening of the American West.* New York.

Anderson, B. 1991. *Imagined communities: Reflections on the origin and spread of nationalism.*[2] London and New York.

Anderson, W. S. 1972. *Ovid's Metamorphoses: Books 6–10.* Norman.

Ando, C. 2001. The Palladeum and the Pentateuch: Towards a sacred topography of the later Roman empire. *Phoenix* 55: 369–410.

Appadurai, A. 1981. The past as a scarce resource. *Man* 16: 201–19.

Argetsinger, K. 1992. Birthday rituals: Friends and patrons in Roman poetry and cult. *CA* 11: 175–93.

Arnason, J. P. 2005. The axial age and its interpreters: Reopening a debate. In *Axial civilizations and world history,* ed. J. P. Arnason, S. N. Eisenstadt, and B. Wittrock, 19–49. Leiden.

Arnold-Biucchi, C. 2002. Review of *Siracusa ellenistica: Le monete 'regali' di Ierone II, della sua famiglia e dei Siracusani,* ed. M. Caccamo Caltabiano, B. Carroccio, and E. Oteri. *BMCR* 2002.08.05.

Asheri, D. 1983. Il millennio di Troia. In *Biblioteca di Athenaeum 2: Saggi di letteratura e storiografia antiche,* 53–98. Como.

———. 1988. *Erodoto: Le storie.* Vol. 1. Milan.

———. 1991–92. The art of synchronization in Greek historiography: The case of Timaeus of Tauromenium. *SCI* 11: 52–89.

Atkinson, R. F. 1978. *Knowledge and explanation in history.* Ithaca and London.

Aubet, M. E. 2001. *The Phoenicians and the West: Politics, colonies, and trade.*[2] Trans. M. Turton. Cambridge.

Aveni, A. 1989. *Empires of time: Calendars, clocks, and cultures.* New York.

Ax, W. 2001. Dikaiarchs Bios Hellados und Varros De vita populi Romani. In Fortenbaugh and Schütrumpf 2001, 279–310.

Badian, E. 1969. Cicero and the commission of 146 B.C. In *Hommages à Marcel Renard I,* ed. J. Bibauw, 54–65. Brussels.

Baier, T. 1997. *Werk und Wirkung Varros im Spiegel seiner Zeitgenossen von Cicero bis Ovid.* Stuttgart.

Bakker, E. J., I. J. F. de Jong, and H. van Wees, eds. 2002. *Brill's companion to Herodotus.* Leiden.

Baldry, H. C. 1952. Who invented the Golden Age? *CQ* 2: 83–92.

Baldwin, B. 1995. Better late than early: Reflections on the date of Calpurnius Siculus. *ICS* 20: 157–67.

Balsdon, J. P. V. D. 1969. *Life and leisure in ancient Rome.* Oxford.

Barchiesi, A. 1981. Letture e trasformazioni di un mito arateo (Cic. Arat. XVII Tr.; Verg. georg. 2,473 sg.). *MD* 6: 181–87.

———. 1989. L'epos. In *La produzione del testo,* ed. G. Cavallo, P. Fedeli, and A. Giardina, 115–41. Vol. 1 of *Lo spazio letterario di Roma antica.* Rome.

———. 1991. Discordant Muses. *PCPhS* 37: 1–21.

———. 1997. *The Poet and the prince: Ovid and Augustan discourse.* Berkeley and Los Angeles.

———. 1999. Ovid and the Homeric Hymns. In Hardie, Barchiesi, and Hinds 1999, 112–36.

———. 2005a. Learned eyes: Poets, viewers, and image-makers. In Galinsky 2005, 281–305.

———. 2005b. Mobilità e religione nell' *Eneide* (Diaspora, culto, spazio, identità locali). In *Texte als Medium und Reflexion von Religion im römischen Reich*, ed. D. Elm, J. Rüpke, and K. Waldner, 13–30. Stuttgart.

Barchiesi, M. 1962. *Nevio epico*. Padua.

Barkan, L. 1986. *The gods made flesh: Metamorphosis and the pursuit of paganism*. New Haven and London.

Barker, D. 1996. "The Golden Age is proclaimed?" The *Carmen Saeculare* and the renascence of the Golden Race. *CQ* 46: 434–46.

Barnett, J. E. 1998. *Time's pendulum: From sundials to atomic clocks, the fascinating history of timekeeping and how our discoveries changed the world*. New York.

Basto, R. 1982. Horace's propemptikon to Vergil: A re-examination. *Vergilius* 28: 30–43.

Bayly, C. A. 2004. *The birth of the modern world, 1780–1914: Global connections and comparisons*. London.

Beard, M. 1987. A complex of times: No more sheep on Romulus' birthday. *PCPhS* 33: 1–15.

Beard, M., J. North, and S. Price. 1998. *Religions of Rome*. Vol. 1, *A history*. Cambridge.

Beck, H., and U. Walter. 2001. *Die frühen römischen Historiker*. Bd. 1, *Von Fabius Pictor bis Cn. Gellius*. Darmstadt.

Belkin, L. 2002. The odds of that. *New York Times Magazine*, August 11, 33–46.

Bennett, C. 2003. The early Augustan calendars in Rome and Egypt. *ZPE* 142: 221–40.

Benson, M. 2005. Just hang on a second. *New York Times*, 5 November.

Bettini, M. 1991. *Anthropology and Roman culture: Kinship, time, images of the soul*. Trans. J. van Sickle. Baltimore and London.

Bichler, R. 1985. Der Synchronismus von Himera und Salamis: Eine quellenkritische Studie zu Herodot. In *Festschrift für Artur Betz*, ed. E. Weber and G. Dobesch, 59–74. Vienna.

———. 1995. *Von der Insel der Seligen zu Platons Staat: Geschichte der antiken Utopie*. Bd. 1. Vienna.

Bickerman, E. J. 1952. Origines gentium. *CPh* 47: 65–81.

———. 1980. *Chronology of the ancient world.*[2] London.

Binder, G. 1971. *Aeneas und Augustus: Interpretationen zum 8. Buch der Aeneis*. Meisenheim.

Blackburn, B., and L. Holford-Strevens. 1999. *The Oxford companion to the year: An exploration of calendar customs and time-reckoning.* Oxford.

Bloch, M. 1989. *Ritual, history, and power: Selected papers in anthropology.* London.

Blundell, S. 1986. *The origins of civilization in Greek and Roman thought.* London.

Boardman, J. 1977. The Parthenon frieze—another view. In *Festschrift für F. Brommer,* ed. J. Höckmann and A. Krug, 39–49. Mainz.

———. 2002. *The archaeology of nostalgia: How the Greeks recreated their mythical past.* London.

Bodel, J. 1993. Chronology and succession 1: *Fasti Capitolini* Fr. XXXIId, the Sicilian *Fasti,* and the suffect consuls of 36 B.C. *ZPE* 96: 259–66.

———. 1995. Chronology and succession 2: Notes on some consular lists on stone. *ZPE* 105: 279–96.

Boedeker, D. 2001. Paths to heroization at Plataea. In Boedeker and Sider 2001, 148–63.

Boedeker, D., and D. Sider, eds. 2001. *The new Simonides: Contexts of praise and desire.* Oxford.

Bömer, F. 1957–58. *P. Ovidius Naso: Die Fasten.* Heidelberg.

Boyd, B. W., ed. 2002. *Brill's companion to Ovid.* Leiden.

Boyle, A. J., ed. 1983. *Seneca tragicus: Ramus essays on Senecan drama.* Berwick, Victoria.

———. 1987. *Seneca's Phaedra.* Leeds.

Boys-Stones, G. R. 2001. *Post-Hellenistic philosophy: A study of its development from the Stoics to Origen.* Oxford.

Bramble, J. C. 1970. Structure and ambiguity in Catullus LXIV. *PCPhS* 16: 22–41.

Braund, D. 1996. *Ruling Roman Britain: Kings, queens, governors, and emperors from Julius Caesar to Agricola.* London and New York.

Braund, D., and C. Gill, eds. 2003. *Myth, history, and culture in Republican Rome: Studies in honour of T. P. Wiseman.* Exeter.

Bremmer, J. N., and N. M. Horsfall. 1987. *Roman myth and mythography.* London.

Brettler, M. 2004. Cyclical and teleological time in the Hebrew Bible. In Rosen 2004, 111–28.

Brind'Amour, P. 1983. *Le calendrier romain: Recherches chronologiques.* Ottawa.

Briscoe, J. 1991. Review of Radke 1990. *CR* 41: 404–6.

Brown, T. S. 1958. *Timaeus of Tauromenium.* Berkeley and Los Angeles.

———. 1962. The Greek sense of time in history as suggested by their accounts of Egypt. *Historia* 11: 257–70.

Buchheit, V. 1965. Tibull 2.5. *Philologus* 109: 184–200.

Buchner, E. 1982. *Die Sonnenuhr des Augustus.* Mainz.

Burde, P. 1974. *Untersuchungen zur antiken Universalgeschichte.* Erlangen-Nuremburg.

Burgess, R. W. 1999. *Studies in Eusebian and Post-Eusebian chronography.* Vol. 1, *The*

Chronici Canones of Eusebius of Caesarea· *Content and chronology, A.D. 282–325.*
Stuttgart.

———. 2002. Jerome explained: An introduction to his *Chronicle* and a guide to its
use. *AHB* 16: 1–32.

Burkert, W. 1995. Lydia between East and West or how to date the Trojan War: A
study in Herodotus. In *The ages of Homer: A tribute to Emily Townsend Vermeule*,
ed. J. B. Carter and S. P. Morris, 139–48. Austin.

Burkhard, K. 1991. *Das antike Geburtstagsgedicht*. Zurich.

Burnett, D. G. 2003. Mapping time: Chronometry on top of the world. *Daedalus* 132:
5–19.

Cairns, F. 1972. *Generic composition in Greek and Roman poetry*. Edinburgh.

Calame, C. 2003. *Myth and history in ancient Greece: The symbolic creation of a colony.*
Trans. D. W. Berman. Princeton.

Campbell, G. 2003. *Lucretius on creation and evolution: A commentary on* De Rerum
Natura *5.772–1104*. Oxford.

Canfora, L. 1991. L'inizio della storia secondo i Greci. *Quad. Stor.* 33: 3–19.

Carandini, A. 1997. *La nascità di Roma: Dèi, lari, eroi e uomini all'alba di una civiltà.*
Turin.

Carlstein, T., D. Parkes, and N. J. Thrift, eds. 1978. *Timing space and spacing time.*
London.

Cartledge, P. 1993. *The Greeks: A portrait of self and others*. Oxford.

Cartledge, P., P. Garnsey, and E. Gruen, eds. 1997. *Hellenistic constructs: Essays in
culture, history, and historiography*. Berkeley and Los Angeles.

Cartledge, P., and E. Greenwood. 2002. Herodotus as a critic: Truth, fiction, polarity.
In Bakker et al. 2002, 351–71.

Casson, L. 1971. *Ships and seamanship in the ancient world*. Princeton.

Cavarzere, A. 1975/6. Virgilio, Orazio e il "motto iniziale" (quarta bucolica e
sedicesimo epodo). *AAPat* 88.3: 35–42.

Champion, C. 2000. Romans as BAPBAPOI: Three Polybian speeches and the politics of cultural indeterminacy. *CPh* 95: 425–44.

Champlin, E. 2003a. Agamemnon at Rome: Roman dynasts and Greek heroes. In
Braund and Gill 2003, 295–319.

———. 2003b. *Nero*. Cambridge, Mass.

———. 2003c. Nero, Apollo, and the poets. *Phoenix* 57: 276–83.

Chaniotis, A. 1988. *Historie und Historiker in den griechischen Inschriften: Epigraphische
Beiträge zur griechischen Historiographie*. Stuttgart.

Chaplin, J. O. 2000. *Livy's exemplary history*. Oxford.

Charpak, G., and H. Broch. 2004. *Debunked! ESP, telekinesis, and other pseudoscience.*
Trans. B. K. Holland. Baltimore and London.

Chassignet, M. 1986. *Caton: Les origines*. Paris.

———. 1996. *L'annalistique romaine.* Vol. 1. Paris.

———. 1999. *L'annalistique romaine.* Vol. 2. Paris.

Clare, R. J. 1996. Catullus 64 and the *Argonautica* of Apollonius Rhodius: Allusion and exemplarity. *PCPhS* 42: 60–88.

Clarke, K. 1999a. *Between geography and history: Hellenistic constructions of the Roman world.* Oxford.

———. 1999b. Universal perspectives in historiography. In Kraus 1999, 249–79.

Classen, C. J. 1963. Zur Herkunft der Sage von Romulus und Remus. *Historia* 12: 447–57.

Clauss, J. J. 2000. Cosmos without imperium: The Argonautic journey through time. In *Apollonius Rhodius*, ed. M. A. Harder, R. F. Regtuit, and G. C. Wakker, 11–32. Hellenistica Groningana 4. Leuven.

Clay, J. S. 1983. *The wrath of Athena: Gods and men in the* Odyssey. Princeton.

———. 1986. *The politics of Olympus: Form and meaning in the major Homeric hymns.* Princeton.

Coarelli, F. 1992. *Il Foro Romano: Periodo arcaico.*[3] Rome.

Cobet, J. 2000. Die Ordnung der Zeiten. In *Europa: Die Gegenwärtigkeit der antiken Überlieferung*, ed. J. Cobet, C. F. Gethmann, and D. Lau, 9–31. Essen.

———. 2002. The organization of time in the *Histories.* In Bakker et al. 2002, 387–412.

Cole, T. 1967. *Democritus and the sources of Greek anthropology.* Chapel Hill.

———. 2004. Ovid, Varro, and Castor of Rhodes: The chronological architecture of the *Metamorphoses. HSCPh* 102: 355–422.

Coleman, K. M. 1988. *Statius: Silvae IV.* Oxford.

———. 2000. Entertaining Rome. In *Ancient Rome: The archaeology of the eternal city*, ed. J. Coulston and H. Dodge, 210–58. Oxford.

Collins, J. J. 1998. *The apocalyptic imagination: An introduction to Jewish apocalyptic literature.*[2] Grand Rapids and Cambridge.

Commager, S. 1962. *The odes of Horace: A critical study.* Bloomington.

Connor, W. R. 1968. *Theopompus and fifth-century Athens.* Washington, D.C.

Connors, C. 1998. *Petronius the poet: Verse and literary tradition in the* Satyricon. Cambridge.

———. 2002. Chariton's Syracuse and its histories of empire. In *Space in the ancient novel: Ancient narrative supplementum 1*, ed. M. Paschalis and S. Frangoulidis, 12–26. Groningen.

Cornell, T. J. 1975. Aeneas and the twins: The development of the Roman foundation legend. *PCPhS* 21: 1–31.

———. 1983. Gründer. *RAC* 12: 1107–45.

———. 1986. Review of Skutsch 1985. *JRS* 76: 244–50.

———. 1989. Rome and Latium to 390 B.C. *CAH*[2] 7.2: 243–308.

————. 1995. *The beginnings of Rome: Italy and Rome from the Bronze Age to the Punic Wars (c. 1000–264 B.C.)*. London.

————. 2001. Cicero on the origins of Rome. In *Cicero's Republic*, ed. J. G. F. Powell and J. A. North, 41–56. London.

Courtney, E. 1987. Imitation, chronologie littéraire et Calpurnius Siculus. *REL* 65: 148–57.

Cowan, R. W. 2002. "In my beginning is my end": Origins, cities, and foundations in Flavian epic. DPhil thesis. Oxford University.

Crawford, M. H. 1996. Italy and Rome from Sulla to Augustus. *CAH*² 10: 414–33.

Cronon, W. 1995a. The trouble with wilderness; or, getting back to the wrong nature. In Cronon 1995b, 69–90.

————, ed. 1995b. *Uncommon ground: Toward reinventing nature*. New York.

Curti, E. 2002. Fra mito e storia: Gli indigeni e la percezione del passato. In *Mito e immagine nella Basilicata Antica*, ed. M. L. Nava and M. Osanna, 47–62. Venosa.

Daffinà, P. 1987. Senso del tempo e senso della storia: Computi cronologici e storicizzazione del tempo. *RSO* 61: 1–71.

Damasio, A. 2002. Remembering when. *Scientific American* 287, no. 3, September, 66–73.

Damon, C. 2003. *Tacitus: Histories Book 1*. Cambridge.

Darbo-Peschanski, C. 1987. *Le discours du particulier: Essai sur l'enquête hérodotéenne*. Paris.

D'Arms, J. H. 1981. *Commerce and social standing in ancient Rome*. Cambridge, Mass.

Davidson, J. 2005. Adrift from locality. *London Review of Books*, 3 November, 10–14.

Davis, N. 1996. *Europe: A history*. Oxford.

Davis, P. J. 1983. A reading of Seneca's *Phaedra*. In Boyle 1983, 114–27.

De Cazanove, O. 1992. La détermination chronographique de la durée de la période royale à Rome. In *La Rome des premier siècles: Légende et histoire (Actes de la Table Ronde en l'honneur de Massimo Pallottino)*, 69–98. Florence.

Degrassi, A. 1947. *Inscriptiones Italiae*. Vol. 13, *Fasti et Elogia*. Fasc. 1, *Fasti Consulares et Triumphales*. Rome.

————. 1963. *Inscriptiones Italiae*. Vol. 13, *Fasti et Elogia*. Fasc. 2, *Fasti Anni Numani et Iuliani*. Rome.

Della Corte, F. 1976. L'idea della preistoria in Varrone. *Atti del Congresso Internazionale di Studi Varroniani*, 1:111–36. Riete.

Delz, J. 1966. Der griechische Einfluss auf die Zwölftafelgesetzgebung. *MH* 23: 69–83.

Dench, E. 1995. *From barbarians to new men: Greek, Roman, and modern perceptions of peoples from the Central Apennines*. Oxford.

————. 2003. Beyond Greeks and barbarians: Italy and Sicily in the Hellenistic age. In *A companion to the Hellenistic world*, ed. A. Erskine, 294–310. Oxford.

————. 2005. *Romulus' asylum: Roman identities from the age of Alexander to the age of Hadrian*. Oxford.

Derow, P. S., and W. G. Forrest. 1982. An inscription from Chios. *ABSR* 77: 79–92.

Desideri, P. 1992. La formazione delle copie nelle "Vite" plutarchee. *ANRW* 2.33.6: 4470–86.

Detienne, M. 1981. The "Sea-Crow." In *Myth, religion, and society: Structuralist essays*, ed. R. L. Gordon, 16–42. Cambridge.

Diamond, J. 1997. *Guns, germs, and steel: The fates of human societies*. New York.

Dilke, O. A. W. 1967. Do line totals in the *Aeneid* show a preoccupation with significant numbers? *CQ* 17: 322–26.

Dillery, J. 2002. Quintus Fabius Pictor and Greco-Roman historiography at Rome. In *Vertis in usum: Studies in honor of Edward Courtney*, ed. J. F. Miller, C. Damon, and K. S. Myers, 1–23. Munich.

————. Forthcoming a. Clio's "other" sons: Berossus and Manetho. In *Duckworth's companion to ancient historiography*, ed. J. Marincola. London.

————. Forthcoming b. Roman historians and the Greeks, audiences and models.

Dionisotti, A. C. 1988. Nepos and the generals. *JRS* 78: 35–49.

Donalson, M. D. 1996. *A translation of Jerome's* Chronicon *with historical commentary*. Lewiston.

Döpp, S. 1968. *Virgilischer Einfluss im Werk Ovids*. Munich.

Dougherty, C. 1991. Linguistic colonialism in Aeschylus' *Aetnaeae*. *GRBS* 32: 119–32.

————. 1993. *The poetics of colonization: From city to text in archaic Greece*. Oxford.

Douglas, A. E. 1966a. *M. Tulli Ciceronis Brutus*. Oxford.

————. 1966b. Oratorum aetates. *AJPh* 87: 290–306.

Dowden, K. 1992. *The uses of Greek mythology*. London and New York.

Dreizehnter, A. 1978. *Die rhetorische Zahl: Quellenkritische Untersuchungen anhand der Zahlen 70 u. 700*. Munich.

Drew, D. L. 1927. *The allegory of the* Aeneid. Oxford.

Duff, T. 1999. *Plutarch's Lives: Exploring virtue and vice*. Oxford.

Dumézil, G. 1970. *Archaic Roman religion*. Trans. P. Krapp. Chicago.

Dunbar, N. 1995. *Aristophanes: Birds*. Oxford.

Dunn, F. M. 1998a. Tampering with the calendar. *ZPE* 123: 213–31.

————. 1998b. The uses of time in fifth-century Athens. *AncW* 29: 37–52.

Dupont, F. 1999. *The invention of literature: From Greek intoxication to the Latin book*. Trans. J. Lloyd. Baltimore and London.

DuQuesnay, I. M. LeM. 1977. Vergil's fourth *Eclogue*. *PLLS* 1: 25–99.

————. 1995. Horace, *Odes* 4.5: *Pro reditu imperatoris Caesaris divi filii Augusti*. In *Homage to Horace: A bimillenary celebration*, ed. S. J. Harrison, 128–87. Oxford.

Edelstein, L. 1967. *The idea of progress in classical antiquity*. Baltimore.

Edwards, C. 1996. *Writing Rome: Textual approaches to the city.* Cambridge.

Eigler, U., U. Gotter, N. Luraghi, and U. Walter, eds. 2003. *Formen römischer Geschichtsschreibung von den Anfängen bis Livius: Gattungen, Autoren, Kontexte.* Stuttgart.

Elias, N. 1992. *Time: An essay.* Trans. E. Jephcott. Oxford.

Errington, R. M. 1989. Rome and Greece to 205 B.C. *CAH*² 8: 81–106.

Erskine, A. 2001. *Troy between Greece and Rome: Local tradition and imperial power.* Oxford.

Evans, R. 2003. Searching for paradise: Landscape, utopia, and Rome. *Arethusa* 36: 285–307.

Fabian, J. 1983. *Time and the other: How anthropology makes its object.* New York.

Fantham, E. 1981. The synchronistic chapter of Gellius (*NA* 17.21) and some aspects of Roman chronology and cultural history between 60 and 50 B.C. *LCM* 6: 7–17.

———. 1985. Ovid, Germanicus, and the composition of the *Fasti. PLLS* 5: 243–81.

———. 1997. Images of the city: Propertius' new-old Rome. In Habinek and Schiesaro 1997, 122–35.

Farrell, J. 1995. The structure of Lucretius' "Anthropology." *MD* 33: 81–95.

———. 2001. *Latin language and Latin culture from ancient to modern times.* Cambridge.

Feeney, D. 1984. The reconciliations of Juno. *CQ* 34: 179–94.

———. 1986. Stat magni nominis umbra: Lucan on the greatness of Pompeius Magnus. *CQ* 36: 239–43.

———. 1991. *The gods in epic: Poets and critics of the classical tradition.* Oxford.

———. 1992a. "Shall I compare thee . . . ?" Catullus 68 and the limits of analogy. In *Author and audience in Latin literature,* ed. A. J. Woodman and J. Powell, 33–44. Cambridge.

———. 1992b. *Si licet et fas est:* Ovid's *Fasti* and the problem of free speech under the principate. In Powell 1992, 1–25.

———. 1993. Horace and the Greek lyric poets. In *Horace 2000, a celebration: Essays for the bimillennium,* ed. N. Rudd, 41–63. London.

———. 1998. *Literature and religion at Rome: Cultures, contexts, and beliefs.* Cambridge.

———. 1999. *Mea tempora:* Patterning of time in the *Metamorphoses.* In Hardie, Barchiesi, and Hinds 1999, 13–30.

———. 2002. The odiousness of comparisons: Horace on literary history and the limitations of synkrisis. In *Horace and Greek literary poetry,* ed. M. Paschalis, 7–18. Rethymnon.

Feldherr, A. 1998. *Spectacle and society in Livy's History.* Berkeley and Los Angeles.

———. 2003. Cicero and the invention of "literary" history. In Eigler et al. 2003, 196–212.

Felperin, H. 1990. *The uses of the canon: Elizabethan literature and contemporary theory.* Oxford.

Ferguson, N. 2003. *Empire: How Britain made the modern world.* London.

Fink, R. O., A. S. Hoey, and W. F. Snyder. 1940. *The Feriale Duranum.* New Haven.

Finley, M. I. 1973. *The ancient economy.* London.

———. 1975. *The use and abuse of history.* New York.

———. 1985. *Ancient history: Evidence and models.* London.

Fitzgerald, W. 1995. *Catullan provocations: Lyric poetry and the drama of position.* Berkeley and Los Angeles.

Flower, H. I. 1991. Herodotus and Delphic traditions about Croesus. In *Georgica: Classical studies in honour of George Cawkwell,* ed. M. A. Flower and M. Toher, 57–77. London.

———. 1995. *Fabulae Praetextae* in context: When were plays on contemporary subjects performed in Republican Rome? *CQ* 45: 170–90.

———. 2003. "Memories" of Marcellus: History and memory in Roman Republican culture. In Eigler et al. 2003, 39–52.

Flower, M. A. 1994. *Theopompus of Chios: History and rhetoric in the fourth century B.C.* Oxford.

Flower, M. A., and J. Marincola. 2002. *Herodotus: Histories Book IX.* Cambridge.

Flusser, D. 1972. The four empires in the Fourth Sibyl and in the Book of Daniel. *Israel Oriental Studies* 2: 148–75.

Ford, A. 1992. *Homer: The poetry of the past.* Ithaca and London.

Fordyce, C. J. 1961. *Catullus.* Oxford.

Fornara, C. 1983. *The nature of history in ancient Greece and Rome.* Berkeley and Los Angeles.

Forsythe, G. 2005. *A critical history of early Rome: From prehistory to the First Punic War.* Berkeley and Los Angeles.

Fortenbaugh, W. W., and E. Schütrumpf, eds. 2001. *Dicaearchus of Messana: Text, translation, and discussion.* Rutgers University Studies in Classical Humanities, Vol. 10. New Brunswick and London.

Fowler, D. 2000. *Roman constructions: Readings in postmodern Latin.* Oxford.

Fowler, R. L. 2000. *Early Greek mythography.* Vol. 1, *Text and introduction.* Oxford.

Fox, M. 1996. *Roman historical myths: The regal period in Augustan literature.* Oxford.

Fraschetti, A. 1990. *Roma e il principe.* Rome and Bari.

Fraser, P. M. 1970. Eratosthenes of Cyrene. *PBA* 56: 175–207.

———. 1972. *Ptolemaic Alexandria.* 3 vols. Oxford.

Frier, B. W. 1975. Licinius Macer and the *consules suffecti* of 444 B.C. *TAPhA* 105: 79–97.

———. 1999. *Libri annales pontificum maximorum: The origins of the annalistic tradition.*[2] Ann Arbor.

Fukuyama, F. 1999. It could have been a German century. *Wall Street Journal*, December 31.

Fyfe, H. 1983. An analysis of Seneca's *Medea*. In Boyle 1983, 77–93.

Gabba, E. 1991. *Dionysius and the history of archaic Rome.* Berkeley and Los Angeles.

———. 2000. *Roma arcaica: Storia e storiografia.* Rome.

———. 2001. Ancora sulle origini di Roma. *Athenaeum* 89: 589–91.

Gaisser, J. H. 1995. Threads in the labyrinth: Competing views and voices in Catullus 64. *AJPh* 116: 579–616.

Gale, M. R. 2000. *Virgil on the nature of things: The* Georgics, *Lucretius, and the didactic tradition.* Cambridge.

Galinsky, K. 1996. *Augustan culture: An interpretive introduction.* Princeton.

———, ed. 2005. *The Cambridge companion to the age of Augustus.* Cambridge.

Gallia, A. Forthcoming. Reassessing the "Cumaean Chronicle": Greek chronology and Roman history in Dionysius of Halicarnassus.

Gamble, C. 1986. Hunter-gatherers and the origin of states. In *States in history*, ed. J. A. Hall, 22–47. Oxford.

Garbini, G. 1980. Gli "Annali" di Tiro e la storiografia fenicia. In *Oriental studies presented to Benedikt S.J. Esserlin*, ed. R. Y. Ebied and M. L. Young, 114–27. Leiden.

Gatz, B. 1967. *Weltalter, goldene Zeit und sinnverwandte Vorstellungen.* Hildesheim.

Gauthier, P. 1966. Le parallèle Himère-Salamine au Ve et au IVe siècle av. J.C. *REA* 68: 5–32.

Gee, E. 2000. *Ovid, Aratus, and Augustus: Astronomy in Ovid's* Fasti. Cambridge.

———. 2001. Cicero's astronomy. *CQ* 51: 520–36.

Geiger, J. 1985. *Cornelius Nepos and ancient political biography.* Stuttgart.

Gell, A. 1992. *The anthropology of time: Cultural constructions of temporal maps and images.* Oxford.

Gellner, E. 1983. *Nations and nationalism.* Ithaca and London.

Gera, D. L. 2003. *Ancient Greek ideas on speech, language, and civilization.* Cambridge.

Geus, K. 2002. *Erastosthenes von Kyrene: Studien zur hellenistischen Kultur- und Wissenschaftsgeschichte.* Munich.

Gibson, B. J. 1995. Catullus 1.5–7. *CQ* 45: 569–73.

Gibson, R. K. 2003. *Ovid: Ars amatoria Book 3.* Cambridge.

Gildenhard, I. 2003. The "annalist" before the annalists: Ennius and his *Annales*. In Eigler et al. 2003, 93–114.

Gildenhard, I., and A. Zissos. 2004. Ovid's "Hecale": Deconstructing Athens in the *Metamorphoses*. *JRS* 94: 47–72.

Ginsburg, J. 1981. *Tradition and theme in the* Annals of Tacitus. New York.

Ginzel, F. K. 1906. *Handbuch der mathematischen und technischen Chronologie: Das Zeitrechnungswesen der Völker.* 3 vols. Leipzig.

Godwin, J. 1995. *Catullus: Poems 61–68.* Warminster.

Goldberg, S. M. 1995. *Epic in Republican Rome*. Oxford.

Goldhill, S. 1991. *The poet's voice: Essays on poetics and Greek literature*. Cambridge.

Gomme, A. W. 1945. *A historical commentary on Thucydides*. Vol. 1. Oxford.

Gomme, A. W., A. Andrewes, and K. J. Dover. 1970. *A historical commentary on Thucydides*. Vol. 4. Oxford.

Gordon, R. L., ed. 1981. *Myth, religion, and society*. Cambridge.

Gosden, C. 1994. *Social being and time*. Oxford.

Gott, J. R. 2001. *Time travel in Einstein's universe: The physical possibilities of travel through time*. Boston and New York.

Gould, J. 1989. *Herodotus*. New York.

Gould, S. J. 1987. *Time's arrow, time's cycle: Myth and metaphor in the discovery of geological time*. Cambridge, Mass.

Gow, A. S. F., and D. L. Page. 1968. *The Greek anthology: The garland of Philip*. 2 vols. Cambridge.

Gowing, A. 2005. *Empire and memory: The representation of the Roman Republic in imperial culture*. Cambridge.

Graf, F. 1996. Römische Kultaitia und die Konstruktion religiöser Vergangenheit. In *Retrospektive: Konzepte von Vergangenheit in der griechisch-römischen Antike*, ed. M. Flashar, H.-J. Gehrke, and E. Heinrich, 125–35. Munich.

———. 1997. *Der Lauf des rollenden Jahres: Zeit und Kalender in Rom*. Stuttgart and Leipzig.

Grafton, A. 1993. *Joseph Scaliger: A study in the history of classical scholarship*. Vol. 2, *Historical chronology*. Oxford.

———. 1995. Tradition and technique in historical chronology. In *Ancient history and the antiquarian: Essays in memory of Arnaldo Momigliano*, ed. M. H. Crawford and C. R. Ligota, 15–31. London.

———. 2003. Dating history: The Renaissance and the reformation of chronology. *Daedalus* 132: 74–85.

Grafton, A. T., and N. M. Swerdlow. 1985. Technical chronology and astrological history in Varro, Censorinus, and others. *CQ* 35: 454–65.

———. 1986. Greek chronology in Roman epic: The calendrical date of the fall of Troy in the *Aeneid*. *CQ* 36: 212–18.

———. 1998. Calendar dates and ominous days in ancient historiography. *JWI* 51: 14–42.

Grafton, A. T., and M. Williams. 2006. *Researching revelation: Origen, Eusebius, and the library of Caesarea*. Cambridge, Mass. and London.

Grandazzi, A. 1997. *The foundation of Rome: Myth and history*. Trans. J. M. Todd. Ithaca and London.

Gransden, K. W. 1976. *Virgil: Aeneid Book VIII*. Cambridge.

Grant, M. 1950. *Roman anniversary issues: An exploratory study of the numismatic and medallic commemoration of anniversary years 49 B.C.–A.D. 375.* Cambridge.

Gratwick, A. S. 1979. Sundials, parasites, and girls from Boeotia. *CQ* 29: 308–23.

———. 1982. Ennius' *Annales.* In *The Cambridge history of classical literature,* vol. 2, *Latin literature,* ed. E. J. Kenney and W. V. Clausen, 60–76. Cambridge.

Green, P. 1997. "These fragments have I shored against my ruins": Apollonios Rhodios and the social revalidation of myth for a new age. In Cartledge, Garnsey, and Gruen 1997, 35–71.

Greenway, D. E. 1999. Dates in history: Chronology and memory. *Historical research* 72: 127–39.

Griffin, J. 1977. The epic cycle and the uniqueness of Homer. *JHS* 97: 39–53.

———. 1997. Cult and personality in Horace. *JRS* 87: 54–69.

Griffith, M. 1999. *Sophocles: Antigone.* Cambridge.

Griffiths, A. 1998. Where did early Roman history come from? http://www.ucl.ac.uk:80/GrandLat/people/griffiths/collatin.htm

Grimal, P. 1951. Énée à Rome et le triomphe d'Octave. *REA* 53: 51–61.

Grotefend, G. J. 1845. Miscellen. *RhM* 3: 152–53.

Gruen, E. S. 1984. *The Hellenistic world and the coming of Rome.* Berkeley and Los Angeles.

———. 1992. *Culture and national identity in Republican Rome.* Ithaca and London.

———. 1998. Rome and the myth of Alexander. In *Ancient history in a modern university,* ed. T. W. Hillard, R. A. Kearsley, C. E. V. Nixon, and A. M. Nobbs, 178–91. Grand Rapids and Cambridge.

Gurval, R. A. 1995. *Actium and Augustus: The politics and emotions of civil war.* Ann Arbor.

Habinek, T. 1998. *The politics of Latin literature: Writing, identity, and empire in ancient Rome.* Princeton.

———. 2002. Ovid and empire. In *The Cambridge companion to Ovid,* ed. P. Hardie, 46–61. Cambridge.

Habinek, T., and A. Schiesaro, eds. 1997. *The Roman cultural revolution.* Cambridge.

Hall, E. 1989. *Inventing the barbarian: Greek self-definition through tragedy.* Oxford.

Hall, J. 2004. How "Greek" were the early western Greeks? In Lomas 2004, 35–54.

Hanell, K. 1946. *Das altrömische eponyme Amt.* Lund.

———. 1956. Zur Problematik der älteren römischen Geschichtsschreibung. In *Histoire et historiens dans l'antiquité: Entretiens sur l'antiquité classique* 4: 149–84. Vandoeuvres-Geneva.

Hannah, R. 2005. *Greek and Roman calendars: Constructions of time in the classical world.* London.

Hardie, A. 2002. The *Georgics,* the mysteries, and the Muses at Rome. *PCPhS* 48: 175–208.

Hardie, P. 1986. *Virgil's* Aeneid: *Cosmos and imperium.* Oxford.

———. 1990. Ovid's Theban history: The first "anti-*Aeneid*"? *CQ* 40: 224–35.

———. 1991. The Janus episode in Ovid's *Fasti. MD* 26: 47–64.

———. 1992. Augustan poets and the mutability of Rome. In Powell 1992, 59–82.

———. 1993. *The epic successors of Virgil: A study in the dynamics of a tradition.* Cambridge.

———. 1994. *Virgil Aeneid: Book IX.* Cambridge.

Hardie, P., A. Barchiesi, and S. Hinds, eds. 1999. *Ovidian transformations: Essays on Ovid's* Metamorphoses *and its reception.* Cambridge.

Harrell, S. 1998. Cultural geography of East and West: Literary representations of archaic Sicilian tyranny and cult. PhD diss., Princeton University.

Harris, W. V. 1971. *Rome in Etruria and Umbria.* Oxford.

Harrison, S. J. 2005. Decline and nostalgia. In *A companion to Latin literature*, ed. S. J. Harrison, 287–99. Oxford.

Harrison, S. J., and S. J. Heyworth. 1998. Notes on the text and interpretation of Catullus. *PCPhS* 44: 85–109.

Harrison, T. 2000a. *Divinity and history: The religion of Herodotus.* Oxford.

———. 2000b. Sicily in the Athenian imagination: Thucydides and the Persian Wars. In *Sicily from Aeneas to Augustus: New approaches in archaeology and history*, ed. C. Smith and J. Serrati, 84–96. Edinburgh.

Hassig, R. 2001. *Time, history, and belief in Aztec and colonial Mexico.* Austin.

Haubold, J. 2002. Greek epic: A Near Eastern genre? *PCPhS* 48: 1–19.

Hedrick, C. W. 2002. The prehistory of Greek chronography. In *Oikistes: Studies in constitutions, colonies, and military power in the ancient world, offered in honor of A. J. Graham*, ed. V. B. Gorman and E. W. Robinson, 13–32. Leiden.

Heilmann, W. 1989. "Goldene Zeit" und geschichtliche Zeit im Dialogus de oratoribus. *Gymnasium* 96: 385–405.

Heinberg, R. 1989. *Memories and visions of paradise: Exploring the universal myth of a lost golden age.* Los Angeles.

Helm, R. 1956. *Die Chronik des Hieronymus. Hieronymi Chronicon.* Die Griechischen christlichen Schriftsteller der ersten Jahrhunderte, vol. 47. Berlin.

Henderson, J. 1998. *Fighting for Rome: Poets and Caesars, history, and civil war.* Cambridge.

Herman, A. 1997. *The idea of decline in Western history.* New York and London.

Herz, P. 1978. Kaiserfeste der Prinzipatszeit. *ANRW* 2.16.2: 1135–1200.

Heydenreich, T. 1970. *Tadel und Lob der Seefahrt: Das Nachleben eines antiken Themas in den romanischen Literaturen.* Heidelberg.

Heyworth, S. J. 1988. Horace's second *Epode. AJPh* 109: 71–85.

Higbie, C. 2003. *The Lindian chronicle and the Greek creation of their past.* Oxford.

Hillen, H. J. 2003. *Von Aeneas zu Romulus: Die Legenden von der Gründung Roms.* Düsseldorf.

Hinds, S. 1987. *The metamorphosis of Persephone: Ovid and the self-conscious muse.* Cambridge.

———. 1992. Arma in Ovid's *Fasti. Arethusa* 25: 81–149.

———. 1998. *Allusion and intertext: Dynamics of appropriation in Roman poetry.* Cambridge.

———. 1999. After exile: Time and teleology from *Metamorphoses* to *Ibis.* In Hardie, Barchiesi, and Hinds 1999, 48–67.

———. 2005a. Dislocations of Ovidian time. In *Zur Poetik der Zeit in Augusteischer Dichtung,* ed. J. P. Schwindt, 203–30. Heidelberg.

———. 2005b. Venus, Varro, and the *vates:* Toward the limits of etymologizing interpretation. *Dictynna* 3. http://www.univ-lille3.fr/portail/index.php?page = Dictynna.

Hobsbawm, E. 1994. *Age of extremes: The short twentieth century, 1914–1991.* London.

Hobsbawm, E., and T. Ranger, eds. 1983. *The invention of tradition.* Cambridge.

Holford-Strevens, L. 2003. *Aulus Gellius: An Antonine scholar and his achievements.*[2] Oxford.

———. 2005. *The history of time: A very short introduction.* Oxford.

Hölkeskamp, K.-J. 2004. *Senatus populusque romanus: Die politische Kultur der Republik—Dimensionen und Deutungen.* Stuttgart.

Hollis, A. S. 1977. *Ovid Ars amatoria: Book I.* Oxford.

Hopkins, K. 1991. From violence to blessing: Symbols and rituals in ancient Rome. In *City states in classical antiquity and medieval Italy,* ed. A. Molho, K. Raaflaub, and J. Emlen, 479–98. Ann Arbor.

Horden, P., and N. Purcell. 2000. *The corrupting sea: A study of Mediterranean history.* Oxford.

Hornblower, J. 1981. *Hieronymus of Cardia.* Oxford.

Hornblower, S. 2001. Epic and epiphanies: Herodotus and the "New Simonides." In Boedeker and Sider 2001, 135–47.

Horsfall, N. 1972. Varro and Caesar: Three chronological problems. *BICS* 19: 120–28.

———. 1973–74. Dido in the light of history. *PVS* 13: 1–13.

———. 1974. Virgil's Roman chronography: A reconsideration. *CQ* 24: 111–15.

———. 1976. Virgil, history, and the Roman tradition. *Prudentia* 8: 73–89.

———. 1981. Virgil's conquest of chaos. *Antichthon* 15: 141–50.

———. 1982a. Prose and mime. In *The Cambridge history of classical literature,* vol. 2, *Latin literature,* ed. E. J. Kenney and W. V. Clausen, 286–94. Cambridge.

———. 1982b. Virgil's 2000th deathday: 1981 or 1982? *Omnibus* 3: 13.

———. 1989a. Aeneas the colonist. *Vergilius* 35: 8–27.

―――. 1989b. *Cornelius Nepos: A selection, including the Lives of Cato and Atticus.* Oxford.

―――. 1991. Review of *Collectanea*, by W. Wimmel. *RFIC* 119: 354–57.

―――. 1993. Empty shelves on the Palatine. *G&R* 40: 58–67.

―――. 1994. The prehistory of Latin poetry: Some problems of method. *RFIC* 122: 50–75.

―――. 1995. *A companion to the study of Virgil.* Brill.

―――. 1997. Criteria for the dating of Calpurnius Siculus. *RFIC* 125: 166–96.

―――. 2000. *Virgil, Aeneid 7: A commentary.* Leiden.

―――. 2003. *The culture of the Roman plebs.* London.

―――. 2006. *Virgil, Aeneid 3: A commentary.* Leiden.

Housman, A. E. 1927. *M. Annaei Lucani Belli civilis libri decem.*[2] Oxford.

How, W. W., and J. Wells. 1912. *A commentary on Herodotus.* Oxford.

Howie, J. G. 1998. Thucydides and Pindar: The *Archaeology* and *Nemean 7. PLLS* 10: 75–130.

Hubaux, J. 1945. *Les grands mythes de Rome.* Paris.

―――. 1958. *Rome et Véies: Recherches sur la chronologie légendaire du moyen âge romain.* Paris.

Huber, L. 1965. Herodots Homerverständnis. In *Synusia: Festgabe für Wolfgang Schadewaldt*, ed. H. Flashar and K. Gaiser, 29–52. Pfullingen.

Hughes, J. D. 1994. *Pan's travail: Environmental problems of the ancient Greeks and Romans.* Baltimore and London.

Hunter, V. 1982. *Past and process in Herodotus and Thucydides.* Princeton.

Jackson, S. 1997. Argo: The first ship? *RhM* 140: 249–57.

Jacoby, F. 1902. *Apollodors Chronik.* Berlin.

―――. 1904. *Das Marmor Parium.* Berlin.

―――. 1949. *Atthis: The local chronicles of ancient Athens.* Oxford.

―――. 1954. *Die Fragmente der griechischen Historiker: Dritte Teil: (b) Supplement.* 2 vols. Leiden.

Jaeger, M. 2003. Livy and the fall of Syracuse. In Eigler et al. 2003, 213–34.

James, P., et al. 1991. *Centuries of darkness: A challenge to the conventional chronology of Old World archaeology.* London.

Janan, M. 1994. *"When the lamp is shattered": Desire and narrative in Catullus.* Carbondale and Edwardsville.

Jaspers, K. 1953. *The origin and goal of history.* New Haven.

Jocelyn, H. D. 1967. *The tragedies of Ennius.* Cambridge.

―――. 1972. The poems of Quintus Ennius. *ANRW* 1.2: 987–1026.

Johnston, W. M. 1991. *Celebrations: The cult of anniveraries in Europe and the United States.* New Brunswick, N.J.

Kallet-Marx, R. M. 1995 *Hegemony to empire, The development of the Roman imperium in the East*. Berkeley and Los Angeles.

Kermode, F. 1967. *The sense of an ending: Studies in the theory of fiction*. New York.

Kidd, C. 2004. Hybridity. Review of Bayly 2004. *London Review of Books*, 2 September. 14–15.

Kidd, D. 1997. *Aratus: Phaenomena*. Cambridge.

Kidd, I. G. 1988. *Posidonius, Volume II. The commentary*. Cambridge.

Klodt, C. 2001. *Bescheidene Grösse: Die Herrschergestalt, der Kaiserpalast und die Stadt Rom: Literarische Reflexionen monarchischer Selbstdarstellung*. Göttingen.

Knapp, R. 1986. Cantabria and the *era consularis. Epigraphica* 48: 115–46.

Konstan, D. 1977. *Catullus' indictment of Rome: The meaning of Catullus 64*. Amsterdam.

Kraus, C. S. 1994a. *Livy Ab urbe condita Book VI*. Cambridge.

———. 1994b. "No second Troy": Topoi and refoundation in Livy, Book V. *TAPhA* 124: 267–89.

———. 1998. Repetition and empire in the *Ab urbe condita*. In *Style and tradition: Studies in honor of Wendell Clausen*, ed. P. Knox and C. Foss, 264–83. Stuttgart and Leipzig.

———, ed. 1999. *The limits of historiography: Genre and narrative in ancient historical texts*. Leiden.

Kraus, C. S., and A. J. Woodman. 1997. *Latin historians*. Oxford.

Krischer, T. 1965. Herodots Prooemium. *Hermes* 93: 159–67.

Kroll, W. 1922. *Catull*. Stuttgart.

Kubusch, K. 1986. *Aurea saecula: Mythos und Geschichte: Untersuchungen eines Motivs in der antiken Literatur bis Ovid*. Frankfurt.

Kuhrt, A. 1987. Berossus' *Babyloniaka* and Seleucid rule in Babylonia. In Kuhrt and Sherwin-White 1987, 32–56.

Kuhrt, A., and S. Sherwin-White, eds. 1987. *Hellenism in the East: The interaction of Greek and non-Greek civilizations from Syria to Central Asia after Alexander*. London.

Kuttner, A. 1999. Culture and history at Pompey's museum. *TAPhA* 129: 343–73.

Labate, M. 1991. Città morte, città future: Un tema della poesia augustea. *Maia* 43: 167–84.

Lacey, W. K. 1979. *Summi fastigii vocabulum:* The story of a title. *JRS* 69: 28–34.

Lachmann, K. 1848. *Die Schriften der römischen Feldmesser*. Vol. 1. Berlin.

Lamberton, R. 1997. Plutarch and the Romanizations of Athens. In *The Romanization of Athens*, ed. M. C. Hoff and S. I. Rotroff, 151–60. Oxford.

Lane Fox, R. 1973. *Alexander the Great*. London.

La Penna, A. 1977. *L'integrazione difficile: Un profilo di Properzio*. Turin.

Laurence, R., and C. Smith. 1995–96. Ritual, time, and power in ancient Rome. *Accordia Research Journal* 6: 133–51.

Le Goff, J. 1960. Au moyen âge: Temps de l'Église et temps du marchand. *Annales* 15: 417–33.

Lehoux, D. Forthcoming. *Astronomy, weather, and calendars in the ancient world.*

Leschhorn, W. 1993. *Antike Ären: Zeitrechnung, Politik und Geschichte im Schwarzmeerraum und in Kleinasien nördlich des Tauros.* Stuttgart.

Leuze, O. 1909. *Die römische Jahrzählung: Ein Versuch ihre geschichtliche Entwicklung zu Ermitteln.* Tübingen.

———. 1911. Das synchronistische Kapitel des Gellius (*Noct. Att.* XVII 21). *RhM* 66: 237–74.

Levene, D. S., and D. P. Nelis, eds. 2002. *Clio and the poets: Augustan poetry and the traditions of ancient historiography.* Leiden.

Linderski, J. 1985. The "Libri Reconditi." *HSCPh* 89: 207–34.

———. 1997–98. Review of Rüpke 1995b. *CJ* 93: 464–68.

Livrea, E. 1973. *Apollonii Rhodii Argonauticon liber quartus.* Florence.

Lloyd, G. E. R. 1979. *Magic, reason and experience: Studies in the origins and development of Greek science.* Cambridge.

———. 1987. *The revolutions of wisdom: Studies in the claims and practice of ancient Greek science.* Berkeley and Los Angeles.

Lomas, K., ed. 2004. *Greek identity in the western Mediterranean: Papers in honour of Brian Shefton.* Leiden.

Long, A. A., and D. N. Sedley. 1987. *The Hellenistic philosophers.* 2 vols. Cambridge.

Lott, J. B. 2004. *The neighborhoods of Augustan Rome.* Cambridge.

Lovejoy, A. O., and G. Boas. 1935. *Primitivism and related ideas in antiquity.* Baltimore.

Lowenthal, D. 1985. *The past is a foreign country.* Cambridge.

Lowrie, M. 1997. *Horace's narrative* Odes. Oxford.

Luraghi, N., ed. 2001. *The historian's craft in the age of Herodotus.* Oxford.

Lynch, K. 1972. *What time is this place?* Cambridge, Mass.

Lyne, R. O. A. M. 1989. *Words and the poet: Characteristic techniques of style in Vergil's Aeneid.* Oxford.

Ma, J. 1999. *Antiochos III and the cities of Asia Minor.* Oxford.

MacCormack, S. 1990. *Loca sancta:* The organization of sacred topography in late antiquity. In *The blessings of pilgrimage,* ed. R. Ousterhout, 7–40. Urbana.

Macey, S. L. 1991. *Time: A bibliographical guide.* New York.

MacLean, G., D. Landry, and J. P. Ward, eds. 1999. *The country and the city revisited: England and the politics of culture, 1550–1850.* Cambridge.

Macleod, C. 1979. Horace and the Sibyl. *CQ* 29: 220–21.

Magdelain, A. 1969. Praetor Maximus et Comitiatus Maximus. *Iura* 20: 257–86.

Malamud, M. A., and D. T. McGuire 1993. Flavian variant: Myth: Valerius' *Argonautica*. In *Roman Epic*, ed. A. J. Boyle, 192–217. London.

Malkin, I. 1998. *The returns of Odysseus: Colonization and ethnicity*. Berkeley and Los Angeles.

Maltby, R. 1991. *A lexicon of ancient Latin etymologies*. Leeds.

———. 2002. *Tibullus: Elegies*. Leeds.

Mancuso, U. 1909. Il sincronismo fra le battiglie d'Imera e delle Termopili secondo Timeo. *RFIC* 37: 548–54.

Mankin, D. 1995. *Horace: Epodes*. Cambridge.

Mann, C. C. 2005. *1491: New revelations of the Americas before Columbus*. New York.

Marincic, M. 2001. Der Weltaltermythos in Catullus Peleus-Epos (*C.* 64), der Kleine Herakles (Theokr. *Id.* 24) und der römische <Messianismus> Vergils. *Hermes* 129: 484–504.

Marincola, J. 1997. *Authority and tradition in ancient historiography*. Cambridge.

———. 2005. Marcellus at Syracuse (Livy XXV,24,11–15): A historian reflects. In *Studies in Latin literature and Roman history XII*, ed. C. Deroux, 219–29. Brussels.

Martin, R. H., and A. J. Woodman. 1989. *Tacitus: Annals Book IV*. Cambridge.

Martindale, C. 1993. *Redeeming the text: Latin poetry and the hermeneutics of reception*. Cambridge.

Mattern, S. P. 1999. *Rome and the enemy: Imperial strategy in the principate*. Berkeley and Los Angeles.

Mayer, R. 2001. *Tacitus: Dialogus de oratoribus*. Cambridge.

Mazzarino, S. 1966. *Il pensiero storico classico*. 2 vols. Bari.

Mazzoli, G. 2001. Quali preistorie? Catullo, Lucrezio. In *L'antico degli antichi*, ed. G. Cajani and D. Lanza, 133–40. Palumbo.

McKeown, J. C. 1998. *Ovid: Amores*. Vol. 3, *A commentary on Book two*. Leeds.

McKie, D. 1984. The horrible and ultimate Britons: Catullus 11.11. *PCPhS* 30: 74–78.

Meadows, A., and J. Williams. 2001. Moneta and the monuments: Coinage and politics in Republican Rome. *JRS* 91: 27–49.

Meister, K. 1989–90. The role of Timaeus in Greek historiography. *SCI* 10: 55–65.

Mendels, D. 1981. The five empires: A note on a propagandistic *topos*. *AJPh* 102: 330–37.

Mendelssohn, L. 1876. Quaestionum Eratosthenicarum Caput Primum, quod est de mortis anno Sophoclis et Euripidis. *Acta Societatis Philologae Lipsiensis* 2: 159–96.

Michels, A. K. 1967. *The calendar of the Roman Republic*. Princeton.

Mikalson, J. D. 1996. Birthday. *OCD*³, 244.

———. 2003. *Herodotus and religion in the Persian Wars*. Chapel Hill.

Miles, G. B. 1986. The cycle of Roman history in Livy's first pentad. *AJPh* 107: 1–33.

———. 1995. *Livy: Reconstructing early Rome*. Ithaca and London.

Millar, F. 1997. Hellenistic history in a Near Eastern perspective: The Book of Daniel. In Cartledge, Garnsey, and Gruen 1997, 89–104.

———. 2000. The first revolution: Imperator Caesar, 36–28 B.C. In *La Révolution romaine après Ronald Syme: Entretiens sur l'antiquité classique* 46: 1–38. Vandoeuvres-Geneva.

———. 2002. *Rome, the Greek world, and the East.* Vol. 1, *The Roman Republic and the Augustan revolution,* ed. H. M. Cotton and G. M. Rogers. Chapel Hill and London.

Miller, J. F. 2002. The *Fasti:* Style, structure, time. In Boyd 2002, 167–96.

Miller, S. G. 1975. The date of Olympic festivals. *MDAI(A)* 90: 215–31.

Mirhady, D. C. 2001. Dicaearchus of Messana: The sources, text, and translation. In Fortenbaugh and Schütrumpf 2001, 1–142.

Moles, J. 1983. Fate, Apollo, and M. Junius Brutus. *AJPh* 104: 249–56.

———. 1984. Review of Woodman 1983. *JRS* 74: 242–44.

———. 1993a. Livy's Preface. *PCPhS* 39: 141–68.

———. 1993b. Truth and untruth in Herodotus and Thucydides. In *Lies and fiction in the ancient world,* ed. C. Gill and T. P. Wiseman, 88–121. Exeter.

———. 2001. A false dilemma: Thucydides' *History* and historicism. In *Texts, ideas, and the classics: Scholarship, theory, and classical literature,* ed. S. J. Harrison, 195–219. Oxford.

Möller, A. 2001. The beginning of chronography: Hellanicus' *Hiereiai.* In Luraghi 2001, 241–62.

———. 2003. Review of Geus 2002. *BMCR* 2003.05.14.

———. 2004. Greek chronographic traditions about the first Olympic games. In Rosen 2004, 169–84.

Möller, A., and N. Luraghi. 1995. Time in the writing of history: Perceptions and structures. *Storia della Storiografia* 28: 3–15.

Momigliano, A. 1977a. Athens in the third century B.C.E. and the discovery of Rome in the *Histories* of Timaeus of Tauromenium. In *Essays in Ancient and Modern Historiography,* 37–66. Oxford.

———. 1977b. Time in ancient historiography. In *Essays in ancient and modern historiography,* 179–204. Oxford.

———. 1987. *On Pagans, Jews, and Christians.* Hanover, N.H.

———. 1989. The origins of Rome. *CAH*[2] 7.2: 52–112.

———. 1990. *The classical foundations of modern historiography.* Berkeley and Los Angeles.

Mommsen, T. 1859. *Die römische Chronologie.*[2] Berlin.

Morello, R. 2002. Livy's Alexander digression (9.17–19): Counterfactuals and apologetics. *JRS* 92: 62–85.

Morgan, L. 1998. Tacitus, *Annals* 4.70: An unappreciated pun. *CQ* 48: 585–87.

Morris, I. 1997. Periodization and the heroes: Inventing a dark age. In *Inventing ancient culture: Historicism, periodization, and the ancient world*, ed. M. Golden and P. Toohey, 96–131. London and New York.

Morris, S. P. 1992. *Daidalos and the origins of Greek art*. Princeton.

Mosshammer, A. A. 1979. *The* Chronicle *of Eusebius and Greek chronographic tradition*. Lewisburg and London.

Most, G. W. 1997. Hesiod's myth of the five (or three or four) races. *PCPhS* 43: 104–27.

Moyer, I. S. 2002. Herodotus and an Egyptian mirage: The genealogies of the Theban priests. *JHS* 122: 70–90.

Mueller, H.-F. 2002. The extinction of the Potitii and the sacred history of Augustan Rome. In Levene and Nelis 2002, 313–29.

Munich, M. 2003. The texture of the past: Nostalgia and Catullus 64. In *Being there together: Essays in honor of Michael C. J. Putnam*, ed. P. Thibodeau and H. Haskell, 43–65. Afton, Mich.

Munson, R. V. 2001. *Telling wonders: Ethnographic and political discourse in the work of Herodotus*. Ann Arbor.

Munz, P. 1977. *The shapes of time: A new look at the philosophy of history*. Middleton, Conn.

Münzer, F. 1905. Atticus als Geschichtschreiber. *Hermes* 40: 50–100.

Murgia, C. E. 2000. "The most desperate textual crux" in Lucretius—5.1442. *CPh* 95: 304–17.

Murphy, T. 2004. *Pliny the Elder's* Natural history: *The empire in the encyclopedia*. Oxford.

Murray, L. 1991. *Collected poems*. Carcanet Press: Manchester.

Murray, O. 2001. Herodotus and oral history. In Luraghi 2001, 16–44. (Originally published in 1987.)

Mynors, R. A. B. 1990. *Virgil: Georgics*. Oxford.

Newlands, C. E. 1995. *Playing with time: Ovid and the* Fasti. Ithaca and London.

Nicolai, R. 2001. Thucydides' Archaeology: Between epic and oral traditions. In Luraghi 2001, 263–85.

Nicolet, C. 1991. *Space, geography, and politics in the early Roman empire*. Ann Arbor.

Nilsson, M. P. 1920. Saeculares Ludi. *RE* 2R 1A.2: 1696–1720.

Nisbet, R. G. M. 1978a. Notes on the text of Catullus. *PCPhS* 24: 92–115.

———. 1978b. Virgil's fourth *Eclogue*: Easterners and Westerners. *BICS* 25: 59–78.

———. 2002. A wine-jar for Messalla: *Carmina* 3.21. In *Traditions and contexts in the poetry of Horace*, ed. T. Woodman and D. Feeney, 80–92. Cambridge.

Nisbet, R. G. M., and M. Hubbard. 1970. *A commentary on Horace: Odes Book I*. Oxford.

———. 1978. *A commentary on Horace: Odes Book II*. Oxford.

Nisbet, R. G. M., and N. Rudd. 2004. *A commentary on Horace: Odes Book III.* Oxford.

Nixon, C. E. V. and B. S. Rodgers. 1994. *In praise of later Roman emperors: The Panegyrici Latini.* Berkeley.

Norden, E. 1927. *P. Vergilius Maro: Aeneis Buch VI.*³ Leipzig and Berlin.

North, J. 1989. Religion in Republican Rome. *CAH* ² 7.2: 573–624.

———. 1995. Religion and rusticity. In *Urban society in Roman Italy,* ed. T. Cornell and K. Lomas, 135–50. New York.

Oakley, S. P. 1997–98. *A commentary on Livy Books VI–X.* Vols. 1–2. Oxford.

Ogilvie, R. M. 1965. *A commentary on Livy Books 1–5.* Oxford.

O'Gorman, E. 2000. *Irony and misreading in the* Annals *of Tacitus.* Cambridge.

O'Hara, J. J. 1994. They might be giants: Inconsistency and indeterminacy in Vergil's war in Italy. *Colby Quarterly* 30: 206–26.

———. Forthcoming. *Inconsistency in Roman epic: Studies in Catullus, Lucretius, Vergil, Ovid, and Lucan.* Cambridge.

Osborne, R. 1998. *Archaic and classical Greek art.* Oxford.

Pais, E. 1905. *Ancient legends of Roman history.* Trans. M. E. Cosenza. New York.

Parker, R. 1996. *Athenian religion: A history.* Oxford.

Pasco-Pranger, M. 2000. *Vates operosus:*Vatic poetics and antiquarianism in Ovid's *Fasti. CW* 93: 275–91.

———. 2006. *Founding the year: Ovid's* Fasti *and the Roman calendar.* Leiden.

Paul, G. M. 1982. *Urbs capta:* Sketch of an ancient literary motif. *Phoenix* 36: 144–55.

Pearson, L. 1975. Myth and archaeologia in Italy and Sicily—Timaeus and his predecessors. *YCS* 24: 171–95.

———. 1987. *The Greek historians of the West: Timaeus and his predecessors.* Atlanta.

Pease, A. S. 1955–58. *M. Tulli Ciceronis De natura deorum.* Cambridge, Mass.

Pelling, C. 1999. Epilogue. In Kraus 1999, 325–60.

———. 2002. *Plutarch and history: Eighteen studies.* London.

Perkell, C. 2002. The Golden Age and its contradictions in the poetry of Vergil. *Vergilius* 48: 3–39.

Pfeiffer, R. 1949. *Callimachus.* Oxford.

———. 1968. *History of classical scholarship: From the beginnings to the end of the Hellenistic age.* Oxford.

Pfligersdorffer, G. 1982. Fremdes und eigenes in Senecas 90: Brief an Lucilius. In *Aspekte der Kultursoziologie: Aufsätze zur Soziologie, Philosophie, Anthropologie und Geschichte der Kultur (zum 60. Geburtstag von Mohammed Rassem),* ed. J. Stagl, 303–26. Berlin.

Piérart, M. 1983. L'historien ancien face aux mythes et aux légendes. *LEC* 51: 47–62, 105–15.

Pighi, G. B. 1965. *De ludis saecularibus p.r. Quiritium.*² Amsterdam.

Pinsent, J. 1988. Notes on Livy 6 (1.1). *LCM* 13: 2–6.

Plüss, T. 1913. Horazens *Beatus Ille. Sokrates* 1: 83–92.

Pomeroy, A. 1991. *The appropriate comment: Death notices in the ancient historians.* Frankfurt am Main.

Porter, J. 2004. Homer: The history of an idea. In *The Cambridge companion to Homer,* ed. R. Fowler, 318–37. Cambridge.

Potter, D. S. 1990. *Prophecy and history in the crisis of the Roman empire: A historical commentary on the* Thirteenth Sibylline Oracle. Oxford.

Poucet, J. 1985. *Les origines de Rome: Tradition et histoire.* Brussels.

———. 1986. Albe dans la tradition et l'histoire des origines de Rome. In *Hommages à Jozef Veremans,* ed. F. Decreus and C. Deroux, 238–58. Brussels.

———. 1987. Temps mythique et temps historique: Les origines et les premiers siècles de Rome. *Gerion* 5: 69–85.

Powell, A., ed. 1992. *Roman poetry and propaganda in the age of Augustus.* London.

Prinz, F. 1979. *Gründungsmythen und Sagenchronologie.* Munich.

Purcell, N. 1994. South Italy in the fourth century B.C. *CAH*² 6: 381–403.

———. 1995. On the sacking of Carthage and Corinth. In *Ethics and rhetoric: Classical essays for Donald Russell on his seventy-fifth birthday,* ed. D. Innes, H. Hine, and C. Pelling, 133–48. Oxford.

———. 1997. Review of Wiseman 1995. *BMCR* 1997.5.18.

———. 2003. Becoming historical: The Roman case. In Braund and Gill 2003, 12–40.

———. 2005. Romans in the Roman world. In Galinsky 2005, 85–105.

Putnam, M. C. J. 1961. The art of Catullus 64. *HSCPh* 65: 165–205.

———. 1986. *Artifices of eternity: Horace's fourth book of Odes.* Ithaca and London.

Quint, D. 1993. *Epic and empire: Politics and generic form from Virgil to Milton.* Princeton.

Raaflaub, K. 1987. Herodotus, political thought, and the meaning of history. *Arethusa* 20: 221–48.

Radke, G. 1990. *Fasti romani: Betrachtungen zur Frühgeschichte des römischen Kalendars.* Münster.

Rambaud, M. 1953. *Cicéron et l'histoire romaine.* Paris.

Rauk, J. 1996–97. Time and history in Catullus 1. *CW* 90: 319–32.

Rawson, E. 1985. *Intellectual life in the late Roman Republic.* London.

———. 1989. Roman tradition and the Greek world. *CAH*² 8: 422–76.

———. 1991. *Roman culture and society: Collected papers.* Oxford.

———. 1994. Caesar: Civil war and dictatorship. *CAH*² 9: 424–67.

Reynolds, J. M. 1982. *Aphrodisias and Rome: Documents from the excavation of the theatre at Aphrodisias.* London.

Rich, J. 1997. Structuring Roman history: The consular year and the Roman historical tradition. *Histos* 1. www.dur.ac.uk/Classics/histos/1997/rich1.html.

―――. 1998. Augustus's Parthian honours, the temple of Mars Ultor, and the arch
in the Forum Romanum. *PBSR* 66: 71–128.

Richard, J.-C. 1978. *Les origines de la plèbe romaine: Essai sur la formation du dualisme
patricio-plébéien.* Rome.

Richardson, J. S. 1986. *Hispaniae: Spain and the development of Roman imperialism,
218–82 B.C.* Oxford.

Ridgway, D. 1992. *The first Western Greeks.* Cambridge.

―――. 2004. Euboeans and others along the Tyrrhenian seaboard in the 8th century B.C. In Lomas 2004, 15–33.

Ridley, R. T. 1980. Fastenkritik: A stocktaking. *Athenaeum* 58: 264–98.

Ritter, S. 1995. *Hercules in der römischen Kunst von den Anfängen bis Augustus.*
Heidelberg.

Rodger, N. A. M. 2004. *The command of the ocean: A naval history of Britain, 1649–
1815.* London.

Romm, J. S. 1992. *The edges of the earth in ancient thought.* Princeton.

Rosen, R. M. 1990. Poetry and sailing in Hesiod's *Works and Days. CA* 9: 99–113.

―――, ed. 2004. *Time and temporality in the ancient world.* Philadelphia.

Rossi, A. 2000. The tears of Marcellus: History of a literary motif in Livy. *G&R* 47:
56–66.

―――. 2004. *Contexts of war: Manipulation of genre in Virgilian battle narrative.* Ann
Arbor.

Rostovtzeff, M. 1988. *Histoire économique et sociale de l'empire romain.* Trans. O.
Demange. Paris.

Roussel, D. 1970. *Les Siciliens entre les Romains et les Carthaginois à l'époque de la pre-
mière guerre punique.* Paris.

Rouveret, A. 1991. Tacite et les monuments. *ANRW.* 2.33.4: 3051–99.

Rüpke, J. 1995a. *Fasti:* Quellen oder Produkte römischer Geschichtsschreibung? *Klio*
77: 184–202.

―――. 1995b. *Kalendar und Öffentlichkeit: Die Geschichte der Repräsentation und
religiösen Qualifikation von Zeit in Rom.* Berlin and New York.

―――. 1995c. *Quis uetat et stellas . . . ?* Les levers des étoiles et la tradition cal-
endaire chez Ovide. In *Les Astres: Actes du colloque international de Montpellier,
23–25 mars 1995,* ed. B. Bakhouche, A. Moreau, and J-C. Turpin, 293–306. Montpellier.

―――. 1997. Geschichtsschreibung in Listenform: Beamtenlisten unter römischen
Kalendern. *Philologus* 141: 65–85.

Russell, D. A. 1996. Genethliacon. *OCD*³: 629–30.

Russell, D. A., and M. Winterbottom. 1972. *Ancient literary criticism: The principal texts in new translations.* Oxford.

Sacks, K. S. 1981. *Polybius on the writing of history.* Berkeley.

———. 1990. *Diodorus Siculus and the first century.* Princeton.

Salzman, M. R. 1990. *On Roman time: The codex-calendar of 354 and the rhythms of urban life in late antiquity.* Berkeley and Los Angeles.

Samuel, A. E. 1972. *Greek and Roman chronology: Calendars and years in classical antiquity.* Munich.

Sanders, H. A. 1908. The chronology of early Rome. *CPh* 3: 316–29.

Saunders, T. J. 2001. Dicaearchus' historical anthropology. In Fortenbaugh and Schütrumpf 2001, 237–54.

Scaliger, J. J. 1583. *Opus novum de emendatione temporum in octo libros tributum.* Paris.

Scheid, J. 2003. *An introduction to Roman religion.* Trans. J. Lloyd. Bloomington.

Scheidel, W. 2004. Human mobility in Roman Italy, I: The free population. *JRS* 94: 1–26.

Schiesaro, A. 2003. *The passions in play:* Thyestes *and the dynamics of Senecan drama.* Cambridge.

Schmidt, W. 1908. *Geburtstag im Altertum.* Giessen.

Schröder, W.A. 1971. *M. Porcius Cato: Das erste Buch der Origines: Ausgabe und Erklärung der Fragmente.* Meisenheim am Glan.

Schultze, C. 1995. Dionysius of Halicarnassus and Roman chronology. *PCPhS* 41: 192–213.

Schütrumpf, E. 2001. Dikaiarchs Βίος ῾Ελλάδος und die Philosophie des vierten Jahrhunderts. In Fortenbaugh and Schütrumpf 2001, 255–77.

Schütz, M. 1990. Zur Sonnenuhr des Augustus auf dem Marsfeld: Eine Auseinandersetzung mit E. Buchners Rekonstruktion und seiner Deutung der Ausgrabungsergebnisse, aus der Sicht eines Physikers. *Gymnasium* 97: 432–57.

Schwegler, A. 1867. *Römische Geschichte im Zeitalter der Könige.* Tübingen.

Scodel, R. 1982. The Achaean wall and the myth of destruction. *HSCPh* 86: 33–50.

Scullard, H. H. 1981. *Festivals and ceremonies of the Roman Republic.* London.

Segal, C. 1983. Dissonant sympathy: Song, Orpheus, and the golden age in Seneca's tragedies. In Boyle 1983, 229–51.

Sehlmeyer, M. 1996. Review of Rüpke 1995b. *BMCR* 96.3.7.

Sellar, W. C., and R. J. Yeatman. 1930. *1066 and all that: A memorable history of England.* London.

Serres, M. 1991. *Rome: The book of foundations.* Trans. F. McCarren. Stanford.

Shackleton Bailey, D. R. 1965–70. *Cicero's Letters to Atticus.* Cambridge.

———. 1977. *Cicero: Epistulae ad familiares.* Cambridge.

———. 1980. *Cicero: Epistulae ad Quintum fratrem et M. Brutum.* Cambridge.

Sharrock, A. 1994. *Seduction and repetition in Ovid's* Ars amatoria *2.* Oxford.

Shaw, P.-J. 2003. *Discrepancies in Olympiad dating and chronological problems of archaic Peloponnesian history*. Stuttgart.

Sherwin-White, S. 1987. Seleucid Babylonia: A case study for the installation and development of Greek rule. In Kuhrt and Sherwin-White 1987, 1–31.

Shimron, B. 1973. Πρῶτος τῶν ἡμεῖς ἴδμεν. *Eranos* 71: 45–51.

Sider, D. 1997. *The epigrams of Philodemos*. Oxford.

Sinclair, P. 1994. Political declensions in Latin grammar and oratory 55 B.C.E.–C.E. 39. *Ramus* 23: 92–109.

Skutsch, O. 1980. Notes on Ennius, V. *BICS* 27: 103–8.

———. 1985. *The* Annals *of Q. Ennius*. Oxford.

Slater, C. 1995. Amazonia as Edenic narrative. In Cronon 1995, 114–31.

Slater, D., and P. Taylor. 1999. *The American century*. Oxford.

Slatkin, L. M. 1991. *The power of Thetis: Allusion and interpretation in the* Iliad. Berkeley and Los Angeles.

Small, J. P. 1997. *Wax tablets of the mind: Cognitive studies of memory and literacy in classical antiquity*. London and New York.

Smart, J. D. 1986. Thucydides and Hellanicus. In *Past perspectives: Studies in Greek and Roman historical writing*, ed. I. S. Moxon, J. D. Smart, and A. J. Woodman, 19–35. Cambridge.

Smith, J. Z. 1990. *Drudgery divine: On the comparison of early Christianities and the religions of late antiquity*. Chicago.

Smith, K. F. 1913. *The Elegies of Albius Tibullus*. New York.

Stern, S. 2003. *Time and process in ancient Judaism*. Oxford.

Strasburger, H. 1968. *Zur Sage von der Gründung Roms*. Sitzungsberichte der Heidelberger Akademie der Wissenschaften, phil.-hist. Kl. 1968.5. Heidelberg.

Suerbaum, W. 1980. Merkwürdige Geburtstage: Der nicht-existierende Geburtstag des M. Antonius, der doppelte Geburtstag des Augustus, der neue Geburtstag der Livia und der vorzeitige Geburtstag des älteren Drusus. *Chiron* 10: 327–55.

———, ed. 2002. *Handbuch der lateinischen Literatur der Antike I: Die archaische Literatur: Von den Anfängen bis Sullas Tod, Die vorliterarische Periode und die Zeit von 240 bis 78 v. Chr*. Munich.

Sumner, G. V. 1973. *The orators in Cicero's* Brutus: *Prosopography and chronology*. Toronto.

Susemihl, F. 1891–92. *Geschichte der griechischen Literatur in der Alexandrinerzeit*. Leipzig.

Syme, R. 1939. *The Roman Revolution*. Oxford.

———. 1958. *Tacitus*. Oxford.

———. 1978. *History in Ovid*. Oxford.

Syndikus, H. P. 1972. *Die Lyrik des Horaz: Eine Interpretation der Oden*. Bd. 1, *Erstes und zweites Buch*. Darmstadt.

————. 1990. *Catull: Eine Interpretation. Zweiter Teil: Die grossen Gedichte (61–68).* Darmstadt.

Taub, L. 2003. *Ancient meteorology.* London.

Taylor, L. R., and L. A. Holland 1952. Janus and the *Fasti.* *CPh* 47: 137–42.

Theodorakopoulos, E. 2000. Catullus, 64: Footprints in the labyrinth. In *Intratextuality: Greek and Roman textual relations,* ed. A. Sharrock and H. Morales, 117–41. Oxford.

Thomas, N. 1996. *Out of time: History and evolution in anthropological discourse.*[2] Ann Arbor.

Thomas, R. 2000. *Herodotus in context: Ethnography, science, and the art of persuasion.* Cambridge.

————. 2001. Herodotus' *Histories* and the floating gap. In Luraghi 2001, 198–210.

Thomas, R. F. 1982a. Catullus and the polemics of poetic reference. *AJPh* 103: 144–64.

————. 1982b. *Lands and peoples in Roman poetry: The ethnographic tradition.* Cambridge.

————. 1988. *Virgil: Georgics.* Cambridge.

————. 2004. Torn between Jupiter and Saturn: Ideology, rhetoric, and culture wars in the *Aeneid. CJ* 100: 121–47.

Timpe, D. 1972. Fabius Pictor und die Anfänge der römischen Historiographie. *ANRW* 1.2: 928–69.

————. 1988. Mündlichkeit und Schriftlichkeit als Basis der frührömische Überlieferung. In von Ungern-Sternberg and Reinau 1988, 266–86.

Tissol, G. 1997. *The face of nature: Wit, narrative, and cosmic origins in Ovid's* Metamorphoses. Princeton.

Traina, A. 1975. Allusività Catulliana (due note al c. 64). In *Poeti latini (e neolatini): Note e saggi filologici,* 131–58. Bologna.

Trompf, G. W. 1979. *The idea of historical recurrence in Western thought: From antiquity to the Reformation.* Berkeley and Los Angeles.

Twain, M. 1968. *Life on the Mississippi.* New York. (Originally published in 1883.)

Valvo, A. 1988. *La <Profezia di Vegoia>: Proprietà fondiaria e aruspicina in Etruria nel I secolo A.C.* Rome.

van Groningen, B. A. 1953. *In the grip of the past: Essay on an aspect of Greek thought.* Leiden.

Vannicelli, P. 2003. *Erodoto e la storia dell'alto e medio arcaismo (Sparta-Tessaglia-Cirene).* Rome.

van Wees, H. 2002. Herodotus and the past. In Bakker et al. 2002, 321–49.

Vattuone, R. 1991. *Sapienza d'Occidente: Il pensiero storico di Timeo di Tauromenio.* Bologna.

————. 2002. Timeo di Tauromenio. In *Storici greci d'Occidente*. ed. R. Vattuone 177–232. Bologna.

Verbrugghe, G. P. 1989. On the meaning of *Annales*, on the meaning of annalist. *Philologus* 133: 192–230.

Vernant, J.-P. 1981. Sacrificial and alimentary codes in Hesiod's myth of Prometheus. In Gordon 1981, 57–79.

Versnel, H. S. 1994. *Inconsistencies in Greek and Roman religion*. Vol. 2, *Transition and reversal in myth and ritual*. Leiden.

Veyne, P. 1988. *Did the Greeks believe in their myths? An essay on the constitutive imagination*. Trans. P. Wissing. Chicago.

————. 1999. Prodiges, divination et peur des dieux chez Plutarque. *Revue de l'histoire des religions* 216: 387–442.

Vidal-Naquet, P. 1981. Land and sacrifice in the *Odyssey:* A study of religious and mythical meanings. In Gordon 1981, 80–94.

————. 1986. *The Black hunter: Forms of thought and forms of society in the Greek world*. Trans. A. Szegedy-Maszak. Baltimore.

von Holzinger, K. 1912. Diokles von Peparethos als Quelle des Fabius Pictor. *WS* 34: 175–202.

von Leyden, W. M. 1949–50. Spatium historicum. *Durham University Journal* 11: 89–104.

von Ungern-Sternberg, J. 1988. Überlegungen zur frühen römischen Überlieferung. In von Ungern-Sternberg and Reinau 1988, 237–65.

von Ungern-Sternberg, J., and J. Reinau. 1988. *Vergangenheit in mündlicher Überlieferung: Colloquium Rauricum Band 1*. Stuttgart.

Walbank, F. W. 1957–79. *A historical commentary on Polybius*. 3 vols. Oxford.

————. 1972. *Polybius*. Berkeley and Los Angeles.

————. 1975. *Symploke:* Its role in Polybius' Histories. *YCS* 24: 187–212.

————. 1989–90. Timaeus' views on the past. *SCI* 10: 41–54.

Wallace-Hadrill, A. 1982. The golden age and sin in Augustan ideology. *Past and Present* 95: 19–36.

————. 1987. Time for Augustus: Ovid, Augustus, and the *Fasti*. In *Homo viator: Classical essays for John Bramble*, ed. M. Whitby, P. Hardie, and M. Whitby, 221–30. Bristol.

————. 1988. Greek knowledge, Roman power: Review of Rawson 1985. *CPh* 83: 224–33.

————. 1990. Roman arches and Greek honours: The language of power at Rome. *PCPhS* 36: 143–81.

————. 1997. *Mutatio morum:* The idea of a cultural revolution. In Habinek and Schiesaro 1997, 3–22.

Walsh, P. G. 1961. *Livy: His historical aims and methods*. Cambridge.

Wardman, A. E. 1960. Myth in Greek historiography. *Historia* 9: 403–13.

Watkins, C. 1995. *How to kill a dragon: Aspects of Indo-European poetics.* New York and Oxford.

Watson, L. C. 2003. *A commentary on Horace's* Epodes. Oxford.

Weber, C. 1983. Two chronological contradictions in Catullus 64. *TAPhA* 113: 263–71.

Webster, G. 1969. *The Roman imperial army.* London.

Węcowski, M. 2004. The hedgehog and the fox: Form and meaning in the prologue of Herodotus. *JHS* 124: 143–64.

Weidkuhn, P. 1977. The quest for legitimate rebellion: Towards a structuralist theory of rituals of reversal. *Religion* 7: 167–88.

Weinstock, S. 1971. *Divus Julius.* Oxford.

West, D. 1995. *Horace* Odes *I:* Carpe diem. Oxford.

———. 2002. *Horace* Odes *III:* Dulce periculum. Oxford.

West, M. L. 1978. *Hesiod: Works and days.* Oxford.

———. 1997. *The east face of Helicon: West Asiatic elements in Greek poetry and myth.* Oxford.

Wheeler, S. M. 1999. *A discourse of wonders: Audience and performance in Ovid's* Metamorphoses. Philadelphia.

———. 2002. Ovid's *Metamorphoses* and universal history. In Levene and Nelis 2002, 163–89.

White, H. 1978. *Tropics of discourse: Essays in cultural criticism.* Baltimore and London.

———. 1987. *The content of the form: Narrative discourse and historical representation.* Baltimore and London.

White, P. 1993. *Promised verse: Poets in the society of Augustan Rome.* Cambridge, Mass.

Whitmarsh, T. 2001. *Greek literature and the Roman empire: The politics of imitation.* Oxford.

Whitrow, G. J. 1989. *Time in history: Views of time from prehistory to the present day.* Oxford.

Wilcox, D. J. 1987. *The measure of times past: Pre-Newtonian chronologies and the rhetoric of relative time.* Chicago and London.

Williams, B. 1993. *Shame and necessity.* Berkeley and Los Angeles.

———. 2002. *Truth and truthfulness: An essay in genealogy.* Princeton.

Williams, G. 2002. Ovid's exilic poetry: Worlds apart. In Boyd 2002, 337–81.

Williams, G. W. 1969. *The third book of Horace's Odes.* Oxford.

Williams, J. H. C. 2001. *Beyond the Rubicon: Romans and Gauls in Republican Italy.* Oxford.

Williams, R. 1973. *The country and the city.* London.

Williamson, C. 1987. Monuments of bronze: Roman legal documents on bronze tablets. *CA* 6: 160–83.

Wills, J. 1996. *Repetition in Latin poetry: Figures of allusion.* Oxford.

Wiseman, T. P. 1979. *Clio's cosmetics: Three studies in Greco-Roman literature.* Leicester.

————. 1992. Julius Caesar and the *Mappa mundi.* In *Talking to Virgil: A miscellany,* 22–42. Exeter.

————. 1995. *Remus: A Roman myth.* Cambridge.

————. 1998. *Roman drama and Roman history.* Exeter.

————. 2000. Liber: Myth, drama, and ideology in Republican Rome. In *The Roman middle Republic: Politics, religion and historiography,* ed. C. Bruun, 265–99. Rome.

————. 2002. History, poetry, and *Annales.* In Levene and Nelis 2002, 331–62.

Wissowa, G. 1912. *Religion und Kultus der Römer.* Munich.

Wodehouse, P. G. 1987. *Joy in the morning.* London. (Originally published in 1947.)

Woodman, A. J. 1975. Questions of date, genre, and style in Velleius: Some literary answers. *CQ* 25: 272–306.

————. 1977. *Velleius Paterculus: The Tiberian narrative (2.94–131).* Cambridge.

————. 1983. *Velleius Paterculus: The Caesarian and Augustan narrative (2.41–93).* Cambridge.

————. 1988. *Rhetoric in classical historiography: Four studies.* London and Sydney.

————. 1989. Virgil the historian: *Aeneid* 8.626–62 and Livy. In *Studies in Latin literature and its tradition in honour of C. O. Brink,* ed. J. Diggle, J. B. Hall, and H. D. Jocelyn, 132–45. Cambridge.

————. 1998. *Tacitus reviewed.* Oxford.

————. 2003. Poems to historians: Catullus 1 and Horace, *Odes* 2.1. In Braund and Gill 2003, 191–216.

————. 2004. *Tacitus: The Annals.* Indianapolis.

Woodman, A. J., and R. Martin. 1996. *The Annals of Tacitus: Book 3.* Cambridge.

Worsley, P. 1997. *Knowledges: Culture, counterculture, subculture.* New York.

Zanker, P. 1988. *The power of images in the age of Augustus.* Trans. A. Shapiro. Ann Arbor.

Zeitlin, F. 1986. Thebes: Theater of self and society in Athenian drama. In *Greek tragedy and political theory,* ed. J. P. Euben, 101–41. Berkeley and Los Angeles.

Zerubavel, E. 1981. *Hidden rhythms: Schedules and calendars in social life.* Chicago.

————. 1985. *The seven day circle: The history and meaning of the week.* New York.

————. 2003. *Time maps: Collective memory and the social shape of the past.* Chicago.

Zetzel, J. E. G. 1983. Catullus, Ennius, and the poetics of allusion. *ICS* 8: 251–66.

————. 1994. Looking backward: Past and present in the late Roman Republic. Jackson Knight Lecture. *Pegasus* 37: 20–32.

———. 1995. *Cicero: De re publica.* Cambridge.

———. 1996. Natural law and poetic justice: A Carneadean debate in Cicero and Virgil. *CPh* 91: 297–319.

———. 1997. Rome and its traditions. In *The Cambridge companion to Virgil*, ed. C. Martindale, 188–203. Cambridge.

INDEX

Page references in italics refer to illustrations.

Argetsinger, K., 278n76

Argo (ship), 118–20; Apollonius on, 264n60; in Catullus 64, 119, 123–26, 264n55; Ennius on, 119, 125; as harbinger of culture, 264n58; as harbinger of Iron Age, 263n52, 266n81, 267n85; as originary moment, 125; primacy of, 118, 119, 263n52, 264n55, 268nn96,99; sea nymphs and, 123, 267n86

Argos: decline of, 284n160; priestesses of, 17–18, 19, 223n54; ruins of, 164

Aristocracy, Roman: perception of time, 16; view of commerce, 265n73

Aristodemus, tyranny of, 224n63

Aristotle: on epic, 43; on synchronism, 43–44, 59

Artemis, burning of Ephesus temple, 275n33

Artemisium, battle of: synchronism with Thermopylae, 44

Asheri, David, 142

Asia: antiquity of, 63; Greek triumphalism over, 144; synchronism with Mediterranean, 59–65

Asinius Quadratus, 248n105; on foundation of Rome, 87; *Rōmaikē Chilietēris*, 144

Astrologers, time charts of, 219n13

Astronomy: in *Fasti*, 295n133; invention of, 263n42. *See also* Constellations

Athens: Boulē, 195; calendars of, 58, 195–96; cultural influence of, 237n83; imperial status of, 234n47; in *Metamorphoses*, 237n83; mirroring by Thebes, 235n62; Olympiad chronicle from, 247n90; Parthenon, 71–72; Roman interest in, 237n83; Sicilian expedition, 229n120; synchronism with Rome, 58; synchronism with Sicily, 44–47, 49, 230n125

Atticus, Cicero's correspondence with, 14, 15–16

—*Liber Annalis*, 23, 35, 63, 227nn94–95;

Cicero's use of, 26–28, 221n31; layout of, 27–28; parallelisms in, 27; synchronism of, 25, 26

Aubet, M. E., 254n171

Augustalia festival, 185, 189

Augustus: assumption of *imperium*, 159, 291n83; birthday of, 149, 154, 155, 280n107, 281n122; calendrical years of, 184–89; civil time under, 169; conquest of Egypt, 31; continuity of Republic under, 160; cult of Mars Ultor, 176, 289n52, 291n66; death of, 158, 169; as *Divi filius*, 291n70; entry into Rome, 161, 282n141; Fasti Consulares under, 172–83, 285n1, 288n37; Forum temporal complex of, 167, 169, 172, 197; Golden Age of, 131, 133, 134–35, 163, 166; horologium complex of, 197; iconography of, 133; on length of *saecula*, 277n65; on Ludi Saeculares, 277n66; mythology of Fall under, 112–13; obituaries of, 158; as Pontifex Maximus, 197; *tribunicia potestas* of, 180, 181, 290n64; triumphs of, 282n140. *See also* Fasti Capitolini; Principate

Axial Age, 232n7

Aztecs, calendar of, 218n10, 299n188

Balbus, Cornelius, 181

Barbarism: Hellenistic struggle against, 45, 51; Rome as foe of, 55–57

Barchiesi, A., 97, 135, 149, 298n168; on Ennius, 205

Bassus, Caesellius, 135–36, 272n158

Battles, reckoning from, 140

B.C./A.D.: adoption of, 7–9, 12, 219n4; in European languages, 273n1; synchronism of, 13; zero in, 275n46

Beard, M., 149, 209

Bede, Venerable: chronography of, 7

Bellerophon, 241n4

Benson, M., 294n120

Bettini, M., 2, 16
Bible, Hebrew: linear time in, 3
Bilingualism, Latin-Etruscan, 146
Biological rhythms, 4, 218n17
Birthdays, Greek, 278n76
Birthdays, Roman, 148–49, 278nn83–84;
as anniversaries, 156–58; Augustus's,
149, 154, 155, 280n107, 281n122;
Caesar's, 189; Caligula's, 278n79;
Cicero's, 150, 157; commemorations
of, 158, 189; D. Brutus's, 149, 189,
278n83; in *fasti*, 189; in Julian calen-
dar, 151, 154–56; Livia's, 156; M.
Antonius's, 155–56; M. Brutus's, 149,
278n84; Nero's, 192; Ovid's, 157–58,
211; poems on, 158, 281n122; Pom-
pey's, 148, 222n36; Virgil's, 150
Blackburn, B., and Holford-Strevens, L.,
231n5, 279n89
Blundell, S., 270n118
Boardman, J., 72
Bodel, J., 290n66
Boëdromion (month), 10
Boundaries, human/divine, 122, 123
Bovillae, battle of, 140
Boyne, battle of, 151
Brundisium, birthday of, 148
Brutus, D.: birthday of, 149, 189, 278n83
Brutus, M., 189; birthday of, 149, 278n84
Buchner, E., 295n139, 296n140
Burkert, W., 91
Burrus, influence on Nero, 192

Caesar, Julius: authority of, 196–97;
birthday of, 189; building works of,
295n134; on Clodius, 273n9; consulship under, 290n62; *De Analogia*, 197,
295n135; emulation of Alexander, 62;
in *fasti*, 203; first regnal year of, 31;
honors voted for, 188; invasion of
Britain, 63; Parthian campaign prepa-
rations, 239n109; Pliny the Elder on,
60–61; as Pontifex Maximus, 197;

rebuilding of Carthage, 145; reforms
of, 295n134; "the Great," 63, 239n108;
universalism of, 60. *See also* Calendar,
Julian
Calendar, Gregorian: adoption in
Britain, 151, 279n91, 281n118, 295n132;
and Julian calendar, 150, 225n77; leap
years in, 278n87
Calendar, Julian, 6, 12, 101, 215; adjustments to, 150, 295n138; anniversaries
in, 156–60; birthdays in, 151, 154–56,
279n92; in British colonies, 151;
Cicero on, 196–97; civil calendars
and, 198; civil time in, 193–94, 205;
days in, 158–60, 162, 163; in Eastern
empire, 209–10; effect on imperial
authority, 196–97, 296n140; *fasti* and,
167, 185; festivals in, 151, 153–54,
279n93; and Gregorian calendar, 150,
225n77; honorifics in, 188; impact of,
193–96, 204; imperial family in, 185–
89; inauguration of, 152, 196; in Latin
West, 209; leap years in, 280nn103–4;
Livy's use of, 257n197; months in, 153;
natural time in, 193–94, 205; parapegmata and, 198, 296n142; Plutarch on,
295n133; recalibrations following, 151–
52; role in religious reform, 189; role
in Roman identity, 210, 211; Romano-
centrism of, 209–11; and Romans'
time perception, 281n120; Scaliger
on, 193, 194; Suetonius and, 154, 197;
Varro on, 200–201, 207
Calendars: Aztec, 218n10, 299n188;
Chinese, 209; *versus* chronologies,
288n29; cities', 9–10; civil, 198;
harmonization of, 10; Italian, 300n195;
lunar, 195; Macedonian, 225n77;
Muslim, 139; solar, 195; as time measurement schemes, 193–96; World,
159, 282n131
Calendars, Greek, 17; archon's, 195;
Athenian, 58, 195–96; calculation of

date in, 279n96; Cicero on, 196; correlations among, 230n2; of Delphi, 300n206; festival, 195, 294n122; lunar, 195, 298n174; Plutarch on, 211; prytany, 195; solar, 195; Syracusan, 230n2

Calendars, Roman, 2; anniversaries in, 6, 138, 142–45, 148, 162; in cultural memory, 209, 211; *dies Alliensis* in, 103, 106; of Dura Europa, 300n197; festivals in, 6, 118, 153, 296n150; Greek understanding of, 94; historical movement in, 169–70; in Horace, 207–8; Ides in, 152, 153; Kalends in, 152, 153; Nones in, 152, 153; Numa's, 188, 283n147; Romulus's, 188, 297n158; state festivals in, 194; symbolic power of, 210; synchronization of events in, 171

—Republican, 150–51, 152–56; beginning of year in, 204; civil function of, 294n122; final year of, 196; intercalary months in, 157, 280nn102,104,106, 281n119, 296n148; months in, 153; semiotic power of, 291n75; Suetonius on, 200; Varro on, 198–99. *See also Ab urbe condita*; Calendar, Julian; Consular dating system, Roman; *Fasti*

Caligula, birthday of, 278n79

Calliades, 221n35

Callimachus, 268nn97–98; *Hecale*, 124; on months, 300n207

Calpurnius Piso, 141

Calpurnius Siculus, 136–37

Camarina (Sicily), capture of, 233n41

Camillus, refoundation of Rome, 101–2, 257n198

Campanians, Roman citizenship of, 143

Campus Martius (Rome), 94; horologium complex at, 197, 206

Cantabrian era, 140

Capitoline: Palazzo dei Conservatori, 172; temporal power of, 274n31

Capitoline temple, 104, 258n214; ceremonial nails in, 176; dating from, 141–42, 249n119; dedication of, 89; inauguration of, 104, 274nn26–27; Jupiter cult at, 142, 168, 176, 177; refoundation of, 259n218

Capua, as second Rome, 234n45, 235n62

Carandini, A., 91

Carmentalia festival, 184; in Fasti Antiates, 292n84

Carneades, embassy to Rome, 11, 14, 15, 221n30, 229n116

Carroll, Charles, 44

Carthage: coexistence with Sicilian Greeks, 56; fall of, 256n192; foundation of, 53, 92, 95, 96–97, 252n152; Greek view of, 53–54; imperial status of, 234n47; as Other, 56; rebuilding of, 145; Roman sack of, 54–55, 59; synchronism with Rome, 92–93, 250n135, 251n138; Syracuse's victories over, 52

Cassius (tyrannicide), birthday of, 149

Cassius Hemina, 256n196, 274n21

Castor of Rhodes: *Chronica*, 20, 63–64, 81; chronography of, 80; impact on Varro, 239n120; as *philorōmaios*, 63; on Pompey, 65; synchronism of, 239n113; universalizing of, 63

Cato the Censor, censorship of, 143

—*De Agricultura*, civil calendar in, 200

—*Origines*, 221n28; chronography of, 99–100, 142, 246n83

Cato Uticensis, judgment on Catiline, 162

Catullus: on Cornelius Nepos, 21, 228n103; Dicaearchus's influence on, 267n85; originality of, 268n99; on Roman *imperium*, 61–63, 238n106

—*Carmen* 64: Argo in, 123–26, 267n85; Argo's primacy in, 119, 264n55; chronological anomie in, 123–26; Golden Age in, 132; heroism in,

Catullus, *Carmen* 64 *(continued)*
269n105; Medea in, 124; Minos in, 125,
126; nostalgia in, 126, 132; opposites
in, 123, 124; originary moments in,
125; Parcae in, 126; Peleus and Thetis
in, 123, 124, 125–26, 267nn88–89;
Prometheus in, 269n102; temporal
demarcations in, 125–27; Theseus in,
124–25, 126; transitions in, 267n91;
Trojan War in, 126

Censorinus: on civil time, 202; epochal
demarcations of, 81–82; on foundation
of Rome, 225n77; on natural time, 202;
on *saecula*, 145–46, 147; textual corruption in, 246n81; time divisions of,
77–78, 79; use of Varro, 276n55

Censors: in Fasti Antiates, 176–77; in
Fasti Capitolini, 172, 176, 289n42; in
Hercules Musarum temple, 287n24;
lustrations by, 176–77

Centauromachy (Parthenon), 71

Centuries: commemoration of, 276n50;
modern orientation toward, 9

Cereal grains, grinding of, 111

Cerealia festival, 207

Chaeronea, battle of, 40; synchronism
with Italian wars, 47

Champlin, E., 135, 136

Charts, spatio-temporal, 1

The Chauci, Seneca on, 260n7

Christ, calculation of birth, 7, 8

Chronography, Christian, 78, 80; B.C./
A.D. in, 7–9, 12; Bede's, 7; Eusebius's,
5, 29; Jerome's, 5, 29–32, 225n77;
synchronism in, 28–32

Chronography, Greek: Apollodorus's,
58, 80; Athenocentric, 20; of Castor
of Rhodes, 80; Cicero's use of, 21;
of Dionysius of Halicarnassus, 93,
251n139; Plutarch's, 10; Roman use
of, 5; Thucydides', 17–18, 221n26,
222nn42,45, 223n46, 293n101;
Timaeus's, 18–19, 223n51

Chronography, Hellenistic: on foundation of Rome, 249n114; Panhellenic,
4–5, 18, 223n45

Chronography, Roman: appearance of,
225n68; Cato's, 99–100, 142, 246n83;
Cicero's, 14–16, 21, 26–28; Polybius
on, 47; regal period, 90; Velleius
Paterculus's, 22, 225n73

Chronology: Asian, 10, 13; Christian, 11;
in demarcation of history, 244n47;
universal, 11. *See also* Synchronism

Chronology, Roman: constitutional
changes in, 249n120; of Republic,
150–51

Cicero, 227n97; on birthday commemorations, 189; birthday of, 150, 157;
chronography of, 14–16, 21, 26–28;
cultural parallels of, 25, 26–28,
227n97; on Dicaearchus, 262n23;
on Greek calendar, 196; intellectual
career of, 25; on intercalation,
296n148; on Julian calendar, 196–97;
on natural time, 297n154; on oratorical history, 227nn99–100; reckoning
by eras, 140; return from exile, 148;
on rivals of Rome, 234n45; on Roman
literature, 35; synchronism of, 25–28;
on Ten Commissioners, 222n37;
on Timaeus, 233n39; use of Aratus,
261n23; use of Greek chronography,
21; use of language of power, 292n95
—*Academica*, 14
—*Brutus*, 16, 26, 27; Atticus in, 221n31,
227n94; Ennius in, 240n131; Solon in,
222n40
—*De Oratore*, 26, 227n97
—*De Re Publica*, 26, 227n95, 248n107;
Rome's limits in, 285n166; Romulus
in, 87

Cincius Alimentus, 254n168

Circadian rhythms, 4

Cities, ancient: calendars of, 9–10; eras
of, 139; rebuilding of, 145

Darius: Herodotus on, 73; Marathon expedition, 233n41

D'Arms, J. H., 265n73

Dates, chronological: "according to the god," 195, 295n124; correlation with events, 12–15; as symbols, 9

Days, Roman: anniversaries of, 148–49; counting of, 152–53; in Fasti Anni, 168; in Julian calendar, 158–60, 162, 163; legal status of, 170; lunar, 207, 298n174

D-Day (1944), synchronistic dating of, 22–23

De Cazanove, O., 90

Decemvirate: establishment of, 259n217; institution of, 141

Degrassi, Attilio: on Fasti Anni, 285n2; *fasti* transcriptions of, 167, 180, 185

Delphi: barbarian dedications at, 73; calendar of, 300n206

Demetrius of Phalerum, 55

Demosthenes, 28

Dendrochronology, 250n129

Diamond, Jared, 111

Dicaearchus: *Bios Hellados*, 113; Cicero on, 262n23; on Golden Age, 117, 261n23; influence on Catullus, 267n85; primitivism of, 262n23; on stages of decline, 119; Varro's use of, 262n35

Dido, death of, 235n66

Dillery, John, 254n168

Dio Cassius: on fall of Rome, 276n47; on Nero, 105; on rebuilding of cities, 145

Diocles of Peparethus, 96, 97, 98; Fabius Pictor's use of, 250n126, 253nn154–56

Diodorus Siculus: chronography of, 10, 245n59; mythic material of, 79, 81; periodization of, 65; synchronism of, 46

Dionysius Exiguus, chronography of, 7

Dionysius of Halicarnassus: on Cato's chronography, 99; chronography of, 93, 251n139; on foundation of Rome,

91; knowledge of Timaeus, 250n135; on mythical time, 78; rationalizations of, 95

Dionysius of Syracuse: birth of, 232n23; siege of Rhegium, 47; synchronism with Euripides, 48; war with Carthaginians, 46

Dionysus, Greek historiographers on, 78

Divus Julius, temple of, 285n1

Dreizehnter, A., 256n191; *Die rhetorische Zahl*, 100

Drusus, German campaign of, 159

Dunn, F. M., 294n122

Dura Europa, Roman calendar of, 300n197

Duris, on Alexander the Great, 142

Durkheim, Emile, 217n9

East: coins of, 299n189; Hellenized, 67; Latin language in, 300n192; local calendars of, 209–10

Easter, calculation of, 7

Egypt: antiquity of, 29, 262n24; Augustus's conquest of, 31; incorporation into Roman empire, 65; Latin language in, 300n192; synchronism with Near East, 220n18

Emperors, Roman: anniversaries of accession, 276n52

Empire, British: decline of, 285n166

Empire, Roman: Golden Age in, 131–34; Hellenized East in, 67; laissez-faire in, 210; and Parthian empire, 240n127; Roman religion in, 299n192; time structures of, 2. *See also* Principate

Eneuma elis (cosmogony), 70

Ennius: Greekness of, 255n182; interest in Pythagoreanism, 275n44; on rape of Silvia, 205; Roman citizenship of, 143; Sicilian models of minor works, 57

—*Annales*, 256n185; ; closure point of, 66; consuls in, 287n22; end point of,

240n131; on fall of Troy, 143, 256n190; on foundation of Rome, 99; ; Livy's use of, 256n194; Muses in, 144, 275n42; numeric symbolism of, 101; refoundation of Rome in, 100, 101; sacred time in, 170; Virgil's use of, 293n109

—*Medea exul*; on the Argo, 119, 125; Golden Age in, 264n54

Ephors, Spartan: dating by, 18, 19, 223n54

Ephorus: on mythical time, 78; synchronism of, 44

Epic, Aristotle on, 43

Epicharmus, 57

Epicurus, synchronism with Fabricius, 35

Epimethius, 111

Eponymity: principles of, 168; in reckoning of time, 174–75, 176. *See also* Consular dating system, Roman; Magistrates, Roman: eponymous

Equirria festival, calculation of, 280n106

Equus October (Roman festival), 94

Eras: honorific, 140; in reckoning of time, 139–42

Eratosthenes: chronological boundaries of, 80, 224n55; dating system of, 85; on fall of Troy, 19, 86, 142, 223n53, 253n159, 283n144; on first Olympiad, 84, 85; Hellenism of, 49; on Olympiads, 223n54; on Roman-Carthaginian parallels, 54; on Roman events, 38; Varro's use of, 247n92

—*Chronographiae:* organization of, 13; publication of, 253n156; terminus of, 19

Etesian winds, 206

Etruscans, absorption into Rome, 146

Euhemerus, 57

Euripides: *Medea*, 118, 119; on seafaring, 120; synchronism with Dionysius of Syracuse, 48

Eusebius of Caesarea: chronography of,

y, 29; chronological boundaries of, 80; on *translatio imperii*, 37; use of Macedonian calendar, 225n77; use of tables, 29, 228n104

Evander: and Aeneas, 162, 163, 164, 284nn155,157; as postlapsarian man, 166

Experience, lived *versus* imagined, 109

Fabian, Johannes, 1; on allochrony, 25

Fabius Pictor: annalistic method of, 190; on foundation of Rome, 95–96, 97, 98, 255n182; *History*, 99; Naevius's knowledge of, 255n178; as originator of annals, 190, 293n100; reckoning system of, 253n153, 258n205; sources of, 96; synchronism of, 48; use of Diocles, 250n126, 253nn154–56

Fabricius, censorship of, 35

Fall of man, 112–13; Augustan poets on, 261n20; Judaeo-Christian, 112; Seneca on, 129; ships as agents of, 127–31

Fasti: aedilicii, 286n8; birthdays in, 189; of city of Rome, 206; of Cn. Flavius, 291n82; etymology of, 286n5; exegetical material in, 170; honorifics in, 185–89; Horace on, 185; imperial, 184, 185–89, 210; interdependence among, 168–70, 286nn8,13; and Julian calendar, 167; monumental, 168; power of, 139; Republican and imperial, 184; Social war in, 290n63; synchronized time in, 210; Tacitus's use of, 191, 193; in temple of Hercules Musarum, 144; transformations to, 167; *tribunicii*, 286n8

Fasti Amiternini, 184

Fasti Anni, 167, 168, 285n2; astronomical information in, 296n142; cyclical time in, 169; fixing of days, 168; parapegmata and, 296n142; relationship to Fasti Consulares, 171–72; in temple of Hercules Musarum, 168, 169–70

Fasti Antiates, 103, 170, 258n210; for 164–37, *178*; beginning of, 287n25; Carmentalia in, 292n84; for 1–16 C.E., *183*; censors in, 176–77; consuls suffect in, 290n59; foundation of Rome in, 184; and Fulvian *fasti*, 287n25; Ides in, 184; and imperial *fasti*, 184; Kalends in, 184; Nones in, 184; state festivals in, 184; temple cults in, 184, 287n25; Tiberius in, 292n84

Fasti Capitolini, 172–83, 289nn40–42; in *ab urbe condita* dating, 175; Agrippa in, 180, 181; for 173–154 B.C.E., *174*, *175*; for 260–154 B.C.E., *173*; for 1–7 C.E., *179*, *182*; censors in, 172, 176, 289n42; consuls suffect in, 290n65; foundation of Rome in, 174; iconography of, 177; imperial aspects of, 174; location of, 285n1; Ludi Saeculares in, 181–82; magistrates in, 176–77, 180, 191; Tiberius in, 180–81; wars in, 173

Fasti Consulares, 167, 168, 170–72; under Augustus, 172–83, 285n1, 288n37; dating from, 141; events in, 171; fixing of years, 168; in *Historia Augusta*, 285n2; historians' use of, 287n23; purpose of, 170–71, 286n4; relationship to calendar year, 171–72; symbolic power of, 170; in temporal space, 222n36; utility of, 170–71

Fasti Praenestini, 184; imperial family in, 185, 292n84; for 6–15 January, *186*, *187*

Fasti Tauromenitani, suffects in, 290n61

Fasti Triumphales, 167, 172; Barberiniani, 285n1, 291nn69–70; cycles in, 181; Romulus in, 181; Urbisalvienses, 285n1, 291n69

Fasti Venusini, 290n63

Fasti Verulani, 155, 281n111

Feriae. See Festivals

Festivals: calculation of, 280n106; in Fasti Antiates, 184; of Hercules Invic-

tus, 161; in imperial *fasti*, 188–89; in Julian calendar, 151, 153–54, 279n93; public, 188–89, 292n92; in Roman calendars, 6, 118, 153, 296n150; seed-sowing, 199, 203; Varro on, 199–200, 296n146. *See also* Anniversaries; Birthdays

Finley, M., 79

Fitzgerald, W., 120

Flamen Dialis, 199

Flavius, Cn.: aedileship of, 89; *fasti* of, 291n82; sanctuary of Concordia, 141–42

Flood, Ogygus's, 83

Fortune, mutability of, 235n68

Forum, Roman: *comitium* area in, 213; during Middle Ages, 164; temporal complex of, 167, 169, 172, 197

Foundations: double, 252n147; myths of, 255n174

Fowler, R. L., 241n7

Francken, C. M., xii

Freud, Sigmund, 85

Fulvius Nobilior, M., 66, 143, 168; consular fasti of, 169–70, 184, 287nn23–25, 291n82

Gabba, E., 93

Gaisser, J. H., 267n91

Galba, Servius, 191

Games, anniversary, 145, 148

Games, Panhellenic, 247n96; synchronization of, 231n2

Gatz, B., 262n38; *Weltalter*, 116

Gauls. *See* Sack of Rome, Gallic

Gell, Alfred, 4, 209, 260n6

Gellius, Aulus: "amateurism" of, 34; Athenocentrism of, 23, 40–41, 58, 226n81; on Coriolanus, 38; dating systems of, 38; on Greek literature, 35, 36–37; knowledge of Accius, 229n115; knowledge of Christianity, 32; on Punic wars, 37; on Pyrrhus, 38, 39; on

Roman literature, 14 393 subject mat-
ter of, 33–34; synchronistic essay of,
5, 11, 32–42
Gellner, Ernest, 129
Gelon (tyrant of Syracuse), 45–46,
233n35; negotiations with Greeks, 50
Genethliaca (birthday poems), 158
Genius, cult of, 148
Germanicus, in Ovid, 169
Geus, K., 223n55
Gibbon, Edward: *Decline and Fall*,
284n156
Gigantomachy: on Parthenon, 71; as
struggle with barbarians, 56–57
Gildenhard, I., 170, 287n25
Gilgamesh (epic), 70
Ginsberg, J., 190–91
Glabrio, M.' Acilius, 172
Gods: departure of, 263n46; genealogies
of, 117; relations with men, 117–18;
state deities, 176; temporality of, 75,
117–18, 263n49
Gold: in city of Rome, 272n151; moral
associations of, 133–34
Golden Age: *absentia* in, 116; in the
Aeneid, 133, 134, 163, 166; agriculture
in, 270n118; Aratus on, 270n118; ban
on plowing in, 263n40; communication with, 127; constellations of, 128,
206; cyclical, 163–64; Dicaearchus on,
117, 261n23; divine recurrence in, 117;
in Ennius, 264n54; freedom from seafaring, 120; Hesiod on, 111, 112, 117,
131, 261n15; in Horace, 132, 133–34;
human-divine relations and, 117–18,
263n46; as hunter-gatherer society,
110–11; legitimacy of, 132, 271n135;
Near Eastern origins of, 112; Nero's,
131, 135–37; nostalgia for, 137; Posidonius on, 270n124; returns to, 271n129;
in Roman empire, 131–34; in Roman
literature, 115–16; in Roman myth,
112; of Saturn, 114, 163; Seneca on,

128, 135; shift from Golden Race, 115,
263n38; as sloth, 114; Tacitus on,
261n21; temporality in, 116, 127; transition to Iron Age, 6, 69, 107, 108,
119–20, 132; Varro on, 113; Virgilian,
131–33, 262n33
Golden Age, Augustan, 131; desirability
of, 133; Ovid on, 134–35; in Virgil,
133, 134, 163, 166
Golden Race, 111; shift to Golden Age,
115, 263n38; tension with Iron Race,
261n11
Gow, A. S. F. and Page, D. L., 284n159
Grafton, A., 58, 215, 219n13, 220n18,
224n55
Grandazzi, A., 91
Grant, M., 148
Gratwick, A., 143
Great Britain: adoption of Gregorian calendar, 151, 279n91, 281n118, 295n132;
beginning of year in, 297n164; Caesar's invasion of, 63; regnal years in,
225n78
Greece: ; cultural influence of, 224n67,
229n114; East-West rivalry in, 49–50,
59; Roman triumphalism over, 144;
parallelism with Akkadia, 241n6; synchronism with Orient, 239n113. *See
also* Athens; Cities, Greek
Greek language, as lingua franca,
300n192
Greeks, Sicilian: Hellenicity of, 236n70
Griffin, J., 278n73, 299n181
Gruen, E. S., 5, 60, 249n15

Habinek, T., 27
Hall, E., 70–71
Hamilcar, ancestry of, 56
Hanell, K., 52–53, 168, 286n6
Hannibal: death of, 231n6; defeat of, 104;
threat to Roman alliances with Magna
Graecia, 98
Harrell, S., 236n73

Harrison, T., 74

Hecataeus of Miletus, 29; rationalizing by, 242n21

Hegira, in Muslim calendar, 139

Heilmann, W., 261n21

Hellanicus of Lesbos, 17; on foundation of Rome, 248n99

Hellas, link with West Greece, 232n22

Hellenism: Athenocentrism in, 58; decadence of, 54; Eastern, 67; *oecumene* of, 57–59; struggle against barbarism, 45, 51. *See also* Panhellenism

Hellenization, *synkrisis* in, 24

Hellenization, Roman, 24, 57, 58–59; synchronization in, 5

Helm, Rudolf, 30

Heracleidae, return of, 78

Heraclides Ponticus, 53

Hercules: antiquity of, 243n32; Antonius's cultivation of, 161, 282n141; and Augustus, 161; Livy on, 252n149; in underworld, 122

Hercules Invictus, festival of, 161

Hercules Musarum, temple of, 240n130; calendrical fasti in, 168, 169–70; censors in *fasti* of, 287n24; *fasti* in, 144, 168, 169–70, 184, 287nn23–25, 291n82; Muses in, 275n40; sacred time in, 170; temporal power of, 143

Herodotus: authorial self-presentation of, 77, 244n44; chronology of, 79, 223n47; conception of time, 75; on Croesus, 72, 73, 76, 242nn19–21; on Darius, 73; and datability of myth, 245n62; on divine action, 75; double past of, 242n15; Egyptian sources of, 75; geographical knowledge of, 246n66; on Hamilcar, 56; historical time in, 72–76; inaccessible time in, 74; knowledge claims of, 74–75, 76, 242n25; mythic time in, 72–76; Pan in, 245n53; on Sicily, 236n73; synchronism of, 43, 45–46; Thucydides' use

of, 244n34; on Trojan War, 74, 243n28; use of Homer, 242n23; use of *muthos*, 242n22; view of divine forces, 243n30; view of nature, 244n35

Heroes, genealogies of, 79

Hesiod: on Golden Age, 111, 112, 117, 131, 261n15; in Ovid, 299n183; on sailing, 266n78

Heyworth, S. J., 208, 299n179

Hieron of Syracuse, 45

Hieronymus of Cardia, 250n134

Himera, battle of: ambassadors before, 233n35; synchronism with Salamis, 43–44, 45, 46, 51, 231n11; synchronism with Thermopylae, 51

Hinds, S., 157

Hipparchus, murder of, 40

Hippias of Elis, 84

Hippocratics, 85

Historia Augusta, "Fasti Consulares" in, 285n2

Historians: constitution of subjects, 245n54; use of Fasti Consulares, 287n23

Historiography, ancient: boundary with myth, 69, 79; intergeneric boundaries in, 78–79; and science, 76–77, 244nn39,45; *translatio imperii* in, 236n68

Historiography, Greek: Athenian, 49; foundation of Rome in, 89, 91, 99; knowledge claims in, 77; Moses in, 63; myth in, 68, 78; Punic Wars in, 236n71; Roman use of, 5; shift of power from, 99

Historiography, Roman: foundation of Rome in, 89–91; myth in, 68; parallelism in, 20–21, 224n64; periodization in, 248n106; under Principate, 190–93; shift of power to, 99; synchronism in, 52; in transition to empire, 6; universal, 65–67, 240n122. *See also* Annalistic history, Roman

History: monumental sources of, 247n95, and myth, 241n2, 245n53; Panhellenic, 18, 85; progressive view of, 114; similes in, 24–25; universal, 63, 65–67

History, sacred: continuous, 241n3; synchronization with profane, 29

Hobsbawm, E., 219n11

Homer: *akmē* of, 21; Herodotus's use of, 242n23; Scipio's use of, 55; time stratification in, 241n4

—*Iliad*: eyewitnesses in, 74; past time in, 70, 74

—*Odyssey*, shipmaking metaphor in, 120

Horace: anniversary celebrations by, 149, 277n73; bimillenary of death, 275n46; on *fasti*, 185; on human progress, 266nn80,84; on Ides, 279n97; immortality themes, 214, 217n6; ode to Virgil, 121; on sailing, 121–22; transgression imagery of, 122; Trojan War in, 83, 84; use of anniversaries, 159; use of Castor of Rhodes, 63

—*Carmen* 4.7, cyclical time in, 214

—*Carmen Saeculare*, 214; Golden Age in, 133–34

—*Epode* 2: calendar in, 207–8, 299n181; Terminalia in, 208, 299n180; Virgil and, 299n179

—*Epode* 16: Blessed Isles in, 260n8; Golden Age in, 132

Horden, P. and Purcell, N.: *The Corrupting Sea*, 264n62

Horsfall, Nicholas, 219n9, 238n104, 261n16; on historical allegory in Virgil's *Aeneid*, 282n139

Housman, A. E., xii

Huber, L., 242n24

Hunter, V., 15, 221nn34–35

Ides (Roman calendar), 152, 153; in calculating birthday celebrations, 155; in Fasti Antiates, 184; Horace on, 279n97; position of, 279n101, 280n104

Imperium, Roman: Augustus's, 159, 291n83; Catullus on, 61–63, 238n106; incorporation of East into, 60; pan-Mediterranean, 59; under Pompey, 63; role of universal history in, 66; Timaeus on, 236n69. *See also Translatio imperii*

Incarnation: dating of, 7, 8; in Scaliger's *Emendatio Temporum*, 218n1; era of, 273n16. *See also* B.C./A.D.

Industrial Revolution, impact on time, 217n4

Iron Age: agriculture in, 111; *artes* of, 129–30; escape from, 128; harbingers of, 119, 121, 128, 263n52, 266n81, 267n85; in Italy, 250n129; Near Eastern origins of, 111; in Roman myth, 112; Rome during, 91; in Seneca, 127–31; time in, 117; transition from Golden Age, 6, 69, 107, 108, 119–20, 132; in Virgil, 114–15, 128, 262n33

Iron Race, 112; Ovid on, 272n145; tension with Golden Race, 261n11

Isthmian games, dating of, 248n96

Italy: Greek colonies in, 254nn160,167,170; Iron Age, 250n129

Italy, southern: non-Greeks of, 254n170

Iuno, cult of, 148

Iustitia Augusta, image of, 292n84

Jackson, S., 263n52

Jacoby, Felix, 13–14, 246n76, 250n133; *Apollodors Chronik*, xii; on Eratosthenes, 84; on Hieronymus of Cardia, 250n134; on Timaeus, 250n135, 274n33

Janus: closing of gates of, 292n84; Roman ruins of, 164; sacrifices to, 168, 192, 286n10

Jason of Pherae, 231n6

Jaspers, Karl, 232n7

Jefferson, Thomas, 44

Jerome, Saint: chronography of, 5, 29–32, 225n77; historical space of, 242n15

Jerome, Saint *(continued)*
—*Chronicle:* fall of Troy in, 83; Olympiads in, 29–30, 247n91; tables of, 29–32, *30–36*, 242n14
Jerusalem, Titus's capture of, 32
Jocelyn, H. D., 255n181
Judaism, ancient, conception of time in, 221n34
Julius Africanus, 80
June, as Germanicus, 292n88
Juno Moneta, 274n31; temple of, 142
Jupiter: Capitoline cult of, 142, 168, 176, 177; and Thetis, 117–18
Justice, departure from earth, 114

Kalends (Roman calendar), 152, 153, 279n99; in birthday celebrations, 155; in Fasti Antiates, 184
Ker, James, 2, 217n6
Kings, Alban, 89, 249n114; Diocles of Peparethus on, 96
Kings, Hellenic: birthday celebrations of, 278n76
Kings, Tarquin: expulsion of, 90, 141, 224n63, 249n121, 259n218; in Livy, 190
Knapp, R., 140, 273n15
Knowledge: geographical, 246n66; technological control of, 76–77
Knowledge, historical: ascertainable, 108; limits of, 69; Thucydides on, 84; time divisions in, 77–78
Knowledge systems, 217n9; encyclopedic, 215; multiplicity of, 217n7
Knowledge systems, Greek: Roman control of, 206
Kraus, C. S., 102, 293n101; on foundation of Republic, 104–5
Kuttner, A., 60

Lacey, W. K., 290n64
Lamberton, R., 237n83
Larentalia festival, date of, 296n146
Lares Augusti, 160, 282n134

Lares Praestites, 160, 282n134
Latin War (340–338 B.C.E.), 143
Laurence, R. and Smith, C., 280n102
Lavinium, Trojan objects in, 94
Laws, development of, 113
Leap seconds, 294n120
Leap years: in Gregorian calendar, 278n87; in Julian calendar, 280nn103–4
Leges Annales, 16; impact of, 222n39
Le Goff, J., 3
Lehoux, D., 198
Leibniz, Gottfried Wilhelm: on spatio-temporal measurement, 220n21
Lepidus, as Pontifex Maximus, 295n138
Leuctra, battle of, 47
Lévi-Strauss, Claude, 217n9, 260n6; on hot and cold societies, 110; model of time, 3, 4
Lewis and Clark, 164–65
Liber, ideology of, 21
Licinius (tribune), 190
Lindian Chronicle, 224n61, 246n67
Literature, Greek: Gellius on, 35, 36–37; early development of, 26
Literature, Latin: Augustan, 230n127; Cicero on, 35; Gellius on, 34–35; late arrival of, 26–27, 34, 225n85; prelapsarian society in, 115–16; and Roman religion, 217n7
Livia (wife of Augustus), birthday of, 156
Livy: on Aeneas, 275n38; annalistic format of, 190; demarcation points of, 105, 141, 274n19; end point of, 240n134; on fall of Troy, 82; ; on foundation of Rome, 78–79, 88, 257n197; on Gallic sack, 101–2, 141, 257n205; good and bad repetition in, 256n188; on Hercules, 252n149; on Marcellus, 234n50; numeric symbolism of, 101; parallels of, 40, 230n123; reckoning system of, 141, 171, 190,

Mommsen, T., 168, 286nn4,8

Months, Greek, 220n15, 279n96; Callimachus on, 300n207

Months, Roman: etymologies of, 170;
intercalary, 157, 280nn102,104,106,
281n119, 296n148; in Julian calendar,
153; Quintilis, 197, 296n143; renaming
of, 292n88; Sextilis, 161, 185

Morgan, L., 192, 294n115

Moses, in Greek historiography, 63

Mos maiorum, 35–36

Munz, P., 260n4

Murray, Les: "The C19–20," 9

Muses: in Ennius, 144, 275n42; Homeric,
74; Pyrrhus's statues of, 144; in temple
of Hercules Musarum, 275n40

Musical pitch, local standards for, 220n14

Mycale, battle of: synchronism with
Platea, 44, 231n8

Mycenae, decline of, 164, 284nn159–60

Myth: datability of, 79, 80, 245n62; Fall
of man in, 112–12; genealogies in, 80,
245n63; and history, 241n2, 245n53;
knowability of, 76; in Roman culture,
87; in Roman historiography, 68–69.
See also Time, mythic

Myth, Greek: Persian version of, 72, 73–
74; Roman use of, 138; Timaeus's use
of, 94–95

Naevius, 56–57; on foundation of Rome,
99, 255nn181–82; and Greek/barbarian
paradigm, 56-57; Greekness of,
255n182; knowledge of Fabius Pictor,
255n178

Nationalism: homogenous time in, 210;
temporal aspects of, 66–67

Nature: *versus* artifice, 270n118; estrangement from, 120–22, 129; harmony
with, 109, 127, 128, 259n1;
Herodotus's view of, 244n35; Seneca
on, 130–31; in Stoicism, 127, 128,
269n108. *See also* Time, natural

Naupactus, treaty of, 237n89

Nepos, Cornelius: *Chronica*, 21–23, 63;
Cicero's use of, 227n95; *De Excellentibus Ducibus Exterarum Gentium*, 24;
parallels of, 226n84

Nero (emperor of Rome): birthday of,
192; burning of Rome, 106–7; Golden
Age of, 131, 135–37; myths concerning,
105; posthumous reputation of, 136;
quinquennial games, 136; Seneca's influence on, 192; subversion of temporal
distinctions, 105; Tacitus on, 105–7,
135, 191, 259n219, 293nn108,113; tour
of Greece, 294n113

Nicolaus of Damascus, *Life of Augustus*,
239n109

Ninus of Assyria, 65–66

Nones (Roman calendar), 152, 153; in
birthday calculations, 157; in Fasti
Antiates, 184

North, J., 296n150

Nostalgia, for rural life, 113

Nostoi (homecomings from Troy): dating
of, 90; as epochal demarcation, 86;
foundation of Rome in, 92, 251n134;
in Timaeus, 94

Numa (king of Rome), 88; calendar of,
188, 283n147

Nundinal days, 184, 300n204

Oecumene, Hellenistic, 57–59, 238n94

Ogulnii brothers, 91

Olympiad, first: date of, 223n54; as
epochal demarcation, 81, 84–85; and
foundation of Rome, 95–96; ; use in
synchronism, 85

Olympiads: Athenian chronicle of,
247n90; dating by, 19, 22, 139, 219n7,
247n92; Eratosthenes on, 223n54;
fixing of date of, 223n48; in Jerome's
Chronicle, 29–30

Olympics, in Panhellenic history, 85

Opici, 254n170; time frame of, 98

Oral tradition, transition to literate, 109
Orosius, 256n192
Ovid: birthday of, 157–58, 211; on Iron
    Race, 272n145; and Lucretius, 298n165
—*Ars Amatoria*, days in, 208–9
—*Fasti:* astronomy in, 295n133; begin-
    ning of year in, 204–5; Caesar's
    reforms in, 203; civil time in, 202–4,
    205–6; continuity in, 282nn132,135;
    cyclical time in, 169; Day of Sowing
    in, 203; death of Augustus in, 169;
    foundation of Rome in, 103; German-
    icus in, 169; Golden Age in, 135; Hes-
    iod in, 299n183; identity of days in,
    159, 160; Ides of March in, 149; impe-
    rial family in, 187–88; Mars in, 205;
    natural time in, 202–6, 297n159,
    298n169; Romulus in, 203, 205; space
    in, 215; technique of, 283n143; time in,
    6, 169, 288n37
—*Metamorphoses:* Argo in, 268n96;
    Athens in, 237n83; Castor of Rhodes's
    influence on, 239n120; foundation of
    Rome in, 103; linear time in, 169; rise
    of Rome in, 165
—*Tristia:* birthdays in, 157–58; city of
    Rome in, 284n158; time in, 211

Paganicae (Country-District Holiday),
    199
Pais, E., 20
Palamedes, invention of astronomy,
    263n42, 223n45
Pan, in Herodotus, 245n53
Panaetius (Stoic), 11
Panhellenism, 45; chronography of, 4–5,
    18
Papus, Aemilius: censorship of, 35
Parallelism: East/West, 232n16; Greek/
    Roman, 24, 27, 225n85; in Roman
    historiography, 20–21. *See also*
    Synchronism
Parapegmata, 296nn141–42, 298n174;

forms of, 198; lunar days in, 207,
    298n174; as meteorological index,
    200–201; Varro's use of, 201
Parcae, in Catullus 64, 126
Parilia, feast of, 22, 103, 149, 258n208
Parthenon, Athenian: past time on,
    71–72
Past, Roman: synchronism with Greek
    past, 67
Past time: in Attic tragedy, 70; Augus-
    tus's redrawing of, 183; on Parthenon,
    71–72; shaping of, 147
Pattern, in human perception, 44
Peleus, gold palace of, 272n146
Peleus and Thetis: in Apollonius,
    267n89; divorce of, 123–24, 267n89,
    268n93; marriage of, 123, 125–26,
    268n96; meeting of, 124, 125, 267n88
Pelling, C., 88, 242n21
Peloponnesian War: synchronism with
    Carthaginian wars, 46; synchronism
    with Roman wars, 39
Pendulum, invention of, 301n205
Periodization, 246n73; of Diodorus
    Siculus, 65; in Roman historiography,
    248n106
Persian Wars: Athenocentric representa-
    tion of, 233n34; in Attic tragedy, 70–
    71; dating from, 18; in Fasti Capi-
    tolini, 173; synchronism with Volscian
    war, 27, 38
Persius (king of Macedon), 173, 221n28
Petavius, Domenicus: *Opus De Doctrina
    Temporum*, 8
Petronius, 265n72
Phaedrus, on the Argo, 268n97
Pharsalus, battle of, 140
Philinus of Acragas, 56
Philip of Macedon, 40
Philippi, battle of: synchronisms of,
    231n8
Philip the Arab, 144, 275n46
Philodemus, invitation to Piso, 158

Philopoemon, 231n6

Philosophy: as original condition, 130; Posidonius on, 270n121; Seneca's view of, 130, 131

Phoenicians, settlement of Western Mediterranean, 252n140, 254n162

Pindar: on Alpheius River, 232n22; *First Pythian*, 45, 49; layering of time in, 283n143

Platea, battle of, 17, 18; dating of, 10; synchronism with Mycale, 44, 231n8; and Trojan War, 71

Plautus: on reckoning of time, 116–17; use of Menander, 263n44

Plebiscitum Claudianum, 265n73

Pliny the Elder: on Julius Caesar, 60–61; on seasons, 201

Plüss, T., 299n177

Plutarch: Athenocentrism of, 237n86; chronography of, 10; on departure of gods, 263n50; on Julian calendar, 295n133; on mythical time, 78; on Numa, 88; on Roman months, 220n15; on Syracuse, 52; use of *synkrisis*, 24, 41

—*Quaestiones Graecae et Romanae:* beginning of year in, 204; calendar in, 211, 300n206

Polybius: chronography of, 47; closure point of, 66, 240n134; on geography, 80; and Hellenization of Rome, 58; organization of narrative, 293n101; on Roman-Carthaginian parallels, 54; on sack of Carthage, 54–55; synchronisms of, 48, 256n189; on Timaeus, 49–51, 94; universalism of, 59; use of ring composition, 55; vision of Rome, 236n68

Polycrates: Herodotus on, 73, 75; Minos and, 73

Pompeius Trogus: on East/West duality, 240n127; on Pyrrhus, 229n120; universal history of, 65–66

Pompey: Appian on, 240n126; birthday of, 148, 222n36; Eastern conquests of, 59, 60, 63, 64, 65; emulation of Alexander, 62; impact on Hellenistic literature, 238n104; as king of kings, 238nn98,101; Lucan on, 238n103; pirate command of, 238n94; in reckoning of eras, 140

Poplifugia festival, 280n105

Porta Mugonia (Rome), 164, 284n157

Poseidon, on Parthenon, 71

Posidonius, 129; on Golden Age, 270n124; on philosophy, 270n121; on state of man, 130

Postumius Albinus, L., 172

Potidaea, battle of, 17, 18

Potitii (family), 282n141

Primitivism, hard and soft, 115

Principate: *ab urbe condita* dating in, 289n48; consuls under, 177, 289n56, 290n63; *fasti* of, 185, 189, 210; historiography under, 190–93; in Julian calendar, 185–89; reconfiguring of time under, 172–89, 288n37. *See also* Empire, Roman; Fasti Capitolini

Probability, statistical, 44, 231n7

Prometheus: in Catullus 64, 269n102; culpability of, 111; symbolism of, 266n84; theft of fire, 122

Propertius, 258n208, 278n73; on bucolic past, 284n161

Prosopography, Roman, 222n37. *See also* Fasti Consulares

Ptolemy II Philadelphus, 229n120

Punic War, First: in Fasti Capitolini, 173; as Gigantomachy, 57; in Naevius, 56-57; seafaring in, 121; Timaeus on, 250n135

Punic War, Second: Gellius on, 37

Punic Wars, Greek historians on, 236n71

Purcell, N., 57, 59, 142; on synchronism, 226n87

Putnam, M., 2

Pydna, battle of, 55, 66, 235n67

Pyrrhus, 229n120; agate ring of, 275n41; defeat of, 104; Gellius on, 38, 39; invasion of Italy, 25, 53; statues of Muses, 144

Pythagoreanism, 275n44

Pythian games, dating of, 248n96

Quinquatrus, date of, 296n146

Quintilis (July), 197, 296n143

Raaflaub, K., 242n19

Races: Golden, 111, 115, 238n68, 261n11; Iron, 112, 261n11, 272n145; prelapsarian, 111–12; Silver, 111–12

Raleigh, Sir Walter, 65, 240n125; *History of the World*, 8

Rawson, E., 25, 57

Regifugium festival, calculation of, 280n106

Remoteness, geographical/chronological, 110, 260n7

Republic, Roman: and Capitoline temple of Jupiter, 258n214; chronology of, 150–51; corporatism of, 3; establishment of, 21, 40; foundation of, 104–7, 175, 274n26; honorific system of, 292n91; intellectual achievements of, 65; Lucan on, 170; temporal dimension of, 170; time systems of, 183

Revolutions, nineteenth-century, 232n7

Rhegium, siege of, 47; synchronism with sack of Rome, 48

Rhome (granddaughter of Aeneas), 86

Rich, J., 190, 191, 293n101

Ridley, R. T., 286n6

Robigalia festival, 199, 296n145

Rome: Alexander-imitation in, 238n105; divorce in, 229n114; domination of Italy, 58; fall of, 276n47, 277n64, 284nn156,166; as foe of barbarism, 55–57; Greek view of, 53–54; Hellenization of, 24, 57, 58–59; impact of Greek culture on, 224n67, 229n114; intellectual culture of, 34; interest in sailing, 118, 120–21; maritime trade of, 121, 265nn70,72–73; parallelism with Sicily, 52–57; personal luxury in, 115; population migration in, 265n72; prophecies of doom, 276n47; relationship with Greeks, 55–56; rivals of, 234n45; sack of Carthage, 54–55, 59; synchronism with Athens, 58; synchronism with Carthage, 92–93, 250n135, 251n138; tax revenues of, 60; technology in, 2; war against Pyrrhus, 25, 53. *See also* Empire, Roman; Principate; Republic, Roman

Rome (city): before Aeneas, 164; in the *Aeneid*, 134, 160–66, 282n136; archaeology of, 91, 250nn129,132; Augustan, 272nn151–52; burning of, under Nero, 106-7; Campus Martius, 94, 197, 206; colonization by Alba Longa, 98; Colosseum, 259n218; eras of, 140–42; *fasti* of, 206; Forum, 164, 167, 169, 172, 197, 213; gold in, 272n151; as Greek city, 53; historical monuments of, 2; in Iron Age, 91; *loca sancta* of, 283n150; millennial celebrations of, 142–45; ; Porta Mugonia, 164, 284n157; refoundation of, 69, 100–104, 252n151, 256n196, 257nn198,203–4, 258n205; relationship to sea, 266n74; relationship with Greeks, 96–97; Roman time outside, 211; sack by Visigoths, 104; *saecula* of, 146

—foundation of: bibliography on, 248n98; Carthage and, 95; Censorinus on, 225n77; dating from, 38; Dionysius of Halicarnassus on, 91; Ennius on, 99; Fabius Pictor on, 95–96, 97, 98, 255n182; ; in Fasti Antiates, 184; in Fasti Capitolini, 174; and first Olympiad, 95–96; following fall of Troy, 88, 89, 90, 94, 213, 252nn142,152,

Rome, foundation of (continued)
255n182; foundation of Republic as,
175; and Gallic sack, 103–4; gradual
nature of, 91; and Greek colonies, 95,
97–98; Greek failure to mention, 24;
in Greek historiography, 86, 89, 91,
99; Hellenistic chronography on,
249n114; historical, 86–100, 250n134;
and life archonships, 239n116; Livy
on, 78–79, 88, 257n197; mechanical
calculation of, 253n159; myth in, 68–
69, 86–88; Naevius on, 99, 255nn181–
82; Nepos on, 21; during *nostoi* period,
92, 251n134; in Ovid, 103; in Roman
historiography, 89–91; on Roman
stage, 91, 249n126; Sallust on, 105;
Servius on, 252n140; Tacitus on, 105;
Timaeus on, 53, 92–97, 249nn119,122,
251n135; time shift in, 88–89, 250n133;
tradition in, 91, 250n127; Varro on, 23;
in Virgil, 88. *See also* Sack of Rome,
Gallic
Romulus: apotheosis of, 26, 258n208;
calendar of, 188, 297n158; Cicero on,
87; civil year of, 291n69; in Fasti Triumphales, 181; Greek Eastern tradition on, 248n108; in historical time,
87–88; Livy on, 87, 248n108; myth
of, 90–91; in Ovid, 203, 205; as proto-
Augustus, 188; Trojan ancestry of, 86,
99, 255n177; twelve vultures of, 147
Rostovtzeff, M., 279n92
Rüpke, Jörg, 184, 185, 189, 287n25; on
triumphal *fasti*, 291n69; on Varro,
297n152
Rutilius Namatianus, 104

Sabbath, Jewish, 159, 209
Sabinus, death of, 192, 193
Sack of Rome, Gallic, 39, 47, 48, 100;
on Aeneas's Shield, 102; as epochal
demarcation, 100–104, 258n205; and
foundation of Rome, 103–4; geese at,

258n207; Greek knowledge of,
230n122; Livy on, 101–2, 141,
257n205; and Nero's fire, 106;
synchronisms of, 48, 232n17; and
Tarpeia, 258n208
Saecula, 145–48, 219n9; eschatological
power of, 146; Etruscan, 146–47;
length of, 145–46, 277n65. *See also*
Ludi Saeculares
Sailing: as crime, 265n63; as epochal
demarcation, 118–31; estrangement
from nature through, 120–22; in First
Punic War, 121; and flying, 266n81;
Hesiod on, 266n78; Horace on, 121–
22; origin of, 118–19; Lucretius on,
263n43; Roman interest in, 118, 120–
21; Seneca on, 129–30, 270n123; suspicion of, 120. *See also* Seafaring
Salamis, battle of: coincidences attend-
ing, 231n8; synchronism with Himera,
43–44, 45, 46, 51, 231n11
Salii, processions of, 162
Sallust, on foundation of Rome, 105
Samnites: as barbarians, 236n73; defeat
of, 104; time frame of, 98
Samuel, A. E., 204
Saturn, 267n91; Age of, 131; arrival in
Latium, 272n150; Golden Age of, 114,
163; in Ovid's *Fasti*, 135; Roman wall
of, 164. *See also* Cronus
Scaliger, Joseph, 220n18; *De Emenda-
tione Temporum*, 8; incarnation era in,
218n1; *Isagogici Chronologiae Canones*,
219n4; on Julian calendar, 193, 194;
Thesaurus Temporum, 219n4
Schütz, M., 295n139
Science, and historiography, 76–77,
244nn39,45
Science, Greek: methodology of, 77
Scipio, Q. Caecilius Metellus Pius: death
of, 276n51; defeat in Libya, 145
Scipio, P. Cornelius Aemilianus
Africanus Minor, 11; conquest of

Carthage, 145; on fortune, 235n67; on
sack of Carthage, 54, 55, 165, 235n68
Scipio, P. Cornelius Africanus Maior, 11;
death of, 231n6; on Sicily, 57; at
Zama, 235n67
Scipio Nasica, P. Cornelius, 15
Seafaring: in antiquity, 265n68; freedom
from, 120; plowing metaphor for,
264n59. *See also* Sailing
Seasons: harmonization with civil time,
297n153; in Horace, 214; Pliny the
Elder on, 201. *See also* Time, natural
Sejanus, 192
Seleucid era, 273nn5–6; dating by, 139
Seleucids, 31; conquest of, 60, 64
Sellar, W. C., and Yeatman, R. J., 79–80
Senators, ban on commerce for, 121,
265n73
Seneca: on the Chauci, 260n7; on Fall of
man, 129; on Golden Age, 128, 135;
influence on Nero, 192; Iron Age in,
127–31; on sailing, 129–30, 270n123;
on state of nature, 130–31; view of
philosophy, 130, 131
—*Epistle* 90, 129; night sky in, 269n112;
relationship to Posidonius in, 270n124
—*Phaedra*, 128–29; human nature in,
270n116; Theseus' cultural demarca-
tions in, 269n115
Servius, on foundation of Rome, 252n140
Servius Danielis, on Virgil's *Eclogues*,
277n62
Servius Tullius, 177; census under,
289n55
Sestius, L., 180
Sextilis (August), 161, 185
Sextius (tribune), 190
Shaw, P.-J., 9, 15, 221n35
Shimron, B., 242nn15,17
Shipbuilding, as emblem of intelligence,
265n65
Ships: as agents of Fall of man, 127–31;
symbolism of, 120, 127; transgressive-

ness of, 121, 122, 123, 127. *See also*
Argo; Sailing
Sicily: Greek coexistence with Carthage
in, 56; Herodotus on, 236n73; impor-
tance in Mediterranean, 47–52; paral-
lelism with Rome, 52–57; Romans in,
56; synchronism with Athens, 44–47,
49, 230n125
Sigonio, Carlo: *Fasti Consulares*, 285n2
Silenus (Greek historian), 56
Silvanus, cult of, 283n151
Silver Race, 111–12
Simile, historical, 24–25
Simmias of Rhodes, 300n207
Simonides, 241n9; "New," 70–71
Skutsch, O., 258n208, 275n42
Smart, J. D., 222n45
Smith, Jonathan Z., 98
Smith, Vance, 219n9
Social War, 146; in *fasti*, 290n63; in Livy,
190
Societies: development from communi-
ties, 260n4; hot and cold, 110
Society, prelapsarian, 109–10; in Roman
literature, 115–16
Society, Roman: agrarian basis of, 2;
time in, 1–2
Solar eclipses, 193–94
Solinus, chronography of, 246n83
Solon: Cicero on, 222n40; on seafaring,
120
Sophistic, Second: Athenocentrism of, 58
Sosigenes (astronomer), 197
Sowing, Day of, 199, 203
Sparta, extinction of, 100–101
Stage, Roman: foundation of Rome on,
91, 249n126
Statius, on Nemean games, 223n48
Stern, S., 221n34
Stoicism: on corrupting civilization,
264n56; harmony with nature in,
127, 128, 269n108

Strabo, on foundation of Croton, 97
Suerbaum, W., 155, 156
Suetonius: and Julian calendar, 154, 197;
   on Republican calendar, 200
Sullan War, 146
Sundial, of Campus Martius, 94
Sybaris, foundation of, 97
Syme, Ronald, 145; on anniversary men-
   tality, 276n49; *Roman Revolution*,
   158–59
Syncellus, George, 80–81
Synchronism: Aristotle on, 43–44, 59;
   Asian/Hellenistic, 63; Asian/
   Mediterranean, 59–65; Athenian/
   Sicilian, 44–47, 49, 230n125; B.C./A.D.,
   13; Christian, 28–32; Cicero's, 25–28;
   difficulties of, 41–42; East/West, 46–
   47; Fabius Pictor's, 48; in first Olympiad, 85; Gellius's, 5, 11, 32–42; historical depth in, 68; lateral, 68; Panhellenic, 18; Pan-Mediterranean, 229n110;
   Platea/Mycale, 44, 231n8; Roman/
   Carthaginian, 92–93, 250n135,
   251n138; in Roman historiography,
   20–23, 52; Salamis/Himera, 43–44,
   45, 46, 51, 231n11; selection process in,
   25; symbolism of, 45; Thermopylae/
   Himera, 51; Timaeus's, 19, 47–52,
   230n125, 232n20; in *translatio imperii*,
   68. *See also* Parallelism
Synchronism, Greek: first instruments
   of, 16–20
Synchronism, Hellenistic, 20; Athenocentric, 23
Synchronism, Roman: first instruments
   of, 20–23
Synchronization: mnemonic, 300n194;
   Panellenic, 4–5; in Roman Hellenization, 5
Syndikus, H. P., 269n105
Synkrisis: in Hellenization, 24; Plutarch's
   use of, 24, 41
Syracuse: calendar of, 230n2;

Deinomenid rulers of, 236n73; as
   failed Rome, 234n44; imperial pretensions of, 51–52; Marcellus at, 52,
   234n50; power of, 46; Roman capture
   of, 52; Timaeus on, 49; victories
   against Carthage, 52

Tablets, bronze: legal documents on,
   288n27
Tacitus: on annalistic technique, 190; on
   Bassus, 272n158; on Capitoline temple, 259n218; on development of laws,
   113, 115; on Golden Age, 261n21;
   numerology of, 106; on stages of
   decline, 119; time reckoning of, 171,
   190–93; use of annalistic format, 191–
   92, 293n106, 294n114; use of *fasti*,
   191, 193; on Vespasian, 115; view
   of decline, 115
—*Annales:* burning of Rome in, 106;
   epochal demarcations in, 105; Nero
   in, 105–7, 135, 191, 259n219,
   293nn108,113; Syme's prequel to, 158–
   59; Tiberius in, 192, 293n108
—*Germania*, heroic epoch in, 246n66
Tarentines: battles with barbarians,
   231n11; war with Lucanians, 47
Tarpeia, 258n208
Technē, knowledge claims for, 76–77
Technology: control of, 76–77; Roman,
   2; transgressive, 121–22
Temporality: in Catullus 64, 125–27; of
   epochal demarcations, 109; of gods,
   75, 117–18, 263n49; in Golden Age,
   116, 127; in nationalism, 66–67; of
   Republic, 170
Terminalia: calculation of, 280n106; in
   Horace, 208, 299n180; Varro on,
   296n143
Thebes: founding of, 113; mirroring of
   Athens, 235n62
Themistocles, 27
Theodorakopoulos, E., 268n99

Theopompus of Chios, 49; use of myth, 244n51

Thermopylae, battle of, 20; synchronism with Artemisium, 44; synchronism with Himera, 51

Theseus: in Catullus 64, 124–25, 126; as normal man, 269n115; on Parthenon, 71; return to Aegeus, 268n94

Thetis: myth of, 117–18. *See also* Peleus and Thetis

Thomas, N., 260n6

Thucydides, 39; authorial self-presentation of, 77; chronography of, 17–18, 221n26, 222nn42,45, 223n46, 293n101; on historical knowledge, 84; on mythic time, 243nn33–34; use of Herodotus, 244n34

Tiberius: on calendars, 188; in Fasti Antiates, 292n84; in Fasti Capitolini, 180–81; German campaign of, 159; Tacitus on, 192, 293n108; as *VIIuir epulonum*, 292n84

Timaeus of Tauromenium: on Aeneas, 95; on Alexander the Great, 142; chronography of, 18–19, 223n51; Cicero on, 233n39; Dionysius of Halicarnassus's knowledge of, 250n135; on fall of Troy, 94, 250n136, 274n33; as father of Roman historiography, 53; on first Olympiad, 84, 85; on First Punic War, 250n135; on foundation of Carthage, 92, 95, 96–97, 252n152; on foundation of Rome, 53, 92–97, 249nn119,122, 251n135; Polybius on, 49–51, 94; *Pyrrhica*, 250n135; on Roman *imperium*, 236n69; on Rome-Carthage conflict, 55–56; on Sicilian achievement, 49–50, 233n39; on Sicilian colonies, 97; Sicilian point of view, 93, 94; synchronism of, 19, 47–52, 230n125, 232n20; on Syracuse, 49; use of columns, 228n104; use of Greek myth, 94–95; use of *nostoi*, 94

Time: absolute, 15, 221n34, 297n157; anthropological study of, 4, 220n22, 260n6; Aztec view of, 218n10; brain physiology of, 12; cosmogonic, 79–80; cultural dimension of, 3, 4, 218n14; European obsession with, 215; in fall from innocence, 109; Herodotus's conception of, 75; holistic, 3; homogenous, 210; impact of Industrial Revolution on, 217n4; individual experience of, 213; International Atomic (T.A.I.), 294n120; in Iron Age, 117; Lévi-Strauss's model of, 3, 4; lunar, 194, 195, 207, 298n174; measurement of intervals, 13, 221n27; medieval, 3; objective, 218n15; and place, 1; pre-Promethean, 117; as process, 221nn34–35; public/private, 12; relative, 15, 221n35; Renaissance, 215, 300n205; ritual representations of, 218n10; scientific measurement of, 294n120; sociology of, 260n6; solar, 194; and space, 1; Universal 1 (U.T.1), 294n120

Time, civil: and absolute time, 297n157; under Augustus, 169; Censorinus on, 202; Greek, 195; in Julian calendar, 193, 205; and natural time, 147, 193–94, 202–6, 296n144; in Ovid, 202–4, 205–6; in Varro, 202, 276n55

Time, cyclical, 110; Greek, 3; in Horace, 214; and linear time, 169–70; non-calendrical, 198; Roman, 169, 184

Time, Greek: advantages of reckoning, 8; civil, 195; cyclical, 3; *versus* Egyptian time, 75; of gods and men, 75; natural, 195; and Roman time, 3, 5

Time, historical, 5; definition of, 69; foundation of Rome in, 86, 88–100; in Herodotus, 72–76; and historical truth, 245n61; organization of, 12–15; Romulus in, 87–88; transition from mythic time, 6, 68–70, 77–86, 88–95, 108, 119; Trojan War in, 83

Time, linear, 3; in consulships, 171; and cyclical time, 169–70; Roman, 184

Time, mythic, 5; Diodorus Siculus on, 79; Dionysius of Halicarnassus on, 78; foundation of Rome in, 68–69, 86; Greek historiographers on, 78; in Herodotus, 72–76; Thucydides on, 243nn33–34; transition to historical time, 6, 68–70, 77–86, 88–95, 108, 119

Time, natural: Censorinus on, 202; Cicero on, 297n154; and civil time, 147, 193–94, 202–6, 296n144; in *Georgics*, 207; Greek, 195; in Julian calendar, 193, 205; markers in, 223n48; in Ovid, 202–6, 297n159, 298n169; Varro on, 198–200, 202, 276n54

Time, Roman, 1–2; annalistic, 2; aristocrats' perception of, 16; cultural debate on, 202; cyclical, 184; effect of empire on, 193; extension of, 138; in *Fasti*, 6; and Greek time, 3; influence of, 213; linear, 184; metaphors, 217n6; modern aspects of, 2, 215; outside city, 211; in post-Roman Europe, 193; premodern aspects of, 2; in private sphere, 217n6; public/private dimensions of, 2; reconfiguring under Principate, 172–89, 288n37; Romans' obsessions with, 215; rural and urban, 206–9; sacred, 2, 170

Time events, contiguity between, 220n22

Time travel, through contemplation of ancient objects, 283n153

Time zones, international, 10

Timoleon, synchronism with Alexander the Great, 50

Timpe, D., 250n126

Titus, capture of Jerusalem, 32

Tomis, Iron Age, 264n52

Tönnies, Ferdinand, 260n4

Tradition, invention of, 252n145

Tragedy, Attic: past time in, 70; subject matter of, 241n7

Translatio imperii, 229n118; Augustus on, 229n110; in classical historiography, 236n68; fall of Troy as, 82; Gellius on, 37, 41; Polybius on, 55; synchronism in, 68

Tribuni militum, in Fasti Capitolini, 172

Trojan War: Cato on, 100; in Catullus 64, 126; Cretan participation in, 74, 243n28; historical time in, 83; homecomings from, 86; Lucretius on, 83–84; on Marmor Parium, 82; and Platea, 71

Troy: archaeology of, 91; as prototype of Rome, 55

Troy, fall of: date of, 142, 274n33; Ennius on, 143, 256n190; as epochal demarcation, 78, 79, 81–84, 107, 108, 109, 117, 118, 142–45; Eratosthenes on, 19, 86, 142, 223n53, 253n159, 283n144; foundation of Rome following, 88, 89, 90, 94, 213, 252nn142,152, 255n182; Jerome on, 83; Livy on, 82; millennial celebrations of, 142, 143, 144, 275n39; on Parthenon, 71; in Roman tradition, 82; Timaeus on, 94, 250n136, 274n33; as *translatio imperii*, 82; Varro on, 82–84; in Virgil, 83

Twain, Mark, 12–13

Tyrants, Athenian: expulsion of, 21

Tyrian annals, 250n138

United States, dating from Independence, 226n81

Universalism, Roman, 59–63

Valerius Flaccus, on the Argo, 266n81, 268n99

Varro: Castor of Rhodes's influence on, 239n120; chronography of, 291n78; chronological researches of, 63;

demarcations of past time, 81; on fall
of Troy, 82–84; historical time in, 81–
82; mythical time in, 81; on nature versus artifice, 270n118; on *saecula*, 147;
on stages of decline, 119; synchronism
of, 25; on Terminalia, 296n143; time
divisions of, 77–78, 79, 246n74,
247n92; use of Dicaearchus, 262n35;
use of Eratosthenes, 247n92
—*De Gente Populi Romani*, 23, 227n95
—*De Lingua Latina:* calendar in, 198–
99; civil time in, 202, 276n55; festivals
in, 199–200, 296n146; natural time in,
198–200, 202, 276n54; Republican
calendar in, 198
—*De Re Rustica:* date of, 297n152;
Golden Age in, 113; Julian calendar
in, 200–201, 207; parapegmata in,
201; progress in, 262n30
—*Imagines*, 226n84
Vattuone, R., 48, 232n19; on Timaeus,
252n152
Vediovis, temple of, 159
Vegoia, prophecy of, 146
Veii: capture of, 235n64; as Rome's twin,
284n161
Velleius Paterculus, 222n36, 229n111;
on Athenian constitution, 230n125;
chronography of, 22, 225n73
Verbrugghe, G. P., 293n101
Versnel, H. S., 267n91, 271n127
Vespasian, 140; *antiquus* lifestyle of, 115
Vettius, on fall of Rome, 277n64
Vinalia (Wine Festival), 199; date of,
296n146
Virgil: audience of, 163, 166; bimillenary
of death, 275n46; birthday of, 150;
death of, 133; on refounding of Rome,
102; on sailing, 121–22; sea voyage of,
121; use of Ennius, 293n109; use of
Livy, 257n199
—*Aeneid*: Arcadians in, 161, 162–63;

chronological displacement in, 161–
66, 210; city of Rome in, 160–66,
282n136; fall of Troy in, 83; foundation of Rome in, 88, 255n83; funeral
games in, 148; Golden Age in, 133,
134, 163, 166; historical time in, 163;
Lucan's parody of, 165; mythic time
in, 163; numerology in, 276n57; primitivism in, 115; publication of, 133; rise
and fall in, 285n167; Roman connectivity in, 300n196; Shield of Aeneas
in, 102, 162; wormhole effect in,
161–66
—*Eclogues*, Golden Age in, 131–33
—*Georgics:* and Horace's second Epode,
299n179; Iron Age in, 114–15, 128;
natural time in, 207; parapegmata
and, 298n174; sexuality in, 270n116
Visigoths, sack of Rome, 104
Visual arts, Greek, 241n7
Volscian war, synchronism with Persian
Wars, 27, 38

Walbank, F. W., 48, 90
Wallace-Hadrill, Andrew, 296n140;
"Time for Augustus," xiii
Washington, George: birthday of, 151,
156–57
Watson, L. C., 299n179
West, Martin, 219n12, 277n68
White, Hayden, 79, 245n54
Wilcox, D. J., 15, 19, 218n1, 221nn32,35
Williams, Bernard, 245n61; on Thucy-
dides, 244n34; *Truth and Truthfulness*,
75–76
Williams, Raymond, 113, 211
Williamson, C., 288n27
Winter solstice, beginning of year at, 204
Wiseman, T. P., 21
Wodehouse, P. G., 13
Woodman, A. J. and Martin, R. H.,
261n16

Wormholes, 283n143

Worsley, P., 217n9

Xerxes: Herodotus on, 72–73; invasion of, 41

Yanomamo Indians, 110

Years: anniversaries of, 142–45; under Augustus, 184–89; beginning of, 22, 204–5; consular *versus* calendar, 288n33; in Fasti Consulares, 168; numbered, 8, 9, 219n7; sidereal, 150; tropical, 150, 279n89. *See also* Civil years

Y2K, 148, 277n68

Zanker, P., 133

Zeitlin, F., 259n226

Zeno, synchronism with Fabricius, 35

Zerubavel, E., 29, 36; on Jewish Sabbath, 159

Zetzel, J. E. G., 26, 165

INDEX LOCORUM

Horace, *Carmina (continued)*

4.7.23–24	214
4.9.25–28	84
4.11.14–16	279n97
4.14.3–4	185
4.14.34–38	159

Epodes

2	207–8
2.59	208
2.67–70	207–8
16	132–33, 260n8
16.1	132

Justin

Epitome

6.6.5	232n17
41.1.1	240n128
42.5.10–12	240n127
44.5.8	240n127

Livy

Pref. 4	101
Pref. 6	78–79
Pref. 6–7	87
Pref. 7	87, 248n108
1.1.1	82
1.4.2	87
1.7.3–14	252n149
1.41.1–2	289n55
2.1.7	104
3.33.1	141
4.7.1	141
5.30.1–3	256n196
5.49.7	258n206
5.51–54	101
5.51.6	257n204
5.54.5	101, 141
6.1.1	257n201
6.1.2	102
6.1.3	102
6.35.10	190
9.17–19	4
10.23.12	91

21.63.2	265n73
25.24.11–13	234n49
30.30–31	235n67
37.4.4	294n118
39.44.10	275n37
39.50.10	231n6
44.37.8	294n118

Livy

Periochae

47	288n34

Lucan

5.398–99	290n62
6.817–18	238n103
7.440–41	170
7.441	16
9.961–99	165

Lucretius

1.459–63	83, 220n21
1.464–77	83
1.469–72	247n86
5.14	260n7
5.17	260n7
5.324–29	83–84
5.1436–39	116
5.1440–45	116
5.1446–47	84
5.1448–49	116

Macrobius

Saturnalia

1.12.16	287n20
1.14.7	281n115
1.14.8–9	280n105
1.14.11	280n106
1.15.17	279n97

Marmor Parium

FGrH 239

1	246n65
3	246n65

Romulus

3.1–2	253n154
12.2	220n15

Sulla

7.3	146

Theseus

1	78

Polybius

1.2	55
1.3.1–6.1	58
1.3.2	59
1.3.4	58
1.5.1	50
1.6.1–2	47
1.6.2	256n189
1.20.12	265n70
2.37.4	237n88
3.3.8–9	240n132
3.58–59	80
4.28.3–4	237n89
5.31.6	237n88
5.105.4–9	237n89
6.51–56	54
6.51.1–2	54
12.4b–c1	252n144
12.11.1	247n89
12.23.7	50
12.26b.4–c.1	50–51
14.12	293n112
15.6.4–7.9	235n67
15.35.6	237n82
23.12.1–14.12	231n6
29.21	55
38.21–22	54–55
39.8.6	240n133

Pompeius Trogus
See Justin, *Epitome*

Posidonius

F 284	270n124

Propertius

4.1.1 ff	284n161
4.4.73	258n208
4.10.27–30	284n161

Quintilian

10.1.93	229n112

Res Gestae

11	292n86

Rutilius Namatianus
De Reditu Suo

121–28	104
139–40	104

Sallust
Bellum Catilinae

6.1	105
10.1	235n65

Historiae

fr. 8	221n28

Bellum Jugurthinum

41.2–3	235

Seneca
Epistles

77.1–2	270n123
90	129–31
90.4–6	129
90.5	130
90.9	270n120
90.9–23	129
90.11	270n120
90.24	129–30
90.35–36	130
90.36	130
90.37	270n120
90.42	269n112
90.44	130, 131
90.44–46	130–31
115.12–13	272n156
115.13	135

13.10–11	191–92	F 36	252n144
13.10.1	197	F 40	233n33
13.11.1	192	F 41b	232n22
15.25.3	238n95	F 59	252n143
15.38.41	106	F 60	234n53
15.39.3	106, 108	F 94	234n42
15.40.2	106	F 105	232n23
15.41.1	106	F 106	233n29, 274n33
15.41.2	106	F 119a	233n40
15.74.1	292n88	F 138	233n38
16.1.1	135–36	F 150	233n28, 274n33
16.2.4	136	F 164	233n38
16.3.2	272n158		
16.12.3	292n88	Valerius Maximus	
Dialogus		1.5.7	278n83
12.1–4	261n21		
Germania		Varro	
3.3	246n66	*De Lingua Latina*	
46.4	246n66	6.1–11	198
Historiae		6.8	300n2
1.1.1	191	6.12	198–99, 202,
4.40.2	188		276n55
4.53	259n218	6.12–26	199
		6.13	296n143
		6.14	296n146
Theopompus		6.16	199
FGrH 115		6.17	296n146
F 153	233n34	6.20	199, 296n146
F 381	244n51	6.23	296n146
		6.25–26	199
Thucydides		6.27	279n99
1.1.3	84	6.27–32	199
1.4.1	268n97	6.33	287n20
1.21.1	84, 243n33	6.34	296n143
2.2.1	17–18	*De Re Rustica*	
6.2.1	243n34	1.1.1	297n151
		1.2.9	274n26
Tibullus		1.28.1	200
1.7	278n79	1.29.1	297n155
2.5.25	284n161	1.29.2	264n59
		1.30	297n155
Timaeus		2.1.3–5	113
FGrH 566		3.1.2	113
T 10	247n89		

Varro, *De Re Rustica (continued)*

3.1.4	113, 270n118
3.1.5	262n35

Velleius Paterculus

1.2.1	22
1.4.1–3	254n161
1.5	22
1.6.4–5	22
1.7.1	22
1.8.1	22
1.8.4	22
1.12.5	22
1.16–17	22, 229n111
2.36	229n111
2.53.3	278n80
2.53.4	222n36

Virgil

Aeneid

1.12–28	247n84
1.257–72	276n57
2.255	223n53
3.301	278n74
3.302	283n152
4.669–70	235n66
6.792–94	133
6.851	271n142
8.99–100	281n136
8.102	163
8.102–4	161
8.104	163
8.269	283n141, 163
8.271	163
8.271–72	162
8.281	283n141
8.312	164
8.324–25	134
8.326–27	134
8.337–38	283n148
8.348	134, 282n348, 165

8.355–57	163
8.356–58	164
8.360–61	164
8.361	164
8.601	283n151
8.635	102
8.635–36	162
8.652–62	102
8.663	162
8.668–70	162
8.671–713	102
8.671–708	162
8.714–29	162

Eclogues

4	131–33
4.4	132
4.6	131
4.15–16	131
4.31–36	131
4.34–35	131
4.35–36	131
4.38–39	131
4.39–41	131

Georgics

1.122–49	114
1.125–28	270n120
1.134–48	121
1.139–40	128, 270n120
1.144	270n120
1.217–18	298n175
1.276–86	207
1.276	207
1.276–77	299n183
1.286	207
1.338–39	207
2.458–74	114
2.513–40	114
3.244	270n116

Xenophanes

DK 21 B 22.5	13

Text	10.25/14 Fournier
Display	Fournier
Indexer	Roberta Engleman
Compositor	BookMatters, Berkeley
Printer and binder	Thomson-Shore